THE DEVIL GETS HIS DUE

THE·DEVIL GETS·HIS·DUE

The Uncollected Essays of

LESLIE FIEDLER

Edited by Samuele F. S. Pardini

COUNTERPOINT BERKELEY

Every effort has been made to secure permissions. We regret
any inadvertent omission.

Library of Congress Cataloging-in-Publication Data
Fiedler, Leslie A.
The devil gets his due : the uncollected essays of Leslie Fiedler / Leslie Fiedler;
edited by Samuele F. S. Pardini.
p. cm.
Includes bibliographical references.
ISBN-13: 978-1-59376-188-2
ISBN-10: 1-59376-188-0
1. American literature—History and criticism. 2. English literature—History
and criticism. 3. Popular literature—United States—History and criticism.
4. Literature—Philosophy. 5. Popular culture—Philosophy. I. Pardini, Samuele F. S.
II. Title.
PS3556.I34D48 2008
814'.54—dc22   2007044754

Paperback ISBN: 978-1-59376-266-7

Cover design by Jacob McMurray
Interior design by David Bullen
Printed in the United States of America

COUNTERPOINT
2560 Ninth Street
Suite 318
Berkeley, CA 94710

www.counterpointpress.com

To Tara and Dante

"L'amor che move il sole e l'altre stelle"

Contents

Acknowledgments

Thanks to the following people for helping with this project: first and foremost my "caro maestro" Leslie Aaron Fiedler, for his friendship, his teaching, and for writing until the very end of the journey; Sally Fiedler for granting permission for the essays and for keeping the door open—always; Geoffrey Green, for his suggestions, advice, encouragement and, more importantly, for his friendship; Lawrence P. Rapp and Joyce Troy for compiling and updating a bibliography of Leslie Fiedler's works; the librarians of the Lockwood Library at SUNY Buffalo, of the Jean and Alexander Heard Library at Vanderbilt University, and of the Belk Library at Elon University; Matthew Schwartz, the hardest-working man in the copyright business; Luke Gerwe, the hardest-working man in the copyediting business; my very patient and dedicated editor at Counterpoint/Soft Skull Press and fellow immigrant Richard Nash, "Erin go bragh"; Roxanna Aliaga who can pronounce my first name, and everybody else at Counterpoint/Soft Skull Press; Dr. Frank Haraf, Jr. and Dr. Jill Roberts, who help turn people's hopes into reality; my parents, Giorgio and Dania Pardini, and my brother Stefano and his family for their continued support over the years; Tara and Dante Leslie Pardini, for their patient support (including the help with the title!), and for the love and joy they bring into my life every day.

Publication credits: "Toward an Amateur Criticism," *The Kenyon Review*, vol. 12, no. 4, Autumn 1950. Reprinted by permission of *The Kenyon Review*; "'Giving the Devil His Due,'" *The Journal of Popular Culture*, vol. 12, no. 2, 1979. Reprinted by permission of Blackwell Publishing; "Explication de Texte *Inferno* Canto XXVI," *New Directions*, 1942. Reprinted by permission of the author's estate; "D. H. Lawrence on D. H. Lawrence *As Told to Leslie A. Fiedler*," *The New Leader*, December 1953. Reprinted by permission of *The New Leader*; "Introduction" by Leslie Fiedler to *The Deerslayer* by James Fenimore Cooper (Modern Library, 2002). Reprinted by permission of Modern Library, a division of Random House, Inc.; "Come Back to the Raft Ag'in, Huck Honey!", *The Partisan Review Collection*, Howard Gotlieb Archival Research Center at Boston University. Reprinted by permission of Boston University; "New England and the Invention of the South," *American Literature: The New England Heritage*, eds. James Nagel and Richard Astro (Garland Publishing, 1981). Reprinted by permission of James Nagel; "*Huckleberry Finn*: The Book

We Love to Hate," *Proteus*, vol. 1, no. 2, 1984. Reprinted by permission of the author's estate; "'As Free as Any Cretur . . . ,'" *The New Republic*, August 1955. Reprinted by Permission of *The New Republic*; "Afterword" by Leslie Fiedler, from "*1601* and *Is Shakespeare Dead?*" by Mark Twain, in *Oxford Mark Twain Series*, ed. Shelley Fisher Fishkin (Oxford University Press, 1996); "The State of Writing," *The Partisan Review Collection*, Howard Gotlieb Archival Research Center at Boston University. Reprinted by permission of Boston University; "Edmund Wilson's Criticism: Re-examination," *The New Leader*, December 1947. Reprinted by permission of *The New Leader*; "The Ordeal of Criticism," *Commentary*, 8, November 1949. Reprinted by permission of *Commentary*; "Love is not Enough," *Yale Review*, vol. 42, March 1953. Reprinted by permission of Blackwell Publishing; "The Intellectual Roots of Anti-Intellectualism," *The Pacific Spectator*, 10, Summer 1956. Reprinted by permission of Stanford University Press; "A Fortyish View," *The New Leader*, May 1957. Reprinted by permission of *The New Leader*; "Intellectual Uncles," *The Guardian* (UK), October 1967. Reprinted by permission of *The Guardian* (UK); "The Canon and the Classroom: A Caveat," *English Inside and Out: The Places of Literary Criticism*, eds. Susan Gubar and Jonathan Kamholtz (Routledge, 1992). Reprinted by permission of Routledge Publishing, Inc. (Taylor & Francis Group, LLC); "Ezra Pound: The Poet as Parodist," *Scripsi* (University of Melbourne, 1987). Reprinted by permission of the author's estate; "Francis Scott Fitzgerald" (Essay 24) (Thomas Cooper Library at University of South Carolina, 1991). Reprinted by permission of the author's estate; "Pop Goes the Faulkner: In Quest of *Sanctuary*," *Faulkner and Popular Culture*, eds. D. Fowler and A. J. Abadie (University Press of Mississippi, 1998). Reprinted by permission of the author's estate; "Looking Back After 50 Years," *San Jose Studies*, vol. 16, no. 1, Winter 1990. Reprinted by permission of the author's estate; "Robert Penn Warren: A Final Word," *South Carolina Review*, vol. 23, no. 1, Fall 1990. Reprinted by permission of the author's estate; "Capote's Tale," *The Nation*, April 2, 1949. Reprinted by permission of *The Nation*; "The City and the Writer," *The Partisan Review Collection*, Howard Gotlieb Archival Research Center at Boston University. Reprinted by permission of Boston University; "Style and Anti-Style in the Short Story," *The Kenyon Review*, vol. 13, no. 1, Winter 1951. Reprinted by permission of *The Kenyon Review*; "The Higher Unfairness," *Commentary*, May 1952. Reprinted by permission of *Commentary*; "Encounter with Death," *The New Republic*, December 1957. Reprinted by Permission of *The New Republic*; "A Homosexual Dilemma," *The New Leader*, December 1956. Reprinted by permission of *The New Leader*; "The Noble Savages of Skid Row," *Reporter*, July 12, 1956, Max Ascoli Collection, Howard Gotlieb Archival Research Center at Boston University. Reprinted by permission of Boston University; "Up from Adolescence," *The Partisan Review Collection*, Howard Gotlieb

Archival Research Center at Boston University. Reprinted by permission of Boston University; "The Divine Stupidity of Kurt Vonnegut: Portrait of the Novelist as Bridge over Troubled Water," *Esquire*, September 1970. Reprinted by permission of the author's estate; "Notes on Philip José Farmer" by Leslie Fiedler from *The Book of Philip José Farmer* by Philip José Farmer (Berkley Publishing Group, 1982). Reprinted by permission of Berkley Publishing Group, a division of Penguin Group (USA) Inc.; "The Return of James Branch Cabell; Or, the Cream of the Cream of the Jest," *James Branch Cabell: Centennial Essays*, eds. M. Thomas Inge and Edgar E. MacDonald (Louisiana State University Press, 1983). Reprinted by permission of Louisiana State University Press; "Who Really Died in Vietnam? The Cost in Human Lives," *Saturday Review*, December 1972; "James Fenimore Cooper: The Problem of the Good Bad Writer," *James Fenimore Cooper: His Country and His Art*, ed. G. A. Test (SUNY Oneonta Conference Papers), 1978. Reprinted by permission of the SUNY Oneonta English Department and The James Fenimore Cooper Society; "Mythicizing the Unspeakable," *Journal of American Folklore*, vol. 103, no. 410, October–December 1990. Reprinted by permission of The American Folklore Society; "The Legend," *Buffalo Bill and the Wild West* (New York: The Brooklyn Museum, 1981). Reprinted by permission of The Brooklyn Museum; "Getting It Right: The Flag Raisings at Iwo Jima," *Princeton Library Chronicle*, 2002. Reprinted by permission of the author's estate; "Mythicizing the City," *Literature and the Urban Experience*, eds. M. Jaye and A. Chalmers Watts (Rutgers University Press, 1981). Reprinted by permission of the author's estate; "Whatever Happened to Jerry Lewis? *That's* Amore . . . ," *Enfant Terrible: Jerry Lewis in American Film*, ed. Murray Pomerance (New York University Press, 2002). Reprinted by permission of New York University Press.

Introduction

Sympathy for the Devil.
Looking Backward for a
New Tradition.

Freedom from bias—the first condition of criticism.
FRIEDRICH ENGELS

To think I did all that,
And may I say, not in a shy way
Oh no, oh no not me, I did it my way.
PAUL ANKA, "My Way," as sung by Frank Sinatra

Tell me how do I begin again? My city is in ruins.
BRUCE SPRINGSTEEN, "My City of Ruins"

Literary criticism is in crisis. Gone are the beneficial effects of Cultural Theory, Neo-Marxism, Feminism and Post-Colonial Studies, the main critical practices of the last few decades. The brightest days of "gender-race-nation" (the triad that occupied the front stage of the critical scene in the most recent past) are behind us. Working-class studies (and a renewed attention to documentary) seem to be gaining a long-overdue attention. Yet this occurs mainly in the area of cultural studies that favors the analysis of cultural consumption over that of the production of the object of study. More importantly, working-class studies still lack widespread organized institutional backing.[1] The absence of new, homegrown public voices with a background in literary studies is yet another indication of the depth of the crisis for literary criticism. The last true public intellectuals of this kind, say Stanley Fish and Camille Paglia, belong to the generation of the thirties and forties respectively.

The clearest indication of the crisis of literary criticism, however, is the lack of proper memorialization of scholars who are part of and makers of the *history* of this valuable profession. One such case is that of Leslie Fiedler. Here is a critic and an intellectual who over the course of more than fifty years has produced a body of work that, for both depth of analysis and range of fields covered, is hardly equaled in post–World War II literary criticism and theory this side of the Atlantic. There is virtually not one area of critical studies today that the author of *Love and Death in the American Novel*—that imperishable study of classic American fiction that originated in "the most influential single essay ever written about American literature,"[2] "Come Back to the Raft Ag'in, Huck Honey!"—has not either written about or opened to investigation *before* it became an established field of research. The *OED* credits Fiedler as the first critic to use the word "Post-Modernism" in the literary field. At least two of the most significant books of American studies of the most recent past, Eric Lott's *Love and Theft* and Michael Rogin's *Blackface, White Noise*, acknowledge their debt to Fiedler's work. One could trace the history of twentieth-century literary criticism in the United States by following Fiedler's biographical-critical trajectory, from his education and coming of intellectual age during the rise of the Popular Front (as Michael Denning rightly insists in *The Cultural Front*) in response to 1920s white Nativism and the Rooseveltian nation described by Gary Gertle as "the American crucible"[3] to the advent of Post-Structuralism and the turn from "class" to "difference" in a large segment of the profession. No less important is Fiedler's impact beyond the academy, his international reputation and his highly regarded work on several foreign literary traditions and authors.

Unlike other recently deceased or retired scholars who have been rightly saluted and celebrated both by colleagues and in academic journals (Edward Said and Jacques Derrida come to mind), five years after his death no serious attempt has been made to properly memorialize Fiedler's work. None of the major academic journals has published anything about Fiedler. None of his essays appears in any of the major anthologies of theory *and* literary criticism, the frighteningly heavy and costly volumes on which thousands of undergraduate and graduate students all over American campuses are required to base their knowledge of the history and the state of the profession. This void reveals a larger problem: a more general lack—in today's academy as well as in much of the intellectual debate that takes place in the public sphere—of the historical sense and role of the teaching profession, of the multiplicity of critical approaches and of the intellectual traditions available in the United States.

The idea of unearthing Fiedler's archives and proposing a new book of essays responds to this void. My goal is to present Leslie Fiedler to a new, hopefully younger generation of readers—perhaps for the first time. At the same time, I hope to re-introduce him to older readers who may not realize the vitality and life in his voice. Ideally, *The Devil Gets His Due* should expose a Fiedler beyond Fiedler rather than the historically minded New Critic turned to popular mythic power as Denning still has it—a trajectory that described in these terms seems to me rather incomplete, one that narrows and undermines the political potential of the theoretical presuppositions of Fiedler's critical work that I want to address here. For this reason I have selected and assembled a collection of articles that covers almost sixty years of critical work, from Fiedler's first published piece of criticism—an exuberant take on Dante's *Inferno* XXVI that dates back to 1944—to his last article, the introduction to the Library of America 2002 edition of *The Deerslayer*.[4] For the same reason I have preferred a thematic organization over a mere chronological order.

The book is composed of seven sections. All but one of the pieces, "Come Back to the Raft Ag'in, Huck Honey!", are previously uncollected. I have included this essay in the first place because history deserves respect and because I hope that in this new context this little meditation may reveal some of the undisclosed potential disseminated underneath any classic piece of writing, thereby shedding some light on the other pieces of the book. The first section is the historical-theoretical section. It includes essays on criticism, the role of the critic and the role of popular culture, the previously mentioned commentary on *Inferno* XXVI, a piece on D. H. Lawrence, "Come Back to the Raft Ag'in, Huck Honey!" and an article on *Uncle Tom's Cabin* titled "New England and the Invention of the South." The second is the Mark Twain section, with essays on *Huckleberry Finn*, *Pudd'nhead Wilson*, *1601* and *Is Shakespeare Dead?* The latter takes us to the section on the intellectuals and literary criticism in the United States, which deals with figures and topics such as Edmund Wilson, Philip Rahv, F. O. Matthiessen, Katherine Anne Porter, anti-intellectualism in the United States and a response to Norman Podhoretz on the issue of the young generations of US intellectuals in the fifties as part of a symposium promoted by and hosted in the pages of the magazine *The New Leader*. This part finishes with a review of works by Charles Olson and the godfathers of French Structuralism, Roland Barthes and Claude Lévi-Strauss, and an article on the literary canon, "The Canon and the Classroom: A Caveat." Next comes the most "literary" of the sections, the one on pop modernism. It incorporates full essays on and reviews of books by Ezra Pound, William Faulkner, John Steinbeck, Robert Penn Warren, Truman Capote, Alfred Kazin, as well as a brief, delightful sketch of Francis Scott Fitzgerald. From modernism we move on to the fifties and the sixties, to the short stories and novels of Conrad Aiken, Raymond Chandler, Mary McCarthy, James Agee, James Baldwin, Nelson Algren, J. D. Salinger, the late Kurt Vonnegut, Jr., Philip J. Farmer, and a reconsideration of James Cabell. The last section groups social commentaries together with cultural studies

and whiteness studies articles. It includes writings on the Vietnam War, Buffalo Bill, *The Last of the Mohicans*, some classic Vietnam movies (*Apocalypse
Now*, *The Deer Hunter* and *Rambo*), an autobiographical piece on the battle
of Iwo Jima and the flag raisings immortalized by Joe Rosenthal, a meditation
on the significance of the city in literature, and the concluding essay on Jerry
Lewis, according to Fiedler "one of the makers of that mulatto culture that is
America's gift to itself and the rest of the world" (312).[5]

The first thing that strikes the reader is a remarkable, enduring public commitment to his work as critic that equaled the development of literary criticism in the United States for more than fifty years, a testimony to the fact that
literary criticism in the United States has a very long *history*, of which Fiedler
is at once an inheritor and a maker. The long history of literary criticism in
the United States is something that seems to me to go unnoticed all too often.
By looking at the cultural developments and the issues Fiedler debated one
cannot help noticing the existence of a variety of different critical traditions,
their complexity and their richness. The careful reader will realize that one
of the things that Fiedler achieves in these writings is precisely his scripting
the history of literary criticism by way of engaging previous traditions. If one
took the time to research these traditions in depth, study them, and connect
on the one hand issues and critical trajectories, on the other hand cultural
institutions, journals and biographical trajectories, one would discover that
many of the topics that have been debated in the last decades after the arrival
or the founding in the United States of Structuralism, Post-Structuralism,
New Historicism and other critical theories were already part of the debate
in the United States, in many cases as part of a larger international context
and debate.[6]

Fiedler was an extraordinarily brilliant critic and intellectual gifted with a
spectacular sense of the avant-garde. This sense made him and continues to
make him today, especially today, a member of the critical community of his
times. At a symposium organized in 1950 by *Kenyon Review*, where he delivered
the essay that opens this collection, "Toward an Amateur Criticism," Fiedler
called for a comprehensible critical vocabulary and language. He declared
his preference for a criticism that adopted "the language of conversation—
the voice of the dilettante at home." He rejected the "contempt of the imagination" and the "bureaucratization" of criticism (10, 3). He invited his colleagues
to distance themselves from the tortuous jargon of both self-declared and
true specialists, the latter embodied in those days by Kenneth Burke. Several
decades later, addressing the need of a language capable of speaking to both
the specialist and the general reader would become a cliché evoked by many
in and out of academic circles. Fiedler's noted take on homosexuality is usually
associated with "Come Back to the Raft Ag'in, Huck Honey!" which appeared

in 1948 in *Partisan Review*, the historical journal largely responsible for fueling the reputation of the so-called New York Intellectuals. Yet, four years earlier in "Explication de Text" Fiedler raised this same issue in relation to the symbol of the flame that unites, literally, Diomede and Ulysses in *Inferno XXVI*. Fiedler created this symbolic union and linked it to the achievement of "the West" in a sort of prelude to the idea of the West that he would further develop in *The Return of the Vanishing American* at the end of the 1960s. "Explication de Text" appeared first in James Laughlin's avant-garde publication *New Directions*. The same volume published a Latin American section, a Federico García Lorca section and, among others, writings by William Carlos Williams, Paul Goodman, Kenneth Rexroth and Tennessee Williams.[7]

Fiedler belongs to this long, complex and in need of recharting (from a post–Cold War perspective) history, which brings up and brings us to a second element of his criticism. This is Fiedler's inexhaustible curiosity for and openness toward the new, whether the new appears in the guise of new forms, new possibilities for interpretation or new media altogether. The reader needs to put all this in context in a historical perspective. What today is almost cliché in and out of academic circles—say, writing about sex in *Uncle Tom's Cabin* or the merits of science fiction—was extreme novelty when Fiedler started writing about such topics. Often writing about those topics was even taboo. However, Fiedler did not apply this way of examining literature and culture solely to contemporary works. He approached the classics in the same vein, as he did with Dante's Ulysses or with Shakespeare in *The Stranger in Shakespeare*, his groundbreaking full-length study of the Bard. This methodology allowed him to cover an impressive range of issues, fields and authors *in order* to put them all together in a sort of uninterrupted dialogue among them as well as between his voice as literary critic—always historically updated, so to speak—and the voices of the works under scrutiny. In turn, such a method reveals a notion of culture conceived as a whole that Fiedler read as historically contingent and geographically local rather than as a series of formally separated and auto-referential spheres. He could write about and link Dante's Ulysses and the achievement of the West to *The Last of the Mohicans*, the Vietnam War, Rambo, the flag raisings at Iwo Jima and the American invasion of Afghanistan in 2001.

Fiedler used his voice as a kaleidoscopic tool to join together different genres and styles, art and the society, the art novel and pop fiction, modernism and mass culture, history and politics. The starting point of the *theoretical presuppositions* of his criticism was the notion of a dialogical, open-ended and diversified unity of the human experience in the West that revolved around and radically questioned the political possibilities of the human expression we call culture—especially literary culture—at once conceived *vis-à-vis* personal freedom and as a potentially democratic act. There is no separation of politics from culture here. The latter does not substitute for the former. In 1948 in "The State of Writing," where the act of writing is depicted as *work*, Fiedler concluded that "the absolute claim to freedom in the creative act, in *going on writing* as we understand it, challenges many political systems and is challenged by them" (103). In 2002 he started what was destined to be his last complete essay of literary criticism, the previously mentioned "Introduction" to Cooper's *The Deerslayer* stating that in the United States politics had preceded the formation of a national literary culture: "In 1789, the year James Fenimore Cooper was born, the thirteen North American colonies of Great Britain had declared their political independence, but their literature was still colonial, chiefly belated imitations of styles and genres formerly fashionable in the homeland" (37).

Fiedler's insistence on personal voices submitted to the notion of universal singularity as the unifying element of literature intended as a form of human expression—what he called literary anthropology. Fiedler did not submit to the theory of a subject ontologically antagonistic that supposedly would transform history for the good of the human collectivity, a notion that history has proven if not entirely wrong, certainly hardly desirable. He submitted to the specificity of each subject as the foundation of the unity of the human experience. That is to say, he submitted to the idea of equality as the condition of difference. The continuous research of and emphasis on the voice of the critic, of the authors, as well as of the fictional or real characters he wrote about distinguished and characterized the universal singularity at the basis of his collective vision. "This is a speech" we read (and hear) Fiedler declaring in the "Explication de Text" of *Inferno XXVI*, a canto that already in his original presents a multitude of voices that continue to resonate in the head of the reader after its last terzina as do the voices of any of the best of Faulkner's novels long after one has put it back on the library's shelf. Fiedler populates this canto with new voices such as the antiwar voice, the voice of the homosexual, the "singular tongue" of "the essential orator" that dislikes the "suety prose" of previous translators. "What did they know of the yelling crowd," we continue to read him thundering. Roughly forty years later he identified the distinguishing feature of Ezra Pound's poetry with its "one hundred borrowed voices" of an America that has always lacked a traditional standard poetic language (27, 31, 142). The fact that the emphasis on singular voices is accentuated in what is largely a translation of Canto XXVI and in a piece on a poet that made an art of translation is hardly coincidental.

Translation is by definition a linguistic, hermeneutic, and cultural act. Its precondition is grounded in multiplicity, in the knowledge of or at least the skilled acquaintance with more than one language, with one's native language as well as with the language spoken and written by somebody else, by other people, by other subjects, and not by chance, alas, a notoriously and supremely damaging lack in the educational system, the social fabric, and the culture at large of the United States, beginning with the field of American Studies right at the moment when transnationalism and transatlantism seem to emerge as its new critical horizon. Translation entails dialogism and dialectics. In a way, perhaps by way of metaphor, translation may be considered as the closest thing to historical representation and the representation of the real in literature. It is an act of appropriation that evolves and becomes a rendition. It implies an ever-present condition of transformation that, quite appropriately, opened Fiedler's critical career. In fact, from time to time Fiedler continued to practice translation. He refashioned such an art in theoretical terms when he wrote that "literary criticism is always becoming 'something else,' for the simple reason that literature is always 'something else,'" and that "every position is the occasion for another and the end is never attained," which also denies the possibility of reading his criticism, including, let me be very clear on this, *The Devil Gets His Due*, as an invocation to return to the past (5, 9). The same theoretical presupposition implies the recognition of an external subject, of an Other whose presence inevitably modifies the ontological as well as the epistemological being of the translator and its subject, of its voice. Translation highlights the relational condition of the human condition and of the literary act, including literary criticism, throwing them both squarely into the realm of politics.

Fiedler inscribed this same notion into the voice and the language of the critic *in order* to connect with the public, whose presence is at once acknowledged and required in his writings. He argued that ideally the critic and literary theorist should write for the *"general reader,"* that category of people for whom, after all, books are written, as one too many critics seems to forget. He insisted that the critic must try "to speak *as if* to men and not to specialists" (4). The main motivation behind his argument was not a mere polemic against those who employ a critical jargon and those who write a "gray, standard, glutinous prose." Fiedler chastised the use of such a jargon and the glutinous prose *because* they reflect and increase an ongoing problem in the social realm. "What discourages sociability discourages style," he maintained. Criticism must be "resisting the atomizing impulse" of our society because it is an art intended to be practiced as a commitment to "communication and sociability" (10). Criticism should expose the relational dimension of the human condition explored in literature since literature too is relational, since literature too embodies, is part of, and expresses a sociopolitical condition. The failure to confront literature in these terms for Fiedler "is often a failure to *connect*" (5).

Fiedler turns literature and literary criticism into forces of opposition against the atomizing impulse of society. The failure of politics and the failure of love he talks about in the section on literary criticism and the intellectuals are not an invitation to disarticulate intellectual work from the politics inherent in cultural formations and social relations. Fiedler does not assign literature and culture a redeeming, cathartic power in the strict Aristotelian sense, although it is from Aristotle's *Poetics* and (especially) *Politics* that he starts out. He wants us to use literature and criticism to try to re-engage politics, well aware of the risk of failing in such an effort. It is precisely because of this risk that he warned that a critic that is isolated aggravates "an endemic weakness of our atomized world" (5). The point of criticism for Fiedler is posing different and new questions rather than giving answers—which of course are nothing but a way to give time-bound answers, the truths of the critic's own time. As Fiedler liked to say,

> Our special need is the interpretation of these [critical] minds. In a world where they do not ordinarily find it possible to communicate, there is work enough for the critic. Perhaps in the end it will turn out that the divorce is too utter to be healed by his resources, but, modest fellow, he will be content to have mitigated a little the cleavage of our mind, or even just to have told the truth about a few books. (12)

The mediating function Fiedler ascribes to the critic witnesses to this position. Criticism relates by way of engaging the production of the cultural work in its complexity as well as by addressing the wide range of traditions the work entails, in the fashion of a humanist conception of the society whereby the new does not displace and destroy the old because understanding and knowledge are the accumulation of voices from the past handed down to the present. This criticism relates to the medium that expresses it, to its language, to its audience and to its history in order to open new critical spaces, to engage and challenge the reader.

"Vestigial Marxist" that he was, as he wrote in *What Was Literature?*[8] he knew that any modern form of communication, including the literary arts and the novel to begin with, equals sociability because it is a form of development of the same forces of production that shape social relations. Cultural formations of any sort—literary, visual, pop—and, no less important, the standards that critics applied to them are also forms of development of the forces of production and the social relations they enact. In "*Huckleberry Finn*: The Book We Love to Hate" Fiedler argues that derogatory terms such as "nigger" "remind us of not just our troubled history but of attitudes and values created by that history of which most of us have learned to be ashamed, yet from which none of us can feel wholly free" (72). Similarly, in "Giving the Devil

His Due" he reiterates the importance of the mechanism and the dynamics of cultural production in modern Western society when he describes the interconnectedness of mass communications, mass-production technologies, the marketplace, the commodity status of the work of art and the pop artifact, as well as the class-defined aesthetic hegemony of any given society.

For this reason Fiedler insists almost obsessively on dealing with popular culture, especially with those works that by any accepted standard are indeed bad and yet resonate with vast, at times immensely vast, audiences. For the same reason he insists on dealing (or pretends to deal?) with High Literature in the same fashion he treated popular literature. This kind of approach allowed him to create a mobile axis that methodologically challenged the reader to confront its personal critical standards. At the same time, it allowed him to question the accepted rules of the culture of a given society and recuperate to the text history and historical memory in a system of production that tends to erase them—and yet it cannot entirely. Throughout the book we can easily note Fiedler's insistence on the fact that the forces of production of a society and their media possess a culturability of their own. They produce culture in a multiplicity of forms—for example the novel and its offspring, the motion picture—that necessarily reflect the politics of the atomized world in which these forms come to existence and are entangled. They produce hegemony. Texts, Frederic Jameson wrote, "come before us as the always-already-read; we apprehend them through sedimented layers of previous interpretations, or—if the text is brand-new—through the sedimented habits and categories developed by those inherited interpretive traditions."[9] It is on the basis of these premises that when he deals with the issue of war in Vietnam movies such as *Apocalypse Now, The Deer Hunter* and the first two *Rambos*, Fiedler starts off with literary texts such as Dos Passos's *Three Soldiers*, E. E. Cummings's *The Enormous Room* and Hemingway's *A Farewell to Arms*, books traditionally enlisted in the modernist canon, and then reaches back to the "good bad" writer James Fenimore Cooper, the founding father of the American novel, with *The Deerslayer*, whose subtitle is, quite properly, *or, the Path to War.*

What is at work in this critical attitude is another fundamental theoretical presupposition of Fiedler's mode of being as a critic and writing about literature and culture. In the fashion of some of the most acute critics of modernity from Henry Adams to Hannah Arendt, Michel Foucault and Marshall Berman, Fiedler assigns to experience and knowledge, regardless of the form in which they are expressed, a *public* dimension that *precedes* any notion of time, space, cultural artifact, literary objects and, no less important, myth without disarticulating them from one another. One of the constant features of his writings is an ever increasing interconnection among these various elements at any level of interpretation, which he grounds in the idea of a shared public dimension of the human experience and the literary and pop work and "other areas of human experience" that sustains his concept of the work of art as "a total human experience" (6). A brief look at his vocabulary is quite telling in this respect.

Over and over again Fiedler addresses the reader in a collective fashion as if he were directly speaking to the reader. He writes of "*our* atomized world," "*our* writers"; he speaks of "*communal* dreams," "*collective* unconscious"; he talks of archetypes as "*shared* patterns of beliefs and feelings beneath consciousness"; he reminds us that slavery is a "*public* issue." In "Robert Penn Warren: A Final Word," he writes that "the underlying mythos" of *All the King's Men* "not merely enters the *public domain* almost immediately, but seems to have been there even before the work which embodies it appeared" (179; all italics mine). He concludes "New England and the Invention of the South" as follows:

> But what has begun as a private fantasy . . . has become a national myth: a perceptual grid through which we continue to perceive slavery, abolition and the ante-bellum South, indeed, our whole country and culture. But this is to say that finally *Uncle Tom's Cabin* is a social, a cultural, fact, quite as real as *public* documents like the Fugitive Slave Law or the Emancipation Proclamation. (63; my italics)

Given the obsessive presence of the word "myth" in many of these essays as in all of his critical writing, it is all the more noteworthy to recall that what attracted Fiedler to Cesare Pavese (one of the Italian writers whose fictional and critical works helped Fiedler discover American literature during his "Roman Holiday" in the early fifties as a Fulbright Scholar in Italy) was Pavese's abandonment of a rigid, bureaucratic communist perspective and his embracement of myth in order to open a "colloquy with the masses."[10]

Fiedler put his notion of universal singularity at the service of the public, of the common interest interconnecting and contextualizing the two, as if the work of writing, in the form of literary criticism, were a public service, a civic duty that reproduces and re-affirms the relationality of the private and the public realms, of the inner and the outer selves, the alignment between the private and the public sphere in relation to literary fiction and history, thereby recuperating history to fiction and popular culture, form (the social) to aesthetics (the public). One such example is the link between the singular and the plural in the title of his book *Freaks: Myths and Images of the Secret Self*, especially in light of the superexposed public dimension of the freaks whose history Fiedler took great pains to reconstruct and analyze before anybody else. Fiedler concludes the introduction to that truly magnificent book warning the reader that the "distinction" between "we and them, normal and Freak, is revealed as an illusion, desperately, perhaps even necessarily, defended, but untenable in the end."[11] In the closing essay of this book, "Whatever Happened to Jerry Lewis?", quite tellingly (for those willing to read it) subtitled "*That's Amore*," Fiedler reads in Jerry Lewis's comic representation of disability— possibly the ultimate limit of subjectivity, otherness and political citizenship for a democratic community—the exposure of the "otherness of the suffering as the sameness to our own" condition (307).*

Ultimately, Fiedler's criticism has a subversive goal. His target was (and, I would argue, remains even more so for us today) the politics of the hegemonic discourse of and in the West, the traditions that over the course of *history* translated, acted out, and thus reified and reinforced the hegemony of the "universally valid standards," the "attitudes and values created" by history. For Fiedler the critical struggle was first and foremost over beliefs, which he judged as the outcome of a historical process fueled primarily by class hier-archy. In the light of this it is profitable to recall French political philosopher Etienne Balibar's note that "a hierarchy of communal references is hegemony within the ideology,"[12] by which, of course, he meant the dominant ideology. The struggle involves identity, including class identity, on the basis of this historical process *and* as a result of it.

In this perspective what one needs to load in his critical baggage is first of all a thorough knowledge of the previous (critical) traditions and the history they belonged to, especially the most influential in the institutions of culture such as universities, literary journals, popular magazines, the cultural sections of newspapers and, I would contend, publishing houses. That is the reason why Fiedler continuously engaged various critical traditions, whether that of D. H. Lawrence's *Studies in Classic American Literature*, the rare and not very memorable criticism by Mark Twain, the "self-declared Marxists" identified by Granville Hicks, the populism of DeVoto and Parrington, the antifascist *American Renaissance* of F. O. Matthiessen, the New Critics, Structuralism, Deconstruction or the trajectories of *Partisan Review*. Likewise, the idea of dealing with hugely popular works or figures such as *Rambo* and Buffalo Bill and linking them to the Leatherstocking Tales and the Western genre does not mean to put these works on the same level of the aesthetic scale as, say, Dante, T. S. Eliot or, as Fiedler put it in "Encounter with Death," "the essentially religious" poetry of James Agee's posthumous *Death in the Family* (203). It means to challenge the ideology of reality that is enacted especially in the pri-vate mind, the one space that, as Fiedler points out in "New England and the Invention of the South," is only apparently private, whose effect reverberates in

---

*For the record, by the time of the writing of this article Fiedler was severely limited in his physical movements and well-being by Parkinson's disease.

the public sphere across gender, class, race or, for that matter, religion, as well as across continents.* It means to ask younger critics, as Norman Podhoretz was in the fifties, to refuse the comfort zone of the "ideas and attitudes" of the previous generations of critics as Fiedler asked him to do in "A Fortyish View." It means to be critically avant-garde. In his "*Postscript to* The Name of the Rose" Umberto Eco explained Fiedler's intent when he pretended to align on the same aesthetic ladder high literature and "junk scorned by the critics," otherwise known as pop literature:

> We all know that he [Fiedler] is too keen of a critic to believe these things. He simply wants to break down the barrier that has been erected between art and enjoyability. He feels that today reaching a vast public and capturing its dreams perhaps means acting as the avant-garde, and he still leaves us free to say that capturing readers' dreams does not necessarily mean encouraging escape: it can also mean haunting them."[13]

This is precisely what Fiedler meant when he invited his fellow scholars and teachers to give the Devil his due! He wanted to return to the literary and popular arts their subversive dimension by asking the apparently easy and indeed quite difficult question of why we like what we like, why certain truly awful books and pop artifacts appeal to vast, national and transnational masses alike, what is hidden underneath the mythopoeic power of these works, what fuels such a power. Although he kept insisting on the need to satisfy our all too obvious animal side, our emotions, he sustained his argument with the reasoning mind of the Cartesian tradition. After all, what is to like in a novel like William Faulkner's *Sanctuary*, whose credo Fiedler defined as "women are completely impervious to evil" and to which female readers too respond despite (or because of?) the unspeakable indignity of the numerous rapes inflicted on Temple Drake? (153). And how do we explain the fact that of all novels it was *Sanctuary* to save the career of such a gifted writer and sell more than any of his previous ones at the onset of the Great Depression? Or, to update this a little, what is so appealing about a criminal such as Tony Soprano, his "famiglia," and their conduct and "lifestyle"? This is what Fiedler is after when he gives the Devil his due. He is avant-garde and hunts the audience's values, attitudes and standards. For if the values, the attitudes and the standards of the dominant traditions are "created" by history, then

---

*As I write, the news report that a small town south of Belgrade, an area heavily bombed by American and NATO military jets less than ten years ago, recently erected a statue of Rocky Balboa in the central public square. If this is for me somehow in the range of the amusing and the conceivable, I must confess that I was stunned when I learned that a Hamas-controlled television channel picked Mickey Mouse's character for a program aimed at the anti-Israeli indoctrination of Palestinian children. God works in mysterious ways. Apparently, so does Satan.

challenging these values, attitudes and standards means to confront both them *and* their history. Leslie Fiedler means to challenge, from the standpoint of intellectual work, the literary anthropology and the historical narratives that produced them, to create not a counter critical tradition, "the anti-tradition of traditionlessness" of Whitman and Twain (139). Fiedler means to attempt to change radically the hegemonic tradition, to envision and begin to forge a new traditionalism upon which to rebuild humanism in place of the classist liberal humanism that is centered on bourgeois individualism of Protestant heritage and the Universalist messianic theology of Christianity.

Fiedler's goal was NOT to enlarge that center to make room for previously exploited and marginalized groups as many among those groups eventually did.[14] He wanted to move the axis of hegemony toward a plural center that did away on the one hand with the historical violence of monotheistic universalism, in this case Christian universalism, on the other with what historian Warren I. Sussman called "the modal psychological type" of the American middle class,[15] the one whose "positive values" are "duty and hard work, heroism and honor . . . home, school and church, which is to say, bourgeois domesticity and Christian humanism" that according to Fiedler Mark Twain tears apart with "the universal solvent of laughter" in *Huckleberry Finn* (74). It is this kind of humanism that in Fiedler's view presents as "liberalism" what really is "a smug, conservative sort of optimism" and as "radicalism" what really is a "religious point of view" (200). This evaluation seems to echo Karl Polanyi's thesis according to which with the great transformation of the twentieth century political economy entered human consciousness and the realm of the universal assuming at once the form of progress and damnation. It was this social environment that fueled the first generation of immigrants in the twentieth century to substitute "Success-America" for their original dream once "the first easy vision of stepping from shipboard to belongingness had failed," the one that, as Fiedler writes in "The Return of James Branch Cabell," built "the bourgeois world of compromise and accommodation, but with the best sellers that celebrated its values," which, once again, explains why it is important to read bestsellers and give their inherent Devil his due (184, 244).

To be sure, Fiedler did not attack work. After all, he worked hard since early in his life and continued to do so until his very last day, writing and teaching. And there was nothing that Fiedler loved more than his home in Buffalo. His target was the crystallization of the classist and messianic narrative that is intolerant, if not altogether inimical, of different cultures and that reified those values to cleanse, enslave, exploit and exclude the groups that originally inhabited the future political entity called the United States of America and others on whose shoulders the country was built, while at the same time posing those values as the founding values of the narrative of the home of the free and the resilient individual (preferably white and male). That is to say, in the name of *liberal democracy as we have historically and theoretically experienced and known it* and, of course, private (NOT personal) property. It is the divisive, hierarchical politics of this narrative that produced a country "divided against itself" as *Huckleberry Finn* is, even structurally, which is what makes it the sacred holy book of America and explains why it is on the raft, away from the community of "sivilization," that one is able *to imagine* "a kind of love compatible with freedom" after he has managed to "establish a community of two, temporary and foredoomed perhaps, but providing for as long as it lasts a model for the reconciliation of blacks and whites in an America otherwise ethnically divided against itself" (73). It is hardly a coincidence, I think, that reflecting in strict sociopolitical terms on the Vietnam War, the watershed of modern American history and, according to Leo Marx,[16] of post–World War II American literary criticism and intellectual political debate, Fiedler made the crucial assertion that "we endure the pangs of a society that has outlived a value system whose mythological foundation remains firm" (250).

War, the twin brother (the gender is not an option) of violence and synonym of death and destruction, of both physical and social ties, highlights a historical gap between society and its value system with his mythological foundations. War functions exactly as the "love compatible with freedom" of *Huckleberry Finn* in "Come Back to the Raft Ag'in," where love highlights on the one hand the heteronormativity of the nation's laws—the one element that Hannah Arendt argued produces the space where human relationships and social ties are experienced[17]—"our laws on homosexuality and the context of prejudice they objectify," and on the other hand collective loneliness, "that compelling anxiety, which every foreigner notes, that we may not be loved, that we are loved for our possessions and not our selves, that we are really—alone" (52). Fiedler establishes a link between violence and lack of social ties on the one hand, and the politics of possessions and the narrative of identity that underwrite them on the other. As he unveils these myths, he attempts to pose, if not the foundation, at least the question of a humanism capable of sustaining a politics of sharing for a "love compatible with freedom" rather than with killing, indifference and exploitation.

On the basis of these theoretical presuppositions—unity of vision of culture and the human experience, universal singularity, equality as the basis of difference, public dimension of writing and the mode of being a critic, oppositional re-framing of politics and intellectual work, historical perspective, interconnectedness of the various levels of interpretations—one can read Fiedler's criticism as work at the service of what James Cox called "a democratic freedom."[18] Fiedler's criticism is a civic and civilizing effort to promote a humanism able to recuperate history to a different project than the one that brings back history as memory in the form of guilt toward the formerly oppressed. For such a project, what better symbol and metaphor than the Devil—New England's synonym for enslaved labor and deprived humanity in the cotton fields as well as in the kitchen and the bedroom— to begin again? It is only too apt and, as I hope I have been able to show, not a coincidence that Fiedler's critical career began in the Devil's home, Dante's *Inferno*, right where the informed imagination challenges the limits of knowledge, of the physical world and man's place in it. To look backward at a criticism based on these critical presuppositions and give the Devil his due may as well be a way out of the crisis of literary criticism. At the same time, such a criticism may also reveal itself as a valid tool to (re)fashion what we desperately need *right now right here*—and what is literature, the art of telling stories and singing songs, most urgent duty and responsibility (first of all toward itself) in these days of dying "from the halls of Montezuma to the shores of Tripoli" as the Marine Corps hymn has it, quite tellingly. That is to say, reintroducing an idea and an actual possibility of a humanism that says yes to the politics of sharing affirmed in "the mulatto culture that is America's gift to itself and the rest of the world," and "No! In Thunder" as Melville's line adopted by Fiedler for one of his books reads, to the hate embedded in the empty rhetoric of freedom and God at the service of our criminal, shameful, arrogant "and futile wars" (303). That's the truth of *The Devil Gets His Due*. That's Amore.

Burlington, NC
Labor Day 2007

NOTES

1. See Terry Eagleton, *After Theory* (London: Allen Lane, 2003). The Center for Working-Class Studies at Youngstown University is one exception, as it is the work of Janet Zandy, alone as editor or author, and with Robert Coles. See Janet Zandy, *Hands: Physical Labor, Class, and Cultural Work* (New Brunswick, NJ: Rutgers U.P., 2004); Janet Zandy, ed., *What We Hold in Common: An Introduction to Working-Class Studies* (New York: The Feminist Press at the CUNY, 2001); Janet Zandy, ed., *Liberating Memory: Our Work and Our Working-Class Consciousness* (New Brunswick, NJ: Rutgers U.P., 1995); Janet Zandy, ed., *Calling Home: Working-Class Women's Writings; An Anthology* (New Brunswick, NJ: Rutgers U.P., 1990); Janet Zandy and Nicholas Coles, eds., *American Working-Class Literature: An Anthology* (New York: Oxford U.P., 2007).

2. Ross Posnock, "Innocents at Home," in *Book Forum* (Summer 2003), 6.

3. Gary Gerstle, *American Crucible: Race and Nation in the Twentieth Century* (Princeton, NJ: Princeton U.P., 2001).

4. At the moment of his death Fiedler was working on an introductory piece for a volume of D. H. Lawrence's works. He last worked on this piece on January 23, 2003, six days before his death. The article focused on Lawrence's *Studies in Classic American Literature*. Fiedler begins by calling that little book "the best critical work ever written by anyone, even Americans. Moreover, no one ever since has surpassed Lawrence's book, though one American at least, F. O. Matthiessen, has come close."

5. Leslie Fiedler, *The Devil Gets His Due: The Uncollected Essays*, ed. and with an introduction by Samuele F. S. Pardini (Berkeley: Counterpoint Press, 2008), 312. All following parenthetical page numbers refer to this collection.

6. See Johannes Willem Bertens, *The Idea of the Postmodern: A History* (London: Routledge, 1995); Alan Wald, *The New York Intellectuals: The Rise and Decline of the Anti-Stalinist Left from the 1930s to the 1980s* (Chapel Hill: U. of North Carolina P., 1987).

7. See *New Directions 1944*, ed. by James Laughlin (Norfolk, CT: New Directions), xi.

8. Leslie Fiedler, *What Was Literature? Class Culture and Mass Society* (New York: Simon and Schuster, 1982), 17.

9. Fredric Jameson, *The Political Unconscious: Narrative as a Socially Symbolic Act* (Ithaca, NY: Cornell UP, 1981), 9.

10. Leslie Fiedler, "Introducing Cesare Pavese," in *No! In Thunder: Essays on Myth and Literature* (Boston: Beacon Press, 1960), 148.

11. Leslie Fiedler, *Freaks: Myths and Images of the Secret Self* (New York: Simon and Schuster, 1978), 36.

12. Etienne Balibar, *The Philosophy of Marx*, transl. by Chris Turner (London: Verso, 1950), 45.

13. Umberto Eco, *Postscript to* The Name of the Rose, transl. by William Weaver (San Diego: Harcourt Brace Jovanovich, 1984), 72.

14. See Eric Foner, *The Story of American Freedom* (New York: W. W. Norton, 1998).

15. Warren I. Sussman, *Culture as History: The Transformation of American Society in the Twentieth Century* (New York: Pantheon Books, 1984), 81.

16. Leo Marx, "Believing in America," *Boston Review* (December 2003/January 2004).

17. Hannah Arendt, *The Promise of Politics*, ed. and with an introduction by J. Kohn (New York: Schocken Books, 2006).

18. James M. Cox, "Celebrating Leslie Fiedler," in *Leslie Fiedler and American Culture*, ed. by Steven G. Kellman and Irving Malin (Newark: U. of Delaware P., 1999), 151.

THE·DEVIL
GETS·HIS·DUE

Toward an
Amateur Criticism

Looking back over my own brief critical practice, I find that it has been rather consistently based on presuppositions fashionably called "obscurantist." Though not always consciously, I have been searching for strategies to oppose that "scientific criticism whose methods are mining, digging or just plain grubbing," and which assumes that the work of art is essentially a social function or a function of language, amenable to analysis in terms of the currently honorific vocabularies of various sciences. Though I should hate to call myself a Romantic, I am opposed to the dogged anti-Romanticism of much contemporary criticism which leads to a contempt for the imagination, and is often grounded in a kind of *lumpen*-nominalism that would grant only a second-class "reality" to works of art. The discrepancy between the metaphors typical to the creative mind and those typical to the critical mind in our world (and this is true often in the single individual who practices both as poet and critic) indicate a quietly desperate cleavage. I propose a mode of criticism more congruous with the sort of literature we admire, a criticism as wary of bureaucratization, as respectful to the mythic and mysterious, as dedicated to a language at once idiosyncratic and humane as, say, *Moby Dick* or the novels of Kafka.

Some great works of criticism *are*, of course, great works of art: *Don Quixote, Werther, The New Eloise, The Man with a Blue Guitar, Madame Bovary;* but even discursive critical comment dares not forget its relationship with literature. To remember that affiliation is to enlist criticism against the chief enemy of literature today, the "liberal" or scientific mind, with its opposition to the frivolous and the tragic, its distrust of such concepts as God, the Devil, Genius and Taste, and its conviction that it is impertinent to ask just how many children Lady Macbeth *did* have. To insist that criticism be occasional, pleasurable and inexact is to keep it out of the hands of those for whom it is, whatever their avowed intentions, a weapon *against* poetry.

The role of the critic resembles that of the poet in two important respects beyond the elementary obligation to provide an overbalance of pleasure. First, he must join in irony and love what others are willing to leave disjoined, and second, he must be willing to extend awareness beyond the point where the lay reader instinctively finds that quality profitable or even possible. Unlike the poet, however, the critic has an obligation to be explicit, patient and humble (humble *enough,* at least); for in choosing his role he has chosen to endure as a necessity what remains for the poet an option, namely, being comprehensible. The critic, indeed, is responsible for all misinterpretations of what he asserts except those arising from absolute stupidity, but including those possible to deliberate malice. The poet, on the other hand, need feel guilty for only those misconceptions of his work which he has secretly desired.

With wit and grace, the critic must mediate between the poem and the platitude, forbidden the insolent freedom of the one and the reassuring dull-ness of the other, yet required to be faithful to both. Loyal to the work of art and pledged to good faith toward an audience conditioned to banalities, he must somewhat betray both. It is a question of balance and discretion.

These days we are all the time decrying "reductive" criticism (I, too, have joined in the chorus), that is, being more fearful of treason toward the poem than toward the platitude. But we must not forget that as critics we engage to reduce works of art, and that our only defense against *hubris* toward the poem is humility and confession: a recognition and public declaration that the textual-semantic analysis, or the biographical-psychoanalytic interpretation, is not more fundamental, not "truer" than the poem.

An excessive fear of the platitude is as harmful to the critic as an excessive contempt for the poem. The mastery of Doctor Johnson as a critic lies in his masterful control of the commonplace. His "technical" vocabulary is a sta-bilization of common speech, and he is constantly illustrating in his critical practice that redemption of the platitude which is more spectacularly accom-plished in poetry. By the same token he speaks directly to that *general reader* for whom the critic ideally writes.

In *intent,* the good critic addresses the common reader, not the initiate, and that intent is declared in his language. That in fact there are in our own time few general readers in the Johnsonian sense is completely irrelevant. The primary act of faith which makes criticism possible compels the critic under any circumstances to speak *as if* to men and not to specialists. The compul-sory comprehensibility of the critic is not a matter of pandering to indolence, prejudice or ignorance, but of resisting the impulse to talk to himself or a congeries of reasonable facsimiles of himself. In an age of declining sociability and the widespread failure of love, it is difficult to be an *amateur;* but at last one remembers that the opposite of the *amateur* is the onanist, and though an occasional voice is raised for "autotelic" criticism, most writers are prepared to admit, in theory at least, that the critic must be, in love and exasperation, a mediator.

Many, persuaded as I am that in a time of mass culture and debased taste, the critic, neither condescending nor snubbing, must continue to pretend that rational communication is possible, would still restrict the area of his mediation in terms of his subject. They regard with polite horror the critic who concerns himself with other platitudes tangent to the work of art, besides the formal ones. To specify any clichés beyond those dealing with the relations of the parts of a work to the whole and to each other is damned as "extrinsic!" But surely, the duty of the critic is to mediate between the lay public and any area of experience which illuminates or is illuminated by a work of art. The general failure to come to terms with works of literature is often a failure to *connect;* and the critic who chooses to deal with the work in isolation aggravates an endemic weakness of our atomized world. The critic's job is the making of mediate metaphors that will prepare the reader for the more drastic metaphors of the poet; and such metaphor-making is his concern because he knows that the relationships he clarifies are real relationships.

In becoming a general critic, the literary critic does not betray his vocation but fulfills it. The "pure" literary critic, who pretends, in the cant phrase, to stay "inside" a work all of whose metaphors and meanings are pressing outward, is only half-aware. And half-aware, he deceives; for he cannot help smuggling unexamined moral and metaphysical judgments into his "close analyses," any more than the "pure" literary historian can help bootlegging unconfessed aesthetic estimates into his chronicles. Literary criticism is always becoming "something else," for the simple reason that literature is always "something else."

The point is not to choose between the complementary blindnesses of the "formalists" and the "historians," but to be more aware than either: to know, if possible, when one is making aesthetic judgments and when philosophical or ethical ones, or, at least, to realize when one is confused. It is not an easy problem. In which category, for instance, do the estimates of Milton by T. S. Eliot and Johnson belong? To *know*—there is the difficult and damnable point of criticism. How much easier it is to be a Parrington, thinking one has dismissed Henry James, when one has dealt with a few of his "ideas" torn from their context of felt life; or to be a scorner of Parrington, believing one has demolished Wordsworth for his "imprecise language," when one has turned from him out of a distaste for Romantic Pantheism; or even to assert that there is neither "Romanticism" nor "Pantheism," only poems. How easy and how ultimately uninteresting!

In criticism as in art, the false is most often the boring; and after all, the critic's unforgivable sin is to be dull. What is less amusing than fumbling history or sociology pretending to be literary discussion, except those "close analyses" or tabulations of imagery become machines for the mindless to manipulate? And what is more irrelevant to the work of art?

The work of art remains still a total, human experience, form and arche-type, daemonic and rational, immune to categorization, and incapable of being produced by organized and divided labor. But criticism aspires these days in almost all camps to become a field of specialization, or rather a series of specialized fields, each tied by its vocabulary to one of the social sciences: the "formalist" approaches tied to semantics, the historical to sociology, psychology etc. The act of total criticism becomes merely a sum of all these ventures, the end-product of a bureaucratized "team." Until our own century, criticism had resisted the atomizing impulse; now it seems to have lost faith in the validity of its traditional humane vocabulary, and its inherited modes of intuition and generalization, in favor of more "scientific" modes. Oddly enough, the quasi-sciences it emulates have just recently remade themselves in the image of the biological and physical sciences. The difference between a Longinus and a Kenneth Burke is analogous to that between Plato and, say, Allport and Parsons, involving a surrender of the humane to the scientific under the shadow of Darwin and the physical theorists.

The various modes of specialized analysis current today, however inimical to each other, share a basic insecurity about the validity of traditional values, and indeed, finally question the very possibility of evaluation. The act of evalu-ation remains nonetheless the vital center of criticism; but to practice it one must believe in the reality of the true, the good and the beautiful, as well as in the existence of men of taste, in whom a disciplined sensibility is capable of making discriminations among experiences in terms of those absolutes. Lacking these beliefs, one can only fall back on relativism, or make intrinsic, formal evaluations, that is, disguise the source of one's judgments in a scien-tific jargon or a parody of one, talking of structure and texture, satisfaction of affective impulses, etc. etc.

To talk of "autonomous" judgments of works of art is not only to aggravate the compartmentalization of our moral lives, which many of the practitioners of such judgments elsewhere deplore, but also to darken counsel. In fact, we respond totally to works of art as their modes of experience jibe or fail to jibe with our *weltanschauung*. Even the terms of "aesthetic" criticism, complexity, irony, simplicity, concreteness, betray themselves as metaphors one element of which rests on ethical preconceptions. Judgments about literature arise always from some larger system, some "religion," in most cases where the debt is not openly confessed, on the prevailing Art Religion of our time, that worship of good works, which is actually a debased Protestantism.

If possible, the critic should have some religious allegiance. This lets him begin with the conviction that the source of the values which inhere in works of art is elsewhere, and saves him from the idolatrous worship of art objects, or the pursuit of the kind of deep exegesis which secretly assumes that certain texts are Scripture. The critic should believe that the practice of art and its contemplation are goods in themselves, as peculiar ways of knowing the real world in love; but that, on the other hand, individual works are more or less good in reference to a truth which they do not define but to which they refer.

If one can believe that poems make only "pseudo-statements," because, indeed, there is no reality available to any mode of knowing but science, the problem is not posed in this form. But to the realist, evaluation is necessarily double. A piece of literature must be judged first in terms of how far it participates in the essential goodness of art by providing a formal pleasure indistinguishable from an organized apprehension of reality; and second, how mature, consistent, complex, and, alas, *true* is its individually realized apprehension.

It is ridiculous to have to insist that "My luv is lak a red, red rose" for all its formal excellence cannot possibly be as good as Donne's sonnet on death, nor the latter, accomplished performance that it is, as good as the book of Job—and that the grounds of this distinction are not ultimately formal but moral. I must confess that, conditioned as I am in my generation, I find it embarrassing to admit this elementary truth; and even more disturbing to have to confess that there are some aesthetically satisfactory works whose vision of reality is narrow to the point of being contemptible. Sometimes, indeed, the technically best works which an age knows how to produce are mean and despicable in their outlook and underlying *mythos*. This is one of the smaller horrors of our own day. We must honor the best we have, but we must not pretend its meanness is beside the point. The true lover of language can be forgiven a great deal, but not everything. That this truth is dishonored by fools does not excuse us from considering it.

The determination of the goodness and badness of art, involving as it does an adjudication of a congruity both subtle and immense, is risky at best. Certainly at any moment one should not pretend to *know* the graded merit of a whole corpus of work, but one does know that such a ranking exists as a limit toward which the critic aspires. And one is especially aware that the new work of art is the touchstone against which the whole existing body is measured, precisely as the new work is assessed in light of the standards implicit in that accepted body. This perfectly dialectical process is made explicit in the critic, for whom all works exist outside of time except as they achieve contemporaneity in his focus of attention. If it were not for the critic, that ideal reader, no work would exist in any sense but the historical. No wonder humility is enjoined for the critic.

Ever since the eighteenth century and precisely as the potential audience for the work of art has grown, so has the length of time between the composition of the new work and its assimilation; in the interim period, the living work, however splendid and universal in its appeal, is entirely the critic's. No wonder that it is tempting for him to resent the moment at which the work passes out of his sole keeping into the living experience of a large group, as the work of Eliot is passing at the present moment. It is at the moment when he accomplishes what he is after, achieving his intended mediation, that the critic is most likely to be tempted out of modesty into snobbishness—crying out, "This is not what I meant at all!"

The critic is least likely to be the victim of pride and most likely to be thought such a victim when he first opposes majority taste with a new claim. Ignoring the charge of insolence, he must patiently explain in terms of the critical tradition or traditions in which he stands his preference; with whatever strategies he knows, he must make *available* the work of art, and if the lay reader still demurs, he must not hesitate to invoke the sanction of taste, and his own authority as a man of taste. To the liberal mind, to which all theories of Election are anathema, and to the scientific mind, to which all mysteries are distasteful, the invocation of taste, a mystery of the order of inspiration and grace, will seem "obscurantist." But the critic must dare that condemnation.

Unfortunately, there is no substitute for taste and the self-perpetuating academy of men of taste—not study, or intelligence, or statistics or Method. Indeed, the whole modern emphasis on methodology seems sometimes a strategic move to make evaluation seem possible at the hands of the mediocre. Each generation has its own peculiar refuge from the stubborn fact of the inequality of sensibility, a device to obscure the problem of the excellent: source-hunting, rime-counting, in our time close analysis.

Against the aristocratic mystery of taste, certain of our contemporaries hold up the claims of "democracy": professional critics may find, say, Sandburg inadequate as a craftsman and gross in his perceptions, but he is much admired by high-school students and the teachers of high-school students. For the "people" is not Sandburg then better than Wallace Stevens? Even more resolvedly than he opposes the substitution of measurable psychological standards for his intuitions, the critic must stand against the attempt to replace the consensus of expert judgment with popular suffrage. He must resist that deep-rooted hatred of excellence that seeks to pass itself off through sentimental analogies as essential democracy.

Not all deniers of the primacy of evaluation are misguided friends of the people or worshippers of scientific method. Occasionally, a critic with quite honorable obscurantist convictions will assert, for instance, that not "rank" but "use" should be the main concern of the critic. And yet the defenders of this position do not mean, I am sure, that the "use" of Eugene Field rather than Dryden should become the matter of the literary theorist. Before the critic can begin to talk of the use of works of art, he must select, and his selection is *per se* an act of evaluation. The only question is, then, whether he makes his choice without defending, as far as he can, his selection, and making explicit its ethical and aesthetic grounds. Or perhaps such critics really mean to make of "use" an evaluative criterion, their essential criterion.

If the latter is their intention, I feel some sympathy for what they are after. I understand, I think, their revulsion from the claims of the generation before theirs to be establishing "universally valid standards" when they were trying merely to rationalize certain vices acquired in adolescence, like a taste for *Idylls of the King.* All critical positions are in one sense strategic and it is good to be frank about it. At worst, we are tempted to defend the prejudices of childhood; at best, we contrive standards that put in its best light the best writing of our own time, our own writing, if we are ourselves poets.

One of the admirable achievements of recent criticism has been the devaluation of such poets as Shelley and Tennyson, the restoration of Donne, the apotheosis of Melville, etc.; and these revisions of received rankings obviously involve an exaggeration of the merits of writers especially "useful" to us, and conversely, an unfavorable distortion of other writers whose practice seems alien to what we are after. But I take it that we have been *aware* (and this is our peculiar merit) all along that these were "strategies," and that there was another standard, a balance gradually righted by counter-excesses and exaggerations. Having reached the proper age for paying respects to the Absolutes, Mr. Eliot has been publicly confessing the truths about Milton that in his youth he strategically suppressed. The pity has been to watch those squirm who have been confusing the strategic with the absolute, and who have made their orthodoxy of his exaggeration.

I practice and love strategic criticism, but it is for me not a rival to the attempt to achieve final hierarchies, but rather a handmaiden. The only way to find out if a poet is immortal is to kill him; Milton and Wordsworth slain have risen; Cowley and Shelley are rotting in their tombs. The only way to know of what a God's feet are made is to lift him into the air; we have tried it with Whitman and with Poe and with Melville, and we are still looking. The strategist provides us with a ritual pattern, the outward ceremonies of the vegetative rite, to adorn our task. It is an apt and lovely metaphor.

Another advantage of the strategic approach is its polemical overtones; its practitioners are aware always that they are in the midst of a continuous debate in which no assertion is unanswered, and in which nothing less than the truth is at stake. Every position is the occasion for another and the end is never attained. But these are precisely the qualities of living criticism, the antidotes to the pontifical and the pedantic.

I distrust the full-length critical thesis, the ponderously elaborated article, the excruciatingly detailed analysis. The ideal form for critical discourse is the irresponsible, non-commercial book-review, written against time and with the full weight of the generalized tradition pressing in on the aggravatingly present and particular work. The notices by T. S. Eliot that appeared in the *Athenaeum* in 1919 and 1920 seem to me wonderful examples; they contain almost all of his most fruitful insights and stimulating perversities, flashed off whatever book came to hand, but faithful to a continuing concern with the use and ranking of that whole section of French and British literature on which he based his own creative practice. How apt it seems that this is the substance of his achievement and not those full-dress works he was continually promising us and forgetting about.

The occasional piece discourages the framing of elaborate vocabularies, and encourages a tone committed to communication and sociability. How many voices are available and how many languages tempt the critic these days, and how few of them assume the real possibility of communication: the school teacher handing down wisdom or explicating the text he knows is on every desk, the "liberal" condescending to the great simple heart of the people, the commissar thundering finalities from the dais, the misunderstood prophet crying shrilly what he is sure no one will heed. What discourages sociability discourages style; and the failure of style is one of the astonishing facts of our critical writing in general. We are attracted (and God knows I do not exclude myself) to one of two poles; the sort of jargon most grossly typified in Kenneth Burke, a "treason of the clerks" become diction, anti-humane and autotelic in its implications; and opposed to the sort of gray, standard, glutinous prose which can be produced by mass-production methods, and indeed is in such monuments as the recent *Literary History of the United States*. The one threatens to turn language into glossaries and lose it among statistical charts; the other threatens to become an editorial in the *Saturday Review of Literature* or an electioneering speech for the Progressive Party.

The true language of criticism is the language of conversation—the voice of the dilettante at home. Its proper materials are what the civilized, outrageous mind remembers and chooses to connect, not what the three by five cards scrupulously preserve or the printed glossary defines. Its responsibilities are the responsibilities of intelligent social discourse, to be true to the speaker's values and his love for what he discusses, to amuse, to disturb. Criticism must be free to leap, to yoke in the flash of wit what has always seemed alien, to make the seminal generalization, even when the generalization cannot be statistically supported. Not only the 100 percent truth, but the 60 percent, the 51 percent, can be fertile and provocative. The fear of the generalization, like the fear of genius and taste, is an aspect of the cult of the mediocre.

The voice of the critic must be his own voice, idiosyncratic, personal, for without real style (and true style is never safe, choosing always to court extravagance) he carries no conviction except what charts and tables accidentally provide. The voices of "Longinus" or Nietzsche, of Coleridge or D. H. Lawrence, these seem to me all, granting the whole range of their differences, conversational voices in the sense I mean. One feels in their tone and texture an assurance that the works of art being discussed have really *happened* to the men that discuss them, and have been ingested into the totality of their experiences. As in all good conversation, one feels here that the subject has fallen into place, making a new pattern of an already existing universe and becoming one with it, not abstractly, but in the living personality. It is such testimony, testimony to the possibility of literature being assimilated to the experience of the individual in richness and joy, that is vital in our time, not another reassurance that the parts and wholes of individual works cohere, or that the meanings of a single work are multiple and even inexhaustible.

The vocabulary of the critic must be a humane vocabulary—like the Law of God, he must speak in the language of men. This is not to say that he is forbidden the more useful terminology of the sciences, but merely that he is forbidden to make his own speech a jargon in the image of such terminology. Like the poet, he is free to use whatever language has been humanized, or that he can, in an assimilative foray, himself humanize. It is not enough that he know his language, but also that he have made it a part of his habitual conversation, of his whole outlook. A diction that compels him to its habits rather than yielding to his betrays him.

The metaphors of the critic must be congruous with the metaphors of the poet; otherwise, the critic finds himself forced back into his traditional comic role as the enemy of art. To say with Messrs. Wellek and Warren that characters in fiction are "merely words" is to subscribe to a metaphor sanctioned by semantics, and supported ultimately by some current nominalism. To say with Graham Greene that for such characters Christ died on the Cross, or with Pirandello that they have an autonomous existence and will, is to choose a metaphor that begins and ends in the work of art. What common ground does the critic, who tells us that it is absurd to talk of Hamlet's relations with his father or his university days, have with William Faulkner, whom he may pretend to admire? For to Faulkner, as to the great writer-critics like Goethe and Coleridge, the fictive is real, the character exists beyond and above his formal realization. We have yielded up this "Romantic" realization to the heavy-handed doctrine of nineteenth-century Germanic "scientific scholarship," with its fundamental distrust of the imagination and, indeed, of the artist.

In myth-theory the anthropologist, the psycho-analyst, the philosopher and the literary theorist have been rediscovering a common area in which they, who had been almost persuaded they were merely specialists, can speak to each other as men, and it is to myth criticism that I find myself more and more drawn. For here we find not only the recognition that the springs of art creation are ultimately a mystery grounded in truth, but also a new basis for evaluation in the assessment of mythoplastic power, that goes beyond the merely formal without falling into the doctrinal and dogmatic. Writers like Dickens and R. L. Stevenson, who have fared ill at the hands of the historical and formalist critics alike, reveal the source of their persistent power over our imaginations in the light of myth doctrine.

In terms of myth, too, the critic finds it possible to speak of the profound interconnections of the art work and other areas of human experience, without translating the work of art into unsatisfactory equivalents of "ideas" or "tendencies." The myth approach is, of course, no panacea; in the hands of the scientizers it becomes, like many other approaches, merely an excuse for another jargon, just one more strategy for avoiding evaluation.

But intelligently exploited, it can open new possibilities for exploring the meaning of the imagination and the persistence of archetypes; it can provide a fund of new critical metaphors that will not betray too grossly the work of art. And finally it can bolster and nourish that dreamed-of language, common to the creative mind, pledged to the daemonic and the mystery of Truth, and the "liberal" scientific mind, distrustful of absolutes, and incapable either of salvation or the tragic appreciation of its own doom. Our especial need is the interpenetration of these minds. In a world where they do not ordinarily find it possible to communicate, there is work enough for the critic.

Perhaps in the end it will turn out that the divorce is too utter to be healed by his resources, but, modest fellow, he will be content to have mitigated a little the cleavage of our mind, or even just to have told the truth about a few books.

"Giving the
Devil His Due"

The title of my talk is "Giving the Devil His Due." I considered as alternative titles "The Marriage of Heaven and Hell," which would indicate to you who my true master is, and I also considered, I must admit shamefacedly, "Sympathy for the Devil" as a possible title. This will, however, be the last reference to Mick Jagger in my talk, which is going to deal chiefly with older examples of popular culture, since my whole point is to put things like the phenomenon of The Rolling Stones in a much larger context. And in order to establish that context, I must begin, as almost everybody else here has begun, with a definition.

I am going to define for you what I mean by "Popular Culture," and in the course of doing so I will also have to define what I mean by "values," without making it embarrassingly explicit. I am not trying to say to you that I consider my definition of popular culture (which is not a historical one, not a sociological one, not an economic one, but a mythographic or a literary-anthropologic one) the best possible definition of Popular Culture. But I would like you to know what I mean when I use that term, so that you can decide whether or not you agree with me. What I will be describing is what is called sometimes Mass Culture, a term to which I have no objections, though I would really prefer to speak of it as "Majority" Culture—"Modern Majority Culture." But nobody seems to know what I mean when I say that, so I'll settle for "Popular" or simply "Pop Culture."

Actually I am going to confine myself in what follows to talking about popular song and story, mostly story, which is to say popular literature. Ray Browne, who objects to us talking about popular literature rather than to other aspects of popular culture, will have to forgive me, but literature is what I know about, literature is what I am interested in, literature is what I am committed to. I use the term "popular" as opposed to "folk" literature, saving the latter to describe literature of pre-literate society, and the literature of classes excluded from literacy and aristocratic or class-structured society. The former I use to mean majority literature in a mass culture, an industrial and post-industrial society.

Now Popular Literature is, as I use the word, a kind of literature that is not merely mass produced and mass distributed but is written *in order* to be mass produced and mass distributed, or at least, it is written in response, negative or positive, to the possibility of being mass produced and mass distributed. This kind of literature (and the same is true of the other popular arts, or popular culture in general), this kind of literature depends for its very existence, as well as its shape and texture, on certain developments in technology independent of the will or desire of its nominal author or authors; and it therefore changes as technology changes. I base my conclusions on the history of the novel, which I consider from its very origin to have been pop literature. Since it was invented by Samuel Richardson, the novel has changed in response to technological changes. When cheap paper was developed in the 1820s, the novel changed its form in response. When stereotyping was invented, the novel changed its form. When mass produced paperbacks became widespread in the United States, the novel changed its form. Clearly movies at this moment are similarly influenced, by developments in color, sound and so forth. This is point one.

Point two. Since the development of mass production technology is coincident with the rise of capitalism, mass-produced literature has always been dependent upon a marketplace where it is bought and sold, hopefully in very large quantities, in response to the mysterious process of popular demand which makes that marketplace operate. Popular Literature is and always has been since the time of Richardson commodity literature. It is commodity literature—I use that term not pejoratively to blame it but merely to describe it—and like all commodities literature is sold in the marketplace and changes with the conditions of the marketplace, as well as with the advance of technology.

The invention of the railway, for instance, changed the nature of the novel because it was possible to read in a railway car, as it had not been possible to read in a stagecoach, and pretty soon we had railway bookstalls. Popular literature is a commodity, and like all commodities it is intended to be bought and taken home, where one of two things can happen to it. It can be used or played with and then thrown away, like Kleenex or a child's toy; or it can, for reasons hard to identify at least *a priori*, be kept and treasured, like a diamond or a grand piano.

One thing is clear: what determines the survival of such literature is not the critics, guardians of the values presumably implicit in high art, nor is it the lords of the marketplace—the masters of the media. At any point from the beginning of the development of the novel down to the triumph of TV, the naïve of cryptoelitist Marxists of the Frankfurt school, let's say, or Leavis and his followers in England, or Herbert Marcuse and Dwight MacDonald in the United States, have believed that such literature is controlled by the masters of the media. But the truth is that the masters of the media are controlled by the marketplace. The man who sells popular literature or distributes popular music is a man riding a tiger. He never knows where it is going to go. He guesses, more times wrong than right. He hopes for the best, and if he guesses wrong he goes bust and the next man comes along and takes his place.

Now what determines what is consumed is a deep hunger which exists on the level of the unconscious or preconscious, not the conscious, mind. Nobody can control any medium if they think of it in terms of overt or manifest content. What really makes commodity literature or commodity art work is its covert, its encrypted content, which is only available to a cryptoanalytic critic. Yet popular authors, because their work is commodity literature, and because it is distributed in the marketplace, tend to think of it as private property. And in some ways it is. It is protected by law and the courts; it can be bought and sold; it can make a man filthy rich and if not celebrated, famous at least, and all in a moment, not slowly over generations or centuries. But the authors and the critics of popular art are wrong in a certain way because they tend to think of the persistence of popular art in terms of the humanist myth of secular immortality (thank you, Shakespeare). But unlike the high art of the Renaissance, popular art is lacking in qualities which I have called elsewhere "signature elements." For instance, when we see a painting of Christ on the Cross done by an eminent Renaissance artist, we do not say that it is a picture of the Crucifixion; we say that it is a Rembrandt or that it is a Michelangelo, because painted in that work are signature elements: an eccentric, obtrusive or special style, a personal voice or a point of view eccentric enough to seem distorted to the viewer. Everybody knows an El Greco, whatever its nominal subject.

But Gutenberg and post-Gutenberg art, popular literature in this case, is more like the anonymous painting and poetry *before* the Industrial Revolution. More like medieval epic or folk ballad. The novel is even more like what follows it than what went before, more like movies and TV than it is like verse tragedy and classic epic. Gutenberg and post-Gutenberg literature contains *communal* dreams, shared myths or archetypes. And it is distinguished by the mythopoeic color of its creators, their ability to sense what already existed in the popular mind, rather than be any unique vision or ability in executive skills. For this reason popular works of literature tend to pass immediately into the public domain.

This is point number three. Works of popular literature have the disconcerting habit—disconcerting to their authors especially—of passing into the popular domain.

For various reasons I have been reading and meditating on Cervantes's Prologue to the Second Part of *Don Quixote*. Some of you may remember that

Cervantes was buggered because after he had published his first part, it took him eight, nine or ten years to publish the second part; and a false continuer picked up the characters of Don Quixote and Sancho Panza and put them through a series of degrading adventures in which the Don was portrayed as having betrayed his own beloved Dulcinea and having ended up in a mad house. This travesty and vilification of the book was accepted as his and was as successful as Cervantes's original Part One, this driving him, compelling him to write Part Two. There's a marvelous essay on this written by Thomas Mann called "*En Voyage* with Don Quixote," in which Mann, from an elitist point of view, ends up saying that what Cervantes had not come to terms with is the disconcerting fact that a book can be a popular success *though* it is good, just as another book can be a popular success *because* it is bad. This is quite to the point. It illustrates what I mean, leading me to think a little about Dickens as well and about George Reynolds, who did those false continuations of *Pickwick* just after it had come out, continuations in which Pickwick went to France, against his character; in which Pickwick became a teetotaler, against his character; in which Pickwick got married, again against his character. Yet in a certain sense Reynolds and that pseudonymous false continuer of *Don Quixote*, whoever he might have been, were right in a way, because characters in popular literature, as soon as they are created enter, as I have said, the public domain.

Moreover, we read them as if they have always been there, as if we have always known them. All authors can do with characters in popular literature is give them a local habitation and a name. But even the name becomes common property, the names Pickwick and Sam Weller and Don Quixote, for instance, passing into the common language, becoming first metaphors, and then common nouns so that they belong finally to people who have never read such writers as Dickens, much less G. W. M. Reynolds, whom I doubt very many of you have read (though he is still read, I discovered recently, by writers in India).

As a matter of fact, one of the distinctions between popular and high literature can be made on the basis of this, as Edgar Allan Poe, in a review of James Fenimore Cooper, pointed out. There is a certain kind of book, he wrote, which is forgotten though its author is remembered (High Literature); and there is a certain kind of book whose author is forgotten though the work is remembered. And it is indeed true, isn't it, that at the present moment there are far more people today who can identify Hemingway than can identify Lt. Henry or Jake Barnes; while Sherlock Holmes is a familiar name to many people who never heard of Conan Doyle. And the name of Tarzan is known to everybody in the world, including those who never heard of the name Edgar Rice Burroughs.

I come now to point number four. Popular literature, non-elite, mass produced literature is not only independent of its author, but of its original text,
in which changes can be made that not only change but become a part of the
text. I am, for example, currently working on Harriet Beecher Stowe. I have
read *Uncle Tom's Cabin*, I suppose, fifteen or sixteen times. It was the first book
I ever bought, when somebody gave me a little money for the first time when
I was six or seven years old and said, "Go out and buy a book for yourself."
Yet even now I cannot think of that book without thinking of Eliza leaping
from one block of ice to another as she is pursued by bloodhounds. But there
are *no* bloodhounds in Harriet Beecher Stowe's text. These were added in the
dramatic version later on. Popular literature never seems the kind of literature that you are reading for the first time. It always seems like something
you are reading for the second or third or millionth time. It is never finished,
and anything that is added to it is OK. I was amused to hear Stan Lee say the
other day that it didn't make a bit of difference to him whether the name of
the Incredible Hulk (I always have trouble with this: I have a grandson who
loves that program and he always calls it the "Credible Hulk") is changed so
long as the character is not.

Point number five. Not only is popular culture independent of the author
and text, but it is independent of the medium in which it appears. No sooner
was *Uncle Tom's Cabin* published than it was transformed into a stage play.
Henry James is one of the few people, oddly enough, who has ever written
any sensible criticism of *Uncle Tom's Cabin*. He remembered it chiefly from a
stage play he had seen at the P. T. Barnum's American Museum, where *Uncle
Tom's Cabin* was competing with freaks and fake mermaids for the attention
of the audience. Henry James said (and it is clear where the metaphor came
from) that it leaped miraculously into a new element as a fish had leaped out of
the water into the air. It is a characteristic of popular literature that it changes
its medium because it never really belonged to any medium to begin with.
Popular Literature is not "words on the page," as some critics would have us
believe. Like all literature it is finally, essentially, images in the head. Once its
images pass *through* words (the text is transparent, downright irrelevant) into
our heads, such primordial images, or archetypes, or myths (call them whatever name you want that seems congenial) can pass out again easily into any
other medium. They can be portrayed on the stage; they can be painted; they
can be sculpted in stone; they can be turned into stained glass windows; they
can be carved in soap. They still retain their authenticity and the resonance of
feeling that was originally connected with them.

Not only can popular literature in Gutenberg form pass into other media,
but it is *driven* to pass to other media by a kind of inner necessity: *driven* to
pass to media which are accessible to larger numbers of people than can ever

read print with pleasure and profit. You know, one of the things that used to vex me very much, but which I've come to terms with recently, is the rejection of literacy in a world where theoretically universal literacy is the goal. It turns out that most people, though they can learn functional Gutenberg literacy, are never capable of reading print on the page with the kind of immediate pleasure and response they have when reading images on the screen. And there are cultures in the world now where people are passing from pre-Gutenberg culture to post-Gutenberg culture without passing through the Gutenberg stage at all. In India, for instance, there are people who only a generation ago were listening to the storyteller in the marketplace and are now listening to the radio, seeing movies and waiting for TV. Indeed, there is no reason why they should have to pass through the Gutenberg stage at all. One can apply here Trotsky's theory of uneven development and say there is no need to go through any social process stage by stage—we can leap if we like, and sometimes we must.

A kind of inner necessity has brought a situation which—disconcertingly to some, *thrillingly* to me—the novel, the popular novel, the *really* popular novel seems to have become a chrysalis or an embryo, a halfway form on the way to a movie, or to television. It is not completed until it moves into that medium which can reach a larger audience than it could ever touch in its original form. Even in the nineteenth century, as I have said to you, popular works were turned into dramas almost immediately. Not just *Uncle Tom's Cabin*; more people, for instance, also knew the story of "Rip Van Winkle" from its stage version than ever read it in print. And in the process of passing via the popular theater into the movies, which was the next step along the way, a further step in the disintegration of the authority of the individual author, in the humanist sense, occurs.

It is very hard to talk about the author of a moving picture. The first really popular maker of films in the world was D. W. Griffith, whose *The Birth of a Nation* was the first really popular film, shown to a mass audience in the year 1915 at an unprecedented two bucks a head—and they turned out in large numbers to see it. For a while at least he seemed to be trying to substitute the authority of the director-*auteur* for that of the person who had written the original "story." Many of you here, for instance, may think of Griffith as the author of *The Birth of a Nation*, since few of you, I suppose, are aware of the fact that a man by the name of Thomas Dixon, Jr., wrote two books called *The Leopard's Spots* and *The Clansmen*, both moving and immensely popular books, by the way, in their own time—fascist books, misogynist books, racist books, it is true, but so effective still, that I can't read them without a repressive shudder, for which I hate myself.

I once presided over a showing of that film to a bunch of Marxists, a Cine

Club, in Athens, which had asked to see it. It was so left-wing a club that the Communists constituted the Extreme Right. The American embassy had felt considerable embarrassment about the showing of the film, and asked if I could say some words by the way of explanation about the historical moment at which the film had been made, as well as the one it purported to describe. And this I, as it turned out, *needlessly* tried to do, since at the showing of this movie at ten o'clock in the morning, this group of convinced left-wingers rose to their feet and cheered as the Ku Klux Klan rode to the rescue of white womanhood. If Griffith was proud of himself, therefore, he can scarcely be blamed. And he was. If you see his films you will see that around the border of each of his titles, which were a necessary part of the silent film, there's a frame which says "*D. W. Griffith, D. W. Griffith, D. W. Griffith.*" As William Faulkner said in a marvelous funeral elegy to Albert Camus: *The only reason any of us works is to leave our names on the walls of the world, to say We were here.* So Griffith did.

But not all film makers. If you think, for instance, of favorite films of yours and mine like *Gone with the Wind* and *The Wizard of Oz* you will understand. Ask yourselves: "Who is the director of *Gone with the Wind*? Who were the script writers of *The Wizard of Oz*?" And if you don't know you need not be ashamed. The point is that the directors changed and the script writers changed. Nobody knew what he was doing. There was nobody. The archetype and myth wrote itself. Even Margaret Mitchell and L. Frank Baum disappeared in the process.

But there is a further step beyond the movie script. *Gone with the Wind* many of us have seen on the movie screen, but even more have watched it on TV, watched and applauded despite its slander of Black People and defense of the Ku Klux Klan. It had the largest audience of any film ever shown on American television except for *Roots*—which had exactly the opposite views of slavery and Reconstruction, at least as far as overt or conscious ideas are concerned. But in the realm of Popular Art, overt and conscious ideas could not matter less. What matters is the stirring up of the collective unconscious, the evocation of closely shared nightmares of race and sex: the drama of protecting little sister against the rapist, whoever she may be and whatever color: Black/White, White/Black. You can mix them and match them and it makes no difference in popular appeal. Is it white innocence assaulted by black bestiality? Is it black innocence assaulted by white brutality? The audience loves it in any case. And this leads me to my final point about popular culture: It is neither good nor bad—*it is beyond good and evil, as we define the terms, in whatever culture we may live.*

When television finally re-embodies the images of popular culture in flickering light and dark on the countless millions of screens, it thus moves them back to where they began and really belong: to our hearts and our homes and our heads. What we can see on television, we do not watch at the end of an outing, or on a special occasion, as when we go to a theater, but sitting half asleep in our chairs, or lying in our bed somewhere between dreaming and waking. But this represents the fulfillment of all to which the popular arts have aspired from the start.

People used to worry about the taste of the general readers, even in the last decades of the Victorian period, in England, which was the first great period of expansion in Popular Literature. The second, chiefly centered on movies, was the 1930s in the United States. And the third, centered on TV, is right now. Disturbed by the fact that the mass audience was reading not Conrad or James, but Rider Haggard's *She* and Bram Stoker's *Dracula* (which, by the way, are *not* mentioned in official histories of Victorian literature though neither has been out of print for one minute since the time of publication). The critics used to say, "Well, this is pretty sad, but at least they were reading," meaning that mass-culture was tolerable if thought of as a by-product of something that was socially valuable, namely, mass education. If one of the results of everyday education was that the working man, having acquired literacy, decided that he wanted to read junk, well that was all right but not highly encouraging. (Marx, by the way, was disturbed by this. Indeed, almost half of his first book, *The Holy Family*, is an attack on Eugene Sue, because Sue's *Mysteries of Paris* was what working people read, instead of what Marx in his academic German way thought they ought to be reading.) But at least Victorian critics could always console themselves by saying that the pleasures of reading even trash were at least *earned*; because people had sweated to learn their ABCs in school; and like any result of good true-blue Protestant hard work, literacy must, therefore, be good for you, and of value, good for something.

But watching movies and TV is not, in that sense, of value at all. What is fascinating is that nobody has ever been taught in school to read images on the screen. Nobody has to be taught to read images on the screen. And the pleasures of TV are consequently available in a way that makes no separation between the learned and the unlearned, the refined and the gross, the diligent and the indolent—which is carrying the process of democratization too far! I mean, a *little* democratization of culture—OK. But not when one gets to the point where people sitting before their TV sets are typically people without any standards at all, or are (like me) a kind of renegade from high culture, who spends too much of their waking time watching the soaps. Does not this represent a flight to valueless vulgarity, self indulgence? Hedonism! What we find television provides us is unmediated pleasure, instant, unearned, unworked for, unsweated-for gratification: gratification, moreover, that depends on sentimentality, lust, terror, as well as gross burlesque of the social institutions in which we most dearly believe or would like to believe.

Where is "value" to be found, then, in popular literature, if it does, as I have suggested, move relentlessly, inevitably, from *Clarissa* to *Pickwick*, to *Dracula*, to Sherlock Holmes, to *Jaws*, to the *Rocky Horror Shows*, to *Roots*, to *Starsky and Hutch*, to Mick Jagger? Now some of the works I have mentioned possess prized aesthetic qualities—shapeliness, elegance, architechtonic grace. Some of them even express estimable ideas—or at least seem to, though here we must be wary. It is easy to be pious about the lessons *Uncle Tom's Cabin* teaches us, as Tolstoi was pious about it. But essentially Mrs. Stowe's book is more about violence and sentimentality than social justice. If you look hard at her ideas about slavery, for instance, you will discover that her hatred of that institution is based on the same genteel notions as her opposition to smoking, cussing, going to the theater, attending opera, and having sex outside of marriage. And visible just below that sentimentality, as James Baldwin understood, is violence.

Harriet Beecher Stowe may have been read, as Ralph Waldo Emerson—of all people—once said, with equal pleasure in the parlor, the kitchen and the nursery. That is to say, the Lady of the House could read her, the cook could read her, the kids could read her. But at least, once more, they read it, had learned to read. They were, consequently, a little refined. Cultured. But present-day television is available to everybody including the unlettered Lady of the House, the sub-literate cook and kids who don't read. Maybe, then, just *maybe* it is possible for us to say that the value of popular literature, like the popular arts in general, is that it joins together at the level of the unconscious people who are, on every conscious level, in this post-industrial society *divided*. Our religion divides us, our politics divides us, our attitude toward education divides us: the only thing that holds us together is *Kojak, Star Wars, Rich Man: Poor Man.*

Ken Kesey's *One Flew over the Cuckoo's Nest* began as a youth cult book of the sixties, but was turned, almost by mistake, into a popular movie. And I know why, having been present at the showing of this film in an audience which consisted nine/tenths of its original readers grown older, i.e., people who were liberated in all respects. They were, that is to say, against racial discrimination, against male chauvinism, and so forth; but were there cheering with the rest of the racists and sexists in the audience at an anti-Black, hysterically misogynist film, because, I suppose, it touched places in the unconscious of both of which some of us were deeply ashamed. *But at least it joined us all together.*

Now Tolstoi in *What Was Art?* was willing to take the position which tempts me, as I reflect on this aspect of popular art; he was willing to say, OK let's throw out all the old aesthetic values along with the old ethical values; let's grant that the one thing about mass culture which seems of "value" is the fact that it joins everybody together—black and white, young and old, male and female, learned and unlearned, everybody. Tolstoi went so far as to argue that the only literature in the world which was finally endurable was a kind of literature which did join everybody together. And he was willing to substitute for the old snobbism an inverted snobbism; insisting that what pleased the few was probably bad, what pleased the many was good. The old snobbism had taught that all books liked by a large number of people were probably no good; and all books treasured by a minority, like *Paradise Lost*, were good. (Some students of mine once, by the way, when they were practicing something called "pejorative criticism" in the late sixties, criticism which had to be short and negative, used to say of *Paradise Lost*—"Too fucking long.") But to substitute one hard orthodoxy for another is to turn snobbism upside down, means to be willing, as Tolstoi was willing, to deny, not just Shakespeare and Michelangelo, but his own *Anna Karenina*. This seems finally crazy, especially now that Tolstoi has so easily been built into the totalitarian culture of the Soviet Union. A friend of mine recently had a conversation with the greatest of the Americanists in that country and asked him how come they don't publish John Barth's *Sotweed Factor* in the Soviet Union, and this Russian said that it appeals to too few people; the money they have available for translation will be spent on *Rich Man: Poor Man*, which will move everyone.

It turns out, moreover, that Tolstoi was wrong in his assumption that the literature which appealed to everyone would move in the end to be literature based on Christian, humanitarian values. He was simply wrong. Nor was this literature, as the Marxists hoped and now try to enforce by law, based on humanist, egalitarian values. It turns out that literature which in fact does appeal to everyone, appeals not to what is highest in their natures but what is (in the view of most moralists) basest.

I became especially aware of this in an especially troubling way as I was recently reading Hitler's *Table Talk* and discovered that Hitler's favorite book was *The Last of the Mohicans*, that Hitler's favorite movie was *King Kong*. (I'll tell you what Hitler's favorite song was—it's just ridiculous: it was "Who's Afraid of the Big Bad Wolf?") Now the first two of those happen to be favorites of mine. And it is disconcerting to learn thus that popular literature not only joins together the poor and the rich, the educated and the uneducated, male and female, children and adults, *but the good and bad as well*; that in the enjoyment of popular literature one is joined to those people who are felt to be socially reprehensible, wicked, whatever your social code and values may be. *Popular literature joins you with your worst enemies as well as your worst self.* Now that's disconcerting!

The way I deal with this problem, a way which I hope you will find plausible, is by asking myself: Can not the same sort of things which I have been saying about popular literature be said of *all* literature? Are not the things I have said as true, if one reads cryptoanalytically—with attention to their concealed and covert values rather than to their overt and moral values, is not the same thing true of much High Literature as well? In *Paradise Lost* Milton was of the Devil's party without knowing it, as was Whitman even less equivocally in *Leaves of Grass*. And what about *Pickwick* and *Huckleberry Finn*? Is it possible really to read *Pickwick* and Dickens's other Christmas Tales without realizing that under his pietistic posturing, he was bent on taking Christ out of Christmas for all time, and putting Dionysus in his place instead? How do the people celebrate Christmas in Dickens? They eat too much, they drink too much, they dance, they kiss each other under the mistletoe. And when the spirit of Christmas Past enters the scene, he turns out to be Dionysus disguised as Old King Cole!

All literature—all art—is the same. Cervantes was practically unread in the eighteenth century because critics said he was a secret defender of insanity, that the main function of *Don Quixote* was to blur the line between sanity and insanity by suggesting that the mad feel more deeply and are more sensitive than the sane. When I think of the books I have loved best in my life, I realize that what I admire in them is what I love in pop art at its most gross, flagrant, vulgar, brutal and unrefined: the mythopoeic power of the author. Never mind his ability to instruct and delight, to create beautiful, elegant, architechtonic forms to teach those things which we think are important for the future of mankind. Instruction and delight are optional; they can or cannot be present. They are not banned from literature; but they are not essential. What really moves us to transport—what Longinus called *ekstasis*—taking us out of our heads and out of our bodies, out of our normal consciousness is the ability of all great books, great pop books, great elite books, to turn us again into savages and children; and releasing us thus from bondage not merely to the restrictions of conscious or superegos, but to consciousness and rationality, which is to say, the ego itself.

This is the function of all literature, those hallucinations projected with such vividness and authority that we take them for our own, though they were created in fact out of the paranoia of others. The not-so-secret secret motto of all literature is the opposite of Freud's injunction—"Where ego has been so powerfully constructed, let id joyously return."

Now there are many names for this process. Longinus, as I have said, called it poetically *ekstasis*. Aristotle, in a condescending medical metaphor, called it *catharsis*. Later prophets called it "alteration of consciousness" or "desublimation" or "regression in the service of the ego." There are as many names as there are philosophies and psychologies. But the name doesn't matter. What does matter is what the name describes, a therapeutic function of art, which makes it the heir of those communal orgies and blood lettings we have abandoned for the sake of civilization. Literature always carries on an underground war, out of sight but not out of mind, not out of our deep mind: a war against all the values professed by all conformist defenders of whatever reigning culture; against spirit, against civilization, against self-control, against rationality, against sanity, against law and order. The artist, in this sense, was against not just the schoolmaster, the priest, the philosopher, the politician, the statesman, the policeman—but everything in ourselves which responds to that law and order appeal.

The chief value of majority literature is to remind us of what *all* literature is really about. I know that for me the value of reflecting, as I have now for some years, on the popular arts, has been to rescue me from the false notion of what letters mean into which I have been brainwashed by too many courses in English Literature: to deliver me from endless analyses which usually falsify the text, as well as the utopian hopes implicit in the Arnoldian Culture Religion. The function of literature is not to enable us to transcend the flesh. Literature does not come to us in the name of the Holy Ghost. Literature teaches us to remain faithful to our animal existence, to those dark gods, dark only because we have shrouded them, to the dark side of our deepest ambivalence toward violence, toward sex, toward our parents, toward our mates, toward our children, toward our secret selves, toward the daylight deities we are proud to boast we honor alone.

The popular arts are, in short—to come back to my title—a way of giving the Devil his due. And that due we must give him, or die.

Explication de Texte

Inferno Canto XXVI

Godi, Fiorenza, poi che sei sì grande
  Che per mare e per terra batti l'ali,
  E per l'inferno il tuo nome si spande.
Tra li ladron trovai cinque cotali
  Tuoi cittadini, onde mi vien vergogna,
  E tu in grande onranza non ne sali.
Ma se presso al mattin del ver si sogna,
  Tu sentirai di qua da picciol tempo
  Di quel che Prato, non ch'altri, t'agogna.
E se già fosse, non sria per tempo.
  Così, foss'ei, da che pure esser dee;
  Chè piu mi graverà, com' più m'attempo.
Noi ci partimmo, e su per le scalee
  Che n'avean fatte i borni a scender pria
  Rimontò il mio Maestro, e trasse mee.
E proseguendo la solinga via
  Tra le schegge e tra' rocchi dello scoglio,
  Lo piè senza la man non si spedia.
Allor mi dolsi, ed ora mi ridoglio,
  Quand' io drizzo la mente a ciò ch'io vidi;
  E più lo ingegno affreno ch'io non soglio,
Perchè non corra che virtù nol guidi;
  Sì che se stella buona o miglior cosa
  M'ha dato il ben, ch'io stesso nol m'invidi.
Quante il villan, ch'al poggio si riposa,
  Nel tempo che colui che il mondo schiara
  La faccia sua a noi tien meno a scosa,
Come la mosca, cede alla zanzara,
  Vede lucciole giù per la vallea,
  Forse cola dove vendemmia ed ara:
Di tante fiamme tutta risplendea
  L'ottava bolgia, sì com'io m'accorsi
  Tosto ch'io fui là 've il fondo parea.
E qual colui che si vengiò con gli orsi

Explication de Texte

Gentlemen:
Canto twenty-six. Each along this left-hand gyre
Inherits—with specific decorum—the fire:
This is the emblem, the name of their desire.
Not that their mode is *success*, and more,
How each becomes his central metaphor:
Singular tongue, flame's whip, the essential orator.
(This is my circle. My Circle. Confess.)
Understand the orator's limits: the poet, yes,
And professor, perhaps, even, the press,
The obvious abettors of will. But no—no,
Not the animal accomplices, the vegetable, the slow:
Earth, air suffice to damn what we grow
Only or feel. *Fire* rebukes the third,
The enveloping, soul. These, immoderate, preferred
The world's body—words to the Word.

Once more the equivoque, the pause. Line forty-two.
"Each flame *invola*, steals, a sinner." Another clue.
Why *steals*? The meaning's clear: hides, conceals. True,
But what bent figure? What guilt beyond rime's
Exigence. *Steals* them because, when they were time's,
They, too (here penalties not fit but *are* the crimes),
Stole—what? The apple, sirs, the trite, adamic fruit.

I must ask, knowing what you name truth,
Surrender here for a moment, they you impute
To this myth the credence of fact. Believe
You are damned. Pretend there is sin. Leave
Certainty and descend to where two cleave
Together, one flame. Permit me. This is
Diomede (the fire's smaller horn). This is Ulysses.
"Together in His vengeance as in His ire," Vergil hisses,
Remembering the horse's ambush, the broken city,

Vide il carro d'Elia al dipartire,
Quando I cavalli al cielo erti levorsi;
Chè nol potea sì con gli occhi seguire
Ch'ei vedesse altro che la fiamma sola,
Si come nuvoletta, in su salire:
Tal si movea ciascuna per la gola
Del fosso, chè nessuna mostra il furto,
Ed ogni fiamma un peccatore invola.
Io stava sopra il ponte a veder surto
Sì che, s'io non avesse un ronchion preso,
Caduto sarei giù senza esser urto.
E il Duca, che mi vide tanto atteso,
Disse: "Dentro da' fochi son gli spirti:
Ciascun si fascia di quell ch'egli è inceso."
"Maestro mio," rispos'io, "per udirti
Son io più certo: ma già m'era avviso
Che cosi fusse, e già voleva dirti:
Chi è in quell foco che vien sì diviso
Di sopra che par suger della pira
Ov' Eteòcle col fratel fu miso?"
Risposemi: "Là entro si martira
Ulisse s Diomede, e cosi insieme
Alla vendetta vanno come all'ira.
E dentro dalla lor fiamma si geme
L'aguato del caval che fe' la porta
Ond' uscì de' Romani il gentil seme.
Piangevisi entro l'arte per che morta
Deïdamìa ancor si duol d'Achille.
E del Palladio pena vi si porta."
"S'ei posson dentro da quelle faville
Parlar," diss'io, "Maestro, assai ten prego
E riprego, che il prego vaglia mille,
Che non mi facci dell'attender nego,
Finchè la fiamma cornuta qua vegna.
Vedi che del disio ver lei mi piego."
Ed egli a me: "La tua preghiera è degna
Di molta lode, ed io però l'accetto;
Ma fa" che la tua lingua si sostegna.
Lascia parlare a me; ch'io ho concetto
Ciò che tu vuoi. Ch'ei sarebbero schivi,
Perch'ei fur Greci, forse del tuo detto.

Evoking a girl's tears for the dead, the obvious pity,
The god's stolen image—the stock, pathetic entreaty!
Remark it; they're damned, he thinks, for a *trick*.
(The burgher's usual villain: the slick.)
The fool, Fall's denier, sentimental, pious, think,
You see, misses and must the meaning of sin
Beyond the civic disturbance, the plot. You begin
To see what has worried the critics. Between
This and Ulysses' avowal they find (as they *should*)
Contradiction. Vergil is simply wrong. How could
He buy with his tear the ware sold for blood . . .

"Two in one fire . . ." Notice the two: Diomede,
The blue-jawed seducer, loving only the deed,
Male animal, incurious killer; you know the breed,
The bullies on corners who pray for the war,
Eyeing the passers—Ulysses, ambiguous, not sure,
Conscientious objector, incredibly passive before
The world's anguish; his name (*really*) No-man;
By denial ironically, perfectly human,
Image of the poet some say was a woman.
"One fire . . ." Do you think it vain to suggest
The union's symbolic? The meaning is manifest,
I think, frozen in fire forever, confessed
In act—immortal *buggery*! You see, not
The body's overplus, man and maid, hot,
The impatient eruption of sense, but
Mind's invention, shared with no beast, man
Lusting as man, each his own Eve. Understand
How aptly the homosexual symbol can damn.

(*"Their young men shall see visions, and their old*
Shall dream dreams." We are the old, hold
Inviolate the day, deny daylight's controlled
Rapture, permit only the random essays of dreams,
What we have surrendered, this young seeing, seems
Sometimes beyond what our progress redeems—
Grant me daylight's disorder.) I skip now
To line eighty-five. You will notice in passing how
Vergil's small pride cannot help but allow
A bow to his past. *"Alti versi!"* Even in Hell,

Poi che la fiamma fu venuta quivi,
> Dove parve al mio Duca tempo e loco,
> In questa forma lui parlare audivi:
"O voi, che siete due dentro ad un foco,
> S'io meritai di voi mentre ch'io vissi,
> S'io meritai di voi assai o poco,
Quando nel mondo gli alti versi scrissi,
> Non vi movete; ma l'un di voi dica
> Dove per lui perduto a morir gissi."
Lo maggior corno della fiamma antica
> Cominciò a crollarsi mormorando,
> Pur comequella cui vento affatica.
Indi la cima qua e là menando,
> Come fosse la lingua che parlasse,
> Gittò voce di fuori, e disse: "Quando
Mi diparti' da Circe, che sottrasse
> Me più d'un anno là presso a Gaeta
> Prima che sì Enea la nominasse
Nè dolcezza di figlio, nè la pieta
> Del vecchio padre, nè il debito amore,
> Lo qual dovea Penelope far lieta,
Vincer poter dentro da me l'ardore
> Ch'i'ebbi a divenir del mondo esperto,
> E degli vizii umani e del valore:
Ma misi per l'alto mare aperto
> Sol con un legno e con quella compagna
> Picciola, dalla qual non fui deserto.
L'un lito e l'altro vidi infin la Spagna,
> Fin nel Morrocco, e l'isola de' Sardi,
> E l'altra che quell mare intorno bagna.
Io e i compagni eravam vecchi e tardi,
> Quando venimmo a quella foce stretta
> Ov' Ercole segnò li suoi riguardi
Acciocchè l'uom più oltre non si metta.
Dalla man destra mi lasciai Sibilia,
> Dall'altra gia m'avea lasciata Setta.
'O frati, dissi, che per cento milia
> Perigli siete giunti all 'occidente,
> A queste tanto picciola vigilia
De' nostri sensi ch'è del rimanente
> Non vogliate negar l'esperïenza,

Part irony and beyond belief, he must tell
To their unending fire, how *his* verses still spell
Their deeds immortal earth to men. I
Read now, without further comment—call it my
Gesture at the translation, an honest, just adequate try
not to be dull. Remember, this is a *speech*. Those
Who've englished these words before, God knows,
Burned with no flame. Their suety prose,
Fat verse—what did they know of the yelling crowd,
Feet stamping, benches overturned, the loud
Insolence of gesture that bends a thousand men,
The platform, the loneliness, the pride—and then—
Fire—fire—(*This is my circle. Confess. Again.*)

    The greater horn of that ancient fire
Crumpled, began to bend, murmuring
    As if weary, battered by the wind;
    The wavering to-fro motion of the flametip,
Like a tongue that spoke to tried to,
    Urged forth a voice and said: "When
    At last I left Circe, who had kept me
A year-long captive in that place
    Near Gaeta (before Aeneas called it so),
    Not the sweetness of having a son, nor the pious
Claim of an old father, nor the licit love
    That should have made Penelope rejoice
    Could quench in me the burning to become
The world's expert and familiar of
    The vice of men and of man's valor;
    But turned again on to the open sea,
Alone with one small ship and that small band,
    The few who stood beside me still,
    I sought the sands, both shores, as far as Spain
Beyond Morocco and the Sardinian isle
    And other islands bathed by that same sea.

    "We were old and slow, my friends and I,
Old laggards at that narrow strait
    Where Hercules set up his double sign:
    Thus far; no further; no man; none.
On the right Seville fell fast behind,

Diretro al sol, del monde senza gente.
Considerate la vostra semenza:
        Fatti non foste a viver come bruti,
        Ma per seguir virtute e conoscenza.'
Li miei compagni fec'io sì acuti,
        Con questa orasion picciola, al cammino,
        Che appena poscia gli avrei ritenuti.
E volta nostra poppa nel mattino,
        De' remi facemmo ali al folle volo,
        Sempre acquistando dal lato mancino.
Tutte le stele già dell'altro polo
        Vedea la notte, e il nostro tanto basso
        Che non surgeva fuor del marin suolo.
Cinque volte racceso e tante casso
        Lo lume era di sotto dalla luna
        Poi ch'entrati eravam nell'alto passo,
Quando n'apparve una montagna bruna
        Per la distanza, e parvemi alta tanto
        Quanto veduta non n'aveva alcuna.
Noi ci allegrammo, e tosto tornò in pianto;
        Chè dalla nuova terra un turbo nacque,
        E percosse del legno il primo canto.
Tre volte il fe' girar con tutte l'acque,
        Alla quarta levar la poppa in suso,
        E la prora ire in giù, com' Altrui piacque,
Infin che il mar fu sopra noi richiuso."

Leftward Ceuta already had been left.
'Brothers, who through ten thousand straits (I said)
Achieved the West, to that small wake of sense
Left to our lot, dare not deny experience
(Hard at the sun's heel) of the unpeopled world.
Consider your seed, your stock; you were not bred
To live like beasts, but to follow wisdom and
Essential power.'
(*Here is childhood's disclaimer; mere innocence,*
Like the varnished leaf, unpeels its bright pretense,
Reveals its after-all—and I fumble between my penance
And disease. For these we are damned for these: our last
Endemic volupté; knowledge beyond decorum; power past
The simple skills of being man; the knowing that at last
Must love Itself, the Child, the Tower and the Tree,
The City and the Dog, the Rose, the Wolf—the Enemy;
From these and from Despair, my God, deliver me!)
                              And with this little speech
So sharp were my companions for the quest, no hand,
Not mine could hold them. We turned our backs upon
The morning, each oar a wing for that mad flight,
Bearing always leftward, always to the left . . .

And now the night looked on the assembled stars
Of earth's other pole, and ours so low they hardly
Crept above the ocean's floor. Five times re-kindled,
The light beneath the moon had come and gone
Since first we'd entered through that lofty pass,
Five times, when that dim mountain, dark
With distance first appeared, so high it seemed
I had not seen a mountain rear so high before.
He hastened there in joy, but joy was swiftly woe;
For from that new found land, a whirlwind struck,
Struck head-on, hard; spinning the ship three times
And all the seas around; three times about, the fourth
The poop-deck rose, the bow-sprit plunged below
As it pleased Him, that Other, and the sea
Closed over us again . . ."

D. H. Lawrence on D. H. Lawrence

As Told to Leslie A. Fiedler

What is the matter with this Lawrence, anyway—this niggling old maid whose red beard never fooled anyone, this latter-day Jane Austen hounding himself to death about how to keep the clear flame of passion alive after marriage? "Is masturbation so harmless, though? Is it even comparatively pure and harmless? Not to my way of thinking . . ." Not pure enough for D. H. Lawrence, for whom nothing is pure enough.

"Who is Sylvia, what is she?" pornographic poison!!—"Away with such love lyrics, we've had too much of their pornographic poison . . ." Away with the dirty story, the love lyric. Away with the dirty-minded Shaw and Joyce and Tolstoy and Swift. Away with the "emancipated Bohemians," away with the lonely boy masturbating toward madness—"away with the dirty little secret." Hurrah for purity! Hurrah for D. H. Lawrence! And there shall be a new Heaven and a new earth: a place without jazz or Jews or free love or "half-naked women"—or homosexuals or intellectuals or God knows what all. But especially without a majority—no mob, mob, mob! That is to say, no people, no "sticky universal pitch that I refuse to touch," no "*vox populi* . . . hoarse with sentimental indecency."

He's not afraid of the names—you can say that for Lawrence, anyhow. Prude, Puritan, pharisee—whatever epithet comes to your mind he has leveled at himself, but not believing it, not *really* believing, pious D. H. Lawrence, who really knew what obscenity was and what purity. Love without friction, joy without pain, passion without fear, purity, purity, purity! It is all too much: Two hundred pages of Lawrence, and one is ready for the genteel pornography of Henry James; another hundred and we run for relief to *Clarissa Harlowe*!

The absurdity of his dream absolves it—the lovely, human absurdity of his masquerade: the purity of absolute marriage, absolute phallicism; the ultimate purity of the abstract dance frozen on the walls of the Etruscan tombs. Twenty-five hundred years in the zero purity of the absolute dark; the silent dance, motionless, the instruments unheard. These are not real Etruscans, of course, but little Lawrences naked in the purity of painted nakedness: the dark, red, solid Etruscans who do not cough or flee in an endless flight from pain and fear toward the absolute zero of the phallic union. These are the

Lawrences of the incredible dream, the Lawrence that Lawrence could not be—the motionless dancers at peace with blood and death, the aristocrats of the dark. How safe they are in the only purity, in the final non-obscenity of death. But they will not speak the name of death; they will not be ghosts because they will not say the name of ghosts, because they are pure, pure, *pure*!

Oh, come off it, D. H. Lawrence! Butter will melt on your genitals, too. Hater of intellectuals and hater of the higher masturbation, but intellectual and masturbator to the end, nursing the oldest wounds, beating the deadest dogs, nagging, insisting. No sex in the head for Lawrence, but he could talk of nothing else; he had sex-in-the-head in his head, poor Lawrence, poor non-Etruscan, nagger, buttonholer, old maid. One remembers him with the broom in his hand, housecleaning, cleaning up—always after the remaining dirt; but stopping sometimes to lecture on the inferiority of women (with the dustrag in his hand)—on the purity of purity.

Why won't you be dead, Lawrence! We've heard it all before; we've *had* it: the fake Indians, the phony Etruscans, the Leader who calls to the blood, the phallic hunt, the higher friendship among men—wrestling naked, limbs entwined until they faint in Ecstasy. But no homosexuality intended; don't get him wrong! The shrill screams, the nagging should be stilled in the grave. A dead hero should not be a pest, not any more. Why the hell should we be pure when you can't even be dead? Leave us the pain and the glory, the shame, the dirtiness! Let us go to bed for the kicks, for the hell of it—and, not for salvation.

Leave all and follow me. Salvation! We've heard it all before. What does it avail a man if he gain the whole world and lose . . . Follow me. As if what we need is another messiah, another salvation. Oh, you hated the *word*, Lawrence, but that's a quibble; call it regeneration, if you like, or the phallic hunt or nothing. Leave the impotent cripple in the chair and follow me—me, the Gamekeeper, the Etruscan, the Red Indian, Kangaroo, the Man Who Died. The newest messiah, the cocksure savior, as proud as the cock that wakes him, the proud bird with the swollen comb. Oh, we see through the masquerade all right—it is Lawrence leaving Lawrence to follow Lawrence, all parts played by the management, a one-man show. We know you, Lawrence: Connie-Lawrence watching what a big boy Mellors-Lawrence is, while the cripple-Lawrence rolls toward the brink.

What a recommendation! Because Lawrence followed Lawrence, we should follow him, too. But the name is revealed in the end, in the final book, the name the withered body, the scraggly beard had tried to declare: Christ, Christ. The Gamekeeper as Christ, the Etruscan as Savior, Follow me! Christ-Lawrence.

That's what *Lady Chatterley* is about, a *new* New Testament, a pious book (and banned, a Bible banned in America—there's the final jest!). For the risen god, the god erect, leave all ordinary mortality and follow. Eschatology is the old word for it. The end of the world is at hand, at every moment at hand, like a thief in the night. Therefore, leave your old ways, prepare for the sacred marriage, the marriage that will deliver us from sex. For there it is, niggling and nagging behind the phallic message, the half-hidden promise of deliverance: In the true marriage, there is less sex: for some of the saved, there is none. There is no marriage or giving in marriage in heaven. He tells us frankly in the end: Only the Church has known the truth all along. Only the Church and D. H. Lawrence!

This is the book we are not permitted to read! The book banned as obscene. Certainly, it *is* obscene: for there is nothing obscener finally than the fantastic resolve to be pure. And therefore it is bearable—bearable because, like *Ulysses* or "Who is Sylvia" or Swift on Celia, it is a savingly, humanly dirty book after all. The joke on us is that we ban it—ban the ultimate ridiculous reaching for purity.

Enough. Let's have the full *Lady Chatterley*, all the words, all the phallic vanity; let's look together at the boldness and the caution—all that is said out, and the rest that is not said. And let Lawrence be done nagging. Let him lie down! Because he is a pest, and because finally we love him for his madness, his vanity, and his love that survived them all, let him lie down. Because we love him at last even for his nagging, for his refusal to be still, to live anyone else's mistake, to yield one bloody cuticle of his outrageous humanity, let him lie down. Enough!

The Deerslayer

In 1789, the year James Fenimore Cooper was born, the thirteen North American colonies of Great Britain had declared their political independence, but their literature was still colonial, chiefly belated imitations of styles and genres formerly fashionable in the homeland. By 1820, the year in which he published his first novel, American critics found *Precaution* an imitation of Jane Austen and did not even trouble to review it. So, too, critics still ignore that novel, though without understanding it, it is impossible to understand Cooper's treatment of love and marriage in his later books or the fact that he could not write anything at all until he had made close contact with the world of women and the novels they read.

This he did not do until he had entered his thirties, since he had been raised in a patriarchal family presided over by a wealthy, powerful father who believed that literature was the province of women, just as politics was that of men. Even after he first left his father's house he ended up in all-male societies, spending two years at Yale University, from which he was expelled for boyish pranks, and then eight years before the mast, where beginning as an ordinary seaman he ended as a mid-shipman. At that point, however, he resigned from the navy and went back to the place where he had been born and raised to become a gentleman farmer and householder. The one thing he still needed was a proper wife, which he was lucky enough to find in Susan DeLancey. She, as he already knew, came from a family richer and more securely upper class than his own and, as he learned, was also an affable, intelligent woman who was fond of reading. Cooper was content with this, yet at first he did not join her when she was busy with her books but indulged in the male pastimes of hunting and hiking in the nearby hills.

After Susan had given birth to four daughters, to whom she at first read and then taught to read to each other, Cooper would stay close enough to wherever they were reading to hear them. Surely some of the erotic and sentimental passages read in the voices of those he loved must have moved him deeply. But there is no record of any positive responses on his part. A single negative one, however, is recorded in almost everything that has ever been written about him.

One time, those accounts tell us, annoyed by the ineptitude of the text being read, he cried out, "Why do you waste time and money reading trash that anybody who can spell his own name could write better. Even me!" To this Susan is said to have answered jokingly, according to some—"Why don't you give it a try? I'd love to see you try." Cooper responded that he would and, surprisingly enough, did, finally producing a full-length imitation of Jane Austen. When it was in print he would tell anyone who would listen that he was now a professional writer who would write fifty more books—and *sell them*. This almost no one believed he would do, and many wished he would not even try.

Though Cooper was aware that neither the critics nor the general reader were interested in any more Jane Austen clones, he felt he had to keep on writing because the family inheritance on which he had been living had begun to shrink, and at the same time it had become much more expensive to feed, clothe and educate his growing daughters. What he really wanted to write was another book that saw the world through female eyes and talked about it in a female voice. In fact, he continued for a little while to experiment with transvestite fiction, even publishing two such short stories under the female pseudonym of Jane Morgan.

Yet he could not do another novel of the same kind; and to do something different, he knew, he had to find some front-runner, an established and respected writer like Austen, with whom he could catch up and finally pass. Surely there was someone who could play that role, and when looking about he found the recent novels of Sir Walter Scott, who came from another British colony that had gone the opposite way from that of America, declaring its cultural independence before its political one. But the Scots had fought long and hard, though finally unsuccessfully, to free themselves of British rule, and therefore war and politics were major themes in Sir Walter's books. They do not, however, drive out the themes of love and marriage, characteristic of women's fiction, but exist side by side with them. This made it possible for Scott to increase the size of his audience by attracting men who had been hitherto indifferent to novels but not excluding the women who were their first fans.

Though males are usually Scott's point-of-view characters, women play important roles in his fiction, too, usually passive but not inactive ones, since they enter the scene running from pursuing villainous males who want to kidnap, murder or rape them, and they keep running until they are delivered by more virtuous males on whom they are then bestowed as prizes. There is never any doubt in Scott's books about who are the heroes and who will win in the end. As in fairy tales and daydreams, the right side is always victorious. Scott, however, does not present his daydream adventures as make-believe events occurring once-upon-a-time but as verifiable descriptions of recorded periods in "history" with scholarly names like "the Renaissance" and "the

Middle Ages." For him, it should be understood, "history" always means the past, a bygone time in which characters who actually once existed and those created just for the work in hand can see, hear and touch each other.

Scott was often referred to in his own time as the "master of motion," but it must be remembered that his characters move through time as well as space. This poses a problem for Cooper, who had decided to adapt Scott's way of writing to the American scene. Though he found it easy to do so with space, it proved almost impossible to do so with time. After all, the conquest of space has been a central concern for our country from when Columbus sailed over the vast stretches of ocean to when astronauts made the first landing on the desert of the moon.

But America has been settled from the start by people fleeing everything Scott would have called the past, in quest of an eternal present or an endless future. For centuries we have boasted that our country, unlike those of Europe, "has no cemeteries to defend"; and it is certainly true that as we look about our land we do not see the mementos of earlier ages, like the fortresses, castles and churches that are everywhere in Europe. Yet some who landed here realized that there does exist in our land the remnants of an alternative past. This is the ancient culture of Native Americans, which looked to those European immigrants much like what they imagined had been the primitive stages of their own culture. Consequently, they felt that descriptions of exotic Indian teepees, tomahawks and totem poles could produce in the readers the sense of wonder that Scott evoked with his descriptions of medieval or classical ruins.

A generation or two before Cooper, Charles Brockden Brown, the first truly serious novelist in the United States, attempted to write fiction that did just that. He did not, however, succeed in writing such books himself but left behind as a preface to one novel a piece of advice by which Cooper profited: "The incidents of Indian hostility and the perils of western wilderness," Brown wrote, "are far more suitable than castles and chimeras" for a truly American literature.

The union of Cooper and Scott with Brown as a matchmaker turned out to be a marriage made in heaven. In a very short time Cooper was able to write three novels, *The Spy*, *The Pilot* and *The Pioneers*, all of them historical romances in the style of Scott, with American settings. For such books he discovered an eager audience was waiting. *The Spy*, in fact, sold a record 3,500 copies before noon on the day it appeared, and *The Pioneers*, which is the seedling out of which grew the whole Leatherstocking series, is honored and beloved to this day.

This is so because in it appear for the first time the two characters Natty and Chingachgook, the white man and the red man who are the heart and soul of that American epic. When he first introduced them, however, Cooper did not seem to know what he was going to do with them, if indeed there was anything he could do at all; since in *The Pioneers* they seem to represent not the beginning of anything but the end—a dead end. Both of them have already reached the terminal age of three score and ten when we first meet them wandering lost on the busy streets of a settlement built on what was once a trackless wilderness in which they felt at home. Now jobless and homeless and left without the strength to resist, they are pursued in the name of laws that they do not understand.

Their plight, however, is not portrayed as pitiful or tragic but close to comical. The Indian partner is addressed by no one as Chingachgook but is called only Old John Mohegan, an appropriate name for a stereotypical drunken Indian; and of the many poetic names by which Natty was once called by his Redskin family, like Pathfinder and Long Rifle and Deerslayer, none is used by the paleface villagers—for whom his baptismal name seemed more suitable. Though Chingachgook still has enough remnants of woodland beauty to stir awe in some, the face of Natty, always homely but inspiring trust, has turned into a hideous clown's mask with a runny nose and the rotting stump of a single tooth, at which small boys laugh and little girls shudder.

Cooper, I think, when he wrote *The Pioneers* planned a mercy killing of both of the moribund vagrants, and before three of the books in the series had been published they are indeed both dead. Natty, however, would not stay dead, though in *The Prairie* he reached the rim of the Pacific and peacefully expired looking into the setting sun. In *The Last of the Mohicans*, Natty is only thirty-five, the age of Cooper himself when he was writing it. And even after Cooper once more let him die, he was resurrected in two final books, *The Pathfinder* and *The Deerslayer*, in the latter of which he is younger than he is in any part of the series, a year or two past twenty.

In any case, by the time Cooper had written *The Last of the Mohicans* he had won worldwide celebrity. Distinguished fellow writers in Europe, like Conrad and Balzac, praised him extravagantly, and when he died just after the middle of the century, all the living writers of note in the United States, including Washington Irving, Herman Melville, Nathaniel Hawthorne and Ralph Waldo Emerson, gathered together to hail him as the founding father of post-Colonial literature.

Moreover, by the end of the century not only was he recognized by his fellow writers all over the world as one of them, but he had become a required part of the curriculum in university classes in literature. Those who taught his works also wrote critiques about him in scholarly journals, some of them more fulsome praise than scholarly analysis. Two especially outrageous ones by a Professor Lansbury from Columbia University and a Professor Brander Matthews from Cooper's alma mater, Yale, fell into the hands of a writer who at that point many were beginning to think was one of the greatest American novelists—and who thought Cooper was one of the worst.

This was, of course, Mark Twain, who was so outraged by Lansbury's description of the Leatherstocking Tales as "pure works of art" and Brander Matthews's description of Natty Bumppo as "one of the greatest characters in fiction" that he sat down and wrote an outrageous attack on the Leatherstocking Tales, which he signed "Mark Twain, M.A. Professor of Belles Lettres in the Veterinary College of Arizona" to make sure that no one would fail to see that his little piece was in some sense a joke, the target of which was not only the professors in elite universities, whom he distrusted and despised, but also himself and we who are reading it more than a century later—along with the novels it contends shall be forgotten. It is not, finally, the slapstick humor of the piece that annoys me but Twain's pretense that it was only on aesthetic grounds that he was attacking Cooper, when clearly it was also on political grounds. Twain was a man of many prejudices, but strongest of all was that against Native Americans. He did not actually confront any until he went to California, after which he spoke of them as if they were really as vile as native Westerners had always taken them to be.

In his comic critique of Cooper, however, Twain does not mention the Indians. Possibly he thought anybody reading his later piece would remember that earlier, in *The Innocents Abroad*, he had described how looking down at Lake Como in Italy he had been reminded of the even more beautiful Lake Tahoe in America, which in turn reminded him of the "filthy and villainous" Indians who lived on those shores. Of them he wrote:

> People . . . talk about Indian poetry—there never was any in them except in the Fenimore Cooper Indians. But they are an extinct tribe that never existed. I know the Noble Red Man. I have camped with the Indians . . . I have . . . helped them steal cattle . . . I have . . . scalped them, had them for breakfast. I would gladly eat the whole race if I had a chance.

This is, to be sure, not just a joke in bad taste but paranoic racism, and I am glad that Twain excluded it from the piece about the Leatherstocking Tales, since much of what he does include seems to me, finally, both funny and utterly convincing. Certainly I myself agree with every word of his summary of Cooper's faults:

> A work of art? It has no invention . . . no order, system, sequence, or result . . . no lifelikeness . . . no seeming of reality . . . its characters are confusedly drawn . . . its humor is pathetic; its conversations are oh! indescribable; its love-scenes odious; its English a crime against the language.

And so apparently did many others; eventually, by the time I was in high school and college, the Leatherstocking Tales were no longer required at that level. As a matter of fact, they were not even *recommended* after the early years of primary school. Cooper had come to be thought of, thanks in large part to Twain, as primarily a writer for children and, to make this clear to the uninitiated, was shelved only in the children's section of libraries.

This opinion has been revised little since, largely under the influence of D. H. Lawrence, who "kindled by Fenimore Cooper" actually came to America and lived among the Indians for a couple of years. But though Cooper is once again made available to university students, it is never done without some sort of apology. So, for instance, a recent anthology of American literature for use in college-level classes contains a selection from the Leatherstocking Tales prefaced with an apologetic headnote written by a professor from Yale once more, warning the reader that "Cooper's defects as a writer are indeed real and great."

Moreover, at this same moment that Ivy League critics were changing their minds about Cooper, the Leatherstocking Tales were having a much less troubled time in the area of popular culture. In that world Cooper was not only being read and loved, but, inspired by his example, a new genre of popular fiction as uniquely American as hamburgers and blue jeans was achieving spectacular success. This was the "Western," which first appeared as what were then called dime novels, sleazy melodramatic pulp fictions that somehow combined Cooper's notions about the confrontation of red Americans and whites with the formulaic tales of gunmen and marshals shooting it out in the Wild West. These pop novels were then turned into plays, acted out by the actual bandits and lawmen who were their subjects, and those plays in turn were translated into Buffalo Bill's Wild West, a combination of re-created history and feats of roping and shooting that he never allowed anyone to call a "show."

When the Wild West began to die, cowboys who were its graduates rode farther west to Hollywood, where they translated the Western to the medium in which it has succeeded best, the movies. These, of course, we still have with us, though they are perhaps seen more often these days on the small screen rather than the large, interrupted by commercials of which some are themselves "mini-Westerns," in which the Marlboro Man, complete with sombrero and spurs, assures readers that the carcinogens currently under attack are really good for them. There is almost no popular medium in which the Western has not appeared. Not only has it been for a long time a standard subject of comic strips and comic books, but for an even longer time it has been one of children's favorite games: Cowboys and Indians.

What is it, then, in Cooper's ill-written books that has permitted their entry into the collective unconscious of almost everybody in the world, including some who have never read any of them at all? It is, of course, the myth embodied in the two key figures at the center of his five Leatherstocking books, who, like Odysseus and Don Juan, Hamlet and Scarlett O'Hara, Huck Finn and Uncle Tom, have become part of the communal dream that binds together in our atomized societies those whom everything else separates—the old and young, males and females, whites and nonwhites. It is, of course, not just either of them alone but the pair of them, in that unique American relationship thought of as surpassing the love of a man and a woman.

Such interethnic male bonding was originally invented by Cooper to allay the guilt and fear created in ex-European Americans by their treatment of Native Americans and is the central passion that moves the protagonists of other great American love stories, like Melville's *Moby Dick*, Mark Twain's *Huckleberry Finn*, Saul Bellow's *Henderson the Rain King*, and Ken Kesey's *One Flew over the Cuckoo's Nest*. But it has proved useful, too, to those reading the daily newspapers as well as our greatest books; it has helped them understand the relationship of white Americans not just to red Indians but to black Africans, brown Polynesians and those people of Asia who—for lack of a better term—we call yellow, and with whom we have been conducting a long painful series of wars, beginning with Vietnam and still continuing in Afghanistan.

Most of my life it has been the political meaning of interethnic male bonding that has concerned me, but I have recently become aware that it has a religious meaning as well. Though it has no established church like other new faiths invented in our country—Christian Science and Mormonism, for instance—it is, I have come to see, a new heretical version of the basic myth of the fall in the Garden of Eden, with which the Judeo-Christian Bible begins. In its orthodox version, that myth tells of a man and woman living in peace with each other until a wily serpent enters the garden where they live and persuades them to disobey the orders of their God, after which they become aware of their sex as something troubling and are driven from the Garden forever. In the heretic revision of the myth the same three archetypal characters appear, the woman, the man and the serpent, but this time the man is living in peace and love with the serpent, which is to say, with Chingachgook, whose name translated into English, Cooper tells us several times, means "The Great Serpent." And the woman is the interloper, wanting to enter a relationship with the man that will end in driving them both out of the great, good place that Cooper portrays not as a cultivated Garden but as the untracked wilderness. In light of this, we can understand why Natty, though often tempted, has refused to enter into a relationship with anyone of the female gender. This is not because he finds no woman who is suitable for him or because he has somehow come to prize chastity above love, but because he longs to stay in the wild with his faithful companion instead of setting up a home, which he considers being exiled from the earthly paradise. To be sure, Cooper realizes from the start that the sublimated relationship between men of different races cannot last forever. In the very first volume of the series, we are reminded that sooner or later one or another or both of the couple must die.

In all of the novels that deal with their union, Natty and Chingachgook discuss what will happen to them when they are dead. Will they be eternally joined or separated forever? In *The Last of the Mohicans* Cooper poses that same question about a heterosexual couple, Cora and Uncas, who were forbidden to wed in life because of the strict taboo against miscegenation. But when at their funeral the father of the girl insists sentimentally that in heaven the good God will not separate a couple because of the difference of race, Natty scornfully answers, for Cooper as well as himself, that this is like believing the snow will fall in the summer. But whether the same fate awaits those whose love was not consummated in the flesh but only in the spirit is a question for which Natty does not have an answer. He edges closer and closer, however, as the Leatherstocking Tales approach their end, to believing that those who for brief moments were able to sit side by side while still alive would surely be granted a similar privilege in the afterlife.

Posing the question over and over, however, seems natural enough for a young man being initiated into full maturity by confronting not the mystery of sex but rather that of death, which, we remember at this point, has been the theme of the Leatherstocking Tales from the very first volume. In it, Natty, already past the age of seventy, learns how to die just as in the last book of this series when he is just past twenty he learns to kill. And kill he does, taking for the first time the life of a fellow human rather than of the kinds of beasts who had hitherto been his prey and for which he has already been named Deerslayer. For his killing of an Indian, however, he is, for reasons never explained to us, not given a new name at all. What we do learn from *The Deerslayer* instead is what he was called before he was old enough to perform any of the feats for which he was given honorific titles like Straight Tongue, Pidgin, and Lop Ear. These baby names he tells to another refugee from the settlements who, like Natty, has learned the skills and customs of the Indians but who, unlike him, does not practice only those suitable for white Christians. Natty refuses, for instance, to torture prisoners of war, take scalps or shoot women and children. Hurry Harry, however, not only performs such atrocities but boasts of having done so.

So, too, does a third dropout from civilization, an old scoundrel who falsely claims the name of Hutter and is in the end scalped while still alive by Indians he intended to scalp, and who after dying in extreme pain is damned for all eternity. There are two other white characters who also live outside the white settlements, a pair of contrasting sisters, one a gentle blonde and the other a feisty brunette. In *The Last of the Mohicans*, one of such a pair is married off at the end, but in *The Deerslayer* neither of them—in fact, no one—achieves a happily-ever-after, except a young Indian woman who does in fact marry. The blonde girl turns out to be half-witted and is killed by a shot from an Indian rifle, while her black-haired sister disappears before the book ends and is rumored to be living as the mistress of a professional seducer, formerly an officer in the British army.

Finally, these forest dwellers perish or vanish after discovering that they have been lied to by those they thought were their parents but who are really nameless bastards. Those who fare the worst are the most beautiful and vain, and, as mentioned earlier, nobody in the entire cast of characters but the Indian woman who, after saving Chingachgook's life, marries him manages to achieve the happy ending of marriage. This narrative leaves Natty to mourn over the fact that whether or not he will be joined to his beloved Indian friend after death, he will in the meantime be deprived of his company in the long life still ahead of him.

But death is not quite through yet. In a kind of unexpected coda that takes place fifteen years after the main action of the book is done, one more death occurs, the death of Chingachgook's wife, the mother of his son, which enables the two survivors to return and rejoin Natty in an all-male family of three. Their reunion is, however, the sole ray of light that penetrates the gloom of this most melancholy of the Leatherstocking Tales. Before we leave them, we watch them return to the now-deserted places where their old friends and enemies lived and died. They find that not only have the earlier inhabitants gone, but no one remains to remember them—except the author, who, speaking over Natty's shoulder, as it were, tells us that bitterness was well deserved and will be compounded by what follows in the kingdom of death: "The sins of the family have long since been arraigned at the judgment seat of God, or are registered for the terrible settlement of the last great day." And Cooper concludes, defending the tone and content of his melancholy work, "We live in a world of transgressions and selfishness, and no pictures that represent us otherwise can be true . . ."

Come Back to the Raft Ag'in, Huck Honey!

It is perhaps expected that the Negro and the homosexual should become stock literary themes in a period when the exploration of responsibility and failure has become again a primary concern of our literature. It is the discrepancy they represent that haunts us, that moral discrepancy before which we are helpless, having no resources (no tradition of courtesy, no honored mode of cynicism) for dealing with a conflict of principle and practice. It used once to be fashionable to think of Puritanism as a force in our lives encouraging hypocrisy; quite the contrary, its emphasis upon the singleness of belief and action, its turning of the most prosaic areas of life into arenas where one's state of grace is tested, confuse the outer and the inner and make hypocrisy among us, perhaps more strikingly than ever elsewhere, *visible*, visibly detestable, the cardinal sin. It is not without significance that the shrug of the shoulders (the acceptance of circumstance as a sufficient excuse, the sign of self-pardon before the inevitable lapse) seems in America an unfamiliar, an alien gesture.

And yet before the continued existence of physical homosexual love (our crudest epithets notoriously evoke the mechanics of such affairs), before the blatant ghettos in which the Negro conspicuously creates the gaudiness and stench that offend him, the white American must make a choice between coming to terms with institutionalized discrepancy and formulating radically new ideologies. There are, to be sure, stopgap devices, evasions of that final choice; not the least interesting is the special night club: the "queer" café, the black-and-tan joint, in which fairy and Negro exhibit their fairy-ness, their Negro-ness, as if they were divertissements, gags thought up for the laughs and having no reality once the lights go out and the chairs are piled on the tables by the cleaning women. In the earlier minstrel show, a Negro performer was required to put on with grease paint and burnt cork the formalized mask of blackness; while the queer must exaggerate flounce and flutter into the convention of his condition.

The situations of the Negro and the homosexual in our society pose quite opposite problems, or at least problems suggesting quite opposite solutions. Our laws on homosexuality and the context of prejudice they objectify must apparently be changed to accord with a stubborn social fact; whereas it is the social fact, our overt behavior toward the Negro, that must be modified to accord with our laws and the, at least official, morality they objectify. It is not, of course, quite so simple. There is another sense in which the fact of homosexual passion contradicts a national myth of masculine love, just as our real relationship with the Negro contradicts a myth of that relationship; and those two myths with their betrayals are, as we shall see, one.

The existence of overt homosexuality threatens to compromise an essential aspect of American sentimental life: the camaraderie of the locker room and ball park, the good fellowship of the poker game and fishing trip, a kind of passionless passion, at once gross and delicate, homoerotic in the boy's sense, possessing innocence above suspicion. To doubt for a moment this innocence, which can survive only as *assumed*, would destroy our stubborn belief in a relationship simple, utterly satisfying, yet immune to lust; physical as the handshake is physical, this side of copulation. The nineteenth-century myth of the Immaculate Young Girl has failed to survive in any *felt* way into our time. Rather, in the dirty jokes shared among men in the smoking car, the barracks or the dormitory, there is a common male revenge against women for having flagrantly betrayed that myth; and under the revenge, the rather smug assumption of the chastity of the revenging group, in so far as it is a purely male society. From what other source could arise that unexpected air of good clean fun which overhangs such sessions? It is this self-congratulatory buddy-buddiness, its astonishing naïveté that breed at once endless opportunities for inversion and the terrible reluctance to admit its existence, to surrender the last believed-in stronghold of love without passion.

It is, after all, what we know from a hundred other sources that is here verified: the regressiveness, a technical sense, of American life, its implacable nostalgia for the infantile, at once wrong-headed and somehow admirable. The mythic America is boyhood—and who would dare be startled to realize that the two most popular, most *absorbed*, I am sure, of the handful of great books in our native heritage are customarily to be found, illustrated, on the shelves of the children's library. I am referring, of course, to *Moby Dick* and *Huckleberry Finn*, so different in technique and language, but alike children's books or, more precisely, *boys'* books.

There are the Leatherstocking Tales of Cooper, too, as well as Dana's *Two Years Before the Mast* and a good deal of Stephen Crane, books whose continuing favor depends more and more on the taste of boys; and one begins to foresee a similar improbable fate for Ernest Hemingway. Among the most distinguished novelists of the American past, only Henry James completely escapes classification as a writer of juvenile classics; even Hawthorne, who did write sometimes for children, must in his most adult novels endure, though not as Mark Twain and Melville submit to, the child's perusal. A child's version of *The Scarlet Letter* would seem a rather far-fetched joke if it were not a part of our common experience. Finding in the children's department of the local library what Hawthorne liked to call his "hell-fired book," and remembering that *Moby Dick* itself has as its secret motto "*Ego te baptizo in nomine diaboli*," one can only bow in awed silence before the mysteries of public morality, the American idea of "innocence." Everything goes except the frank description of adult heterosexual love. After all, boys will be boys!

What, then, do all these books have in common? As boys' books we should expect them shyly, guiltlessly as it were, to proffer a chaste male love as the ultimate emotional experience and this is spectacularly the case. In Dana, it is the narrator's melancholy love for the *kanaka*, Hope; in Cooper, the lifelong affection of Natty Bumppo and Chingachgook; in Melville, Ishmael's love for Queequeg; in Twain, Huck's feelings for Nigger Jim. At the focus of emotion, where we are accustomed to find in the world's great novels some heterosexual passion, be it "platonic" love or adultery, seduction, rape or long-drawn-out flirtation, we come instead on the fugitive slave and the no-accent boy lying side by side on a raft borne by the endless river toward an impossible escape, or the pariah sailor waking in the tattooed arms of the brown harpooner on the verge of their impossible quest. "*Aloha, aikane, aloha nui*," Hope cries to the lover who prefers him to all his fellow-whites; and Ishmael in utter frankness tells us: "I found Queequeg's arm thrown over me in the most loving and affectionate manner. You had almost thought I had been his wife . . . he still hugged me tightly, as though naught but death should part us twain . . . Thus, then, in our heart's honeymoon, lay I and Queequeg—a cosy, loving pair . . . he pressed his forehead against mine, clasped me around the waist, and said that henceforth we were married."

In Melville, the ambiguous relationship is most explicitly rendered; almost, indeed, openly explained. Not by a chance phrase of camouflaged symbol (the dressing of Jim in a woman's gown in *Huckleberry Finn*, for instance, which can mean anything or nothing at all), but in a step-by-step exposition, the Pure Marriage of Ishmael and Queequeg is set before us: the initial going to bed together and the first shyness overcome, that great hot tomahawk-pipe accepted in a familiarity that dispels fear; next, the wedding ceremony itself (for in this marriage like so many others the ceremonial follows the deflowering), with the ritual of touching foreheads; then, the queasiness and guilt the morning after the *official* First Night, the suspicion that one has joined himself irrevocably to his own worst nightmare; finally, a symbolic portrayal of the continuing state of marriage through the image of the "monkey rope" which binds the lovers fast waist to waist (for the sake of this symbolism, Melville changes a *fact* of whaling practice—the only time in the book), a permanent alliance that provides mutual protection but also threatens mutual death.

Physical it all is, certainly, yet somehow ultimately innocent. There lies between the lovers no naked sword but a childlike ignorance, as if the possibility of a fall to the carnal had not yet been discovered. Even in the *Vita Nuova* of Dante, there is no vision of love less offensively, more unremittingly chaste; that it is not adult seems beside the point. Ishmael's sensations as he wakes under the pressure of Queequeg's arm, the tenderness of Huck's repeated loss and refinding of Jim, the role of almost Edenic helpmate played for Bumppo by the Indian—these shape us from childhood: we have no sense of first discovering them or of having been once without them.

Of the infantile, the homoerotic aspects of these stories we are, though vaguely, aware; but it is only with an effort that we can wake to a consciousness of how, among us who at the level of adulthood find a difference in color sufficient provocation for distrust and hatred, they celebrate, all of them, the mutual love of *a white man and a colored*. So buried at the level of acceptance which does not touch reason, so desperately repressed from overt recognition, so contrary to what is usually thought of as our ultimate level of taboo the sense of that love can survive only in the obliquity of a symbol, persistent, obsessive, in short, an archetype: the boy's homoerotic crush, the love of the black fused at this level into a single thing.

I hope I have been using here a hopefully abused word with some precision; by "archetype" I mean a coherent pattern of beliefs and feelings so widely shared at a level beneath consciousness that there exists no abstract vocabulary for representing it, and so "sacred" that unexamined, irrational restraints inhibit any explicit analysis. Such a complex finds a formula or pattern story, which serves both to embody it, and, at first at least, to conceal its full implications. Later, the secret may be revealed, the archetype "analyzed" or "allegorically" interpreted according to the language of the day.

I find the complex we have been examining genuinely mythic; certainly it has the invisible character of the true archetype, eluding the wary pounce of Howells or Mrs. Twain, who excised from *Huckleberry Finn* the cussing as unfit for children, but who left, unperceived, a conventionally abhorrent doctrine of ideal love. Even the writers in whom we find it attained it, in a sense, dreaming. The felt difference between *Huckleberry Finn* and Twain's other books must lie in part in the release from conscious restraint inherent in the author's assumption of the character of Huck; the passage in and out of darkness and river mist, the constant confusion of identities (Huck's ten or twelve names; the question of who is the real uncle, who the true Tom), the sudden intrusions into alien violences without past or future, give the whole work, for all its carefully observed detail, the texture of a dream. For *Moby Dick* such a point need scarcely be made. Even Cooper, despite his insufferable gentlemanliness, his tedium, cannot conceal from the kids who continue to read him the secret behind his overconscious prose: the childish, impossible dream. D. H. Lawrence saw in him clearly the boy's Utopia: the absolute wilderness in which the stuffiness of home yields to the wigwam, and "My Wife" to Chingachgook.

I do not recall ever having seen in the commentaries of the social anthropologist or psychologist an awareness of the role of this profound child's dream of love in our relation to the Negro. (I say Negro, though the beloved in the books I have mentioned is variously Indian and Polynesian, because the Negro has become more and more exclusively for us *the* colored man, the colored man *par excellence*.) Trapped in what have by now become shackling clichés—the concept of the white man's sexual envy of the Negro male, the ambivalent horror of miscegenation—they do not sufficiently note the complementary factor of physical attraction, the archetypal love of white male and black. But either the horror or the attraction is meaningless alone; only together do they make sense. Just as the pure love of man and man is in general set off against the ignoble passion of man and woman, so more specifically (and more vividly) the dark desire which leads to the miscegenation is contrasted with the ennobling love of a white man and a colored one. James Fenimore Cooper is our first poet of this ambivalence; indeed, miscegenation is the secret theme of the Leatherstocking novels, especially of *The Last of the Mohicans*. Natty Bumppo, the man who boasts always of having "no cross" in *his* blood, flees by nature from the defilement of all women, but never with so absolute a revulsion as he displays toward the *squaw* with whom at one point he seems at the point of being forced to cohabit; and the threat of the dark-skinned rapist sends pale woman after pale woman skittering through Cooper's imagined wilderness. Even poor Cora, who already has a fatal drop of alien blood that cuts her off from any marriage with a white man, in so far as she is white cannot be mated with Uncas, the noblest of redmen. Only in death can they be joined in an embrace as chaste as that of males. There's no good woman but a dead woman! Yet Chingachgook and the Deerslayer are permitted to sit night after night over their campfire in the purest domestic bliss. So long as there is no mingling of blood, soul may couple with soul in God's undefiled forest.

Nature undefiled—this is the inevitable setting of the Sacred Marriage of males. Ishmael and Queequeg, arm in arm, about to ship out, Huck and Jim swimming beside the raft in the peaceful flux of the Mississippi—here it is the motion of water which completes the syndrome, the American dream of isolation afloat. The notion of the Negro as the unblemished bride blends with the myth of running away to sea, of running the great river down to the sea. The immensity of water defines a loneliness that demands love; its strangeness symbolizes the disavowal of the conventional that makes possible all versions of love. In *Two Years Before the Mast*, in *Moby Dick*, in *Huckleberry Finn* the water is there, is the very texture of the novel; the Leatherstocking Tales propose another symbol for the same meaning: the virgin forest. Notice the adjectives—the virgin forest and the forever inviolable sea. It is well to remember, too, what surely must be more than a coincidence, that Cooper, who could dream this myth, also invented for us the novel of the sea, wrote for the first time in history the sea story proper.

The rude pederasty of the forecastle and the captain's cabin, celebrated in a thousand jokes, is the profanation of a dream; yet Melville, who must have known such blasphemies, refers to them only once and indirectly, for it was *his* dream that they threatened. And still the dream survives; in a recent book by Gore Vidal, an incipient homosexual, not yet aware of the implications of his feelings, indulges in the reverie of running off to sea with his dearest friend. The buggery of sailors is taken for granted everywhere, yet is thought of usually as an inversion forced on men by their isolation from women; though the opposite case may well be true: the isolation sought more or less consciously as an occasion for male encounters. At any rate, there is a context in which the legend of the sea as escape and solace, the fixated sexuality of boys, the myth of the dark beloved, are one. In Melville and Twain at the center of our tradition, in lesser writers at the periphery, the archetype is at once formalized and perpetuated. Nigger Jim and Queequeg make concrete for us what was without them a vague pressure on the threshold of our consciousness; the proper existence of the archetype is in the realized character, who waits, as it were, only to be asked his secret. Think of Oedipus biding in silence from Sophocles to Freud!

Unwittingly, we are possessed in childhood by these characters and their undiscriminated meaning, and it is difficult for us to dissociate them without a sense of disbelief. What—these household figures clues to our subtlest passions! The foreigner finds it easier to perceive the significances too deep within us to be brought into focus. D. H. Lawrence discovered in our classics a linked mythos of escape and immaculate male love; Lorca in *The Poet in New York* grasped instinctively (he could not even read English) the kinship of Harlem and Walt Whitman, the fairy as bard. But of course we do not have to be conscious of what possesses us; in every generation of our own writers the archetype reappears, refracted, half-understood, but *there*. In the gothic reverie of Capote's *Other Voices, Other Rooms*, both elements of the syndrome are presented, though disjunctively: the boy moving between the love of a Negro maidservant and his inverted cousin. In Carson McCullers's *Member of the*

Wedding, another variant is invented: a *female* heterosexual romance between the boy-girl Frankie and a Negro cook. This time the Father-Slave-Beloved is converted into the figure of a Mother-Sweetheart-Servant, but remains still, of course, satisfactorily black. It is not strange, after all, to find this archetypal complex in latter-day writers of a frankly homosexual sensibility; but it recurs, too, in such resolutely masculine writers as Faulkner, who evokes the myth in the persons of the Negro and the boy of *Intruder in the Dust*.

In the myth, one notes finally, it is typically in the role of outcast, ragged woodsman, or despised sailor ("Call me Ishmael!"), or unregenerate boy (Huck before the prospect of being "sivilized" cries out, "I been there before!") that we turn to the love of a colored man. But how, we cannot help asking, does the vision of the white American as a pariah correspond with our long-held public status: the world's beloved, the success? It is perhaps only the artist's portrayal of *himself*, the notoriously alienated writer in America, at home with such images, child of the town drunk, the hapless survivor. But no, Ishmael is in all of us, our unconfessed universal fear objectified in the writer's status as in the outcast sailor's: that compelling anxiety, which every foreigner notes, that we may not be loved, that we are loved for our possessions and not our selves, that we are really—*alone*. It is that underlying terror which explains our incredulity in the face of adulation or favor, what is called (once more the happy adjective) our "boyish modesty."

Our dark-skinned beloved will take us in, we assure ourselves, when we have been cut off, or have cut ourselves off, from all others, without rancor or the insult of forgiveness. He will fold us in his arms saying, "Honey" or "Aikane"; he will comfort us, as if our offense against him were long ago remitted, were never truly *real*. And yet we cannot ever really forget our guilt; the stories that embody the myth dramatize as if compulsively the role of the colored man as the victim. Dana's Hope is shown dying of the white man's syphilis; Queequeg is portrayed as racked by fever, a pointless episode except in the light of this necessity; Crane's Negro is disfigured to the point of monstrosity; Cooper's Indian smolders to a hopeless old age conscious of the imminent disappearance of his race; Jim is shown loaded down with chains, weakened by the hundred torments dreamed up by Tom in the name of bulliness. The immense gulf of guilt must not be mitigated any more than the disparity of color (Queequeg is not merely brown but monstrously tattooed; Chingachgook is horrid with paint; Jim is portrayed as the sick A-rab dyed blue), so that the final reconciliation may seem more unbelievable and tender. The archetype makes no attempt to deny our outrage as fact; it portrays it as if meaningless in the face of love.

There would be something insufferable, I think, in that final version of remission if it were not for the presence of a motivating anxiety, the sense always of a last chance. Behind the white American's nightmare that someday, no longer tourist, inheritor or liberator, he will be rejected, refused, he dreams of his acceptance at the breast he has most utterly offended. It is a dream so sentimental, so outrageous, so desperate, that it redeems our concept of boyhood from nostalgia to tragedy.

In each generation we *play out* the impossible mythos, and we live to see our children play it: the white boy and the black we can discover wrestling affectionately on any American sidewalk, along which they will walk in adulthood, eyes averted from each other, unwilling to touch even by accident. The dream recedes; the immaculate passion and the astonishing reconciliation become a memory, and less, a regret, at last the unrecognized motifs of a child's book. "It's too good to be true, Honey," Jim says to Huck. "It's too good to be true."

New England and
the Invention of the South

On a bare northern summit
A pine-tree stands alone.
He slumbers; and around him
The icy snows are blown.

His dreams are of a palm-tree
Who in far lands of morn
Amid the blazing desert
Grieves silent and forlorn.
Ein Fichtenbaum steht einsam

HEINRICH HEINE

Everyone knows that the image of American slavery and the antebellum South was created not by slow accretion, but all at once, overnight, as it were, by a single mid-nineteenth-century book, Harriet Beecher Stowe's *Uncle Tom's Cabin*. Translated from language to language and medium to medium (first to the stage, then the movies, comic books, TV) it created not just certain mythological Black characters, Uncle Tom, Eliza, Topsy, but the mythic landscape through which they still move in the dream of America dreamed by native Americans as well as by Europeans, Africans, and Asians of all ages and all degrees of sophistication.

Mrs. Stowe was not the first American author to have created Negro characters. They had appeared earlier in novels and stories by such eminent writers as James Fenimore Cooper, Edgar Allan Poe and Herman Melville; but somehow they had remained archetypally inert, refusing to leap from the printed page to the public domain. And though the long-lived Minstrel Show (which still survives on British TV) had begun to invent its pervasive stereotypes of plantation life before Mrs. Stowe ever set pen to paper, they, too, failed to kindle the imagination of the world. To be sure, Mrs. Stowe herself was influenced by them; so that before we learn the real name of George and Eliza Harris' small son, Harry, we hear him hailed as "Jim Crow." Many of the minor darkies who surround her serious protagonists are modeled on the clowns in blackface who cracked jokes with a White Interlocutor.

But clearly images of Black Americans could not stir an emotional response adequate to the horrors of slavery so long as they remained merely comic. Small wonder then that Mr. Bones retreated to the wings once Eliza had fled the bloodhounds on the ice (only in the dramatic version, to be sure) and Uncle Tom had been beaten to death in full view of a weeping house. Nor is it surprising that the figure of the martyred Black slave under the lash, too old to be a sexual threat, too pious to evoke fears of violent revenge, captured the deep fantasy of a White world, haunted (since the Haitian revolt at least) with nightmares of Black Insurrection, and needing, therefore, to be assured that tears rather than blood would be sufficient to erase their guilt.

What is puzzling (though somehow few critics have paused long enough to puzzle it out) is that Uncle Tom was the creation not of some son of the South, a literate Black runaway slave, perhaps, or a tormented Byronic White Planter, like Mrs. Stowe's Augustine St. Clare, but of a daughter of New England, who seemed fated by nature and nurture to become the laureate of that region rather than of a Southland she scarcely knew. It was, indeed, as a New England local-colorist that she began and ended her literary career. Her first published story and her first published book were set in that icy and rockbound world, and her final works were genre studies, evoking scenes of her own Connecticut childhood and that of her husband, who had grown up in Maine. Yet no matter how hard hightone critics, who distrust the sentimentality and egregious melodrama of her most popular novel, may tout them, ordinary readers do not remember her for *The Minister's Wooing* or *Old Town Folks*.

What such readers, what I myself, prize her for constitutes in effect an interruption, a detour in her career: a temporary abandonment of her essential subject matter, which was in any case domestic rather than political. Indeed, the sole public issue which ever engaged her as a writer was Slavery, to which she devoted some five or six years of her life, producing finally three books: *Uncle Tom's Cabin* (1852), *The Key to Uncle Tom's Cabin* (1853), *and Dred: A Tale of the Dismal Swamp* (1856), of which only the first is still read with pleasure. After the failure of the last, she abandoned slavery as a fictional theme forever, returning to the South only to sing, in *Palmetto-Leaves* (1873), praises to Florida as a tourist refuge from the rigors of the New England Winter.

But much earlier she had begun to be aware of the South in a way she would never have been if she had never left home—never followed her father to Cincinnati, where she lived for eighteen crucial years of her life between her twenty-first and thirty-ninth birthday. It was there she married Calvin Stowe, there she bore her first six children, losing one in infancy. To be sure Cincinnati thought of itself as a Western rather than a Southern city; but it bordered on the upper South, separated only by the width of the Ohio River from Kentucky, where the action of Mrs. Stowe's immortal novel begins. It was, moreover, a place where Slaves and ex-Slaves were highly visible: on the one hand, a stop on the Underground Railway; on the other, a city of Black-White Conflict, of riot and murder, of rape and rumors of rape. Harriet was, however, somewhat removed from all that, living as she did in the Lane Seminary, a kind of New England missionary enclave, for which slavery was less a fact of daily existence than an occasion for theological debate and schism.

She did not, in any event, write *Uncle Tom's Cabin* in Cincinnati, *could* not write it—or even dream it—until she returned to her native New England, following, or rather preceding her husband, who had been offered a job at Bowdoin College in Brunswick, Maine. Some twenty-five or thirty years before, he had been a student at that unredeemably rural and ferociously Calvinist school, a poor boy then fighting to rise in the world by sheer intellect and energy, a professor of moral theology now and married to one of the aristocratic Beechers. He seems not to have been very happy at his job, however, not finding among his students, perhaps, any to equal those of his own time, who included not just a future president of the United States, Franklin Pierce, but Nathaniel Hawthorne and Henry Wadsworth Longfellow; which is to say, two men who between them created (think of Hester Prynne and her "steeple-crowned" persecutors, of Miles Standish, John and Priscilla Alden) figures as essential to the myth of New England as Uncle Tom, Simon Legree, and Little Eva to the myth of the South.

But it was not of Bowdoin that Harriet wrote even after the child with which she was pregnant on her trip from Ohio had been delivered and she had settled down to writing for popular magazines again in her endless effort to catch up with the household bills. That college, it seemed, was doomed never to be memorialized in literature for all the gifted writers who had inhabited its halls. Hawthorne, it is true, had tried in his first novel, *Fanshawe,* to describe the solitude of its setting: "secluded from the sight and sound of the busy world . . . almost at the farthest extremity of a narrow vale . . . as inaccessible, except at one point, as the Happy Valley of Abyssinia"; but he had suppressed that book immediately after publication. Nor was Mrs. Stowe tempted to emulate him, since in everything she wrote she was more concerned with the spaces inside which men and women live than those through which they move. Moreover, when she did turn her attention outward from houses and furnished rooms, she was more likely to deal with imaginary landscapes than real ones.

In any case, finding herself in a region further northeast than she had ever been before, a kind of ultimate, absolute New England, evoked in her images of ultimate, absolute South: a mythic Louisiana and Mississippi, in which Black field hands and White overseers toiled in cottonfields under a sweltering sun. But she remained unaware of this for many months. At first, indeed, as December storms shook the house around her and she lay sleepless beside her half-frozen babies, she thought instead of the blizzards of her childhood, her parents struggling homeward through mounting drifts. But seated at a Communion Service in the college church of Bowdoin in February of 1852, she saw before her, lit by a meridianal glare brighter than the dim northern light at the windows, the bloody and broken body of an old Black man beaten to death by his White master. And barely repressing her tears, she rushed home to write down (the words are her son's, remembering, echoing hers years afterward) "the vision which had been blown into her mind as by a mighty wind."

Then, the ink scarcely dry, she read the first installment of what was to become *Uncle Tom's Cabin* aloud to her children, who "broke into convulsions of weeping," and only when they were asleep did she permit herself to give way to tears. "I remember," she wrote to one of her sons a quarter of a century later, "weeping over you as you lay sleeping beside me, and I thought of the slave mothers whose babies were torn from them." But surely she was thinking, too, of the child she had lost before leaving Cincinnati: the son she always referred to as "the most beautiful and beloved" of all her brood, since elsewhere—indeed, more than once—she noted for posterity that "it was at his dying bed that I learned what a poor slave mother may feel when her child is torn away from her . . ." And she added, "I felt that I could never be consoled for it, unless this crushing of my own heart might enable me to work out some great good to others . . ."

The "great good" turned out to be, of course, *Uncle Tom's Cabin*, whose serial publication she began almost immediately, not quite knowing at first where she was going or how long it would take her but sustained, it would appear, by other hallucinations as vivid as the first, so that finally she began to believe her book had been *given* from without (by God, she liked to say) rather than invented from within. Yet the essential feeling of the book is that of a bereaved White mother, a kind of latter-day Rachel who weeps for her children and will not be comforted. Very early on in that book she appeals, in fact, to others who, like her, have suffered the loss of a child, as the kindly little Mrs. Bird prepares to give the clothing of her dead son to Eliza's Harry: "And oh! mother that reads this, has there never been in your house a drawer, or a closet, the opening of which has been to you like the opening again of a little grave?" Indeed, Eliza seems in many ways an apter surrogate for Mrs. Stowe than Uncle Tom, being introduced in a chapter called simply "The Mother." Yet though Eliza is threatened with the loss of Harry, she never actually is deprived of him even for a moment, so that we tend to forget the babe in her arms, remembering her not as "The Mother" but as the Fleeing Maiden, an object of inter-racial lust, like Cissy and Emmeline at the book's conclusion.

There are, to be sure, in the chapters between, many Black mothers deprived of their children by slave-traders and driven in despair to drink or self-inflicted death. But somehow the scenes that involve them, though pathetic enough, lack the mythic resonance of the death of Uncle Tom, with which it all began, or even that of Little Eva, which rivaled it in popularity, at least on the boards. Both scenes, of course, provide opportunities for a "good cry," but more than that they have similar theological meanings: the pearl-pale, golden-haired, barely pubescent virgin becoming, like the wooly-headed old Black at the moment of death, a secular avatar of Christ. Both die, that is to say, for our sins, the sins of slavery and blind lust and contempt for the bourgeois family.

But interestingly enough in light of Mrs. Stowe's own deep self-consciousness, there is no mourning Mary figure present at Eva's death, no bereaved mother to weep as Mrs. Stowe had wept. Mrs. St. Clare, who bore Eva, is an anti-Mother: a vain, silly, cruel, hypochondriacal woman, a fading beauty, who loves and pities no one but herself. If she is called "Marie" it is to emphasize the irony of her relationship to the Christ-like child she has borne and lost without ever knowing it. In any case, Eva's death-bed scene is presided over by her Byronic father and Uncle Tom, who must sustain him, too, in his grief, as if he were another child. It is a strange kind of Protestant *Pietà* that Mrs. Stowe portrays: a Daughter, a Father and a Slave. But no mother. Or is it that Tom is revealed in that scene as the symbolic, archetypal, mythological Mother he has really been all along?

It would seem, indeed, that for Mrs. Stowe (and this provides the link between the passion that begot her book and the image in which it became incarnate) Woman=Mother=Slave=Black; or simplifying, Woman=Black, Black=Woman. Perhaps the final formulation most accurately represents Mrs. Stowe's perception of the relationship between race and gender, since, unlike certain hardcore feminists of her time and ours, she was far from believing that women played the role *vis à vis* men of "niggers." Yet Charlotte Brontë seems to have thought so, or at least this is the way Ellen Moers would interpret her comment that "Mrs. Stowe had felt the iron of slavery enter into her heart, from childhood upwards . . ."

It seems to me, however, that Mrs. Stowe, being what we would now call a "sexist" as well as a "racist," believed that just as males and females were intrinsically different, so also were Whites and Blacks, and that, moreover, their differences corresponded exactly, i.e., "the Anglo-Saxon race" possessed those qualities considered in Mrs. Stowe's age "masculine," being "stern, inflexible, energetic . . . dominant and commanding," at their worst, "hot and hasty." "Africans," on the other hand, were—like women as Mrs. Stowe understood them—"naturally patient, timid and unenterprising, not naturally daring . . . but home-loving and affectionate . . ." And Tom, being the most African of all (as opposed, say, to George Harrison, a mulatto with certain *macho* traits inherited from his White father), is the most womanly, most motherly, possessing "to the full, the gentle domestic heart which, woe for them, is characteristic of his unhappy race."

If we understand the sense in which Tom is a White Mother in Blackface, we realize that when Mrs. Stowe sighs "woe for them" she means also "woe for us": we long-suffering, pious WASP mothers, daughters and wives, who respond to the indignities visited upon us with forgiveness and prayer, as is appropriate to *our* "gentle, domestic hearts." There is, then, a sense in which Mrs. Stowe's novel, despite the fact that she rejected radical feminism, even as she rejected radical abolitionism, is—just below its surface—a protest on behalf of women as well as of slaves. In this sense surely she is true to the New England culture, which not only produced certain pioneers of Feminism, real and fictional, like Margaret Fuller and Hester Prynne, but in Harriet's time was characterized by a progressive movement which advocated simultaneously Rights for Women, Freedom for Slaves and the Prohibition of Whiskey, a third major theme of her complexly didactic romance.

It was, I am suggesting, fitting (perhaps even inevitable) that a crusading woman, daughter and sister to crusading clerics, end by mythicizing slavery as an offense not just against the teachings of Christ but more immediately against the bourgeois family and that in the course of doing so she create archetypal images of their owners as well as the dark and lovely land in which flourished what Mrs. Stowe called—with multiple ironies that escaped her control—the "patriarchal institution." But she did not do so, could not do so, until the passing of the Fugitive Slave Law had made manifest the complicity of Massachusetts and Connecticut and Maine in that institution so that it was no longer possible to attribute the guilt of treating humans with Black skins as things solely to alien others in the alien South.

This became especially clear when in the midst of Mrs. Stowe's trek from Cincinnati to Brunswick, on March 7, 1850, Daniel Webster, spokesman for, living embodiment of, the political conscience of New England publicly defended that atrocious law. At that point what had been an inter-sectional conflict became a family quarrel. "So fallen! so lost! the light withdrawn/ Which once he wore!" Whittier wrote of that failed brother, more in sadness than anger, "The glory from his gray hairs gone/ Forevermore!" And at almost the same moment, Mrs. Stowe's sister-in-law was pleading in a letter, "Now, Hattie, if I could use a pen as you can, I would write something that would make this whole nation feel what an accursed thing slavery is."

If this sequence of events does not make it clear, the text of *Uncle Tom's Cabin* does, that when Harriet began to turn her vision into words she was concerned not only with how "accursed" the "patriarchal institution" was, but also—and perhaps most of all—with how ignominious was the moral capitulation before its claims of her own beloved New England. Simon Legree, the chief villain of her novel, is, as everyone knows, not a Southern planter, overseer or trader, but a Vermonter, the faithless son of a saintly New England mother much like what Harriet believed her own son to be, who in a decaying plantation house bereft of white women presides over the murder of a non-resisting Black male while pursuing in drunken lust helpless Black females. And surely Legree was also an actor in Mrs. Stowe's original vision; if not the actual killer (it is unclear what his color was in the first instance; in the book he is split in two and made Black), then the shadowy Third Man, who *was* White from the start and who urged the murderer on, an accomplice before and after the fact.

In any event, it seems to me that both Tom and Simon, the blessed "slave" who dies forgiving his enemies and the damned "master" who drags out his last days unable to forgive even himself, represent aspects of the pious, guilt-ridden and hopelessly divided psyche of Harriet Beecher Stowe. Insofar as she is a woman, she identifies with the loving persecuted slave; insofar as she is a New Englander, she identifies with his brutal persecutor. It is worth recalling at this point that Mrs. Stowe's Grandmother Foote had two indentured Black servants, who, though they could look forward to eventual freedom, were obliged to call their mistress's grand-daughter "Miss Harriet" while to her they were simply Harry and Dinah. That that experience stayed with her we know from the fact that the first named Black character in her book, the threatened Black child of Eliza, is called "Harry" while the cook in the kitchen of the St. Clare house is named "Dinah," though she resembles physically the woman who helped out with Mrs. Stowe's cooking in Cincinnati, "a regular epitome of slave life in herself, fat, gentle, easy, loving and loveable," who, to complicate matters even further, was named Eliza.

Almost all of Harriet's real, close relations with Black people were as a Mistress (however enlightened and benevolent) dealing with servants. That this was a troubling fact one would never gather from her letters on the subject; but when in her novel she attempts to portray ideal or Utopian families, they turn out to be *servantless:* like the orderly Vermont home from which Miss Ophelia comes, where the Lady of the house has cleaned and arranged and provided long before anyone else has arisen or the Quaker household of Rachel Halliday, in which adults and children in peaceful concert handle all the chores. No servants, Black or White, and, I cannot resist adding at this point, no resident Blacks at all, since Mrs. Stowe cannot imagine a world in which Black and White inhabit the same country in peace, much less cohabit and beget in a bi-racial family. Symptomatically, then, at the end of her book, all the major Black characters who are not dead are on their way to Liberia. In

Mrs. Stowe's quite un-utopian households (she was a notoriously disorganized housekeeper) what order was maintained was maintained by servants, a large part of them Black, and the difficulties this caused her, as well as the guilt it bred, can best be understood by looking closely at Miss Ophelia's adventures in New Orleans.

Though Mrs. Stowe believed in repatriating Black Americans, she did not propose to send them back to Africa until they had been educated and converted by White Americans like her, i.e., turned into literate missionaries who would eventually Christianize all of the continent from which they had been so cruelly snatched. Indeed, since she herself had been a teacher before she became a housewife, Mrs. Stowe had known Black people, particularly small children, as students earlier than as servants, and she represents the pathos and comedy (as well as the underlying terror) of her attempts to deal with what sometimes must have seemed their invincible ignorance in the encounters between Miss Ophelia and Topsy. But the figure of Miss Ophelia is more complex and important than that. The only other New Englander besides Legree who is close to, if not quite at the mythic center of the novel, she is clearly another projection of or surrogate for the author as New Englander.

We must not be misled by the superficial differences between this bristling, cold, compulsively orderly Old Maid and the warm-hearted, hopelessly untidy mother of seven who conceived her. She represents a caricature, drawn not without a certain degree of self-hatred, of Harriet Beecher Stowe as do-gooder, meddler in the affairs of others, impotent voyeur. Perpetually outside of everything, essentially unable to communicate with anyone or influence anything (who can really believe in the eventual redemption of Topsy?), Miss Ophelia stands in a particularly absurd relationship to Black slavery since despite her abstract conviction that slaves are fully human, she cannot bear to touch their flesh. Even more equivocal and suspect is her relationship to Southern culture, whose slovenliness, leisurely pace and sensuality she affects to despise, though secretly she is titillated by its beauty, envious of its easy charm. Finally she is, like the rugged landscape of Maine, like Mrs. Stowe (who always deprecated her own looks), like New England piety itself, perhaps, without beauty and without charm but not without guilt, despite her high ideals and blameless life.

To understand the source of that guilt in her and her author, I propose to return once more to Mrs. Stowe's Bowdoin "vision," explicating yet another level of its meaning with the aid of an essay by Sigmund Freud, which actually mentions *Uncle Tom's Cabin* and is called "A Child Is Being Beaten." In it Freud discusses a fantasy which he kept encountering in cases of pathological sadomasochism (a fantasy disconcertingly like one central to many popular books of the nineteenth century, most particularly perhaps Dickens' *Oliver Twist* and *David Copperfield*) in which a small boy or girl is being brutally whipped.

As far as literature is concerned, almost any helpless or relatively powerless victim will do as well: a horse, a dog, an abused wife, a Black Slave; all that is absolutely necessary is a whip, a half-visible wielder and a victim who does not or cannot resist. It is a multi-purpose symbol signifying social injustice and perverse pleasure, and it can stir therefore guilt and self-righteousness, tears and sexual excitement. No wonder it has been exploited to make best sellers and to fuel social reform—in *Uncle Tom's Cabin* both at once.

But, I am tempted to ask at this point (and here Freud does not finally help), with whom does the fantasizer of such scenes, with whom did Mrs. Stowe, identify, the beater, or the beaten? Though my first impulse was to say with the beaten, the child, the wife, the slave, the Black—helpless, perhaps, but not guiltless or wholly sympathetic until beaten to the verge of death or beyond, my second was to say also the beater: the parent, the husband, the master/mistress, the White—guilty without a doubt, but also a victim, powerless to compel submission or to stay his/her own fury. The fantasizer identifies with both then, *both,* and feels guilty on both counts: guilty enough to have been punished in the first instance (and who, Mrs. Stowe's theology asked, is without sin?), but guilty in the last of having dared to punish (vengeance is mine, says Mrs. Stowe's patriarchal God) the offending other. Even this is not the whole truth, however, since—as the figure of Miss Ophelia suggests—the sado-masochistic fantasizer is not just beater, he is also something, someone else: an onlooker, a third party who watches both the sufferer and the inflictor of suffering, finding double pleasure in being, though vicariously both, in fact neither.

But Miss Ophelia is our surrogate in the novel as well as Mrs. Stowe's since we watch what she watches, watch through her, as it were. And this eye-to-the-keyhole effect, this observing at a double remove what is too obscene to be observed firsthand, much less done, constitutes the very essence of pornography. Moreover, the sneaky pleasure it affords us is compounded by the pretense of piety which writers like Mrs. Stowe afford us: a claim that we are looking at such ultimate atrocities even as she is showing them, only in order to bear witness, to protest, maybe to change it all for the better. I have always experienced, in any case, the same sickening revulsion/attraction in reading *Uncle Tom's Cabin* that I do, for instance, watching the films on child-abuse whose current popularity on TV must be explicable, in part at least, because they provide us with vicarious opportunities to relish the maceration of children's flesh while pretending to deplore it—or rather, *really* deploring it.

Nor am I alone in my response to Mrs. Stowe's all-time best seller, which has been read, it seems ironical in this context to remind you, with equal pleasure in the kitchen, the parlor and the nursery. Similar opinions have been expressed by writers as different from each other and me as that Black child of Harlem, James Baldwin, and that White daughter of the early twentieth-century South, Margaret Mitchell, whose belated fictional response to Mrs. Stowe's improbable masterpiece has rivaled it in sales. Baldwin speaks of "the ostentatious parading of excessive and spurious emotion," which he calls "the mask of cruelty," while Mrs. Mitchell, through the mouth of Scarlett O'Hara, refers contemptuously to the "nasty and illbred interest" of Mrs. Stowe and her first Northern female fans in "branding irons, cat-of-ninetails and slave concubinage." Small wonder, then, that some of Freud's sado-masochistic patients, in an attempt to revive and refresh their own flagging fantasies, would while masturbating to climax read that pious and sentimental piece of New England porn.

In any case, we cannot begin to understand *Uncle Tom's Cabin* (as I am always beginning again to understand it in an essentially endless quest) unless we are aware that, gifted with easy access to her own unconscious and trained by her Calvinist forebears in conscious self-examination, Mrs. Stowe was able to draw a triple portrait of her guilt-ridden self at the very heart of her senti-mental, didactic best seller. As a bereaved White Mother, she identified with a victimized and forgiving Black male. As a Beecher, her father's truest heir and, in that sense, a betrayer of her mother, she portrayed herself as an iron-muscled White male, a murderer and rapist. As her sister's sister, another frustrated New England schoolmarm and reformer, she projected herself in the half-comic figure of prurient do-gooder, a spinster with no home of her own.

But what began as a private fantasy disguised, even from herself, as a popu-lar protest novel ("Everybody's protest novel," Baldwin called it with loving bitterness) has become a national myth: a perceptual grid through which we continue to perceive slavery, abolition, and the ante-bellum South, indeed, our whole country and culture. But this is to say that finally *Uncle Tom Cabin* is a social, a cultural, fact, quite as real as public documents like the Fugitive Slave Law or the Emancipation Proclamation and one, moreover, still read rather than merely read about.

Huckleberry Finn:
The Book We Love to Hate

I like to think that it would have tickled Mark Twain that a defender of "sivilization" 1984-style rose at the first major symposium honoring the hundredth anniversary of the publication of *Huckleberry Finn* to demand—piously and solemnly—that it be banned from the school curriculum in State College, Pennsylvania. "Black kids," she contended of a book about a white boy willing to "go to hell" to insure the freedom of a runaway black slave, "can be humiliated by it, white kids who are sensitive feel somehow culpable and guilty, and others have their racial biases reinforced"; and she further urged that an English teacher who had assigned it to a ninth grade class, "be censured for manifestations of racial prejudice . . ." But no one present, as far as I can gather from newspaper accounts of the occasion, had sense enough to laugh.

Instead, some of the other symposiasts seconded her plea, as unaware as she of the absurdity of advocating censorship in the name of "enlightened liberalism"; and apparently equally unaware that some decades earlier the book they advocated keeping out of the hands of the young lest it foster "racism" had been quite as piously and solemnly condemned by unabashed white racists, including a now forgotten congressman called Joseph Shannon and the still infamous Senator Joseph McCarthy. The former, an unreconstructed apologist for the Confederacy, had described Twain as "a foresaker of the interests of the South, a coward and deserter"; while the latter apparently considered him un-American, a source of aid and comfort for the Communist enemy.

To be sure, several of the academic participants in the centennial symposium rose valiantly to its defense; but they scarcely could have done otherwise, considering that they earned their living by teaching it. Besides, there was something almost as ridiculous as the attack in their defense to which credit in their humorless insistence on the moral integrity and classic status of a book to which its author had appended an ironic "Note" warning: "Persons attempting to find a motive in this narrative will be prosecuted; persons attempting to find a moral in it will be banished . . ." In any case, academic critics, as their latter day descendants did not trouble to remind their audience, have not always been so sure about the morality and greatness of *Huckleberry Finn*. As a matter of fact, when it first appeared it was reviewed favorably in only one "serious" literary periodical.

Part of the trouble seems to have been that it was not packaged and distributed like a "serious" book at all—but published by "subscription," which is to say, peddled like the sleaziest "commodity literature" of the time. Moreover, it seems to have disappointed the kind of genteel readers who had been encouraged by Twain's previous novel, *The Prince and the Pauper*, to believe he was shedding the bad habits he had acquired as a Western journalist, contemptuous of elegance and good taste, and learning at long last to produce books suitable for family reading in the civilized East. In *Huckleberry Finn*, however, he seemed to be reverting to inadvertent vulgarity and deliberate irreverence, farce and shameless burlesque. What is more, to make matters worse he had written his new book in colloquial backcountry American, with the deliberate misspellings and grammatical lapses on which newspaper humorists depended for easy laughs.

Small wonder then that most of the few notices he did get were more in the nature of rebukes than proper reviews. "Vulgar and coarse," the avowed enemies of the low comic called it, "trashy and vicious . . . no better than the dime novels . . . not elevating . . . more suited to the slums than to intelligent, respectable people . . ." but even the polite humorists of the time found Twain offensive; a writer in *Life*, the leading comic magazine of the era, for instance, described *Huckleberry Finn* as "coarse and dreary fun"; and after detailing its many scenes of murder and mayhem, observed snidely that such fare was apparently being proffered as "especially suited to amuse children on long, rainy afternoons." But it was the humorless hardline which triumphed and persisted; so that as late as 1920, ten years after Twain's death, a certain Professor John T. Rice is still insisting in the *Missouri Historical Review*, of that state's best-known writer, "he is often coarse, irreverent if not blasphemous . . . Mark Twain lacks the education absolutely necessary to be a great writer; he lacks the refinement which would render it impossible for him to create such coarse characters as Huckleberry Finn; furthermore, he is absolutely unconscious of all the canons of literary art . . ."

By the time Rice had delivered himself of this blanket condemnation, however, a counter-effort to tout *Huckleberry Finn* as "the Great American Novel" had begun in earnest. Starting with the authorized and adulatory autobiography by Albert Bigelow Paine, it had even begun to penetrate the academy. But Twain's chief apologists up to the middle of our own century tended to be not objective critics, but cultural chauvinists bound and determined to find somewhere in our past a supreme American classic, or journalists with a strong populist bias, like Bernard DeVoto, bent on redeeming a homegrown novelist whom European-oriented academic critics had hitherto denigrated or ignored. When DeVoto's *Mark Twain's America* appeared in 1932, however, he was most directly responding to another freelance nonacademic, Van Wyck Brooks. In *The Ordeal of Mark Twain* (1920), Brooks had somewhat grudgingly granted that *Huckleberry Finn* attained a certain measure of greatness, but his chief emphasis was on the fact that it might have been even greater if Twain had not been himself the victim of the same genteel tradition which had found his novel vulgar and unrefined. During the Sexual Revolution of the twenties, that is to say—in one more typically ironic turn of the critical screw—Twain was blamed for expurgating his own work in response to the pressures of his timid family and friends—for failing, in short, to be vulgar and unrefined *enough*.

Moreover, just as he was found lacking by the "liberated" Freudian critics of the post–World War I era, he was adjudged inadequate by the two critical schools which dominated the American cultural scene during the Great Depression and immediately after World War II, the self-declared Marxists first and then the so-called "New Critics." To a hardline Stalinist like Granville Hicks, for instance, Twain seemed never to have fulfilled his promise of becoming "a great social novelist." Failing either to confront the social conflicts of his own time or "to regard the literary life as a serious enterprise," Twain—Hicks contends in *The Great Tradition*, published in 1933—ended bitter and frustrated. Ironically once more, despite their differences on almost every other score, the defenders of High Modernism, most of whom were politically reactionary, agreed. After all, their most admired literary ancestor, Henry James, had dismissed Twain as reading for the immature, and Newton Arvin echoed him in the fifties, writing that Twain's appeal was "chiefly to the very young . . . he is read not because he makes experience more intelligible, but because he cooperates with the desire to play hooky . . ."

It was Hawthorne and Melville whose fiction Arvin found infinitely more sympathetic, as did more of his more serious and sophisticated colleagues in the university and out; not merely teaching them assiduously, but producing numerous full-length studies of *The Scarlet Letter* and *Moby Dick*. They did not, however, perform a similar service for *Huckleberry Finn*. Indeed, Twain remains oddly invisible in the Age of Criticism which climaxed in the fifties. He is, for instance, absent from F. O. Matthiessen's *American Renaissance*, the critical study which established for that time a new canon of American literature, as he was also from an earlier work which much influenced it, D. H. Lawrence's *Studies in Classic American Literature*. Clearly, in the case of Matthiessen (who, unlike Lawrence, admired *Huckleberry Finn*) Twain was excluded for purely chronological reasons; but, in any case, neither Matthiessen himself nor anyone else hastened to fill the gap. To be sure, T. S. Eliot, who was not only the favorite poet of the first generation of New Critics, but a formidable critic as well, in 1950 declared himself convinced of the greatness of *Huckleberry Finn*. Eliot, though, was speaking nostalgically and sentimentally on the occasion of his temporary return from exile to the banks of the Mississippi, where he had been born; and he is, in any event, an erratic and untrustworthy judge of fiction. But Lionel Trilling, most literate and plausible of all American critics influenced by Karl Marx (and Sigmund Freud to boot), had gone on record to the same effect just a couple of years before. Consequently, despite the fact that both of their pieces are slight and occasional, they carried the day, making *Huckleberry Finn* as standard a part of the English curriculum as *Moby Dick* or the *Scarlet Letter*; so that even the far later critics, bent on making a negative case, have felt obligated to come to terms with so odd and formidable a united front.

This, however, is precisely what William Van O'Connor, a second-generation academic New Critic and hardline "Modernist," attempted to do in 1955, in a little essay much reprinted ever since, called "Why *Huckleberry Finn* Is Not the Great American Novel." In it he argues that, in spite of Trilling and Eliot, "Twain, however gifted as a raconteur, however much genius he had as an improvisor, was not, even in *Huckleberry Finn*, a great novelist"; and he suggests as examples of writers who were: Jane Austen and Henry James. It is quite evident by the standards of Modernism that O'Connor finds Twain wanting— deficient in "serious wit," controlled form and precision of language. In light of this, then, it is scarcely surprising that Cyril Connolly, drawing up in 1965 a list of the "one hundred key books" of the Modern Movement, excluded *Huckleberry Finn*, which, he explained, "is over-praised, too involved and sentimental despite its prophetic use of American vernacular—a false dawn . . ."

For a long time, moreover, Twain fared as badly with his fellow-novelists as he had earlier on with the literary critics. His Continental contemporaries by and large ignored him, and even novelists who wrote in his own tongue, both American and English, though more likely to begin by granting that he possessed considerable talent, typically ended by denying his "greatness." The British, in fact, remained skeptical well into the twentieth century: Arnold Bennett, for instance, declaring that though some of Clemens' fictions were "episodically magnificent . . . as complete works of art they are of inferior quality"; and Frank Harris dismissing him even more summarily, with the observation, "I do not think *Huckleberry Finn* among the best boys' books. *Treasure Island* of Stevenson seems to me infinitely better." As late as 1941, V. S. Pritchett though urging an apparently reluctant English audience to read the book which he described somewhat condescendingly as, "granting the limits of a boy's mind in the hero and the author, a comic masterpiece," hastens to add that "It is not a book which grows spiritually, if we compare it to *Don Quixote*, *Dead Souls* or even *The Pickwick Papers*; and it is lacking in that civilized quality which you are bound to lose when you throw over civilization—the quality of pity."

Considering the British inclination to identify their own culture with "civilization" itself, the response is understandable enough. But less understandably for a while at least, Twain was regarded just as suspiciously by eminent writers in his own country. Even William Dean Howells, his life-long advocate, as well as his editor and censor and close friend, though he rushed into print enthusiastically in behalf of *The Innocents Abroad*, *The Prince and the Pauper* and *A Connecticut Yankee in King Arthur's Court*, published no review of *Huckleberry Finn*. Good and sufficient reasons have been offered for this (he had no regular reviewing assignment at the moment; he was too deeply involved with editing the book *etc. etc.*); but his perhaps embarrassed silence is too much like most of his respectable contemporaries to be easily explained away. Certainly, he was aware of the resistance to Twain on the part of the eminent Brahmins of New England, whom he himself had wooed and won, though initially quite as much a suspect outsider as Twain, reporting a little ruefully that "I don't think Longfellow made much of him and Lowell made less."

Henry James, though more nearly of Twain's age and generation, regarded him, as we have already noted, with equal coolness; but this is scarcely surprising in light of the fact that the mass audience which spurned his work had made a rich man of his rival. What is surprising is that Walt Whitman, who one might have supposed would find Twain with his commitment to the vernacular and his populist politics profoundly sympathetic, thought him somehow not really on his side. "I think he misses fire," the Good Gray Poet told Horace Traubel of Twain, "he might have been something; he comes near to being something; but he never arrives." Similarly, the somewhat younger Theodore Dreiser, though he respected and admired Twain for his ideas, especially his religious skepticism and his hostility to American imperialism, found him inadequate as a maker of fictions; "never a novelist," was his final word on that subject, "He could not write a novel."

It seems clear, however, that Dreiser was deeply indebted to Twain in ways he could not confess even to himself. It was only with the emergence of Faulkner and Hemingway in the late 1920s that a generation of novelists appeared willing to acknowledge fully and generously what our literature in general and they in particular owe to Mark Twain. Fittingly enough, it is the judgment of the latter which has been quoted over and over ever since, till it has come to seem an article of faith. "All modern American literature comes from one book by Mark Twain called *Huckleberry Finn*," Hemingway wrote in *The Green Hills of Africa* in 1935, ". . . All American writing comes from that. There was nothing before. There has been nothing as good since."

The grandiloquent overstatement of the conclusion, dismissing as "nothing" all of Cooper and Poe, Hawthorne and Melville, is odd enough and is, there-fore, generally ignored by those citing the passage in Twain's behalf. But even odder is the qualifying proviso, indicated by my three dots just before "All American writing," which most admirers of Twain and Hemingway tend to forget. "If you read it you must stop where the Nigger Jim is stolen from the boys. This is the real end. The rest is just cheating." In the first place (obviously Hemingway had not read the novel he so highly praised in a long time and had rewritten it in his memory), Jim is not stolen from "the boys" at all, only from Huck who is accompanied by Tom Sawyer at that climactic moment.

Moreover, as those of us who *have* read *Huckleberry Finn* recently are uncomfortably aware, the "rest" that is "just cheating"—the long passage full of cruel horseplay and tedious burlesque involving the mock stealing out of cap-tivity of a black slave who Tom knows has long since been freed—constitutes nearly one third of the whole book. One must slog his way through it to reach what is perhaps the most famous pair of sentences in the book (the essential clue, as I hope finally to demonstrate, to why it has bugged so many self-righteous critics ever since): "but I reckon I got to light out for the Territory ahead of the rest, because Aunt Sally she's going to adopt me and sivilize me and I can't stand it. I been there before."

What Hemingway is saying, finally, is that all of American literature comes out of two thirds of a single book, the rest of which is an aesthetic botch and moral failure; and almost all the critics who succeeded him have agreed. Ironi-cally, however, Mark Twain himself did not. After completing the first sixteen or seventeen chapters, which is to say, the part of the novel which critics have found most authentic and moving, he temporarily abandoned the whole proj-ect for five or six years, vowing that he was well-nigh determined to "pigeon hole or burn the MS when it is done." But after he had completed the long anti-climax in which all that is potentially tragic in the work is dissolved into farce, he came to believe that he had produced a "rattling good" book after all, and declared that "*I* shall *like* it, whether anybody else does or not."

But that resolve was soon shaken by the treatment *Huckleberry Finn* received from the self-appointed guardians of public morality, to whom in some ways Twain attended more closely than he did to critics and fellow writ-ers; since their opinions much influenced his wife and his daughters, whose approval was essential to his psychic well being. But Livy and Suzy turned out to be dubious about his new book, and eventually even he came like them to regard it as second best to more refined and pretentious works of his like *The Prince and the Pauper* and especially the almost unreadable *Joan of Arc*.

It was in the very heart of New England where he himself had settled that the voice of outraged moral protest against *Huckleberry Finn* was first raised; ironically enough in Concord, Massachusetts, the very cradle of American

Liberty. It was there that an irate committee banned Twain's book from their shelves as "rough, coarse, inelegant, dealing with experiences not elevating . . . the veriest trash." And a chorus of newspaper editorials—reaching eventually back into the West out of which Twain had emerged—repeated the charges: accusing him not only of a contempt for propriety and a willingness to pander to the gross tastes of the mass audience, but of fouling his own American nest, discrediting his country and culture in the eyes of the "civilized" world.

It was indeed this kind of attack on *Huckleberry Finn* which has persisted the longest. However critics may have changed their opinions and practicing writers altered their attitudes with the passage of time, the do-gooders and righteous book-banners have continued to regard his masterpiece as subversive. As late as the time in which T. S. Eliot grew up, such a view prevailed in his genteel but cultured family (after all, his grandfather had brought enlightenment to the provinces by founding Washington University in Saint Louis). "I suspect," he wrote looking back from 1950, "that a fear on the part of my parents lest I should acquire a premature taste for tobacco, and perhaps other habits of the hero of the story, kept the book out of my way." It is interesting that Eliot discreetly specifies only smoking (not yet under fire from a new wave of puritan repression in his time) rather than lying and stealing and a contempt for school and church which constitute Huck's less venial faults. The truth is that, taken seriously, *Huckleberry Finn* is not merely "rough, coarse, and inelegant" as charged, but also its anti-hero, convinced as he is what parents, preachers and teachers advocate must be rejected at the behest of his own untutored heart, is a dubious sort of model for growing boys and girls.

It was therefore predictable from the start that scarcely a year would pass during the century since its publication that has not seen Twain's book forbidden somewhere in the United States. After all, the self-righteous we have always with us. What is surprising (though finally characteristic of an America, which like that novel is divided against itself) is that even as *Huckleberry Finn* has remained a banned book, it has also become a *required* one; and that this, indeed, has seemed to exacerbate the resistance to it. Truly to understand the impact of Twain's most beloved and feared novel on our culture, then, we must be aware of both sides of our ambivalent response. But from a distance, what is most highly visible is the negative pole of that ambivalence—and the almost habitual scapegoating of poor Huck in which it periodically results.

It was, therefore, possible for a Soviet critic to claim in 1959, at the height of the Cold War, that the relationship of official America to "its greatest writer" is to "try to forget him," and when that fails, to forbid his books. In proof of this, that critic quotes from an English literary journal which a few months before had listed under the heading "Banned in America," *Lady Chatterley's Lover*, the novels of Henry Miller—and *Huckleberry Finn*. The Russian spokesman, proud of the fact that up to that time eleven million copies of Twain's book had been distributed in his country, where everything not forbidden is required, did not mention that the two other authors were (and are still) under official ban there. Nor did he seem aware that, despite the occasional attempts to forbid it, *Huckleberry Finn* had sold even better in the United States. Instead, he alluded to the attacks on Twain by the long-dead Congressman Shannon and the recently discredited McCarthy, citing as a clincher the fact that only two years earlier "The Board of Education of New York City crossed out the book about Huck from the books permitted for reading in elementary and junior schools."

Clearly he was suggesting that Samuel Clemens had become *persona non grata* in the United States because of his satires of American capitalism and imperialism. But the final example scarcely supports this case; since the action of the New York School Board in 1957 was undertaken not at the instigation of the Chamber of Commerce or the Veterans of Foreign Wars, but the NAACP, an organization whose fight against the evils of American racism was then being supported by the American Communist Party. Moreover, in the quarter of a century since, most of the continuing efforts to ban *Huckleberry Finn* have been launched by enlightened liberals, though attacks from genteel conservatives have not utterly ceased.

Every year since 1971, for instance, the *School Library Journal* has given a mock award called the "Huck Finn Pin" to a new book adjudged by its editor to "ill serve the limited reading time of young people." It seems obvious to me that this gallant defender of "good taste" in literature for the young would in 1885 have awarded her booby prize to the book whose anti-hero she describes (explaining why she has thus used his name) as "illiterate and inclined to stay that way." But she feels obliged at least to justify and explain; while the book-banners on the Left have grown even bolder—and more shameless.

When word leaked out in 1957 that *Huckleberry Finn* had been "barred as a textbook" in New York City, school officials felt obliged to lie to the press, explaining that it had been dropped not because of political or ethical objections from anyone, but merely because "it was not really a textbook." The NAACP, however, gave away the game, insisting that they had in effect objected to its "racial slurs" and "belittling racial designations"—meaning its frequent use of the word "nigger." They could not bring themselves to actually say the six-letter word, which at that point was considered "dirtier" than any of the once taboo four-syllable Anglo-Saxon monosyllabics. By 1982, however, the self-righteous anti-racists were out of the closet, and willing, in a good cause, to call a spade a spade.

In that year, for instance, the Human Relations Committee of the Mark Twain (*sic*) Elementary School of Arlington, Virginia, recommending the removal of *Huckleberry Finn* from the curriculum, charged it with being "anti-American," a threat to the Fourteenth Amendment and the very notion that "all men are created equal" because of its "flagrant use of the word 'nigger.'" Nor is there any point in denying that Twain is guilty as charged. That offensive epithet is, indeed, repeated over and over on the pages of his book like a *leitmotif* or an obsession; so that one can understand a black school boy in the midst of whites wincing as he reads.

But how could Twain have done otherwise in a book in which he boasted he had "painstakingly" re-created seven dialects spoken in the Mississippi Basin, in all of which (including that spoken by blacks themselves), the sole name for African-Americans was indeed "nigger." The deeper truth told by America about *Huckleberry Finn*, whose last words are, after all, "*Yours Truly*," depends on its faithfulness to the language we Americans actually speak; especially terms like "nigger," which serve to remind us of not just our troubled history but of attitudes and values created by that history of which most of us have learned to be ashamed, yet from which none of us can feel wholly free. We should therefore prize Twain's dangerous and equivocal novel not in spite of its use of that wicked epithet, but for the way it manages to ironize it; enabling us finally—without denying our horror or our guilt—to laugh therapeutically at the "peculiar institution" of slavery.

One of my own favorite passages in the book is, indeed, the little interchange between Huck and Aunt Sally in Chapter XXXII, in which, after Huck lyingly tells her that the boat he had arrived on had blown a cylinder head, she asks "Good gracious! Anybody hurt?" "No'm," he answers; "Killed a nigger"; to which she responds "Well, it's lucky; because sometimes people do get hurt." What initially makes this passage funny is that both of these essentially good people by thus dehumanizing the negro diminish their own humanity; and what makes it even funnier is that Huck, obtusest of all obtuse narrators, a classically humorless "straight man," does not find it funny at all. But the real cream of the jest is that in our time self-righteous anti-racists still fail to get the joke, making it also a joke on them unto the third and fourth generation.

Ridiculous or not, however, one hundred years later they continue to suppress *Huckleberry Finn*—putting its defenders more and more on the defensive; so that some have even tried to appease the book-banners by expurgating the novel. It would appear, for instance, that in New York in 1957, the publishers of the textbook version then in use had already discreetly substituted "negro" for "nigger" throughout. As always, however, appeasement did not work, the adamant objectors protesting that that anachronistic and tasteless euphemism had not been properly capitalized. And there is no end in sight; since at this point even capital-N-Negro has become suspect by those who, however pale their actual hue, prefer to call themselves "blacks." In any case, the anti-racist objection to *Huckleberry Finn* is not finally to its language, but (once more in the words of the Human Relations Committee of the Mark Twain School) to "the demeaning way in which black people are portrayed in the book."

I must confess I find this second charge harder to grant, in light of the fact that the only black character portrayed fully in it is "Miss Watson's big nigger Jim," who is by all odds the most sympathetic of its characters. A loving parent and husband, a faithful friend, resourceful, courageous, self-sacrificing (he risks his life to save Tom's), he possesses a natural dignity and authority, which in one of the novel's most moving scenes compels Huck—whom Jim has just called "trash" for his heartlessness—to apologize abjectly. "It made me feel so mean," Huck writes. "I could almost kissed *his* foot to get him to take it back. It was fifteen minutes before I could work myself up to go and humble myself to a nigger—but I done it, and I warn't ever sorry for it afterwards, neither." It is an apology for all of white America, which its ironies (triggered once again by the key word "nigger") keeps on the safe side of sentimentality. Moreover, Huck finds on the raft with Jim what he can find nowhere in the "sivilized" white world, a kind of love compatible with freedom. Together they establish a community of two, temporary and foredoomed perhaps, but providing for as long as it lasts a model for the reconciliation of blacks and whites in an America otherwise ethnically divided against itself.

But off the raft (and especially in the long farcical anti-climax which follows Chapter XXXI), the book's detractors protest, Jim is portrayed as ignorant, superstitious and gullible; thus perpetuating certain degrading "stereotypes about blacks" derived from the minstrel show, which—in the words of a professor of Afro-American Studies who testified against *Huckleberry Finn* at the centennial symposium I began by describing—consists of "white men blackening up to entertain other whites at the expense of black people's humanity." Some thirty years earlier the same charges had been made by the eminent black American novelist, Ralph Ellison, who had explained to white readers that the Negro is "made uncomfortable" by Nigger Jim, because "Twain fitted Jim into the outlines of the minstrel tradition." Ellison, however, then went on to add—finally loving Twain's great book (and, he tells us, identifying with Huck, whatever his discomfort with Jim)—that "it is from behind this stereotype mask that we see Jim's dignity and human capacity—and Twain's complexity—emerge."

What he suggests and present enemies of the book fail to recognize, is that Twain not merely reflected but redeemed the "niggershow stereotype"—converting it to an archetype of great resonance and power: a mythic grid of perception through which for a long time the whole world, black as well as white, perceived black Americans. The only two archetypal images of the Negro which can compete with Twain's Nigger Jim are Joel Chandler Harris's Uncle

Remus and Harriet Beecher Stowe's Uncle Tom, both also created by white Americans and derived, directly or indirectly, from the minstrel show. Yet neither of the books in which they appear has ever been banned from libraries or classrooms at the behest of anti-racists. *Uncle Tom*, to be sure, has been the target of Southern white racists, like *Huckleberry Finn*. Only the latter, however, has the unique distinction of having been censored not only by apologists for *both* sides in what eventuated in a bloody civil war—but also by those to whom culture and taste seemed more important than the "Negro Question," or indeed any social issue.

The persistent popularity of Huckleberry Finn has in fact always troubled members of any elite, aesthetic, moral or political, whose members feel that they know better than the unredeemed masses what is good for them. I recall William Burroughs (improbable heir to Mark Twain as literary disturber of the peace) once observing that the world would be vastly improved if a weapon could be invented which would destroy "all those who think they are right," i.e., believe that the values in which they happen to believe are valid for everyone, everywhere and will forever remain so. But *Huckleberry Finn*, it occurs to me, is precisely that weapon; killing no one, to be sure, but undermining all pretensions to final wisdom with ambiguity, irony, farce and burlesque: the universal solvent of laughter.

Without seeming to preach or teach it persuades us—at a level far below full consciousness—of the essential ridiculousness not only of our society's restrictive taboos against lying and stealing, "copping out" and "dropping out," but of its highest positive values as well: duty and hard work, heroism and honor. Moreover, in addition to mocking institutions despised by all right-thinking Americans by the end of the nineteenth century, royalty, aristocracy, slavery, the blood-feud and lynching, it satirizes others still dearly prized, like home, school and church, which is to say, bourgeois domesticity and Christian humanism. Certainly, the teachers and preachers and parents who defend them turn out in its pages always to be hilariously wrong. But it is worse even than this; since finally *Huckleberry Finn* undercuts, as Huck himself tells us (and we must—without ceasing to laugh—take him quite seriously) "civilization" itself: the reign of law and order and sweet reason, without which no community can survive, but for which the price we pay is, from the individual's point of view, in some sense too high.

To be sure, Twain himself did not live by Huck's antinomian, anarchic code but contented himself with dreaming of an orphan boy who did; and in his voice told the tale which—despite all censors—the world will not let die. Not that we who read and love it dare to "light out for the Territory" either; but turning its pages and evoking its images, we release vicariously all we have repressed in the daylight world of respectability and routine; thus therapeutically giving the Devil of our unconscious his due.

Such therapeutic release of the repressed is what all literature which, like *Huckleberry Finn*, pleases many and pleases long, affords us; though not all writers are aware of this. Some indeed aspire to reinforce rather than to deliver us from the "restrictions" of civilization to justify God's ways (i.e. the reigning theology and morality of their time) to man. Mark Twain, however, was of the Devil's party and knew it. He therefore despised, as he did other preachers and teachers, those Apostles of the Art Religion who did not. About Poe and Jane Austen, for instance, he wrote, "I could read his prose on salary, but not Jane's . . . it seems a great pity they allowed her to die a natural death"; and of Henry James he once observed that he would "rather be condemned to Paul Bunyan's Heaven" than be forced to finish *The Bostonians*.

Huckleberry Finn is a travesty of High Art quite as much as of conscience and duty and "sivilization"; and this Twain himself came finally to realize; writing in 1889, with a candor clearly bred by desperation, to Andrew Lang, one of the few critics he hoped might understand:

> Indeed I have been misjudged from the very first. I have never tried in even one single instance to help cultivate the cultivated classes. I was not equipped for it, either by native gifts or training. And I never had any ambition in that direction, but always hunted for bigger game—the masses. I have seldom deliberately tried to instruct them, but have tried to entertain them . . . to amuse them . . .
>
> Yes, you see, I have always catered for the Belly and the Members but have been . . . criticized from the culture standard—to my sorrow and pain, because, honestly, I never cared what became of the cultured classes. They could go to the theater and the opera. They had no use for me and the melodeon.

That he did in fact win the "masses" he wooed, in *Huckleberry Finn* at least, is attested to by their having taken that book to their hearts long before official critics and moralists had managed to come to terms with it. But precisely because it has thus proved from the start available to the undereducated as well as the learned, the naïve as well as the sophisticated, children as well as adults, the many as well as the few, the self-appointed guardians of culture and morality have continued to regard it with suspicion. Indeed, its scapegoating on ethical grounds has, as we have been noticing, never ceased, though those grounds have changed. But, in a sense, those who insist that Twain's novel, written from as well as to "the Belly and the Members," rather than the "Head," is dangerous and "vulgar" speak the truth. What falsifies Huckleberry Finn is the begrudged and belated praise of elitist critics, who have done their best recently to persuade us that Twain's untidy masterpiece, more improvised than structured, is "a great novel" in terms of the "culture standards" by which they also find *Pride and Prejudice* or *The Wings of the Dove* great.

The desperate plea with which Clemens ended his letter to Lang, that is to say, has never been truly or fully answered. "And now at last," he wrote, "I arrive at my object and tender my petition, making supplication to this effect: that the critics adopt a rule recognizing the Belly and the Members, and formulate a standard whereby work done for them shall be judged. Help me, Mr. Lang . . ." Lang did at least try but in years since, and especially on this side of the Atlantic, Twain's anguished appeal has been ignored, and the defense of popular art which underlies it dismissed as "self-serving" and "insubstantial." His cry for help continues, however, to ring in my head, a reproach to me and the profession I practice. I have therefore taken advantage of the centennial celebration of the American book we most love to hate to begin at long last, tentatively—and with appropriate irony—to respond.

"As Free as Any Cretur . . ."

The most extraordinary book in American literature unfortunately has not survived as a whole; but its scraps and fragments are to be found scattered through the works of Mark Twain: a cynical comment ascribed to a small-town lawyer and never printed, the wreck of a comic tale framed by apologies and bad jokes, and finally *Pudd'nhead Wilson*, that has come back down to us, half melodramatic detective story, half bleak tragedy. What a book the original must have been, before *Those Extraordinary Twins* was detached and Pudd'nhead's *Calendar* expurgated—a rollicking atrocious mélange of bad taste and half understood intentions and nearly intolerable insights into evil, translated into a nightmare worthy of America.

All that the surrealists were later to yearn for and in their learned way simulate, Twain had stumbled on without quite knowing it. And as always (except in *Huckleberry Finn*) he paid the price for his lack of self-awareness; he fumbled the really great and monstrous poem on duplicity that was within his grasp. The principle of analogy which suggested to him linking the story of the Siamese Twins, one a teetotaler, the other a drunk, Jekyll and Hyde inside a single burlesque skin—to a tale of a Negro and a white baby switched in the cradle finally seemed to him insufficient. He began to worry about broken plot lines and abandoned characters, about the too steep contrast between farce and horror; and he lost his nerve—that colossal gall which was his essential strength as well as his curse. Down the well went the burlesque supernumeraries and finally out of the story; and the poor separated twins remain to haunt a novel which is no longer theirs.

But something in Twain must have resisted the excisions; certainly they were made with a striking lack of conviction, and the resulting book is marred by incomprehensible motivations and gags that have lost their point with the unjoining of the once Siamese twins. The two stories were, after all, one, and the old book a living unity that could not be split without irreparable harm.

Yet *Pudd'nhead Wilson* is, after all, a fantastically good book, better than Mark Twain knew or his critics have deserved. Morally, it is one of the most honest books in our literature, superior in this one respect to *Huckleberry Finn*; for here Twain permits himself no sentimental relenting, but accepts for once the logic of his own premises. The immoral device of Tom's revelation, the fake "happy ending" of *Huck* are avoided in *Pudd'nhead*. It is a book which deals not only with the public issue of slavery, after all, long resolved—but with the still risky private matter of miscegenation, which most of our writers have chosen to avoid; and it creates in Roxy, the scared mulatto mother sold down the river by the son she has smuggled into white respectability, a creature of passion and despair rare among the wooden images of virtue or bitchery that pass for females in American literature. It is a portrait so complex and unforeseen that the baffled illustrator for the authorized standard edition chose to ignore it completely, drawing in the place of a "majestic . . . rosy . . . comely" Roxana—a gross and comic Aunt Jemima.

The scenes between the mother and her unregenerate son, who passes from insolence and cowardice to robbery and murder, and who ends slobbering at the feet of the woman he despises and plots to sell, have the cruelty and magnificence attained only by a great writer telling us a truth we cannot afford to face in a language we cannot afford to forget. It is a book which will be, I am sure, more and more read; certainly it is hard to believe that so rare a combination of wit and the metaphysical shudder will be considered forever of the second rank. Beside this book, *The Mysterious Stranger*, for the last several years a favorite of the writers on Twain, is revealed as the callow and contrived piece of cynicism it is: the best a cultureless man can do when he chooses to "philosophize" rather than dream.

Perhaps the best way to understand *Pudd'nhead* is to read it as a complement to *Huckleberry Finn*, a dark mirror image of a world evoked in the earlier work. Nearly ten years come between the two books, ten years in which guilt and terror had passed from the periphery of Twain's life and imagination to their center. *Huckleberry Finn* is also steeped in horror, to be sure; but it is easier to know this than to feel it. Though the main fable of the earlier book begins with a boy standing off with a rifle, his father gone berserk with the D.T.'s, and ends with the revelation of that father's death in a seedy and flooded room scrawled with obscenities. In *Pudd'nhead*, however, the lyricism and the euphoria are gone; we have fallen to a world of prose, and there are no triumphs of Twain's rhetoric to preserve us from the revealed failures of our own humanity.

True enough, there is humor in the later book, but on a level of grotesquerie that is more violent and appalling than anything avowedly serious. It is the humor of Dickens' Quilp and Faulkner's idiot Snopes, the humor of the freak. In the chamber of horrors of our recent fiction, the deformed and dwarfed and dumb have come to stand as symbols of our common plight, the failure of everyone to attain a purely fictional norm. Toward this insight, Twain was fumbling almost without awareness, believing all along that he was merely trying to take the curse off of a bitterness he could not utterly repress by being what he liked to think was "funny."

Just as the grotesque in *Pudd'nhead Wilson* tends to break free from the humorous, so the tragic struggles to shed the nostalgic which swathes it still in *Huckleberry Finn*. In the earlier book, it is possible to believe that the flight toward freedom and childhood is more than a flight toward isolation and death. There is always waiting in a bend of the river Aunt Sally's homestead: a utopia of childhood visits and Southern homecooking. But Huck rejected this nostalgic Southland at the end of his own book, and in *Tom Sawyer, Detective*, Twain had introduced death and the threat of madness into that Eden itself.

By the time he was attempting to detach *Pudd'nhead Wilson* from the wreck of his larger book, Twain had decided that the only unthreatened utopia is death itself; and amid the animal jokes and easy cynicism of the Calendar quotations set at the head of each chapter, rings the sybil's cry: *Let me die*: "Whoever has lived long enough to know what life is knows how deep a debt of gratitude we owe to Adam, the first great benefactor of our race. He brought death into the world." When he writes this, Twain no longer finds in freedom the pat happy ending waiting to extricate his characters from their moral dilemmas and himself from the difficulties of plotting. He does not abandon the theme of liberty, but render now the full treacherous paradox, only half of which he had acknowledged earlier.

Everyone remembers the climax of *Huckleberry Finn*, at which Tom, "his eye hot, and his nostrils opening and shutting like gills," cries out of Jim: "They hain't no *right* to shut him up . . . Turn him loose! He ain't no slave: he's as free as any cretur that walks this earth!" As free as any CRETUR . . . the wry joke is there already, but Twain can no more see it than can Tom; and we are not permitted to see it as readers as long as we remain within the spell of the book. But in *Pudd'nhead Wilson*, the protagonist, who is obviously Tom himself grown older and an outcast but about to be reinstated into the community, rises to answer his own earlier cry, in such a situation as he has always dreamed: "Valet de Chambre, Negro and slave . . . make upon the window the finger-prints that will hang you!" The double truth is complete: the seeming slave is free, but the free man is really a slave.

The resolution of *Pudd'nhead Wilson* is, of course, double; and the revelation which brands the presumed Thomas à Becket Driscoll a slave, declares the presumed Valet de Chambre free. We are intended, however, to feel the "curious fate" of the latter as anything but fortunate; neither black nor white, he is excluded by long conditioning from the world of the free, and barred from the "solacing refuge" of the slave kitchens by the fact of his legal whiteness. Really, his is, as Twain himself remarks, quite another story; what is symbolically important is the deposition of Thomas à Becket—and the meaning of this Twain makes explicit in one of the final jottings of his journal, "The skin of every human being contains a slave." We know at last in what bitter sense Tom's earlier boast is true: "As free as any cretur . . ." *Pudd'nhead Wilson* begins and ends in the village where *Huckleberry Finn* began and *Tom Sawyer* was played out, on the banks of the same river and in the same pre–Civil War years. But between "St. Petersburg" and "Dawson's Landing" there is a terrible difference. In the latest book, we see Twain's mythicized Hannibal for the first time *outside*; in the two earlier books, we are already inside of it when the action begins, and there is no opportunity to step back and survey it. But Pudd'nhead comes as a stranger to the place of Twain's belonging; and the author himself takes advantage of this occasion to pan slowly into it, giving us an at first misleadingly idyllic description of its rose-clad houses, its cats, its sleepiness and its fragrance—all preparing for the offhand give-away of the sentence beginning, "Dawson's Landing was a slaveholding town . . ."

The Civil War is the watershed in Twain's life between innocence and experience, childhood and manhood, joy and pain; but it is politically, of course, the dividing line between slavery and freedom. And Twain, who cannot deny either aspect, endures the contradiction of searching for a lost happiness he knows was sustained by an institution he is forced to recognize as his country's greatest shame. It was the best he could dream: to be free as a boy in a world of slavery!

In *Tom Sawyer*, this contradiction is hushed up for the sake of nostalgia and in the name of writing a child's book; in *Huck* it is preserved with all the power of its tensions; in the last book it falls apart into horror. In *Pudd'nhead Wilson*, Hannibal is felt from the beginning not as a Western but as a *Southern* town. The river is no longer presented as the defining edge of the natural world, what America touches and crosses on its way West, but as a passageway into the darkness of the deep South. "Down the river" is the phrase which gives a kind of musical unity to the work—a motif repeated with variations from Roxana's first jesting taunt to a fellow Negro, "If you b'longed to me I'd sell you down the river 'fo' you git too fur gone . . ." to the bleak irony of the novel's final sentence, "the Governor . . . pardoned Tom at once, and the creditors sold him down the river."

A comparison inevitably suggests itself with *Huckleberry Finn* in which the southward motion had served to symbolize (in contempt of fact) a motion toward deliverance. But here the direction of the river that Twain loved is felt only as the way into the ultimate South, the final horror—the absolute pole of slavery. The movement of the plot and the shape of the book are determined by this symbolic motion toward the sea, now transposed from a dream of flight to a nightmare of captivity. It is after she herself has been threatened with such a fate and in order to preserve her son from it, that Roxy switches the children in the cradle. But there is no way to escape that drift downward toward darkness to which the accident of birth has doomed her and her son;

by virtue of her very act of evasion she sets in motion the events that bring both of them to the end she has dreaded.

It is not only as a slave-holding town that Dawson's Landing belongs to the South, but also in terms of the code of honor to which everyone in the book subscribes. Patrician and Negro, American and foreigner, freethinker and churchgoer, all accept the notion that an insult can only be wiped out in blood, and that the ultimate proof of manhood is the willingness to risk death in such an attempt. The real demonstration of the unworthiness of the false Tom is his running to the courts for redress in preference to facing a duel. Ironically enough, this very duel was to have been in the book as originally planned a howling travesty of the values of a gentleman; for one of the parties was to have been half of a Siamese twin—and one can see what mad complications would have ensued. The "serious" Twain was, however, as incapable of doubting the code as Tom Sawyer; he could mock it only in pure farce, when he felt it perfectly clear to everyone that he was just kidding. There is in this book no Huck to challenge the many Colonel Sherburnes by rejecting courage as just another temptation—no absolute outcast armed only with style and success—and so he must pay his Tom Sawyerish respects to chivalry.

In *Huckleberry Finn*, the society which Huck finally rejects, his "siviliza-tion," is essentially a world of the mothers, that is to say, of what Christian-ity has become among the females who sustain it just behind the advancing frontier. It is a sufficiently simple-minded world in which one does not cuss or steal or smoke but keeps clean, wears shoes and prays for spiritual gifts. Above all, it is a world of those who cannot lie—and the truth, too, Huck finds a virtue beyond his budget. In this world the fathers appear generally as outcasts or scoundrels, like the Duke and Dauphin and like Pap himself. At best, the paternal is represented by the runaway nigger, the outcast who was never even offered the bait of belonging.

In *Pudd'nhead Wilson*, however, society is defined by the fathers, last defend-ers of the chivalric code and descendents of the cavaliers. Four in especial represent the world to which Pudd'nhead aspires: York Leicester Driscoll, Percy Northumberland Driscoll, Pembroke Howard and Col. Cecil Burleigh Essex—the names make the point with an insistence that is a little annoying. This is a world continuous with that of Renaissance gallantry, connected with the Court of Elizabeth, which represents for Twain on the one hand a roman-tic legend, and on the other a kind of lost sexual Eden (celebrated in his pri-vately circulated *1601*), whose potency puts to shame a fallen America where the natives "do it onlie once every seven yeares." The religion of such a society is, of course, not Christian at all; of Driscoll, the noble character murdered by the boy to whom he was benefactor and almost a father, we are told "to be a gentleman was his only religion."

One half of the story of Thomas à Becket Driscoll (really the slave Valet de Chambre) is the account of his failing this world of the fathers, first in gambling and thieving, then in preferring the courts to the field of honor, finally in becoming out of greed and abject rage, a quasi-parricide. Twain spares us, perhaps from some reluctance to surrender to utter melodrama, more probably from lack of nerve, the final horror. The logic of the plot and its symbolic import both demand really that Tom be revealed at last as the bastard of the man he killed; but we are provided instead with a specially invented double of the dead Driscoll as the boy's begetter, a lay figure called Cecil Burleigh Essex.

In all of the book, only a single mother is allowed the center of the stage—the true mother of the false Tom, the slave girl Roxana. Just as in *Huckleberry Finn*, Nigger Jim is played off against the world as Aunt Polly–Aunt Sally–Miss Watson, so in this reversed version a Negress is set against the society defined by Driscoll, Howard and Essex. This is, of course, a just enough stroke, which satisfies our sense of the historical as well as our desire for the typical. If the fathers of the South are Virginia gentlemen, the mothers are the Negro girls, casually or callously taken in the parody of love, which is all that is possible when one partner to a sexual union is not even given the status of a person.

The second and infinitely worse crime of Tom is the sin against the mother, the black mammy who threatens him with exposure; and the most moving, the most realized sections of the book deal with this relationship. Throughout his career, Twain returned over and over to this theme of rejection of the mother, the denial by the boy of the woman who has loved him with the purest love Twain could imagine. Of this Tom Sawyer is falsely accused by his Aunt Polly; of this Tom Canty is actually guilty at the tearful climax of *The Prince and the Pauper*, so extravagantly admired by its author. It is as if Mark Twain were trying to exorcise the possibility of himself failing the plea he could never forget, the cry of his own mother, clasping him to her over the death-bed of his father: "Only promise me to be a better boy. Promise me not to break my heart."

In *Pudd'nhead Wilson*, this tearful romance of the boy as a heartless jilt becomes involved with the ambiguous relations of black and white in the United States, with the problems of miscegenation and of "passing," and is lifted out of the sentimental toward the tragic. Twain's own judgment of sexual relations between the races is not explicitly stated; but there seems no doubt that he thought of the union between Roxy and Essex as a kind of fall—evil in itself and the source of a doom on all involved. Paired together, *Huckleberry Finn* and *Pudd'nhead Wilson* express both sides of a deep, un-thought-out

American belief, reflected on the one side of Twain by James Fenimore Cooper and on the other by William Faulkner: that there are two relations, two kinds of love between colored and white, one of which is innocent, one guilty, one of which saves, one damns. The innocent relation can only exist between men, or a man and a boy (Natty Bumppo and Chingachgook, Huck and Jim)—a love unphysical and pure; the other, suspect and impure, tries to join the disjoined in passion, and must end in either frustration and death (Cora and Uncas) or in unhappiness for all (Roxana and Essex).

A further reach of complexity is added to the theme by the symbolic meanings inevitably associated with the colors white and black, meanings which go back through literature (Shakespeare's "Dark Lady," for example) and popular religion (the New England habit of calling the Devil "The Black Man") to the last depths of the folk mind. No matter how enlightened our conscious and rational convictions may be in these matters, we are beset by a buried ambivalence based on the archetypal symbolism of light and dark. Twain himself in this very novel speaks unguardedly of the rain trying vainly to wash soot-blackened St. Louis white; and the implication is clear: black is the outward sign of inward evil. In this sense, the Negro puzzlingly wears the livery of the guilt we had thought the white man's. But *why?* It is a question which rings through the white man's literature in America; and the answer returns in an ambiguity endlessly compounded.

Who, having read it once, can ever forget the terrible exclamation in Melville's "Benito Cereno"—the cry which seems intended to dissolve in irony the problem we had hoped would be resolved in certainty, "It is the Black!" But there are even more terrible lines in *Pudd'nhead Wilson*: the lonely and baffled query of Tom (how hard it is to believe that it is not a quotation from Faulkner), "What crime did the uncreated first nigger commit that the curse of birth was decreed for him . . ." and the still more appalling response of Roxy to the news that her son has failed the white man's code, "It's de nigger in you dat's what it is!" The name of their own lot turned insult in the mouth of the offended—beyond this it is impossible to go; and we cannot even doubt that this is precisely what Roxy would have said!

Perhaps the supreme achievement of this book is to have rendered such indignities not in terms of melodrama or as a parochial "social problem" but as a local instance of some universal guilt and doom. The false Tom, who is the fruit of all the betrayal and terror and profaned love which lies between white man and black, embodies also its "dark necessity"—and must lie, steal, kill and boast until in his hubris he reveals himself as the slave we all secretly are. This tragic inevitability is, however, blurred by the demands of the detective story with which it is crossed. The tragedy of Tom requires that he expose and destroy himself; the melodrama of Pudd'nhead Wilson requires that he reveal and bring to justice the negro who had passed as white; and Twain decided finally that it was Pudd'nhead's book—a success story. Yet there remains beneath the assertion that a man is master of his fate, the melancholy conviction that to be born is to be doomed, a kind of secularized Calvinism.

We have already noticed that Pudd'nhead is Tom Sawyer grown up to be the man who has not surrendered with maturity the dream of being a hero; but it must be added that he wants to be a hero on his own terms, to force himself upon a hostile community without knuckling under to its values; that is to say, he would like still to be as an adult the "good bad boy" who put the finger on Indian Joe. Translated out of the vocabulary of boyhood, this means that he has to become first a rebel and then a detective.

He begins as a pariah, the sage whose wisdom is taken for folly: an outsider in a closed society, a free thinker in a world of conformism, a gadgeteer and crank, playing with palmistry and fingerprints. But he is also, like his creator, a jokester; and, indeed, it is his first quip which earns him a reputation for stupidity and twenty years of exclusion. "I wish I owned half of that dog," he says of a viciously howling beast, "because I would kill my half"—and that is almost the end of him. Yet like his creator he wants to succeed in the world he despises; and he yields to it half-unwittingly even before it accepts him, adjusting to its code of honor, its definition of a Negro—while writing down in private or reading before a two-man Free Thinker's Society his dangerous thoughts.

Typically enough, it is as a detective that he makes a comeback. In three earlier books his prototype, Tom Sawyer, had achieved similar triumphs: exposing Injun Joe, revealing Jim's true status, clearing his half-crazed uncle of the charge of murder; but more is involved than this. Ever since Poe's Dupin, the sleuth has been a favorite guise of the writer in fiction—non-conformist and exposer of evil, the poor man's intellectual. He is the one who, revealing in the moment of crisis "who done it," restores the community (as W. H. Auden has suggested in an acute study of the detective story) to a state of grace.

But Twain has the faith neither of a Chesterton nor a Conan Doyle; and the revelations of David Wilson (the name "Pudd'nhead" is sloughed off with his victory) restore civil peace only between him and the community which rejected him: for the rest, they expose only bankruptcy and horror and shame, and stupidity of our definition of a Negro, and the hopelessness of our relations with him. Wilson's disclosure of Roxy's hoax coalesces with Twain's exposure to America of its own secret self; and the double discovery is aptly framed by Wilson's calendar entries for two of our favorite holidays.

The chapter which contains the courtroom revelation is preceded by the text, "*April 1.* This is the day upon which we are reminded of what we are on the other three hundred and sixty-four." The implication is clear, whether conscious or not, not fools only but slaves! And it is followed by another, even grimmer, "*October 12, the Discovery*. It was wonderful to find America, but it would have been more wonderful to miss it." The Discovery! It is a disconcerting ending for a detective story, which should have faith in all disclosures; but it is the aptest of endings for an American book, the only last word possible to a member of the Free Thinker's Society. Beyond such bleak wisdom, there is only the cry of Roxy at the moment of revelation, "De Lord have mercy on me, po' miserable sinner dat I is!" But this is forbidden to Mark Twain.

1601

It has always seemed to me regrettable that many readers of Mark Twain, including some of his most ardent admirers, are unaware of the existence of his hard-core pornographic skit originally entitled *Conversation, As It Was by the Social Fireside, in the Time of the Tudors*, but later called simply *1601*. Twain himself never kept it a secret—except from his wife and daughters—nor did he ever forget it. Though he wrote it in 1876, at a moment when he had bogged down in his eight-year-long, off-again-on-again writing of *Huckleberry Finn*, he was still reminiscing about its origins until shortly before his death. In his autobiography he explains how, preparing to write *The Prince and the Pauper*, he had been "reading ancient English books with the purpose of saturating myself with archaic English . . . and . . . had been impressed with the frank indelicacies of speech permissible among ladies and gentlemen of that ancient time."

Simultaneously envious of and appalled by the titillating freedom lost in what he considered his own morally superior but less colorful age, he determined "to contrive one of those stirring conversations out of my own head." He chose finally not to report it directly, but as recorded by "a dried up old nobleman," who bitterly remarks on the speech and manners of Queen Elizabeth and her courtiers. The pleasure he found in reproducing their gross conversation, Twain goes on to say, was "as nothing to that which was afforded me by the outraged old cupbearer's comments."

In conclusion, however, Twain confesses that he has not recently reread *1601*; and that he intends, therefore, "to examine that masterpiece and see whether it is really a masterpiece or not." Apparently, he never got around to doing so, but Albert Paine, his official biographer, did, and declared, "*1601* is a genuine classic, as classics of that sort go . . . and perhaps, in some day to come, the taste that justified *Gargantua* and *The Decameron* will give the literary refugee shelter and setting among the conventional writings of Mark Twain."

Alas, this has not come to pass. Despite the much touted "sexual revolutions" of the present century and the disappearance of old verbal taboos, *1601* has continued to lead an underground, semi-respectable life, appearing until now only in sometimes bootlegged and always limited editions. Originally, indeed, it was intended for an audience limited to one, having been sent as a letter to Joseph Twichell, Twain's pastor and lifelong friend. Remote from everyone else, they would read passages from it aloud to each other on their customary weekend walks in the woods, rolling on the fallen leaves and laughing until they were "lame and sore."

Such secret sharing of pornography behind the backs of their womenfolk constituted in Victorian times a ritual of male bonding, like cussing, drinking, smoking cigars and shooting pool. In this case, evidently, it seemed to Twichell too satisfactory a one to be confined to a single pair. Consequently, he sent a copy to a mutual friend, Dean Sage, who in turn dropped it, as if inadvertently, onto the floor of the smoking compartment of a train, then still a male preserve. There it was picked up, passed from hand to hand and so extravagantly praised that Sage felt impelled to make it available to a larger audience. He therefore had "a dozen copies" printed on a press in Brooklyn, and "sent one to David Gray in Buffalo, one to a friend in Japan, one to Lord Houghton in England and one to a Jewish Rabbi in Albany, a learned man . . . and lover of old time literature."

So, at any rate, Twain reported later. But he is notoriously unreliable, as he himself admits elsewhere in the autobiography, warning his readers, "I don't believe the details are right but I don't care a rap. They will do just as well as the facts." In fact, *1601* was not first printed in Brooklyn, but in Cleveland, under the auspices of the Vampire Club, at the behest not of Dean Sage but of John Hay—an older and closer friend of Twain's who later became ambassador to Great Britain and the secretary of state under President McKinley and Theodore Roosevelt. Though his own manuscript copy has been worn to rags by much reading and rereading, when another friend called Alexander Gunn proposed setting it up in type and running off a few proofs, Hay at first demurred, protesting, "I cannot properly consent . . . as I am afraid that the great man would think I was taking unfair advantage." He then added, thus betraying how hypocritical his demurral was, ". . . if in spite of my prohibition, you take those proofs, send me one."

How Hay got hold of a manuscript copy to begin with remains unclear. The best guess is that it was passed on to him by William Dean Howells, to whom Twain had sent it earlier, along with a mocking letter purporting to submit his disreputable little essay for publication in the eminently respectable *Atlantic Monthly*, of which Howells was then the editor. "If you do not need this for the contributor's column," Twain wrote, "will you please return it to me, as they want it for the Christian Union." Since Howells left behind no record of his reaction, we can only surmise what it was from the general comments on Twain's bawdry which he allowed to be printed after his friend's death.

"He had," Howells wrote at that point, "the Southwestern, the Lincolnian, the Elizabethan breadth of parlance . . . which I suppose one ought not to call coarse without calling oneself prudish; and I was often hiding away in discreet holes and corners the letters in which he had loosed his bold fancy to stoop on suggestion." In the case of *1601*, however, instead of hiding it away, Howells sent it on to Hay, thus setting in motion the chain of events which led to its first modest publication, after which Twain was almost overwhelmed by a flood of letters: fulsome praise from those lucky enough to have been recipients of the few printed copies, and urgent requests to see one from those who had not.

What seems to have moved him most deeply was a communication from David Gray, who had been his sole companion and comforter in those terrible fourteen months in Buffalo, following his marriage, when he was plagued by the deaths and illnesses of family and friends. Certainly, Twain never forgot Gray's encouraging missive, actually quoting it word for word twenty-five years later in his autobiography. "Put your name on it," he tells us Gray wrote him. "Don't be ashamed of it. It is a great and fine piece of literature and deserves to live, and will live. Your *Innocents Abroad* will presently be forgotten, but this will survive. Don't be ashamed; don't be afraid. Leave the command in your will that your heirs shall put on your tombstone these words, and these alone: 'He wrote the immortal *1601*.'" To be sure, though this is in some deeper sense finally serious, it is ironic as well; and the irony is further compounded by the fact that before his tragic death in a train accident, Gray had changed so utterly in his basic beliefs that he would have recanted his words of praise.

Though Gray, a poet and the editor of the *Buffalo Daily Courier*, the rival of Twain's *Buffalo Express*, had also been born into "a Presbyterianism of the bluest, the most uncompromising and unlovely shade," Twain recounts in another part of the autobiography, "When I was comrading with him, the Presbyterianism had all gone and he had become a frank rationalist and pronounced unbeliever"; but by the time of their final encounter, "his unbelief had all passed away." Nonetheless, Twain is still able to say of him that "he was great and fine, blemishless in character, a creature to adore." It seems to me that in any event it was Gray's hyperbolic praise that started Twain thinking about producing a larger, authorized edition of *1601*.

What finally made it possible, however, was his chance encounter with Lieutenant Charles Erskine Scott Wood, who was adjutant to the commanding general in 1881; Twain—accompanied by Joe Twichell—made a visit to West Point. There he discovered not only that Wood, like him, was a freethinker, but that he had at his disposal a well-equipped printing plant. Shortly after returning home, Wood later reported, Twain wrote him a letter asking if he would be willing "to print a small thing he has written." This turned out to be, of course, *1601*, after reading which, Wood enthusiastically assented. He was intrigued, first of all, on political grounds, because the pious censors he hated would have found it "obscene"; but on aesthetic ones, too. That is to say, being well versed in the plastic arts as well as the verbal ones, he was able to see ways in which the pseudo-archaics of Twain's mock Elizabethan language could be reinforced typographically.

"I wrote Mark," he recalled, "that for literary effect there should be a species of forgery, though of course there was no effort to actually deceive a scholar." To this Twain responded "that I might do as I liked;—that his only object was to secure a number of copies, as the demand for it was becoming burdensome." Finally, after editing the spelling and diction of Twain's text a little, Wood printed, on deckle-edge vellum dampened with mild coffee to suggest age, and using Old English–style type, fifty copies of what Twain referred to later as "the sumptuous West Point edition."

In light of the fact that Wood was what Shakespeare would have called "the onlie begetter" of *1601*, it was odd that these days he seems to have been forgotten by almost everyone, including many Twain scholars. His name is not listed, for instance, in the indexes even of books which deal at some length with that "obscene" work, like Charles Neider's edition of the autobiography or Walter Blair's *Mark Twain and Huck Finn*. Yet in his own time, Wood was widely known to both academics and the general public; since after leaving the army he had achieved considerable success as an artist, a poet, an essayist, a lawyer, a politician—and especially as a gadfly to self-righteous defenders of the status quo and a champion of persecuted rebels, like Margaret Sanger, Emma Goldman and the anarcho-syndicalists of the IWW.

Mark Twain himself seems to have forgotten Wood in later years, making no mention of his name in his notebooks or his autobiography. Wood, on the other hand, never forgot Twain, though he outlived him by thirty-five years, dying at the age of ninety-two. He makes Twain, in fact, a major character in his *Heavenly Discourse*, which was not published until 1927. An attack on hypocritical piety and false patriotism, this book takes the form of conversations carried on in a kind of post-Christian, multicultural Heaven, the participants including not just Twain but Buddha, Lao Tzu, Rabelais, Voltaire, Satan, Jesus Christ and God Himself. Twain is starred, as seems appropriate considering the occasion for their brief relationship, in a couple of dialogues on obscenity— in one of which he is portrayed as saying, "Nature from manure brings flowers and fruits. It might be that by the same wonderful alchemy she should make from obscenity something vital and fine."

What explains Wood's consequent obscurity is surely, at least in part, the equivocal status of that nearly anonymous "obscene" book over whose production he presided. Unlike most of Twain's other later books, *1601* does not include in its front matter a portrait of the author, nor does his name appear on the title page. Also uncharacteristically, it was never sold—being, indeed, the only one of his works from which Twain never made a cent. But this is fair enough, since—as Twain wrote in 1906 to an inquisitive librarian—he never considered it a true sibling to his more legitimate books, describing it as a "Wandering Offspring" which "I hasten to assure you is *not* printed in my published writing." Taking a cue from Twain, subsequent editors have excluded it from his collective works (the present volume and the Library of America's *Collected Tales, Sketches, Speeches, and Essays* excepted).

It seems to me, however, that *1601* can only be properly understood in the context of Twain's total oeuvre. Placing it in that setting makes clear how much this presumably unique book has in common with what critics considered his more characteristic ones. First of all, it deals with life in a foreign land, like so many other books by this most American of all American writers, beginning with his first, *The Innocents Abroad*, and continuing on until his unfinished last one, *The Mysterious Stranger*. But it takes us on a vicarious journey through time as well as space; and in this it resembles not just that full-fledged time-travel fantasy, *A Connecticut Yankee in King Arthur's Court*, but also the Tom Sawyer–Huck Finn series, with its almost magical resurrection of the endless summers in an antebellum mid-America, otherwise presumably lost forever.

Finally, too, in this wider context it is possible to see *1601* as one of Twain's many linguistic experiments—to which he was driven, I think, though he may not have been fully conscious of it himself, by a need to escape the restrictions of what Victorians considered a proper literary dialect. Sometimes he sought, as in *A Connecticut Yankee in King Arthur's Court* and *The Prince and the Pauper*, to do this by counterfeiting archaic speech; sometimes, as in *Huckleberry Finn*, by attempting to reproduce in writing oral colloquial dialects. In *1601*, he combines both strategies, interlarding the high diction of the Elizabethan court with the gross four-letter words which were then used solely in barrooms, back alleys—and, of course, pornography.

Even considered as pornography, however, *1601* does not stand alone among Twain's works. In addition to jotting down the punch lines of dirty jokes in his notebooks, he wrote for the eyes of men only raunchy poems like "The Mammoth Cod," and to a similar audience he made speeches like the notorious defense of masturbation delivered at the Stomach Club in Paris. Moreover, even in worlds intended for family reading, he flirted with taboos. So, for instance, in *Tom Sawyer* he discreetly describes Becky peeking at nude pictures in her teacher's anatomy book; and in *Huckleberry Finn* he circumspectly hints at the phallic nature of the play put on by the Duke and the King for the yokels of a one-horse town in Arkansas.

Yet even at its hardest, Twain's pornography differs from the run-of-the-mill erotic literature whose popularity was peaking at the moment he wrote

1601. In *The Other Victorians*, Steven Marcus argues that this popular genre was typically distinguished by three things. First, it is only "minimally verbal," which is to say, it tends to make its readers oblivious to rather than conscious of the language in which it is written. Second, it avoids defining specifically the time and place of its action. Third, its characters are invariably young, since its essential fable is a projection of the male fantasy of potency, in which the penis is imagined to be "a magical instrument of infinite powers."

But *1601*, as we have already observed, is conspicuously verbal. Moreover, its time and place are specified in the very title; and many of its characters are old, most notably the aged narrator and the Queen herself, who is at the date of the action sixty-eight. Finally, when it ceases to be basically scatological, as it is from the start, and becomes fully erotic, the male fantasy it projects is not the dream of infinite potency but the complementary nightmare of genital inadequacy, as it is made clear by the mournful last line, ". . . which doing, lo hys member felle, & wolde not rise again."

In the end, *1601* is not only truly American but, like much of Twain's other writing, autobiographical. Of this Sir Walter Raleigh has earlier made us aware, telling of "a people in ye most uttermost parts of America that copulate not until they be five-&-thirty yeeres of age . . . & doe it then but once in seven yeeres"; thus leaving us to remember, as we close the book, that it was approximately at this age that Mark Twain married—for all his foul mouth, probably still a virgin.

Is Shakespeare Dead?

Despite its misleading title, *Is Shakespeare Dead?* deals not with the problem of the poet's mortality but with that of his identity. It attempts, that is to say, to answer the question of who really wrote the works attributed to the actor from Stratford, and therefore should more properly have been called *Is "Shakespeare" Shakespeare?* But death was much on Twain's mind when he wrote this little book in 1909. He was still mourning his favorite daughter, Susy, who had been dead for more than a dozen years, and his beloved wife, Livy, who had been dead for five.

Moreover, the death of another daughter, Jean, lay just ahead, as did his own. The latter, at least, he must have foreseen, since his health was failing rapidly; and Halley's comet, which had flashed across the sky when he was born—and to which he felt bound like a Siamese twin—was due to appear again the following year. It is scarcely strange, then, that the word "dead" intruded into the title of what was to be one of the last of his books published during his lifetime. What is strange, however, is that the test which follows is not melancholy but basically blithe and even at its most irascible moments punctuated with jokes. Indeed, it finally seems as if the mortuary title itself might be just another joke.

After all, we remember, in Twain's first book, *The Innocents Abroad*, he recounts how he and some irrelevant fellow travelers would annoy their guides by asking a question "which never failed to disgust [them]." "We use it always when we can think of nothing else to say," he explains. "After they have exhausted their enthusiasms pointing out to us . . . the beauties of some bronze image . . . we look at it stupidly and in silence for . . . as long as we can hold out . . . and then ask, 'Is he dead?'" It seems reasonable that by playing the same game with the Shakespeare idolators more than four decades later, Twain was able to imagine himself once more a "bad boy," challenging the cultural clichés of his elders.

But he was, of course, in reality a lonely old man, haunted by bad dreams and incapable of finishing any of the fictions in which he thought by embodying them to exorcise them. Only fragments survive of these nightmarish fantasies in which the terrified protagonist is shrunk and trapped in a drop of water, frozen into the eternal ice of the Arctic, overwhelmed by impenetrable darkness or blinded by intolerable light. The most nearly successful of such abortive ventures is the posthumously published pseudo-text called *The Mysterious Stranger*. Cobbled together and shamelessly emended (without acknowledgement) by Fredrick Duneka and Albert Paine, this account of an ambiguously satanic figure who ends by revealing to the young man he has bedeviled that all he has taken as reality is "a grotesque and foolish dream" has come to be accepted not just as one of Twain's major works but as his final word to the world.

Yet though Twain was apparently working to the very end of his life on one or another of its three or four incoherent versions, it is not in fact his valedictory statement. Disconcertingly, that was *Is Shakespeare Dead?*—one of his least well received and most misunderstood works. Part of the problem, surely, is that this little book seems at first glance to belong to a genre which Twain did not customarily write, and not very successfully when he did: literary criticism.

His recorded comments on what he called "belles lettres" are few and far between. His preferred reading was popular history, philosophy and theology; and when he did try to read poetry and fiction it was at the urging of his friend and mentor William Dean Howells, who never ceased trying to induct him into the mysteries of high culture. Typically, however, Twain's responses were negative, brief and in any case intended for Howells's eyes only. Snidely and in few words, for instance, he dismissed both Edgar Allan Poe and Jane Austen, declaring, "To me his prose is unreadable—[like hers]. No, there is a difference. I could read his prose on salary, but not Jane's. Jane is entirely impossible. It seems a pity they allowed her to die a natural death." With almost equal brutality and brevity, he disposed of three other canonical authors, confessing, "I can't stand George Eliot & Hawthorne & those people; I see what they are at, a hundred years before they get to it, & they just tire me to death. And as for the Bostonians, I would rather be damned to John Bunyan's heaven than read that."

Only three times before his essay on Shakespeare appeared did Twain write about literature at greater length. Two of these essays, "Fenimore Cooper's Literary Offenses" and "In Defense of Harriet Shelley," were published in the 1890s; the third, "William Dean Howells," not until 1906. The last of these differs from the other two as well as from Twain's brief epistolary comments, being overwhelmingly positive in tone. But this is scarcely surprising, since it is less objective criticism than a token of gratitude to one who even before they became friends had favorably reviewed Twain's work. In any event, Twain seems to have felt the piece inappropriate to the persona called by his nom de plume, whose function it was to mock everything admired by the respectable and conventional—including high literature. He therefore, uncharacteristically, published it under the name S. L. Clemens.

But "Mark Twain" was the name under which he issued what is surely the best known and most often reprinted of his critical essays, "Fenimore Cooper's Literary Offenses" (1895). As a matter of fact, school dropout and autodidact that he was, he signed it "Mark Twain, M.A., Professor of Belles Lettres in the Veterinary College of Arizona." For a while, moreover, he tried to maintain a proper academic tone; but what begins as a patient *explication de texte* detailing Cooper's lapses in taste and style quickly degenerates into slander and calumny. "Cooper hadn't any more invention than a horse," he writes at one point, "and I don't mean a high-class horse, either; I mean a clothes-horse."

What prompts the most extravagant of these outbursts is not Cooper's literary ineptitude but the failure of certain self-styled experts to notice it. To make this clear, Twain prefixes to his essay what he considers particularly wrong-headed laudatory comments on Cooper by Professor Lounsbury of Yale, Professor Brander Matthews of Columbia and the British novelist Wilkie Collins; and then he observes scornfully, "It seems to me that it was far from right . . . to deliver opinions on Cooper's literature without having read some of it." In any case, what Twain is writing here is not criticism of literature but criticism of criticism—criticism twice removed; and so, too, is his earlier literary polemic against Shelley, published in 1894.

"In Defense of Harriet Shelley," as its title indicates, is primarily a chivalrous attempt to redeem the reputation of that ill-fated lady from what Twain felt to be the unfair representation of her in Professor Edward Dowden's *Life of Shelley*. He was, of course, irked by the good professor's bland assertion that despite having abandoned Harriet and run off with young Mary Godwin, Percy could not be held responsible for Harriet's suicide. But what seems especially to have enraged him was what he had apparently learned when his daughter Susy enrolled in Bryn Mawr, that Dowden's book was "accepted in the girls' colleges of America and its view taught in their literary classes."

To rebut Dowden, Twain not only attempts to reconstruct the true history of the relationship which Dowden falsified; he also tries to demonstrate the falsity of the rhetoric with which Dowden did so. Ironically enough, as he makes his case, his own rhetoric grows ever more hyperbolic and shrill. "The Shelley biography," he writes, "is a literary cake-walk . . . all the pages . . . walk by . . . mincingly in their Sunday best . . . It is rare to find a sentence that has forgotten to dress." This metaphor, he informs us, is drawn from the folk culture of "our Negroes in America." But once into the sort of adversarial criticism of criticism he relished, he draws on white high culture as well, telling us that Dowden's biography is "a Frankenstein with the original infirmity supplemented by a new one; a Frankenstein with the reasoning faculty wanting." This, too, is ironic enough, since the metaphor is drawn from the famous book by the second Mrs. Shelley; but the irony is twice compounded by the fact that Twain does not properly remember her book, confusing her nameless monster with its maker.

What had become evident by 1895, in any case, was that typically Twain was moved to write about literature only when his temper was aroused by critical opinions contrary to his own—especially if those opinions were propagated by academics. Thus, it seems inevitable that sooner or later he would get mad enough to take sides in the ongoing controversy about the authorship of the poems and plays traditionally attributed to "William Shakespeare." Moreover, there seemed little doubt about which side he would support, since the scholars and critics who have determined the canon of Shakespeare's works, as well as edited and commented on them, have by and large ended up believing that their true author is the actor from Stratford.

Yet there has always been a minority of nonbelievers; and there are indeed few of us who are not a little disturbed by the fact that justly or unjustly, among the acknowledged greater writers of the world, Shakespeare is the only one whose identity has been thus challenged over and over. The person who seems to me to have come closest to explaining why is Wyndham Lewis, who in *The Lion and the Fox* wrote, "That there is something equivocal and of a very special nature in the figure of this poet has been felt constantly; and people have always tapped his pedestal, inquisitive and uneasy, peered up into his face, scenting hoax. The authenticity of that face has even been doubted; it has been called 'an obvious mask,' the 'face of a tailor's dummy.'"

When it comes to saying who was the real author, however, there has been widespread disagreement among the anti-Shakespeareans. Francis Bacon has been suggested, and Anthony Bacon; the Earl of Oxford and a host of other earls; Sir Walter Raleigh, Christopher Marlowe, Queen Elizabeth and even a nun called Anne Whatley. Francis Bacon, of course, is the all-time favorite—

as he was Mark Twain's; though Twain could not quite bring himself to endorse him when he finally got around to addressing the Bacon-Shakespeare controversy in 1909. To be sure, he claims in *Is Shakespeare Dead?* that he had "a fifty years interest in the matter—born of Delia Bacon's book—away back on that ancient day—1857, or maybe 1856." But there is no evidence of this in anything he published earlier.

He had, it is true, kept working throughout his career on a burlesque version of *Hamlet,* in which a kibitzer from the nineteenth century breaks into the action of the play. But though this makes it clear that Twain always wanted in some sense to make Shakespeare his own, nowhere does the manuscript betray the slightest doubt about that playwright's identity. Nor does *1601,* which includes both Shakespeare and Bacon in its cast of characters. In fact, in it Bacon is described not as a poet, actual or potential, but as "a tedious sink of learning" [who will] "ponderously philosophize" though "ye subject bee but a fart." On the other hand, "ye famous Shaxpur" is portrayed as reciting verses from *King Henry IV* and *Venus and Adonis,* whose authorship no one challenges, instead bestowing on him "prodigious admiration."

Nonetheless, by 1909 Twain had somehow persuaded himself that his skepticism about Shakespeare dated back half a century and had only been "asleep for the last three years." But he had, as is well known, an immense capacity for self-deceit, so that in this case, as in so many others, the real truth is hard to determine. Probably he really had, as he claims, supported the anti-Stratfordian position back in 1858, in a continuing half-earnest debate with George Ealer, the master pilot to whom he was then apprenticed, and a passionate pro-Stratfordian. But later, with no living opponent to combat, he seems to have lost all interest.

What revived it, apparently, was the chance arrival on his desk of the galleys of a book on Bacon by William S. Booth, which then led him to read George Greenwood's *The Shakespeare Problem Restated,* whose anti-Stratfordian arguments he echoes in *Is Shakespeare Dead?*—even quoting a large section of it verbatim. His enthusiasm he shared with his daughter Jean, telling her, "I am having a good time dictating to a stenographer a day-after-day scoff at everybody who is ignorant enough and stupid enough to go on believing that Shakespeare ever wrote a poem or play in his life." Clearly what pleased him was the opportunity to calumniate once more the kind of scholarly experts he had always despised, this time the historians and biographers whom he calls "these Stratfordolators, these Shakesperiods, these thugs, these bangalores, these troglodytes, these herumfordites, these blatherskites, these buccaneers, these bandoleers . . ." (133–34).

No one else, however, was convinced. Albert Paine, who usually praised uncritically whatever he wrote, was so dubious that Twain felt obliged to reassure him, falsely claiming, "I have private knowledge from a source that cannot be questioned. It is the great discovery of the age." But the finished book contained nothing except a rehash of old arguments about the Stratford Shakespeare's lack of schooling and legal expertise—interlarded with outbursts of vitriolic abuse. Even Isabel Lyon, who after Livy's death was Twain's closest female companion, felt forced to confess that it was "not gentle and not very clever"; agreeing therefore with other of his concerned friends that he was "slipping intellectually," and that it would be wise "*not* to have his ideas made public."

In fact, his publishers finally issued the book only because they were contractually obligated to do so; and as they had foreseen, it received perfunctory notice in the press. One reviewer, trying to beat Twain at his own game, jocularly argued that since, like Shakespeare, he was an autodidact and school dropout, the literary works attributed to him must have been written by somebody else—probably Elbert Hubbard. Even those most deeply involved in the Shakespeare-Bacon controversy did not pay his book much heed. The only response of Greenwood himself, for instance, was a threat to sue Twain for inadequately acknowledging his borrowings. Naturally, with members of the critical establishment, to whom the "Baconian heresy" seemed as absurdly illusory as a belief in UFOs or Bigfoot, *Is Shakespeare Dead?* fared even less well. Typical is its dismissal in a recent Twain handbook intended for classroom use, which describes it as "an exaggerated pitch of a travelling salesman . . . repetitive, sporadic, and totally without direction . . . full of overblown, bombastic pseudo-eloquence."

It is a judgment with which it is hard to disagree if *Is Shakespeare Dead?* is read solely as an inept attempt at literary criticism. But after all, as its subtitle indicates, it is a piece "from my autobiography"; and only by keeping this in mind is it possible to perceive the sense in which it is finally coherent. We must, however, be aware of Twain's unorthodox notion that the right way to do an autobiography was "to wander at your free will all over your life; talk only about the thing which interests you at the moment; drop it the moment its interest threatens to pale." But this means that what pattern it has is unconscious, like that of a reverie or a dream.

Certainly, this is true of *Is Shakespeare Dead?*, which, despite its presumed subject, begins with an apparently irrelevant discourse on "claimants": pretenders of various kinds, including not just Mary Baker Eddy and Louis XVII but (rather astonishingly) the Golden Calf and Satan. To be sure, Shakespeare is mentioned as a "claimant," too, but only in passing; and before Twain manages to treat him at length, he has wandered off into reminiscences about his days as a riverboat pilot and the death on the river of his brother Henry. This in turn somehow segues into a not quite credible anecdote about his days in Sunday school and an explanation of his lifelong interest in Satan.

What is not clear, until he approaches the end of the book, is why Twain started it with the incantatory repetition of the word "claimants." At that point, he reminds us of the pilot's cry "m-a-rk-*twain*," which indicates safe water but is also his nom de plume; and we realize that "claimants," too, is a pun, this time on his given name, "Clemens." Finally, in what he calls a "post-script," he reproduces a clipping from a current edition of his hometown newspaper which identifies him as "Mark Twain or S. L. Clemens as a few of the unlettered call him": thus not merely joining together both of his names, but ironically reversing their claim to authenticity.

Between his two encrypted signatures, Twain not only piles up proof for his anti-Stratfordian brief; but—like a proper autobiographer—tells us much about his own early life. Indeed, if all other records were to disappear, we would know from *Is Shakespeare Dead?* not just when and where Twain was born, when his father died and he left school, but also what trades he practiced before he became a full-time writer and where they took him. Of his later life, however, he tells us little (not even mentioning his wife or daughters, for instance), only that he ended up by being everywhere in the world, but especially in his hometown, honored and loved—his name a byword.

This, he insists, is quite different from the ultimate fate of the pretender from Stratford, remembered and mourned by none of his fellow citizens—his very name forgotten. But why, I am moved to ask, does Twain not merely insist on that difference but feel a need to cite objective evidence to prove it. Could it be that somewhere below the level of full consciousness he had doubts about the identity not just of England's greatest writer but of one he needed desperately to believe was America's greatest, namely, himself—whoever he really was, Mark Twain? or S. L. Clemens? or both? or neither?

Certainly, throughout his writing life he had been obsessed by that question: making the confusion of identities the thematic center of *The Prince and the Pauper* and *Pudd'nhead Wilson,* and ending *Huckleberry Finn* with Huck taken for Tom and Tom not sure who he is supposed to be. His own personal identity crisis, which he projected in those fictional ones, is more clearly revealed in the famous "Whittier Birthday Speech," whose true significance has tended to be lost in subsequent analysis of the question of whether or not that speech scandalized the Boston Brahmins before whom Twain delivered it one ill-fated night in December of 1877.

The somewhat raunchy tale which Twain told in that inappropriate setting deals with a miner whose hospitality has been abused by three drunken louts impersonating three of those Brahmins, Emerson, Longfellow, and Oliver Wendell Holmes. But as Twain observed some years later, he could as easily have had them call themselves Beaumont, Ben Jonson and Shakespeare, since the real point of the story is the plight of the first-person narrator, who arrives at the miner's cabin just after the three hooligans have departed.

After hearing the miner's story, that narrator, who has begun his own story by informing us, "I resolved to try the virtue of my *nom de plume,*" explains that those other "littery" men were only imposters; to which the miner replies, "Ah—imposters, were they?—are *you?*" Small wonder, then, that some thirty years later Twain dreamed that he appeared at a "social gathering" dressed only in his nightshirt, and when he declared, "I am Mark Twain," no one believed him. Surely, it must have been just such a dream that he was dreaming in the three years' sleep from which he woke to write *Is Shakespeare Dead?*

The State of Writing

It becomes easier and easier to *say* these days (we have known it for a long time) that the writer in the forties is essentially concerned with establishing alternatives to naturalism. This involves the re-instatement in his vocabulary of such words as "freedom," "responsibility" and "guilt," words which a little while ago he regarded as obscenities, and which even yet he cannot manage without uneasiness. All the better—that uneasiness redeems him from the possibilities of sentimentality, from the sterile certainty of the New Humanists, whose impertinent attacks on naturalism delayed for years the legitimate revolt of creative writers. It was necessary that we be able honestly to say of Babbitt and More, "Who the hell are *they?*" before a re-assertion of the autonomy of the individual could seem anything but a slogan of the White Terror. It is a help, too, that our leading naturalists have become middle-aged, ripe for ritual slaughter.

But best of all is that fact that our revolt began, as it were, against our wills, with technical annoyance, with offended sensibilities—rather than with a program. It was, for instance, the relentless blur of Farrell's style, the failure of his ponderous honesty; Steinbeck's shameless extortion of sentiment; the shapelessness of the Proletarian Novel, that moved us, protesting, toward the central recognition that failures of style and feeling were signs of the inadequacy of a tyrannical subject-matter, a systematic reduction of meaning, a "scientific" equation of the individual with the sum of his environmental causes. It was good for us *as artists* that our discovery of the need to re-establish focuses of moral responsibility, to be done with the featureless passive sufferer as hero was a function of our desire to write a good sentence and our resolve not to exploit indeterminate feeling. There is for the non-writer, I suppose, something trivial, even offensive in such a point of view, but the writer is convinced of the ultimate humanity, the essential morality, the *necessity* of the practice of his art, and he is tempted to trust his metaphors, his meters more than himself. There is, after all, on his shelf that monument to an opposite approach, *memento mori* and souvenir of his beginnings in one, *Proletarian Literature in the United States.*

Our generation is haunted by the memory of the profane mystique which created that drab memorial; when we were kids becoming a writer seemed, if not synonymous with, at least an aspect of, becoming a Communist; abandoning oneself to the proletariat and finding oneself as an artist seemed a single act—and there was a covert moral satisfaction (we did not have those words then, of course) in what was at once a self-sacrifice and a self-assertion. Our awakening was gradual, though a little faster than our political disenchantment, toward a realization of the enormous *contempt* for art just below the culture-vulturish surface of the John Reed Clubs. In such a critic as Edmund Wilson, the old heresy still persists, that art is a solace of exploitation-ridden societies, a second-best expedient that will disappear with Socialism; and scarcely one of us with such roots is entirely free of the suspicion that in coming to terms with our craft before righting the world, we are guilty. That concept, battered and despised, nags at us a little, whispers from underground "traitor!" because we do not spend ourselves utterly or, at least, first of all in political action; its prick is one of the many despairs of varying magnitudes we call these days "anguish."

"Anguish"—I have avoided the word so far precisely because it covers everything from a cosmic passion to the meanest wringing of the hands. The proper anguish of our generation of writers as writers is compounded chiefly of that social guilt and the uneasiness I spoke of above at having to re-invent the whole vocabulary of ethical responsibility, that stubbornly insists, despite ingenuity and patience, in resembling what our fathers spoke in churches we have foresworn: apostasy and return, it is a contradictory self-reproach that will not somehow cancel out.

The writer has preferred always a foster-father to a father (think of Stephen Dedalus and Bloom); fleshly ancestors embarrass him, but ghostly ancestors he must have even in the periods of extremest experiment, and this is, as everyone knows, not such a period. The experimentalism of the twenties as it has survived in a thin academy of revolt seems a tyranny of the Interesting as perilous as the tyranny of Subject Matter in the thirties. We have legitimized the word "tradition," and though our tradition is open to the point of eccentricity, we have moved from the mere evocation of ancestors toward a pious imitation even of forms. Baudelaire, Rimbaud, Donne, Hopkins, Rilke, Lorca, Proust, Joyce, Eliot, Kafka, James, Dostoevsky—there is scarcely a Culture Hero in the list that first comes to mind whose vogue does not go back to the thirties, some even deep into the twenties and beyond. Only Kafka belongs particularly to us, and behind him the witty anguish of Kierkegaard, but Kafka in especial, polysemous, obsessive, fragmentary—a Jew.

His Jewishness is by no means incidental; the real Jew and the imaginary Jew between them give to the current period its special flavor. In *Ulysses,* our prophetic book of the urbanization of art, the Artist and the Jew reach for each other tentatively and fall apart; but in the Surveyor K. a unity is achieved, a mystic prototype proposed: Jewishness as a condition of the Artist. In America in particular, where the impulse of the Frontier has become the doubtful strength of cities, a generation of writers and critics whose thirtieth year falls somewhere in the forties has appeared: Delmore Schwartz, Alfred Kazin, Karl Shapiro, Isaac Rosenfeld, Paul Goodman, Saul Bellow, H. J. Kaplan, typically urban, second-generation Jews, chiefly ex-Stalinist, ambivalently intellectual, but for all their anguish insolently at home with ideas and words. Before the advantage of their long maturity, forced early in the Movement, the writer drawn to New York from the provinces feels, in the terms Jean Stafford has so aptly exploited, the Rube, attempts to conform; and the almost parody of Jewishness achieved by the gentile writer in New York is a strange and crucial testimony of our time.

It is not surprising that Kafka pre-eminently conditions the revolt against naturalism in a generation with such a core; the obsessive, the parabolic, the irreducible become defining aims of our art. There are other elements to be sure: from Dostoevsky the underground man, the baptism in evil; from Joyce, Eliot or Mann, the exploitation of the Myth; from various Christian sources the concepts of Fall and Original Sin (though in the United States not a full-fledged Christian metaphysical school like that Charles Williams and C. S. Lewis in England have developed out of George MacDonald); from James a morality of style, from Hawthorne and Melville a symbolic audacity and complexity.

It is an unselfconsciously international complex; and indeed the Jew as writer helps mediate a traditional dilemma of the artist in America, the conflicting claims of an allegiance to Europe and to the American scene. But having left behind him the immigrant's drive drastically to deny an abandoned past, the second-generation Jewish writer has learned to be aware of a tradition immediately his that is European and American at once; he is *himself* the guarantee of the singleness of Europe and America, and he escapes completely the polar tugs of a defensive chauvinism and an embarrassed self-abnegation before Continental culture.

In a second act of mediation, too, the Jewish writer plays a role, in the mediation between writer and intellectual. The typical American author in most periods has been almost aggressively anti-intellectual. One thinks of Twain or even of Melville, and in the generation just before ours of Hemingway and Wolfe and Faulkner, and, set against them, the melancholy academicians Spingarn and Babbitt and More. The immense impoverishment caused by that schism, the creative paralysis of the University, and the complementary weakness of ideas in our literature is scandalous; and that strange American invention, the non-academic, non-creative Intellectual, unfrocked, detached, the Comedian of Ideas, is that cleavage made flesh. The urban Jewish writer moving inward from the Schools of Marxism is at least not contemptuous of ideas, and, at best, he is convinced of the unity of his vocation from conversation to creation.

In this mediation to be sure, the great exiles, James and Eliot, and the Southern Agrarians have preceded the writer of our generation, but our situation is perhaps closer to the center than their special cases of expatriation or regionalism.

In the recent migration of writers into the universities this unifying tendency is being sealed. The possible meanings of teachings in a college are, of course, many—and the writer may be quite simply trying to earn a living, but in most cases there is something more: an impatience with the concept of freedom in the term "free-lancer"; an attempt to close the gap between criticism and creation, to make of the teaching of literature a discipline for discriminating readers; a stratagem to mitigate the alienation of the writer by attacking middlebrow culture on its most sensitive flank. For the writer as an individual there are many compensations (though he pays a desperate price in an accommodation to routine and what has been called the "black vacuum" of his students' minds, an accommodation which he fears always may become habitual); he finds an adequate community and the possibility of making himself a better one. For the University, it has been a redemption from historicity and scientism in the study of literature and the arts. And for literature?—it is difficult to say. The average American university is not at all, as the word is conventionally understood, "academic"; there is, I think, little threat from that direction, but much from the appalling and profound weariness, the occasional despair that accompanies the spiritually expensive pursuit of teaching.

The writer in the Lansings, Madisons, Moscows and Lincolns of America schools with his own hand his own audience on a periphery he could not even dream in the centers of New York or San Francisco. We are entering a period, I feel, in which successful strategic raids into middlebrow territory will be increasingly profitable. The decline of experimentalism, and the re-institution of the plot as a concomitant of new notions of freedom and responsibility make possible an extension of the serious writer's audience (Robert Penn Warren is a notable example in this country and Graham Greene in England); and there is the further factor that the production of middlebrow literature can no longer keep pace with the demands of its audience. The opening of the super-slicks to more serious writing, the flirtation of the *Cosmopolitan* with belle-lettres, the association of large commercial publishers with little magazines, the frantic excursions of editors up and down the countryside are not so much tokens of some radical change of heart, as of an incipient panic at a growing discrepancy between mass production methods of distribution and the low supply of popular literature; publishers and editors, abhorring a vacuum, turn in desperation, if not in love, to the more serious writer. This mild revolution will doubtless increase the pressures toward accommodation as well as opportunities for publication, and we must proportionally increase our wariness and our devotion. War, in all its senses, is the condition not the crisis of our lives; this at least we know in the late forties.

It is a dreary and tiny sector from which we as writers fight, and, I suspect it is not even marked on the maps of the General Staff; but there are moments when our struggle to preserve the integrity of play on the adult level, to defend the necessity of ambiguity and irony, to assert the morality of form and to specify feeling, seems to merge with a political conflict, with a *real* (as they say) war. It is not then our duty *as writers* to deny our vocation for a gun or the OWI, or to impugn the autonomy of our fictions with dogmatic assertions or pledges of allegiance. A poem or a story, after all, solves the problem it poses; the war successfully subsumed in a fiction, ends with the fiction; a successful poem is a complete and final act; if it leads outward to other action, it is just so far a failure.

But the absolute claim to freedom in the creative act, in *going on writing* as we understand it, challenges many political systems and is challenged by them, most spectacularly these days by the Soviet Communist world-view. An honest devotion to writing *hypothetically* (is it a Giant or a windmill?) attacks Stalinism, tests its pretensions and our own analysis at once; what cannot endure the practice of the most human of activities is the Enemy. This is our sufficient task as writers; as men, as citizens, though we are required by no iron law to be consistent, we may choose to defend our status and our vocation against the Enemy they have defined, with what weapons come to hand.

Edmund Wilson's Criticism:
A Re-examination

The current re-issue of *The Wound and the Bow* and the promised reprinting of *The Triple Thinkers* make it impossible any longer to avoid a re-examination of the criticism of Edmund Wilson. There is a felt obligation, and a complementary reluctance, periodically to detach a writer important in one's own development from public status and private memory; a certain tenderness re-inforces the reluctance, but it cannot stand against the explicit intent of a re-issue: to be read, not merely recalled.

The first memory of Wilson belongs for many of us to the period when we were discovering at once Marxian doctrine and the New Literature—when Joyce and Lenin presided, with equal authority, over our disavowal of bourgeois values. Our unclarity about what we proposed to substitute (it was *War*, and to define the Enemy seemed enough) kept us from realizing the ultimate conflict of our two revolutions. Besides, we could find in the single authorship of *Axel's Castle* and *The American Jilters* a warrant for believing that, though Proletarian Literature failed to attain artistic distinction, and Eliot, for all his art, persisted in wrong-headed politics, somewhere our two allegiances cohered.

Later, when we had lost faith in the spectacular crudities of Stalinism, there was Wilson at the Finland Station with us, re-defining his social goals—re-examining *Finnegans Wake;* the process was still single. In the latest stage, there was a cue for uneasiness, perhaps; the critical values we had nursed as rebels succeeded (with dignity, it is true) Clifton Fadiman in the *New Yorker,* while the political impulses, turned toward anguish, sought the underground of quasi-fiction in *Hecate County.*

But Wilson's appeal reached not only us for whom he was the critic *par excellence*; those to whom the approach of Eliot or Richards was more congenial, even the Southern Agrarians, whose close analysis Wilson could not achieve and whose politics he openly despised, treated him with respect. He was (it is a hard thing to say of a critic) a Gentleman. The easy perspicuous style, the range of tolerance, the sense of a solid background, Classical and Modern, made him acceptable in circles where other critical advocates of avant-garde literature and the Revolution could not enter.

There is in certain critics who share Wilson's allegiances a disturbing narrowness of culture, an espousal of the contemporaneous *chic,* rooted in their sense of being excluded from the classic past, the property of those with inherited libraries—a feeling that what belongs to them is precisely what has been rejected by those more fortunate in their cultural heritage. Even the radical intellectual could not help feeling a certain begrudged reassurance in finding at his side one as conspicuously non-marginal as Wilson.

Wilson has avoided, too, the second typical narrowness of recent criticism, the academic. Never vocationally bound to the University he is free of pedantry, and what lies at its root—the self-consciousness of the teacher, unable to forget that he can be charged with touting what is, after all, his Bread and Butter.

It is the air of the amateur, the evasion of a professional commitment, that charms us in Wilson—and that protects him from his own method and theories. I think there is a price for such ease: the lack of a real unity in the critical books, the appearance as essays of what might easily have been full-length studies, but in the end it is a partial salvation.

Wilson's customary description of himself as a Historical, or even a Marxian, Critic is a little misleading. On the conscious level, he is a Moralist Critic of the order of Paul Elmer More (on whom he has written one of his most successful pieces), though with quite other ethical standards, derived from the prophetic side of Karl Marx. But he is moved, at the deepest level, by the failure of love in "The Heartbreak House of Capitalism" and his metaphors of decay are chiefly sexual, not social.

In *The Wound and the Bow*, his major analysis is frankly Freudian, and in "The Girl with the Golden Hair," it is suggested that even his own sympathy with the working class is condescending, sentimental, motivated by a kind of class sexual envy. Wilson's almost compulsive drive to this sort of examination can lead on the one hand to the poverty of his exegesis of the *Wasteland,* and, on the other, to such a splendid *tour de force* as his study of "The Turn of the Screw."

It is true, however, that Wilson is often concerned with the social fate of Ideas extracted from works of art, and so far he may be called a historical critic. But he is the least brash of historical critics, surely, in his constant discovery that evaluations, social or moral, of Ideas, have nothing to do with the evaluation of works of art as such. Refusing to submit to *The New Masses* confusion of the two evaluations, he is driven back on—honest confession and his instinctive taste. That taste is good (in prose at least; in verse Wilson has never quite graduated from an early adulation of Edna St. Vincent Millay), and the honesty disarming, but they are not enough. Refusing to develop or espouse any general theory of aesthetics, incapable of close textual analysis,

Wilson most often remains in a critical middle-ground, and cannot solve the discrepancy between his exegesis and judgment.

Is the historical investigation of genesis and background a discipline pleasurable in itself though alien in the fundamental aesthetic experience? Is the critic's only parity with the artist on the level of instinctive taste? Is the work of art more important than the sum of its ideas? These questions Wilson seems sometimes willing to answer affirmatively, though he will not say so clearly.

On the other hand, there are clues throughout his work to a quite different point of view that begins in an impatience with form (it is characteristic that writers in whom the formal element is weaker than the ideological, like Dickens, seem in Wilson's discussions better than they are, while writers like James seem worse) and ends in a total confounding of the arts among themselves and with experience.

The obsessive notion of the dying out of verse in our time that haunts *Axel's Castle* and *The Triple Thinkers* is no mere quirk, but grows out of Wilson's primary belief that attempts to discriminate between poetry and prose in terms more subtle than metrical technique are mystifications. The difference between Dante and Flaubert "is simply that by Flaubert's time the Dantes write their visions as prose fiction . . ." Simply! Surely, that is willful naïveté, and when we are told further that all communication is essentially one, that the poem of "the Symbolist poet is really performing the same sort of function as . . . even the severe technical languages of science," we begin to appreciate the bias that makes Ideas more attractive to Wilson than their formal embodiment in works of art.

But there is a remoter assumption from which these others spring: that the literary arts are second-best, "underground" arts, practiced because our society inhibits the primary art of living, and that the human spirit will, in creating the meta-capitalist state, "transcend literature itself."

This view, with its obvious suggestion of an inverted distaste for literature, is not, of course, Wilson's whole view. In his easy, amateur eclecticism it can live beside a contradictory view; but the double bias, his sundered taste and analysis, the one arising from a love of the arts, the other from a disguised contempt, cannot enrich each other, and in their conflict is the clue to why Wilson's successes are closer to his surface, his failures nearer his core.

The Ordeal of Criticism

In the texture of these essays, there is the manifest intent of reaching a relatively large, amateur audience. Rahv's is an open tone and a vocabulary not deliberately hermetic, both of which set these pieces outside the orbit of the so-called "New" or textual-explicatory criticism, with its highly developed jargon proper to limited intra-academic discourse. On the other hand, there is a certain truculence of statement, a refusal to come to terms with bourgeois or genteel expectations and especially the central American fable of optimism and success succeeding everywhere, that cuts them off from the largest possible area of acceptance, that area in which flourish the *Saturday Review of Literature* and such exponents of official Americanism in art as Howard Mumford Jones.

"Alienation" is always Rahv's key word—a word that expresses at once the possibility of a rich interplay between artist and society and its failure in fact. In his insistence upon asserting in a public voice the difficulty of performing the business of the artist in America (with the further implication that a society is critically tested by its ability to provide the writer with the possibilities of freedom and acceptance that his development requires), Rahv associates himself with the tradition of criticism that includes H. L. Mencken and the early Van Wyck Brooks, and that has found perhaps its finest expression in some of the essays of Edmund Wilson.

The followers of that tradition have sometimes been called the "Ordealists," and it is a name that suggests some of their passionate intensity, though it directs attention too exclusively perhaps to their analysis of the artist's plight, at the expense of the larger criticism of society implied in that analysis, the moral prophetic tone toward which in one way or another they aspire. (The freezing of that moral drive into literary pharisaism in the later Brooks makes a splendid American "case.")

Yet in Rahv, who comes relatively late upon the scene, there is lacking the vigor, the self-assurance verging sometimes on bumptiousness, of the early practitioners of this kind of criticism. He cries out still against the academy, still ultimately distrusts the pious and the priests, still resolutely sallies forth to rescue the more classic American writers from the ikons that respectability makes of them when it can no longer ignore them, still crusades for the ignored contemporary writer, but something has changed.

There is in Rahv a greater subtlety and resiliency, a wider area of critical tolerance—but those qualities have been achieved by sacrificing the liveliness, the vigor, and brute impact found in the early Ordealists and nowhere else in American criticism. It is in part the kind of artist with whom the critic had come to deal that makes the difference; the proper idols of the Ordealists are what Rahv himself would call the "Redskins," *plein-air* types, resolutely barbarous: Whitman and Twain and Dreiser and Farrell. But what is the latter-day Ordealist doing as a leading advocate of Kafka or Henry James (at whom even Wilson sneers as he retreats, and who was to Brooks the essential despised Paleface), or as a reviver of Nathaniel Hawthorne? There is involved here something like what *Partisan Review* enjoys calling "a failure of nerve," as well as a gain of insight and broadening of sensibility.

To understand Rahv's considerable role in recent American literary life, one must see him in a context larger than that of this rather slim volume; first of all, against the background on *Partisan Review,* in which he has long been a controlling force, and beyond that of the parallel, or apparently parallel, interests in radical politics and avant-garde literature out of which that magazine first emerged. One must read back into these essays, selected and revised to represent what Rahv's critical position had now become, the remembered course of his development from a somewhat doctrinaire, though no longer Stalinist, Marxist critic, convinced that there could be no ultimate contradiction between his literary and political allegiances.

He had from the beginning been over-shadowed by the figure of Edmund Wilson, a more productive and ingenious critic, with a subtler and more ingratiating style and a considerably wider group of readers. Rahv, however, represents in more extreme form the critical approach found in Wilson, not mitigated by contact with the university curriculum or the pervasive "gentlemanliness" of the latter.

By the 1930s, Marxism had become at last effective in American intellectual life, overcoming the strong native resistance to a deterministic specification of the role of the intellectual; and it seemed on the verge of organizing coherently all the vaguer anti-bourgeois, anti-genteel notions that had until then existed without a program in the livelier critical minds. The "Revolutionary Movement" seemed for a while capable of providing a true focus for the first wave of "Freudian" protest against conventional sex mores, for Menckenian middle-class baiting, for the espousal of anti-philistine literature, as well as for the political revolutionary impulse proper.

In *Partisan Review,* Philip Rahv and his early associates provided a journal to give visible form to that focus, to express the uneasy but powerful complex without disregarding or falsifying and of its contributory elements. The Ordealist approach, refined by the Marxist dialectic, provided the critical method suitable for such a journal, and in its insistence on the rich inter-penetration of the exigencies of formal statement and social pressures in the personality of the creative artist, managed to resist for a long time the impulse toward anti-literary "Marxism" and anti-political aestheticism. Rahv's under-standing that literary standards could be maintained only outside the totali-tarian circle of Stalinism, enabled him to escape the fatal descent which has led others who began with similar position to the admiration of—Howard Fast!

But the collapse of radical politics on the one hand, and the deflation of the literary reputations of the "radical" writers of the thirties, Dos Passos, Farrell, Caldwell etc. on the other, has finally destroyed the original ideological basis upon which *Partisan Review* and Rahv have attempted to salvage a kind of minimal Marxism committed to no real politics, supplemented by heavier and heavier reliance on the insights of Freud, and most recently revised in the light of Existentialist philosophy. The process has meant a re-definition of the key term "alienation," from a product of social forces, to a resultant of buried disturbances in the individual psyche, to a basic determinant of the human condition. In each case, there had been the prospect of less and less hope, and finally there is that acceptance of anguish as ultimate that has so much vexed recent genteel critics of *Partisan Review.*

Throughout all his adaptations, however, Rahv has clung desperately to a naturalistic and rationalist position, a faith in "scientific method" as the sole criterion of truth, and the almost mythic vision of a dead, God-less universe that provides a common background for Marx and Freud and Sartre.

Yet despite this philosophic predilection, Rahv has come more and more to comment upon, and *Partisan Review* more and more to print, poets and fictionists committed to various supernaturalist positions. It is a fact of our time that such writers have come more and more to do the work of real dis-tinction, and Rahv had stubbornly refused to betray his own fine taste; but his position is ultimately intolerable. The plight of a critic dedicated to natu-ralism devoting his expositions and commentary to Dostoevsky and Tolstoy, Kafka and Hawthorne, reflects on its own level the contradictions of *Partisan Review*, printing T. S. Eliot and Robert Lowell and Robert Penn Warren, while conducting symposiums on "The Failure of Nerve."

Despite himself, Rahv sometimes becomes the victim of a desire to resolve that contradiction by denying the reality or ultimate efficacy in the work of art of religious convictions he finds distasteful. It is the obverse of the pre-dicament of the supernaturalist critic before, say, a poet like Rimbaud—and equally dangerous. Such a process vitiates, I think, much of what Rahv has to say about the notion of sin as salvation in Hawthorne, and even somewhat mars the otherwise penetrating and acute study of Tolstoy.

I find Rahv at his best in the general essays such as "Paleface and Redskin" or "The Cult of Experience in American Writing," which afford real scope for his post-Marxian tough-mindedness, his willingness to make generalizations in an age of "careful scholarship" and narrow textual exegesis and his complete lack of squeamishness before despair, rare among those who write about American literature.

I feel, too, that our intellectual life had profited by the strategic elevation of certain culture heroes in which he and *Partisan Review* have played a leading role: the creation of the contemporary pantheon of Dostoevsky, Hawthorne, Melville, James and Kafka, which we are likely short-sightedly to resent these days as having become merely *chic*, capable of being admired by the culture vulture breathlessly pursuing the up-to-date. Though Rahv's critical system, with its fundamental reliance upon naturalist assumptions, will not permit him to comprehend fully the very writers of whom he has become a leading advocate, he must be given credit for his share in resolution of taste in fiction, as crucial as the parallel one in verse that has uplifted Donne and Metaphysicals.

The publication of Rahv's collected essays coincides with the second decade of *Partisan Review*, and with a growing feeling in all quarters that that magazine has somehow lost its *raison d'être*, or at least its initial vigor and interest. *Image and Idea* provides, beyond the intrinsic pleasures and profits of its discourse, a key to understanding that decline historically.

A kind of critical approach is represented here that may seem to us no longer vital; its realest achievements in Rahv, in Edmund Wilson and in others stir in us rather a comprehension of the recent past than an impulse to future explorations along the same lines. At a point when criticism seems to be going off in a score of directions none of them indubitably forward, it is hard to have to raise such a charge yet once more; and yet it must be said firmly and without irrelevant rancor.

Those of us who were brought up intellectually on *Partisan Review* look to it sometime, I am afraid, unreasonably expecting it to do for us in our present ideological plight what we cannot do for ourselves; reflecting on its limitations, we are obliquely commenting on our own. It is well to remind ourselves that no critical approach can outlive the historical moment that evokes it; the thing is to have justified the moment.

Love is not Enough

We are just now getting used to holding in our minds two uncomfortably complementary notions: first, that we have been living in one of the great ages of criticism, and, second, that much of our criticism, even where not in itself silly or merely exhibitionist, has been harmful in its effects. The success of the new critical theory has meant the creation of a new academy. But this we have really always forknown; the old platitude warns us that nothing succeeds (alas!) like success; and we must not be stampeded into forgetting the excellence of our criticism in our eagerness to get on record our recognition of its harmfulness. The triumphs of the great age of criticism we have been living in are inseparable from the flaws that define them. Surely, no critic since Dr. Johnson has been so magnificently silly as William Empson can be on occasion, nor any at all so blithely exhibitionist as R. P. Blackmur; yet despite their characteristic vices, and indeed by virtue of them, they are splendidly exhilarating. But the exhilaration is running out.

It has usually been assumed that the close-textualists, those aging "New Critics," have sponsored our present difficulties with their compulsive devotion to "structure and texture," their detachment of poems from their contexts and their transformation of works of art into occasions for professional exercise. Indeed, F. O. Matthiessen makes just this point in the title essay of "The Responsibilities of the Critic." Needless to say, he makes it mildly (without either the malice or brilliance of Randall Jarrell's recent sally in the "Partisan Review"); as a friend though not a follower of the New Criticism he offers this reproach: "the little magazines seem now to be giving rise to the conventions and vocabulary of a new scholasticism." And the practitioners of such criticism he calls "pedantic," "grimly thin-lipped" and, finally, "intellectuals without love."

But we are all these days quite suddenly in favor of love. The four books I have before me are prefaced by passionate avowals. Mr. Lehmann assures us that his book deals only with writers "whose work at one time or another, I devoured as the only dish my hunger demanded." Miss Porter's literary essays come imbedded in a context of panegyrics on flowers, birds, and Mexico, all intended to portray "the shape, direction and connective tissue of a continuous, central interest and preoccupation of a lifetime." And Henry Miller speaks of the books in his life as "living moments of joy and plenitude." Four declarations of love, then, each in its author's proper rhetoric—assurances that we are dealing not with the cold excisions of the analysts but with the warm appraisals of amateurs.

Yet, not only are these books not especially good, but the first three share a specific sort of badness with the poor, loveless new scholastics. For, like the latter, they are the victims of our new canon—a brief series of literary works championed over and over in certain expected and unexciting ways. I have never been so aware how most of us, despite our differences, have become inmates of the same infernal circle of taste; busily snapping at each other's skulls, we do not notice how we are all imprisoned from the waist down in the ice of our congealed enthusiasms. This ice, fixed at the temperature of absolute boredom, our approximate passions cannot melt. Another boost for Henry James, another good word for Melville, another cheer for T. S. Eliot—why this is hell, nor are we out of it.

From this circle, Matthiessen himself cannot escape despite the Christian Marxist form of his love, despite the style that declares his humility, his refusal of that bold-mannered dogmatism which characterizes the best current criticism. "Most of the critics I have mentioned now hold academic appointments," Matthiessen begins a typical gambit, "which may or may not have been good for their work." All right, tell us then, the impatient reader cannot help asking—what do *you* think—was it good or not? But there is no answer, and there was never intended to be one. The unnecessary evasion is only a tic, a compulsive mannerism which contributed oddly to Matthiessen's undeniable excellence as a teacher, but which made him even as a literary historian gratuitously involved, and kept him from ever becoming a critic in the fullest sense of the word.

These reviews and essays, a representative sampling of a lifetime of work, are marked always by the seriousness, the generosity, the gentle honesty of the man; but they betray nakedly the inner contradiction that in his best work is decently camouflaged: his failure to close the gap between his literary allegiances and his political-ethical ones. More than any other critic, Matthiessen was the victim of current taste; what a sense of relief we have in coming upon those essays—the piece on Phelps Putnam or on Sarah Orne Jewett—where for once he escapes the compulsion of the mode, indulges some personal fancy. But much more central are his studies within the standard repertory. He accepted beneath the level of thought, through his sensibilities, the canon of Yeats, Eliot, Joyce, James, Melville, that any reader of the literary quarterlies can recite like a litany; but with these his Christian Marxism could not ever really come to terms. He loved them certainly, but with the flesh, as it were, rather than the spirit; and his inconclusive style represents perhaps the stuttering of guilt and doubt. There is something odd and moving about Matthiessen's lifelong championing of Eliot and James; he would have been a wholer man if he could have leaped so unreservedly to the side of Whitman or Dreiser; but his honesty refused him the luxury of such singleness. And beneath the dogged, stifled style we feel the drama of his conflict: not the pure passion for literature, but the more touching, the almost tragic sense of the *need* for that passion.

In John Lehmann's "The Open Night," we find again, this time without uncertainty or strain, the same starred items: Joyce, Yeats, James—with the legitimate extensions to Proust, Virginia Woolf and Rilke. The essential nature of Lehmann's choices is not concealed by a few more personal elections—a handful of editorials in favor of British war poets who died early in both wars, not only the expected tribute to Wilfred Owen, but a word for Rupert Brookes and Alun Lewis. The total effect is of conscious righteousness at work, of one who knows securely that he has chosen the better part. There is a final appeal in a concluding inspirational essay for that Wordsworthian truth "carried alive into the heart by passion," but the passion seems more intended than realized; the choices are so foreseeable that it is hard to *feel* them as the free and dangerous acts of love. The banality of Lehmann is, though, qualified by a kind of relaxed grace, unknown in his more pedantic opposite numbers in America. Compared to our own, British criticism is strangely unfallen; the academic New Criticism (that among us has already bred with terrifying speed three generations!) has never flourished in England, finding instead of the vacuum into which it has rushed in the United States a tradition of perhaps limp but genuinely humane discourse about books. But this tradition has been as helpless before the onslaught of the new canon as Matthiessen's Christian Marxism was.

I am not meaning, of course, to deny the real, the extraordinary merit of the writers in our standard repertory; when Mr. Lehmann speaks of them so dully, he shakes a little my awareness of their genius; but when Katherine Anne Porter asserts that she was "educated by five writers: Henry James, James Joyce, W. B. Yeats, T. S. Eliot and Ezra Pound," the authority of her own achievement as a fictionist reminds me that their merits were equaled once by their uses; each represents a position won in a recent war that was fought for all of us; but we have had enough of listening to the veterans of that war repeating to each other ritual accounts of their victories.

Miss Porter knows this. "If a young writer must choose a master," she tells us, "that choice should be made according to his own needs from the widest possible field." She does not realize what she herself so dramatically demonstrates, how limited is the possibility of free choice in this regard; how the age, the mode impose upon us all the choices we think we freely make. When the revolutionary positions have become clichés this is clear to everyone. To believe with Miss Porter that Henry James's "feelings are more complex than Whitman's; . . . he faced and labored over harder problems," may not be true, but it is certainly standard, and reveals the assumptions which have determined our present canon. We greet Miss Porter's occasional departures from orthodoxy—her case, for instance, for Thomas Hardy—but we have to recognize that her best critical writing (the title piece on Henry James) as well as her more fashionable absurdities (the claim of greatness for the late poetry of Edith Sitwell) are connected with her involvement in a tradition that has outlived its usefulness.

To turn from these books of exegesis on a received scripture to Henry Miller is like turning from the Scholastics to the Book of Mormon. Miller shares with the latter a certain provincial, pseudo-inspired, homemade air; his is the most passionate, the most religious of these books, and at the center of his love and his faith is, as everyone knows, Mr. Miller himself.

Indeed, he solemnly promises us (his truly wonderful sense of humor failing him, as usual, when he confronts himself) his own exegetical works—a second volume listing everything he has ever read, a third containing all the literary references in his own work! But if it is freedom of literary choice, untrammeled love, we have been seeking, surely we have it here, in Miller's praises of H. Rider Haggard and G. A. Henty, J. C. Powys, Erich Gutkind and Blaise Cendrars. We are done with Henry James at last; Miller is squarely in the Whitman camp, in favor of "the direct experience of life"—and theosophy. The opening up of Timbuctoo and the exploration of the kind of large idea which strikes young boys and old women as profound—these are the poles of Miller's passion—with everything in between excluded. "Aye, we must go full swing. *Home* is everywhere and nowhere at the same time."

In such a piece as "Reading in the Toilet," Miller demonstrates that he knows how to be funny, though he does not know how to stop when he is through; but in such a chatty absurdity as his essay "The Story of My Heart" he seems like a sweet though eccentric old lady, who remembers only too well her "advanced" past—somebody's mother. It is amusing to discover his prototype precisely in Ezra Pound's mother. Miss Porter quotes in her essay on Pound a line from a letter of Ezra to his mother, "I am profoundly pained to hear that you prefer Marie Corelli to Stendhal, but I cannot help it." But these are precisely the sentiments of Henry Miller; "The Red and the Black" he vows never to read—and the work of Marie Corelli he ranks only a little behind such a masterpiece as H. Rider Haggard's "She." But this also we cannot help, though we find the play of free preference coinciding with the prejudice of deepest provincialism. Between the exegetes of a tradition become a standard repertory and the exploiters of self-indulgent eccentricity, surely there lies the possibility of the free exercise of taste—and it is at this point that we wait for the authentic critic improbably to appear.

The Intellectual Roots
of Anti-Intellectualism

The intellectual and anti-intellectual not only come into existence at the same moment, but they are inventions of the same mind, the divided mind of the intellectual himself. Needless to say, the enemies of the intellectual invent nothing; they do not even have a name of their own aside from the epithets flung at them contemptuously from time to time by their opponents: philistines, booboisie and so forth. It is their fate to live on the discarded notions of those whom they despise, converting tortured insight into smug banality; and even their self-consciousness is arrived at secondhand by this scavenging process. Perhaps the anti-intellectual is dimly aware of this irony or at least dimly resents it without real awareness; but it is not necessary for him to know it at all. As a matter of fact, it is juster and funnier that he thunder away against intellectuals in blithe ignorance of the truth that all his best invective was ghost-written for him before he was born by precisely the kind of mind he delights in abusing.

The intellectual, on the other hand, must endure the final indignity and joke of knowing that he himself has invented the whole anti-intellectual position. He must see the attacks against him, fear and the violence, as projections of his own self-distrust on record in a thousand novels and poems which his opponents mysteriously absorb without reading. I do not mean to suggest, of course, that the intellectual must hamper his own defense by telling himself that "it's all his own fault!"—merely that he must not allow his justified indignation to blind him to the supreme irony of it all. For this irony he must abide as he abides all the others; and, indeed, this is his distinction among men, the essence of his vocation. Where allegiance exists in others—good citizens, good fathers, good rebels—irony exists in him. He is a terrible ally and the worst of friends.

We must be careful, I think, to reserve the honorable name of intellectual only to the ironical, though there is a growing tendency these days to bestow it on anyone who can read and write gracefully enough to earn the contempt of the vainly ignorant. No one else deserves the title, however, even if he is pilloried by the leading anti-intellectual of the moment. Not everyone martyred by Nero is a Christian; there are some who end up in the mouths of lions by mistake, and this must not be interpreted sentimentally as a sign of their election—not even if they cry out (having nothing further to lose) the name of the Lord.

No, the true intellectual is not faithful even to himself, much less to God; for he knows that any human commitment is a lie, and that even noncommitment, when it becomes a program, is hypocrisy. He does not think that only he is not a joke among the jokes of the world, merely that he is the last and best joke of all; and it is this sense of the ridiculousness even of his own predicament that is used against him by the literal-minded when he cannot resist writing it down. What really stirs the anger of the anti-intellectual is that his opponent evades even that last comforting platitude: "Those who are not for us are against us!"—for the intellectual is neither for nor against in the ordinary sense.

It is possible to love as well as hate the enemy who goes down crying out slogans equal and opposite to your own. By this very act he assures you of the reality of your cause, which is, after all, more important than its rightness or wrongness; but the intellectual dissolves in his irony the reality of the cause itself. The intellectual is the permanent revolutionist of the spirit; even as he straddles one barricade, the red flag in his hand, he is dreaming of the next, when he will raise the black. And worse than that, he is already in his mind writing the book that will reveal just how absurd he and his comrades looked waving the red flag or the black. It is not difficult to despise him; he finds it easy himself; and anyone who undertakes a defense of the intellectual must begin with this depressing realization rather than some melodramatic vision in which a clean and public-opinioned Ivy-Leaguer (looking rather like Adlai Stevenson) stands valiantly against an ill-shaven yahoo (looking not unlike Senator McCarthy).

It is not the witty and polished Adlai Stevenson one must imagine but the stuttering and seedy Jean-Jacques Rousseau. Those who would defend one and not the other are only anti-intellectuals once removed. More is required of the intellectual's friend than loving "eggheads" with good grammar and good manners or despising those to whose manhood such grammar and manners seem a threat. What I mean when I use the word "intellectual" is not merely a person who thinks in public, but that new kind of thinking man produced out of the ferment of shallow rationalism and sentimentalism which shaped the ideology of the French Revolution and whose first embodiment was the truculently "anti-intellectual" Rousseau.

For many hundreds of years the mind of Europe functioned through the "clerk"; but the "clerk," pledged to the past and the Church, gave way briefly when that past and that Church were challenged by force, to the *philosophe*, committed to the future and to abstract Reason. Born with the *philosophe*, however, was a strange milk-brother, at first unnamed, who lived only for the present and for himself. Diderot called him "Rameau's Nephew" and portrayed him in a dialogue as half artist and half underground man, consumed by vanity and self-hatred; but God had already named him Jean-Jacques. His contradictions are implicit in the historical moment that produces him; the disruption of the old hierarchies and the disappearance of the old centers undercut even the rationalists who had dreamed them, leaving the thinker alone and unsustained, his only relationship with the community one of challenge and mockery. But the same catastrophe breeds the dogmas of Democracy and Romanticism, the unwillingness to endure difference or distinction.

The intellectual begins by preaching against the surviving aristocracy an egalitarian creed that the middle class ends preaching against him. The theory that the kitchenmaid's by-blow is as good as the bastard of a king slips inevitably into the belief that the former is a damn sight better: that we are *all* better than anyone else, especially those of us who are worse. One cannot unleash the notion that what was lower should be higher without somehow ending up with the idea that the only stability is in having everything in the middle. The heritage of the Revolution is the hatred of excellence; and that this does not *inevitably* follow is beside the point; in fact, it does. Depressingly enough, even when liberty and fraternity are subverted, equality, understood as leveling, somehow lives on, as it did under Napoleon and as it continues to do under the Jacobin totalitarianisms of fascism and communism—or, indeed, in the minds of our own McCarthys. The fear of distinction and the veneration of mediocrity are common links between governments united by nothing else. And how can the intellectual insist at this late date that when he attacked the aristocracy he meant only a corrupt aristocracy of blood and not the just one of sensibility and talent? He is not even sure that he did.

Moreover, the intellectual begins by raising against the artists who had turned themselves into purveyors of erotic entertainment for the court a demand for commitment which the middle class ends by turning on him. The proud call of David to his fellow painters to serve Reason and the Revolution becomes the pressure of Van Wyck Brooks or Archibald MacLeish against the "irresponsibles," too proud and alienated to serve the "war effort." The demand for spiritual commitment turns into a request for practical contributions: posters, movie scenarios, editorials in favor of democracy and against racial discrimination. And how can the intellectual protest at this point that when he advocated commitment he meant a commitment to what was not yet debased, a commitment *against* conformity? It is hard to remember just what he did mean.

He cannot (or at least should not) forget, however, that it was he who espoused against the respectable of another day the notion of the superiority of the "natural" to the "artificial," the peasant to the courtier, the untutored heart to the overcultured head. For this, even more than for his espousal of egalitarianism and commitment, the intellectual must see himself as the father of anti-intellectualism. It was not only Rousseau, after all, who affected to distrust reason and looked nostalgically back toward the natural, but a host of others, unlike in every respect except this: Diderot and Wordsworth, Whitman and Twain, Dostoevsky and Tolstoi. It is the last writer who gives the game away in a spasm of self-contempt and honesty, who reveals that the cult of the natural, the veneration of the peasant becomes finally anti-art, anti-thought, anti-life. The others, even Twain with his pose of the know-nothing abroad, exempted from their indictment of formal culture such sacred figures as Shakespeare and themselves; in *What Is Art?*, Tolstoi begins with such fair game as the "obscure" decadents but ends by disavowing even *Hamlet* and his own *Anna Karenina.*

No embattled Midwestern congressman, to whom art equals communism and the taste of the "little man" is the court of final appeal, could go further; all that is left him is unconscious plagiarism. And what is the use of the intellectual's crying out after such a development that he meant originally to attack only that "culture" which had been hopelessly compromised by its allegiance to the false values of the past; that he had dreamed all along not the death of all culture but the emergence of a new one, finer and more outrageously honest. How does one ever know just what he does mean?

Even the maddening stereotypes of "the intellectual" and "the Bohemian" that haunt the bourgeois mind, the most sentimental and the most savage, were invented by the intellectuals themselves. In the works of the more passionate or hard-boiled worshipers of "Experience," in D. H. Lawrence, in Sherwood Anderson, in Hemingway himself, one finds caricatures of the intellectual that have served anti-intellectuals ever since: the intellectual as homosexual, as effete Jew, as intelligence without *cojones* or a connection with the soil. Especially in America, with the triumph of Midwestern realism, which is to say, with the victory of the provinces over the center, of improvisation over culture, there has grown up a gallery of parodies of the intellectual, parodies that have by some strange process of cultural osmosis oozed down into the popular mind.

Literary populism, emerging from the political variety, has bred a species of anti-intellectual intellectuals who equal in their voluntary vilification of their own confreres anything forced on the Soviet writers by an officially sponsored "Social Realism." And there is no use pleading that this is only *one part* of the self-portrait of the intellectual. The middle class is willing enough to read the ambiguity of the intellectual as confusion and inconsistency; and besides it finds quite as much ammunition in the intellectual's favorable vision of himself as in the portraiture born of his self-hatred.

If one aspect of the Democratic-Romantic complex out of which the intellectual emerges leads to populism, another develops into dandyism. The

Romantic, who, lying on his right side, dreamed himself the voice of the common man—the articulateness of the inarticulate—rolling over onto his left, endured the nightmare of himself as an outcast, cursed for his very sensibility and honesty, the lonely voice crying in a void. This nightmare he transmuted into art and life in an effort to seem to *choose* what had been thrust upon him. His exclusion he made a point of pride, his *raison d'être,* becoming the very personification of his outsidedness and exaggerating the viciousness imputed to him as a gesture of contempt for the bourgeois world.

In that role as acted out by Byron or half-lived, half-composed by Poe and completed by Baudelaire, the intellectual became everything the middle classes needed him to be, everything they longed and feared to become themselves: drunkard, seducer, dope addict, syphilitic, sadist—failure and poet. The failure of the intellectual was demanded by a world that thought it worshiped only success; as such intellectuals saw themselves, a hostile society saw them, too—for they are the consciousness of that society which can know nothing except through them. To be sure, what was for them evidence of their election was for that society a sign of depravity, but the vision remains the same though the judgment differs.

By themselves and by their enemies alike, the intellectuals came more and more to seem a separate class in a world that had learned from them to aspire to classlessness. Thinking of themselves as a nobility of talent and suffering, as "knights of infinite resignation," they attempted to constitute, at the very moment that the middle classes (taught by other intellectuals) had learned to hate all aristocrats, the world's last aristocracy. And before the dilemma posed by this self-ennoblement, the contemporary intellectual still stands bewildered. How can he know whether he is finally betraying his own cause more flagrantly if, in his charcoal flannels and his university office, he cries out that he is not Edgar Allan Poe; or if, in a shabby sweater and a cold-water flat, he plays the expected role of the futile Bohemian? He must be willing to despise himself in either case, first for choosing however he does and then for despising himself for it; for there is no way out of irony except into deeper irony. At least he must not content himself with righteously despising the anti-intellectuals and finding himself beside their grossness justified even to himself.

> *Man is but a reed, the weakest in nature,*
> *but he is a thinking reed.*
> BLAISE PASCAL

A Fortyish View

"**B**e careful what you wish for in your youth," says an aphorism of Goethe, "for you will get it in your middle age." It is a terrifying enough thought, but at forty I feel capable of amending it into one still more terrifying. "Be careful what you wish for in your youth," my new version runs, "for *the young* will get it in your middle age."

Since what I wished for when I was younger was maturity and an end to innocence—in short, middle age itself—I thought I was playing it safe; and anyhow I always added under my breath: "Not yet, dear God, not quite yet!" First, violence and despair, the flirtation with failure and the commitment to revolution; then, all the savor of slow disenchantment, and only at long last the acceptance of responsibility and success: This was the pattern I imagined and have approximately lived, the pattern of many of us to whom the Depression seemed perversely enough Our Great Good Time and the Spanish Civil War, to which we did not go, *our* war.

God knows, the "not yet!" we prayed under our breath was answered. We have had, notoriously enough, the most prolonged youth on record, a youth wished on us by our predecessors of the twenties, who could conceive of no greater good. To the younger generation now defining itself I am grateful for at least one thing: It has lifted from me the burden of being young. No one after this series of statements will again, I hope, dare refer to my fortyish contemporaries as "young novelists," "young critics," "young intellectuals." We may now become grandfathers in peace.

To be sure, none of us will ever be as old as those who are now around 30, just as none of us were ever as young as, say, Scott Fitzgerald; for the new unyoung are mature with the maturity we dreamed. We ended their innocence before they possessed it; and they passed directly from grade school to middle age with a copy of *Partisan Review* or *Kenyon Review* as a passport, their only youth *our* youth, which is to say, the mythical youth of the thirties.

My own high-school-age son, reliving for a third or a fourth time the attitudes I first remember noticing in my freshman classes just before World War II, complains to me that by anticipation I have robbed him of the possibilities of revolt. He sees clearly enough that for him the revolutionary gesture would be empty mimicry, incongruous in a world that has found there is no apocalypse, and that the threat our society poses is not exclusion and failure but acceptance and success. What he does not yet perceive is that by anticipation my generation has robbed his even of new possibilities of accommodation, of the use of accommodation as a revolt against revolt.

To me, the most appalling aspect of the new generation's writing, as of its life style, is its familiarity. I cannot conventionally deplore its creative sterility and its turning to criticism; each does what he can, and criticizing a poem by John Crowe Ransom is better than biting one's fingernails. Frankly, I *like* criticism; but when I find myself nodding with comfortable approval over some bright new essay by some bright new critic, I force myself to wake to a realization that my approval is *self*-approval, for the ideas and attitudes are my own and those of my contemporaries, unearned intellectual income.

The young, who should be fatuously but profitably attacking us, instead discreetly expand, analyze and dissect us. How dull they are! How dull *we* are without our pasts; how banal our dissent from dissent without the living memory of a commitment to dissent. The young are able to share our Depression experience only vicariously; our reaction from it they can not only live but live on! How soon they prosper on rehashed responses to the Thirties, which they re-echo in magazines invented in those Thirties or earlier.

Here is a clue, surely. For the period of the Twenties had its own magazines, say, *Hound and Horn;* the Thirties, *Partisan Review* and *Kenyon Review.* What comes after has nothing—or worse than nothing, the *Hudson Review,* which is to say, *Kenyon Review* reborn in the full flush of genteel and middle-aged youth. The only "new" political journal is *Dissent,* edited chiefly by aging radicals unwilling to leave the Garden of the Thirties.

The new generation has founded no new journals because it has discovered no new voice, no new themes in which to invest its carefully nurtured sensibility and technique. Indeed, the unyoung need no such journals to be heard; the older quarterlies are open to them, as are the back pages of weeklies like *The New Republic* or *The Nation,* and *The New Yorker* itself is not unfriendly. Opportunities exist everywhere, not only for publication but for study and travel. The great foundations are eager to invest in so predictable a youth, to send them to school or Europe or Asia or up and down America. Whatever the imagination can conceive, there is plenty of money to subsidize. Expatriation is financed with the same even-handed munificence as an academic study of population pressures or right-left asymmetry.

Only one necessity of life no fund can sponsor—failure; only one satisfaction it cannot bring itself to provide—violence. Yet, the sensibility of the young has been conditioned by a literature of the Thirties based on violence and failure; their dreams are possessed by the images life is too good to match.

In a world rent by violence, America remains strangely immune to disaster; and it seems impossible for the young to identify themselves with, say, the

Hungarian revolt as we did with the war in Spain. The daily newspaper falls from their hands which clutch the latest reprinting of Orwell's *Homage to Catalonia*. The dream of violence and the fact of security, the dream of failure and the fact of success—this is our New Comedy which awaits only the writer capable of embodying it.

The trouble is that there are no new social groups out of which a truly new writer might come. The Thirties saw the breakthrough of urban Jews into the centers of American cultural life; indeed, the Communist movement itself became, in a sense not generally noticed, a way for intellectual social climbers, the pathway of the new intellectuals toward status and acceptance. First the Party, then some splinter group, and finally a university job—with the young before us, eager to learn the pattern for themselves: first revolt (*our* revolt revisited), then the academy (*their* instructorships bending over *our* books) and a new group of students, etc., etc. In a similar way, wave after wave of young Southerners emerged from their own areas of deprivation, twin volumes of poetry and criticism proffered in lieu of passports—only to disappear into the colleges of the North, still shouting the slogans of Agrarianism to their own students now interested only in the *poetry* of the Fugitives.

For us at least, it was not all foreknown—the faculty meetings, the salons of upper Bohemia, the suburban peace—and we move in such milieus not really believing in them, winking secretly to each other across the room. But for the young who follow there is *only* the world we have prepared for them—possessed, mapped and cleared for comfortable living.

I have talked so far of the younger generations as if they were a unit, but one internal division I have already suggested—the cleavage into New Yorker and Southerner, urban and agrarian, sociologue and New Critic, *Partisan Review*-er and *Kenyon*-ite. Yet, long since our Augustan peace has blurred the old battle lines. This is, after all, an age of interfaith tolerance, and only an occasional challenge to a duel ruffles the truce that finds Allen Tate and Philip Rahv presiding over the same summertime school for training the literary young.

And yet, for clarity's sake it is worth distinguishing subgroups among the young. First, the New York Jewish academics, who represent the latest form of status-striving among the descendants of Eastern European immigrants. In the first generation, there was a simple-hearted drive for wealth in woolens or ladies' underwear or junk; in the second, a more complicated impulse toward the (still well-paying) respectability of law or medicine; in the third, a timid and sophisticated urge to enter publishing and the universities, to become in the full sense intellectuals. The old tragedy of the poet forced into manufacturing brassieres becomes the new comedy of the proto-tycoon lecturing on the imagery of Wallace Stevens.

The New York intellectual, the *alrightnik* in academia, is typically a product of Columbia who has received certain finishing touches at the Kenyon School of Letters or Downing College or both, and who ostentatiously sports a body of learning so appalling in scope that beside it the sheer ignorance and dullness of, say, a John Aldridge seems like freshness of vision. In addition to contributing toward the Talmudic commentaries on a canon set in the Twenties and Thirties—Faulkner, Stevens, Melville, etc.—such intellectuals normally concern themselves with "popular culture" or the "mass arts." (Here, too, they follow the lead of Riesman or Dwight Macdonald.) Their attitude toward these sub-arts is ambivalent, compounded of one part inverted snobbism and one part social protest. On the one hand, they seek to dissociate themselves from self-conscious culture-vulturism by publicly preferring Westerns to art films and boxing to ballet; on the other, they take an almost political stand against the debasement of values which threatens eventually to engulf their own markets.

The *alrightnik*-academician is flanked on one side by the radical once removed, the youngster who insists on reliving the politics of the Thirties in pious recapitulation. Such belated, symbolic revolutionaries become Trotskyites in 1945 or 1946, subscribe to *Dissent* and save their finest scorn for Lionel Trilling and David Riesman, to whom they are bound in spasms of filial rejection. But, alas, they cannot in role or function distinguish themselves from their colleagues, who admire Riesman and Trilling and subscribe to *The New Leader* or *Encounter*. They, too, sit in the offices of Rinehart or Simon and Schuster; they, too, teach at Columbia or Minnesota or Bard; and the Ford Foundation is only too delighted to subsidize what their politics has in large measure become—the writing of histories of the radical past. Needless to say, their youth is noticeably shopworn even in a world of second-hand youth.

If to his left the academician of the Center finds a *Dissent*-nik, on his right (in, say, R. P. Blackmur's class at the School of Letters) he may find a contributor to *Hudson Review*, solemn before literature with a solemnity scarcely distinguishable from *rigor mortis*, yet finding in Ezra Pound and Wyndham Lewis a manly vulgarity to which his limpness aspires. The Ivy League exegete in search of virility and the Bronx poet in quest of status meet at a common point though in mutual incomprehension. A basic class distinction is involved. The Princeton graduate has no use for the graces of Lionel Trilling but finds in Yvor Winters in art or in Willmoore Kendall in politics a kind of moral ferocity compatible with the ideals of a Christian gentleman. Trained in such a school, he will find the *National Review* more than a little crude; though, indeed, he would be the first to admit that Buckley is "really brilliant," and he dreams of a pure politics of the literary Right, presided over by Cleanth Brooks and Wimsatt, a politics in which the most delicate insights into poetry are blended with a dignified McCarthyism. It is these right-wing purists who sometimes pretend to find themselves isolated among the new young; but for them, too, there is a place on Mike Wallace's program.

Beyond all these and within are the homosexuals, the staunchest party of them all. Indeed, I have the feeling sometimes that homosexuality is the purest and truest protest of the young, not an aberration merely or a disease, but a last politics. Implicit in its way of life is a rejection of the monogamous family and the PTA—the sole remaining protest, perhaps, in a world where adultery has come to seem old hat. But they come so fast and fade faster, queen treading on queen, the seventeen-year-old novelist hard on the heels of the aging nineteen-year-old; and the world is so ready for them, waiting with a tolerance as large and damp as that which smothers the Jews. For each group there is a fitting and proper mode of accommodation: for the queers, publication in *Harper's Bazaar* or *Vogue* or *Mademoiselle* and an entry into a world of chic and good manners, where certain sensitive, effete explorations of the Faulknerian scene and Faulknerian themes supply a necessary music.

What is finally most distressing about all this is not that the devices of the young seem so dismal and unpromising, but that they are not even theirs. If I have drawn as desperate a picture as legitimate distortion can make of their plight, this is not to blame them but to blame *us*. It is disconcerting enough to see a host of little Trillings and Riesmans and Rahvs; it is all the more appalling to catch glimpses of imitation Irving Howes and Willmoore Kendalls; but it is completely unnerving to discover what is surely intended to be oneself—all that innocence so smugly ended, all that maturity buttoned up to the third button! Enough, dear friends and students, *enough!*

And yet it does not matter really; for so long as the imagination lives, any plight is potentially the stuff of a vision that will transcend it by capturing it. It is not generations, thank God, that write books or come to understanding; it is lonely men. The generations are what the books are about, what the understanding dissolves to be re-created in art. At the moment, one has the sense of young writers at a loss for subjects because yesterday's subjects are lost. We are all aware of poets with more technique than audience and more audience than theme, of novelists desperately contriving fictional subjects because their self-respect demands that somehow they make books. But the theme is here, the subject all around us: the comedy of the young in their passionate and absurd relationship with us. When a young writer arises who can treat this matter in all its ridiculous freshness, we will be done with false pathos and symposia; and on that day I will be leaning from my window to cheer that writer and to shake down on his head the torn scraps of all surviving copies of this piece.

Intellectual Uncles

It seems appropriate that a series of modern classics—i.e., of works almost up to date—should be launched with books by Charles Olson, Roland Barthes, and Claude Lévi-Strauss. Each made his first impact some twenty years ago: Barthes with the series of essays in *Combat* that later became *Writing Degree Zero*, in 1947; Olson with *Call Me Ishmael* in the same year; and Lévi-Strauss with a study of the Nambikwara Indians in 1948. Each has had, much more recently, full academic recognition, Lévi-Strauss a professorship in the Collège de France, Barthes a similar post in the Ecole Pratiques des Hautes Etudes, and Olson one at the State University of New York at Buffalo. All, moreover, were educated in the O.K. universities of their respective countries, Barthes and Lévi-Strauss at the University of Paris, Olson at Wesleyan, Yale, and Harvard.

They are, in short, all established academic critics of literature and society, though confusingly enough Barthes talks about books from the asylum of a Department of Sociology, Lévi-Strauss about myth as a Social Anthropologist and Olson about both inside a Department of English Literature. And more confusingly still, all are identified with points of view once thought of as essentially anti-academic, all committed to a defense of a post-modern *avant-garde*.

POINTLESS

Even Barthes, whose style I find so pointlessly and tastelessly abstract, so devoid of grace, blood or even (in spite of his theoretical homage to existentialism) *existenz*, that I shall never willingly read a word of his again, is identified as an expert of the *nouveau roman* and Robbe-Grillet—though, to tell the truth, I consider the neo-classicism of the latter almost as unsympathetic as the exegesis on it. Moreover, he lays claim to the fashionable title of "structuralist" thus identifying himself with Lévi-Strauss, who is to the young—in America, I know, and I suspect elsewhere as well—among the few oldsters felt to be somehow in tune with what is happening or better perhaps, with a semi-mythical version of the present scene a little better than the mere fact. At any rate, I was presented recently by a couple of below-twenty-five-year-old intellectuals (that's the wrong word, I know, but the best in my archaic vocabulary), who wanted both to flatter and educate me, with the newest edition of Kurt Vonnegut, Jr.'s *The Sirens of Titan* and a recent translation of Lévi-Strauss's *La Penseé Sauvage*.

As for Olson, he has become for whole swarms of young poets and editors and writers of fiction—not only for the generation which passed through Black Mountain College when he was its moving spirit (Robert Creeley, for example, and, until he lusted after even black power, Leroi Jones), but for disciples and students of those first disciples and students to the third generation—their truest spiritual Papa.

It is not only in terms of sheer physical bulk and charisma that he appeals to certain too-white sons of strong pale-face mothers and weak paler-face fathers. He also seems to provide them models for a kind of short-breathed verse, closer in style to the letters they write each other than to what their teachers once assured them was poetry; and for a kind of rhapsodic criticism closer to such a poetry.

HOSTILE

Enough, then, for the sociology of Jonathan Cape's series; since, though, such an approach seems apropos under the circumstances, more important by far is the question what *use* are the examples of these three men, whose minds were made in the thirties, to practicing literary criticism in an age as hostile as our own to the practice of their art. Certainly, formalist approaches based on the example of T. S. Eliot (whether in certain Cavalier versions like those of John Crowe Ransom and company in the United States, or more grimly Puritanical ones, like those of the school of F. R. Leavis) have come to seem as quaint and irrelevant as Socialist Realism. And in this regard, Olson seems still alive—suggesting that the lyric and the dithyramb rather than the polite essay or the scientific report provide viable models for the critic in an age which has learned, or at least aspires to learn, to distrust reason and plausible syntax. To be sure, he is a rather dogged dithyrambist in *Call Me Ishmael*, not mad enough for his method by a long shot—not nearly as mad as his friend and colleague Edward Dahlberg or Ezra Pound who is his obvious Master.

The very subject he has chosen and the moment of his choice give the whole game away; for he turned to Melville just after the Second World War, which is to say at the moment he was becoming a respectable academic subject—and the years since, more conventional scholars have gone beyond Olson in the kind of investigation of sources and influences which turns out, unexpectedly, to be the strong point of his book. One thinks by contrast of

Lawrence, who was not only there first, but whose insights remain unrepeatable, unperfectable, whose very errors survive with an authority which shames our best retrospective wisdom.

PROVINCIAL

Yet, how preferable is Olson's earnest simulation of inspired frenzy to Barthes's turgid philosophizing, or his preference of definition to poetry. No American, moreover, could manage to achieve the provinciality that comes to the average Frenchman as an inalienable birthright. Writing of what he calls "the Western art of the Novel," Barthes assures us that it is inseparable from the use of the preterite form of the verb and third-person narration! And in the head of any modern sentences there ring not only those urgent first-person present tense of Richardson's letter-writing heroines (these even such early French critics of the form as Diderot and de Sade knew enough not to forget), but the opening cadence of *Moby Dick* which Olson's title echoes, and the phrase with which Huck Finn comes to life: "You don't know about me without you have read a book by the name of *The Adventures of Tom Sawyer* . . ."

Perhaps Lévi-Strauss escapes the curse because, whatever his initial miseducation, he was reborn among American-Indians, close to the sources of an ancient wisdom and simplicity to which he pays so courtly a tribute in the splendid little book now available for the first time in English, his inaugural lecture as Professor of Anthropology in the Collège de France.

Let him call himself an anthropologist if he will; it is a title to which we all lay claim when we go in search of our submerged selves. He is, for my money, the best literary critic of the three before me—which is to say, as far from *explication de texte* and as close to that border where literature blends into our general experience, to the world of myth in which dreams and poems and artifacts are one, as a man dare venture without losing his conscious self forever. I wish I had written the four or five pages in which (off-hand, as it were, by way of casual example) he simultaneously illuminates the story of Oedipus, an Indian incest myth and the Legend of the Holy Grail. Perhaps, if I am lucky, I will dream tonight I have.

The Canon and the
Classroom: A Caveat

As I was pondering what I might usefully say about the future of literary studies in English—especially its role in establishing and maintaining a canon (which has become, for better or worse, one of its chief functions)—I received a rather disconcerting dispatch from that future. There arrived on my desk, that is to say, a letter from my granddaughter detailing the curriculum in a summer seminar for gifted high school seniors, intended to prepare them, I suppose, not just for college but, in some cases at least, careers as teachers of English. Delighted to have been so honored, she was even more delighted by what she was learning. "Wonderful," she called her courses, which included (all too predictably), "Ideology in Children's Literature," "Black English," "Post-Modernist Theatre," and "Feminist Poetry." Then she concluded by writing, "I feel as if a whole new world is opening up to me": to which I found myself responding (an improbable Prospero in Buffalo, New York), "'Tis new to thee."

It was not merely the cant words in the course title which dismayed me (I am allergic to all words ending in "-ism," particularly those I have been tempted on occasion to use myself), but my sense that I had lived through all of this before, trapped in a half-century-long bad dream. Over and over again, I have watched a presumable critical breakthrough, an opening up of new insights tend first to turn into a fad, then a cliché; and finally on the level of day-to-day pedagogy become a canon, enforced in the totalitarian regime of the classroom, where whatever is not required is forbidden.

I have, indeed, long considered it my special function in the academy to combat that all but inevitable tendency; beginning before I even suspected that I myself might someday end up as an academic expected to impose what was currently canonical in quest of promotion, tenure and the respect of my colleagues. I can remember, for instance, rising in my high school sophomore English class (from whose walls portraits of the Boston Brahmins looked down in silent disapproval) to protest that our poetic horizons should not be bounded by those genteel New England Sages. Nor, I insisted with all the arrogance of youth, should our novel-reading be confined to *Ivanhoe*, *Silas*

Marner and *The Virginian*—a list chosen for us by a committee of college professors, most of them long dead.

Even in graduate school I still found it necessary to continue to fight the good fight, this time against living professors, who thought of themselves as emancipated from the timidity and sentimentality of late Victorianism, but as "historical scholars" found any work published after the mid-nineteenth century (especially, it turned out, American books) unworthy of serious study. But—as I could not resist pointing out—even the canon of the centuries they deigned to treat in learned articles was being changed at the moment by the more recent authors they chose to ignore. John Donne, for instance, was coming to be prized more highly than Milton and Gerard Manley Hopkins, more esteemed than Tennyson and Browning; even as Hawthorne and Melville were threatening to replace Dickens and Thackeray in the pantheon of great novelists.

It was, of course, the pioneers of High Modernism and the "New Critics" who canonized them who inspired me. I had been reading Proust and Joyce behind my timid teachers' backs since the age of thirteen; and by the time I came of legal age, I had not merely begun my lifelong love-hate relationship with Ezra Pound and T. S. Eliot but had already discovered Charles Olson in the pages of an obscure little magazine. I had, moreover, been influenced by critical revisionists like John Crowe Ransom, Allen Tate, and F. R. Leavis. It was they who first awoke in me the hope of creating a kind of meta-canon without limits and forever changing; thus making it possible for the study and even the teaching of literature to become more like literature itself: not an act of conformity and submission to established authority, but a way of challenging and subverting the *status quo* whatever it might be—a way of saying "No! in thunder."

The epigones of Modernism, however, ended by destroying one rigid canon only to create another. At their worst, they defined, like F. R. Leavis, a "great tradition" so narrow that it excluded such long-established classics as *Jane Eyre, Wuthering Heights,* and *Tristram Shandy*. But even at their more generous best, they consigned to the outer darkness many books which had pleased many and pleased long—on the grounds that precisely because they had done so they had proved themselves unredeemable trash. Moreover, such critics had trouble coming to terms with borderline writers, including some who had been my own favorites. I am thinking in particular of Walt Whitman, who theoretically at least wrote for the popular audience; Edgar Allan Poe, who wooed— and eventually won—that audience, though he boasted of spurning it; and especially Harriet Beecher Stowe, who not merely aspired to best-sellerdom but achieved it.

In the two critical works which established the Modernist canon for American Literature, Matthiessen's *American Renaissance* and Lawrence's *Studies in Classic American Literature*, *Uncle Tom's Cabin* was completely ignored. But this was predictable enough, was it not?; since Nathaniel Hawthorne, a special favorite of both Matthiessen and Lawrence, seems to have been thinking chiefly of Mrs. Stowe when he excoriated "the damned female scribblers," against whom, he thought, he and other more serious writers (all male, of course) had to contend for readers. In my own *Love and Death in the American Novel* I tacitly accepted the Matthiessen-Lawrence canon; but over the next decade I became more and more ill at ease with the old blending of snobbism and misogyny which had prompted Mrs. Stowe's exclusion.

It was not, however, until the publication of *What Was Literature?* That I publicly called for opening up the canon to include her—along with Alex Haley, Thomas Dixon, Jr., and Margaret Mitchell, whose *Gone with the Wind* has finally outsold even *Uncle Tom's Cabin*, becoming simultaneously the most widely sold and loved and the most critically despised of American books. In large part because of this, my last full-length critical study has become, ironically enough, the least widely sold and loved of all my own books; most vilified, of course, by certain last-ditch defenders of High-Modernism as Hugh Kenner, a political as well as aesthetic reactionary, and therefore particularly offended by my shameless populism.

I was not utterly dismayed, however, snce Modernism was already obsolescent, if not quite obsolete. Indeed, its successors had already appeared, new aspirants to new canon-making. One wing of the so-called post-Modernists (I was one of the first to call them by that now much abused name), for instance, declared their intent to close the gap which the Modernists had widened between High Art and Pop. They argued, as I myself had done much earlier, that the true mythology of the late twentieth century was to be found in the fast foods rather than the *haute cuisine* of contemporary literature; and, in fact, some among them larded their experimental novels with allusions to and downright emulation of science fiction, comic books, and Class-B horror movies. But did this not mean, I found myself asking, opening the canon, the classroom curriculum to such works, including even the commodity novels of shameless schlock artists like Stephen King?

That most admired post-Modernist novelists of our time thought no such thing, I found out rather painfully when I was moved to observe toward the end of a conference attended by many of them that King's book might still be read and cherished when the experimental fiction we ourselves wrote had long been forgotten. *Misery*, I suggested, might well turn out to be for the eighties and nineties what *Gone with the Wind* had been for the thirties: a reproach to critics, indeed, to any presumptuous making of the canon. My remarks, however, stirred no assent, not even embarrassed laughter. Instead, I was greeted with a hushed silence, as if I had committed some unspeakable sacrilege; and I was assigned to the equivalent of the children's table at the ceremonial banquet which concluded our sessions.

But this should not have surprised me, since I had long since become uncomfortably aware that even in their essays written in praise of Pop the post-Modernists had used the hermetic jargon invented by elite French critics, bent on undermining the authority of primary texts and the autonomy of their authors. Unlike most eminent Anglo-American critics, such critics were not themselves creative writers attuned to a larger audience; and consequently they wrote in a language incomprehensible to any but their academic colleagues—plus, of course, their students who aspired to a similar status. I began, therefore, to look in another direction for possible allies in my quest to redeem the teaching of English by inventing a new canon more congruous with the values of an open society and the writers of song and story, from Sophocles and Shakespeare to Dickens, Twain and Mrs. Stowe, who had pleased its mass readership, whether or not they had passed critical muster.

In *What Was Literature?*, I had contended that this breaking down the boundaries between High Art and Pop would enable us to read without prejudice hitherto despised works by underprivileged groups in our society: women; Black Americans; Native Americans; homosexuals; Hispanics; even Rednecks, the "niggers" of the presumably enlightened. Such works had been underestimated, it seemed to me, because the earlier makers of our canon had been chiefly college-educated, straight WASP males, who (speaking only to each other) had found it possible to identify their parochial prejudices with universal aesthetic standards. With this diagnosis of our cultural plight, militant feminists, gays, Indians, and Afro-Americans seemed at first sight to agree.

They too, however, turned out to be untrustworthy allies—finally, only another kind of enemy. To begin with, some of them, though dedicated to opening up the canon in terms of gender and race, still smuggled in the old elitist distinctions of High and Low. A recent highly respected history of African-American literature, for instance (its author himself black), not only ignores a street writer like Iceberg Slim, but passes over in silence Frank Yerby, the most widely read author of his race; and does not even mention the immensely talented Samuel Delany—presumably because his books, marketed as science fiction, are, whatever their intrinsic merits, generically extra-canonical.

Even more disconcertingly, such "progressive" revisers of the canon end by excluding as well as including works on ideological grounds; so that their new canon is finally even narrower than the reactionary one they began by deploring. On the one hand, they urge teaching works written by members of previously underesteemed groups in our society, along with those written by anyone which present what are considered at the moment in liberal academic circles correct views on ethnicity, sexuality, age and physical impairment. Yet at the same time, and on the same high moral/political grounds, they urge dropping from our curriculum books which support views on the subjects with which they happen at the moment to disagree, labeling them "racist," "sexist," "ageist," "homophobic," etc. etc. The more fanatic and finicky among them even consider the use of the customary colloquial derogatory names for embattled minorities sufficient grounds for snatching books from the hands of students. But it is notoriously hard to keep up with such lexical orthodoxy. "Darky" and "coon," much less "nigger," have long been deemed dirty words by the "enlightened"; but more recently "negro" has become suspect and even "Afro-American" not quite kosher enough.

Worst of all, though, is the demand of some ardent multiculturalists for the proportional representation in the canon of hitherto excluded minorities. Certainly, the drive to include a percentage of, say, Native and African-American novelists and poets equal to what their people make up in the total population has proved a total disaster in our polyethnic United States; since it has led to exclusion of certain writers who have pleased many and pleased long, simply because they happen to be "DWEMs." "Dead White European Males," however, happen to have written most of the books read and loved by such minorities once they have attained literacy. Moreover, these former oppressors have also invented the genres in which the formerly oppressed are presently seeking to render their unique experiences.

Please understand, when I speak of the calamitous resolutes of such misguided book-banning, I am not just thinking of the lunatic political fringe which annually calls for keeping a "racist" *Huckleberry Finn* out of the classroom. Much less am I referring to the yahoos who picket with equal self-righteousness campus buildings where *The Birth of a Nation* is being shown and those in which courses in the Great Books of Western Civilization are being taught. Such protestors are the victims of their own ignorance. Not only are they incapable of reading books or films in any way but ideologically; they are also unaware that the so-called "Western Civilization" has always been multicultural.

In its centuries of imperialist expansion the West, even as it has sought to impose some of its own values on alien cultures it has encountered, has simultaneously assimilated theirs. So Longfellow sought to render Native-American legend in the meter of Finnish epic, at the same historical moment that Thoreau and Whitman and Emerson were attempting to make Persian and Hindu myth available to the world of middle-class WASPs. Nor did the process cease in the age of High Modernism, when Ezra Pound dedicated himself to re-imagining contemporary experience in terms of Zen poetry and Confucian philosophy; while at the same time Picasso was learning from African sculpture new ways to see and render the human face.

But this was only to be expected; since from its very beginnings Western culture was rooted in many cultures. It was born, after all, in the eastern Mediterranean, where the Middle East and Europe, Hebraism and Hellenism, the Semitic and the Japhetic merge. But Hamitic elements were present from the start, too. Not only did the Greeks learn much from the Egyptians, but writers whom we think of as belonging to a world dominated by Greece and Rome were in fact Africans: Aesop, for instance, and Apuleius, Terence, and Saint Augustine. Moreover, even after the invention of nationalist Europe, such canonical writers as Dumas and Pushkin were of African descent. To be sure, they made it into the canon—in this respect, quite like Europeanized Jews, from Spinoza and Heine to Proust and Kafka—not because of their alien ethnic origin, but in bland disregard of that fact.

No, it is not the rabid racist "anti-racists" who disturb me finally. It is rather the well-intentioned and knowledgeable young people, misled by (alas, only half-understood) attempts at opening the canon, including my own. I have just learned, for instance, that the most recently hired young instructor at a private secondary school where my wife teaches in his proposed list of readings for an introductory course in American Literature did not include a single book by Hawthorne, Melville, Twain, Hemingway or Faulkner. But, of course, women and African-American writers—most of lesser distinction—were dutifully included. He was, of course, only trying to be "politically correct," as that term is defined by the liberal academic establishment; yet in doing so he was—perhaps unwittingly—collaborating in the creation of what may well be the most totalitarian of all canons. Not merely is it as narrow as the Modernist canon which preceded it; but, unlike the latter, it is immune to criticism in the sense that anyone who objects to it is morally suspect. That is to say, it is based not on aesthetic standards, about which men of goodwill can disagree; it rests rather on ideological and ethical values, which its advocates believe to be not just something to which they happen to subscribe at the moment but one valued for all times and places, *right* forever.

Confusingly, however, many of those who are opposed to Political Correctness are equally sure that their notions about what the "Western Tradition" is—and therefore what the canon should be—are eternally right. In support of their contention they claim a direct line of descent from Plato and Sophocles; though, in fact, their genteel standards date back no further than Queen Victoria and the Boston Brahmins. Similarly, their opponents would have us believe that their ideological approach is rooted in the teachings of those anti-Victorian Victorians, Marx and Engels; though their rhetoric smacks more of the Fireside chats of Franklin Delano Roosevelt. The current debate about the canon seems, therefore, not a confrontation between eternal verities, but an extension of the journalistic debate between left-wing Democrats and right-wing Republicans. This is only to be expected, in any case, since an overwhelming majority of the elite academic community tends to support the former, while an equal percentage of extra-academic middle Americans continues stubbornly to vote for the latter.

Consequently, most of the spokesmen for the recent backlash against "multiculturalism" are politicians and bureaucrats elevated to power in the Reagan-Bush administrations, plus a handful of hard-line conservative newspaper columnists, whose highest ambition is to be reprinted in *Reader's Digest*. But they include also elitist college professors like Allan Bloom, whose reactionary *Closing of the American Mind* (with an approving introduction by the Nobel Laureate, Saul Bellow) had already become a best seller even before the current pedagogical debate had been reduced to journalistic platitudes. The readership of that ill-tempered diatribe did not consist mainly of arrant yahoos, but included some who buy books and may even read them: primarily, I assume, college-educated parents of the students we are currently teaching.

Like Bloom himself, they may have been permanently traumatized by the cultural revolution of the sixties; and they are therefore profoundly disturbed to discover their children being taught by survivors of those troubled times, now tenured and aging, but dedicated still to the subversive values they then espoused. But surely, such parents end by thinking, if everything such "progressive" teachers teach is wrong, wrong, wrong, everything in the tradition they deny (and which Bloom supports) must be right, right, right—and should therefore be not merely advocated but enforced.

Such self-righteous yea-sayers agree with their self-lefteous opponents on only one thing: that not to choose between them, not to take sides is the ultimate betrayal of culture. I, alas, find little or nothing to choose; but how to say so and be heard has long been and remains for me still a problem. Initially, I thought it would be sufficient simply to keep on repeating the cryptic phrase of Melville's which I have made my *leitmotif* throughout my writing career: "All men who say yes lie . . ." I feared, though, that those I addressed, contemptuous of ambivalence and unprepared to admit that all things—even our most dearly held pieties—change with time, would not listen. And so I ended up repeating in the silence of my troubled head (what I at long last say aloud here) the wish I once heard William Burroughs express: that a toxin might be invented which would destroy all those who think they are right.

It occurs to me, however, as I prepare to conclude, that there is such a toxin, namely, literature itself. To be sure, on the didactic or ideological level, song and story may seem to confirm the values of the social groups by whom and for whom it is written, thus preserving the status quo. But on deeper archetypal levels (and all literature which survives its historical moment is rooted in archetypes), it prepares for change by expressing the otherwise unconfessed dark side of our ambivalence: chiefly our hatred and fear of the Other. That Other is, though customarily defined in terms of race, gender, generation, or class, a projection of all that is unredeemably alien in the depths of our own psyches.

It is for this reason that the books we teach will deliver us (at least so I assure myself) not just from the fashionable methodologies with which we approach them and the currently fashionable canonical distinctions we vainly seek to impose; but finally from the temptation to believe that—unlike our deluded predecessors—we have at long last really got it *right*.

Ezra Pound:
The Poet as Parodist

Everyone knows from childhood on what parody is. Certainly I remember (and I can hardly be unique in this regard) reciting parodies of certain school-anthology poems long before I had encountered the originals. Nonetheless, I feel compelled to begin—though I risk self-parody as a pedant thereby—with a pair of dictionary definitions that distinguish two meanings often blurred in our everyday usage of what is after all an ambiguous term. One kind of parody, which I shall refer to hereafter as intentional, pejorative parody, Webster defines as "a writing in which the language or style of an author is imitated for comic effect . . ."; while the other, which I shall henceforth call inadvertent, honorific (more properly, I suppose, would-be honorific) parody, is described as "imitation that is faithful to a degree but that is weak, ridiculous, or distorted." I am uncomfortably aware, however, that in the latter sense all writing which emulates or pays homage to an earlier model or aspires to establish its credentials as real canonical literature by evoking a tradition runs the risk of becoming parodic—is, I am tempted to say, willy-nilly, parodic or quasiparodic. Yet it took a long time before critics or writers became aware of this fact. Vergil, for instance, seems to have been blissfully unaware that there was anything funny about attempting to write—on order, and for pay—a Homeric Epic in the age of Augustus; as was Dante when he tried to write a Vergilian one—travestying a travesty, as it were, in the time of scholastic Christianity. Perhaps even Shakespeare did not suspect that his *Titus Andronicus* burlesques the Senecan horror drama which it seems to emulate, though in the dying twentieth century it has become impossible, for some of us at least, to sit through that play with a straight face. This is because we are the heirs of Modernism, and our sensibilities are sharpened by poets and novelists defensively self-aware, which is to say, prepared to laugh at themselves before their readers laugh at them. The moment at which the founding fathers of Modernism triumphed was, it should be remembered, also the moment of the triumph of Mass Culture. Consequently, they could scarcely have remained unaware that the traditional High Culture of the West, of which they felt themselves to be the last alienated spokesmen (alienated from the great majority of their contemporaries precisely because of their nostalgia for that dying tradition), could be preserved even for the minority audience of their peers only if the great writers of the past who had established it were ironically undercut even as they were piously evoked. "These fragments I have shored against my ruins," is the classic phrase with which T. S. Eliot described the mode of honorific (a rather, perhaps, ambivalent, bipolar) parody by allusion and quotation central to his own poetic practice and to that of most other modernist masters as well. In *The Waste Land*, for instance, he echoes certain elegant anthology pieces, apparently all that is still recoverable of an admired but irrelevant cultural heritage: "So many I had not thought death but had undone so many . . ."; "The Chair she sat on like a burnished throne . . ."; "Sweet Thames run softly till I sing my song . . ."; "When lovely woman stoops to folly . . ." By placing them in inappropriately banal and sordid contexts, he makes their very elegance seem a little absurd; this managing simultaneously to satirize—however tenderly, lovingly—both those texts themselves, and—more brutally, the modern world of anomie and pop culture, in which not even he can any longer take them quite seriously.

At the same time, moreover, he also parodies pop culture itself, particularly the pop songs which most of the world in which he sought to make himself heard preferred not just to his own verse but to that of Dante and Spenser and Goldsmith and Shakespeare. "O O O O that Shakespearian rag. It's so elegant so intelligent . . ." an anonymous voice sings, parodying his evocation of the Bard. And we recall, as he apparently could not forget, that "The Love Song of J. Alfred Prufrock" and Irving Berlin's "Alexander's Ragtime Band" appeared at the same historical moment. But the bipolar parody of *The Waste Land* cuts deeper than that; since its very structure, what tenuous coherence and form it has, depends on an evocation with similar parodic intent of the archetypal tale of the Quest of the Holy Grail.

That pagan-Christian myth which in times with Europe was still both pagan and Christian, but in any case pious, possessed the deep imagination of both the courtly and folk audience, had, to be sure, not quite died in the secular, skeptical age into which Eliot was born. It persisted, however, chiefly in the nursery and the academy, in illustrated children's books and footnoted studies written by scholars for scholars. The debt of Eliot was chiefly to the latter, as the parodically pedantic footnotes which he appended to his poetic text make clear: confessing that the source of his inspiration was not the *Perceval* of Chrétien de Troyes or Malory's *Morte D'Arthur*—much less Tennyson's *Idylls of the King*—but *The Golden Bough* of James Frazer and, especially, Jessie L. Weston's *From Ritual to Romance*.

So also Eliot's fellow High Modernist, James Joyce, plays in his mock epic *Ulysses* the game of bipolar parody by evoking and travestying the archetypal story of the wanderings of Odysseus on his long way home. Not merely does he pathetically translate the magic kingdoms of the Mediterranean into the squalid urban environment of Dublin; but by suggesting that the comic-pathetic, uncircumcised Jew, Leopold Bloom, is all the Odysseus such a world can produce or afford, he also insidiously suggests that perhaps his Homeric prototype may have been nothing more. Thus he calls into question the very notion not just of the Hero but of the Heroic Poem—perhaps even of poetry itself, the Western tradition of which, after all, begins with Homer. Some, indeed (including Joyce's brother, Stanislaus), have contended that *Ulysses* as a whole must be read as a travesty, a put-on or send-up not just of the myth of Odysseus but also of the ironic book we hold in our hand and of the notion of High Culture to which that book declares its ironic allegiance.

Not that Joyce (though in fact he consumed its products as avidly as any shopgirl) takes popular culture quite seriously either, mocking it, in fact, throughout *Ulysses*. He parodies, for instance, in the "Nausicaa" episode the tone and diction of a sentimental Victorian Ladies' best seller called *The Lamplighter*, a novel which—to compound the joke even more—almost none of the academic critics of Joyce, who do not in general share his taste for *schlock*, would be likely to recognize. But all of them do, of course, recognize the English prose styles, ranging from the Anglo-Saxon Chronicles to Dickens and beyond, travestied in the "Oxen in the Sun" episode, that tour de force of auto-parodic pedantry, which has become an occasion for further pedantry from those too learned to realize the joke is on them.

In any case, I would argue, travesty, parody and burlesque have been the hallmarks of Modernism from the start. It is, therefore, scarcely surprising to discover that they are omnipresent in the poetry (and prose) of Ezra Pound, who is not merely one of the key figures in, but an apologist for and promoter of, that most self-conscious and self-advertised of all literary movements—its impresario-in-chief, as it were.

Pound as a parodist, however, not merely by virtue of his Modernism; but, even more perhaps, by virtue of his Americanism, for he is hopelessly, unre-deemably American—more American by far than T. S. Eliot, as American as Whitman or Longfellow. And this (as I shall try eventually to make clear) not so much despite as because of his long self-exile in Europe, and his shrill, almost hysterically declared allegiance to Old World Culture; in presumed defense of which (as represented by Mussolini!), he risked imprisonment or death as a traitor to his own country. American poets, however, as W. H. Auden once contended, and I do in fact believe, are prone to inadvertent parody of a particular sort. "The danger of the American poet," Auden wrote, reflecting on the resemblances and even more conspicuous differences of a group of such poets which included William Carlos Williams, Vachel Lindsay,

Marianne Moore, Wallace Stevens, E. E. Cummings, Laura Riding and, of course, Pound, "is not that of writing like everybody else but of crankiness and a parody of his own manner."

The poets to whom Auden specifically refers belong to a single generation which came of age in the early twentieth century, and his observation is made in an attempt to define the differences between modernist verse in England and the United States. But, of course, American writers had been falling into the same trap even before the rise of Modernism, indeed, since the very beginnings of literature in English on this side of the Atlantic; and the reasons are obvious. We have never had a standard received literary tradition any more than we have had a standard received literary language. Our writers, therefore, have always had to invent and reinvent both—with, as T. S. Eliot puts it, "great labour," and they have all consequently run the risk (it is a source of their special charm, as well as their peculiar plight) of falling into ridiculous eccentricity.

Nor does it matter whether, like Poe and Melville and Longfellow, they have sought to construct a patchwork pseudo-tradition out of the scraps of European High Culture, which they happened to know and love, or, like Whitman and Mark Twain, they have opted for making an anti-tradition of traditionlessness. If the "barbaric yawp" of Whitman's *Leaves of Grass,* with its vaunt of having canceled out all "old debts to Greece and Rome," trembles eternally on the edge of self-travesty, so also does Longfellow's *Hiawatha,* with its Indian lore dutifully worked up out of scholarly sources and improbably rendered in a meter borrowed from a Finnish Epic known in America only to university professors. Both have, therefore, been more ultimately parodied (which is to say, pushed over that perilous edge) ever since. In Longfellow's case, this has usually been done with deliberate malice or condescension; in Whitman's, most often inadvertently, in inept homage, as in the worst of Carl Sandburg. Indeed, it is hard to emulate either of these two laureates of mid-nineteenth-century America without falling, willy-nilly, into burlesque. Yet Pound tried with both.

Longfellow, who was his great-uncle, he apparently despised but could never quite manage to exorcize from his undermind. In fact, though, as T. E. Lawrence once observed, he tried from early adolescence to define for himself a life-style as diverse as possible from that of his New England Brahmin ancestor; helplessly, hopelessly, he turned into a kind of unwitting caricature of him: a University Professor of Comparative Literature (fired from his first job, to be sure, for sharing his room with a transvestite actress out of a traveling burlesque show) and an apostle of hightone Old World Culture, which he translated from many tongues for the benefit of his philistine compatriots who spoke only their own. Moreover, impelled by God knows what vestigial pieties, Pound published in 1913 what may well be the only straightfaced imitation of *Hiawatha* in print, in which he chants with, apparently, no sense of being ridiculous:

> If you press me for the legend,
> For the story of the maiden
> Of the laughing Indian maiden
> Of the radiant Minnehaha

To be sure, as if to make up for this gaffe, he published some twenty or twenty-five years later, this time with malice aforethought, a parody of the best-known and most anthologized of his great-uncle's patriotic pieces, beginning, "Listen my children and you shall hear/ The midnight activities of What's-his-name..." To this he attached, lest some obtuse reader fail to get the already obvious satirical point, an epigraph written, apparently by A. Orage, but surely at Pound's prompting: "Here's another improvement on a worn-out model. I did it very nearly in my sleep..."

Whitman, who seems to have haunted him waking, as Longfellow did him sleeping, Pound never either imitates so piously or caricatures so wickedly. Nevertheless, he does echo him over and over, even occasionally referring to him by name. As far as I know, however, no mainstream Poundian critic (perhaps because none of them has read Whitman hard and well) has ever dealt adequately with the equivocal but pervasive influence on the author of *The Cantos* of the author of *Leaves of Grass,* another unfinished, unfinishable, cranky, not-quite epic. But Pound himself, of course, had read Whitman hard and well from quite an early time, and he continued to wrestle all his life long with his oedipal ambivalence toward the older poet.

Even before he had publicly made peace with him in "A Poet" ("I come to you as a grown child/ Who has had a pig-headed father/ I am old enough to make friends.")—just after his first arrival in Europe, in fact—Pound wrote a six-page essay called "What I Think of Walt Whitman." In it he confessed, rather grudgingly, "I see him as America's poet..."; he then hastened to add, with characteristic unconsciously comic arrogance, "I honor him because he prophesied me"; after which he went on to assure anyone interested that it was not Whitman's "tricks" (meaning his metrical strategies, his unique diction, tone and voice) that he proposed to make his own, only his "message."

This turns out to be, however, the very reverse of the truth, since Pound in fact tends everywhere to subvert Whitman's "message," his euphoric celebration of democracy and mass society, along with his attack on the traditional High Culture of Europe. But he uses for that purpose (thus simultaneously parodying himself and his model) Whitman's whole bag of "tricks," particularly his metrics: that dactylic or triple falling rhythm, which is characteristic not just of Whitman but of all American as opposed to British speech and provides a viable homegrown alternative to the Old World iambs which Pound prided himself on having broken.

Moreover, Whitman's diction, his odd blend of the adorned rhetorical and the nakedly colloquial, provided Pound with a model he desperately needed in order to escape from the archaizing, studiedly quaint poetic diction that blights his earliest poetry: all those "thees" and "thous" and "haths" which he had learned (twenty years too late, as he himself eventually confessed) from the English Pre-Raphaelites and other exponents of the pseudo-Gothic and the late Victorian "sublime." Some of Pound's first reviewers claimed to detect the influence of Whitman even in his early *fin de siècle* poems; but not until *Ripostes* (1912) does he produce a poem which seems to me even remotely Whitmanian. The very title of "N.Y." is a tribute to the first laureate of Manhattan, and the line "Here are a million people surly with traffic" could not have been written without his example. But Pound is still clinging to the cloyingly affected "thou art" and "thou shalt," still afraid to say, like his not quite acknowledged master, simply "you."

He did finally learn to use unabashed that neutral second-person pronoun, which makes impossible discrimination between stranger and familiar, inferior and superior, even singular and plural, in certain uncollected poems like "To Whistler, American," which appeared in 1912, and "Pax Saturni," which appeared a year later. He thus released in himself the true Whitmanian voice and style, complete with incremental repetitions at the beginning of successive lines that not only establish an incantatory cadence but underscore the paradoxes they contain:

> Say there are no oppressions . . .
> Say that labor is pleasant . . .
> Say that I am a traitor . . .

By 1916 he was able to write in *Lustra* (my own favorite collection, perhaps for this reason, of Pound's poetry) verses so close to the Whitmanian model that they seem counterfeits, impersonations, trembling on the verge of parody.

> Go my songs to the lonely and unsatisfied . . .
> Go to the bourgeoisie who is dying of her ennuis.
> Go to the women in suburbs,
> Go to the hideously wedded . . .

> Go to those who have delicate lust . . .
> Go out and defy opinion . . .

And the joke implicit in such ambiguous imitations is compounded by the continuing attack in them on their unmistakable model:

> There is no use your quoting Whitman against me,
> His time is not our time, his day and hour were different.

Even in those poems in *Lustra* which do not employ so obviously Whitman's "tricks," Pound found himself able at long last to be comic, irreverent and downright vulgar, rather than solemn, hightone and genteel; his posture no longer that of one too *good* for the America which he had abandoned yet could not cease hectoring and haranguing—but of one who is instead, or at least also—too *bad*. It is therefore fitting (after all, Whitman had been labeled "the dirtiest beast of the age") that for the first and, I think, the last, the only time in the career of this self-styled rebel, four of his poems intended for *Lustra* were precensored, discreetly dropped by his timid publisher before the book ever appeared as being—sixty years past the publication date of *Leaves of Grass*—too blasphemous and/or obscene. In these poems, moreover, and others less obviously offensive ("Study in Aesthetics," for instance, "The Lake Isle," "The Bath Tub" and "The Gypsy") he was able, thanks once more to Whitman, to write in easy conversational rhythms and an unpretentious demotic diction, so that one is tempted (I, at any rate, am tempted) to think rereading them, hearing them in my inner ear: Here, if anywhere, is the true voice of Ezra Pound, the man of a hundred borrowed voices.

For a long time I was convinced that Pound had no authentic voice of his own at all—only, like a ventriloquist's dummy, pseudo-voices speaking in pseudo-tongues. I am thinking not only of the mock archaic "British" diction of his earlier poems, his translations from the Provençal and the Italian and, alas, much of *The Cantos* but also of the counterfeit colloquial "American" dialects, which he uses more rarely in *The Cantos*, but almost compulsively in his personal letters, early and late, much of his hard-core pornography and especially in his infamous wartime propaganda broadcasts on the Italian radio.

In a letter to a friend about Eliot's possible reaction to the book with which this symposium is centrally concerned, for instance, he writes in execrable Minstrel Show dialect, "And how you gwine to keep Possum in his feedbox when I brings in the Chinas and blackmen? He won't laak for to see no Chinas and blackmen in a bukk about Kulchur." Similarly unconvincing versions of colloquial American (white rather than black) appear also in some of his earliest "light verse." Nor are they confined entirely to poems written for private consumption, like the one included in a letter to his father, sent just after the granting of his M.A., in which he imagines that beleaguered parent complaining, "While you rushed the can/ And played the man/ Smokin' your fine cheroots,/ I had to pay/ In a hefty way/ for a coon to black your boots." Then speaking for himself, the young poet confesses, "Go little verse, by gumbo, go."

That same pseudo-voice in a similar stage-hick accent is heard in Pound's first published poem as well: a parody of James Whitcomb Riley called "Ezra on the Strike," but with no author's name attached:

> Wal, Thanksgivin' do be comin' round,
> With the price of turkeys on the bound,
> And coal, by gum! that was just found
> Is surely gettin' cheaper.

The title alone is insufficient evidence (fortunately there is other proof) of authorship, since "Ezra" was in the early twentieth century just another disparaging nickname for farmers like "rube" or "hayseed" or "hick." Indeed it is this fact that makes it almost inevitable that one of Pound's favorite parodic voices was, and would remain for as long as he wrote, his version of how subliterate rural Americans talked.

He returns to that voice, at any rate, in the propaganda broadcasts he delivered over the Italian radio during "World War II": those would-be chummy chats in which he tried to persuade his fellow citizens back home that Franklin Delano Roosevelt was stark raving mad and a Jew to boot and that the war into which the "higher kikery" had dragged the unwitting WASPs of England and America was an assault against European culture, civilization itself. That "culture" and "civilization" he conveniently forgot that he himself had described, a war earlier and in a more authentic voice, as "an old bitch gone in the teeth . . . two gross of broken statues . . . a few thousand battered books." Sometimes his language in these broadcasts comes so close to downright travesty of American speech that it is tempting to believe he was only kidding or perhaps deliberately trying to subvert the cause he presumably served, putting one over on Mussolini's intelligence service, which after long soul-searching, had authorized his talks.

But alas, he fooled no one except himself when he said in pseudo-American, "I will teach you kids why you were drugged into the war . . ." or "Democracy has been licked to a frazzle. Property has vamoosed. It has went." If he seems sometimes (not only in these broadcasts but occasionally in *The Cantos* as well, whose paranoiac, obsessive compulsive politics and bigotry are indistinguishable from those expressed in his political prose) like a non-native speaker, a double agent from elsewhere trying to pass as an American, he did not know it. Yet sometimes when he was making poems rather than propaganda, his voice is as authentically, unmistakably American as that of Whitman or Mark Twain, Hemingway or Faulkner.

How seldom, though, even in his verse did he find that voice: throughout *Lustra,* as I have already observed, and the first part of *Hugh Selwyn Mauberley* as well; intermittently in *Cathay* and *The Cantos,* particularly the *Pisan Cantos,* where a pain deeper than politics, and a pathos more genuine than self-pity moved him to forsake crankiness and self-parody. It is, in fact, for the sake of this slim remnant of verse that I have accepted your invitation and have slogged once more through the intolerably incoherent and tedious rest of Pound's work, in which his authentic voice is drowned out by a cacophony of counterfeit pseudo-voices in a macaronic echo-chamber, which blur finally into white noise.

The point is that Pound lost faith in the genuine voice he had discovered in 1916 and betrayed it in what is for me an act of treason against himself and against poetry more reprehensible by far than that against his country with which he was legally charged. Yet the former, like the latter, is excusable perhaps on the grounds of "insanity": which is to say, the obsessions (USURA is the root of all evil, Il Duce is our Savior), the paranoia (the yids are doing us in) and especially the ever-increasing dissociation which afflicted him both in his life and his work. Such disappointment classically manifests itself in the "splitting" of personality, the emergence, once the ego boundaries have been breached, of multiple quasi-personae, speaking in diverse voices for diverse aspects of an intolerably conflicted psyche.

Pound's defenses against such ever-growing dissociation were weapons out of the arsenal of art: the therapeutic acting out of the threatened fragmentation of the self. In his case, this meant the use, on the one hand, of travesty and burlesque and on the other, of translation and "masking," especially the Dramatic Monologue which he had learned from Robert Browning. Finally, even, his defenses became indistinguishable from his symptoms. The puppets took over from the puppet master—their simulated voices drowning out his own real one. Finally, even parody no longer served to exorcise the alien personae which possessed him. Yet he continued compulsively his life-long practice of travesty and burlesque, taking, for instance, one last parodic smack at Browning late in *The Cantos* ("Oh to be in England now that Winston's out"), which is to say, evoking yet again the Ur-mask he had assumed in order to begin: evoking the poet in whose parodied voice he had originally intended—indeed, had begun—to write all of *The Cantos.*

From the mid-thirties on, in any case, Pound seems to have been at least on the borderline of insanity. It was at that point, for instance, that James Joyce begged Hemingway to accompany him—as a kind of bodyguard—to a dinner *chez* Pound; confessing that he thought him "mad" and was "genuinely frightened of him": an opinion in which Hemingway concurred, observing later that at their meal together Pound had spoken "very erratically." In light of this, it seems somehow fitting that Pound's last published collection of shorter verse, *The Poems of Alfred Venison*, which appeared at that very moment, turned out to be, as its title indicates, hardcore parody: nearly a score of mocking reworkings of the favorite anthology pieces of popular Victorian bards—including not only Tennyson but also Kipling and even Longfellow. Despite the inclusion of that eminent American, however, they were all written in what Pound clearly intended to be Cockney dialect, though it bears about as little resemblance to actual lower-class, urban English speech as the dialect of "Ezra on the Strike" had to genuine rural mid-American.

Between his earliest and latest ventures into parody, moreover, Pound had published similar jocular takeoffs, some wicked, some affectionate, of verse by Byron and Burns, A. E. Housman and Swinburne, as well as the Medieval popular lyric and the poetry of the Irish Renaissance. One of the best of these, his travesty of "Lhude sing Cuckoo," whose irreverent refrain "Lhude sing Goddamn" had led to its being dropped from the first edition of *Lustra*, has since become a standard anthology piece, a part of the Pound canon as taught in our schools. This seems not only a wry joke on changing times and tastes but also a clue to the fact—still generally ignored by critics—that such parody is central to Pound's work.

Indeed (it is an equivocal boast that can be made of no other poet with claims to real distinction, even among parody-prone Americans and Modernists), if all Pound's work in this intentionally burlesque mode were gathered together, it would make a substantial and not unimpressive volume. It would be even more substantial and impressive if one were to add a selection of some of the many unintentionally hilarious boners which are to be found in his "translations." Robert Graves speaks somewhere of asking his children, who were at home in Mallorcan, a Romance language closely akin to Provençal, what they thought of Pound's approximately English versions of Arnaut Daniel; at which, he tells us, they laughed and laughed and *laughed*. It is a response, I must confess, to which I (who invested a couple of years of my own graduate-student days in the study of poetry in that tongue) am also tempted; as I am, too, rereading Pound's overstuffed, self-indulgent renderings of the slim and austere verses of the Medieval Italian poet Guido Cavalcanti, in which a simple and straightforward phrase like *morte gentil* becomes the pretentiously archaic "death who art haught."

So others—not all of them pedants by any means—have sniggered at his infamous goof in translating the Old English phrase *eorthen rices* in "The

Seafarer" as "earthen riches," though of course it means "earthly kingdoms," as well as at his apparent belief in a nonexistent poet called Ri Haku—arising from a failure to realize that this "name" represents only a Japanese reading of the ideograms which spell Li Po.

Such absurdities are risked, of course, not just by translators but by all poets (I think once more of Walt Whitman) who like Pound have the chutzpah to rush in where timid and learned scholars fear to tread. Indeed, I honor him for it; honor him all the more, because I realize, as he clearly did not, that by such travesty he subverts unconsciously the high culture for which he was consciously so solemn, and therefore doubly comic, an apologist—campaigning all his life long, for instance, like some parody schoolmaster, for reinstituting compulsory Latin in America's schools.

In light of all this, you will scarcely be surprised to discover that I think the best way of reading (the only way really to redeem) *The Cantos* themselves is by reading them as unintended—or perhaps subintended—parody. His *magnum opus*, I am suggesting, is not a failed Epic, though it seemed so to Pound's most sympathetic advocate, T. S. Eliot, and, for that matter, even to him, who when near his death spoke of the long poem at which he had labored for so many years as *sbagliato*, botched, a mistake from the start. It is rather a mock epic, an anti-epic, a comic travesty of the genre, and consequently (as I would dearly love to believe that at some level he suspected) a joke on himself as well as on the latter-day pious Poundolators who do not realize as much. What else are we to make of the passage in Canto 41, in which he approvingly quotes the comments on a sample of his work by Mussolini: "Ma questo" said the boss "è divertente" (the adjective, of course, means "amusing," not to be taken seriously); then he adds, "catching the point/ before the aesthetes had got there."

After such a warning how can "the aesthetes" still read *The Cantos* with a straight face? Had Pound not revealed his not-so-secret parodic intent, even before the fact, as it were, in the title of an early poem, which travesties the famous opening line of the *Aenead*, "Famam Librosque Cano." This warns us clearly enough, does it not, that he sings, will continue to sing, *not* like his Latin model, Arms and the Man, Warfare and the Hero, but Fame and Books, which is to say, making it by producing literature about literature, a scarcely heroic—though diverting—theme.

The Cantos, moreover, not only lack a heroic theme; they lack a heroic protagonist as well. Indeed, they have no proper protagonist at all, not even a parodic one. For a little while, in the earlier Cantos, Odysseus promises to play such a role. He is ironized from the start, however, by the fact that he appears not in a text translated by Homer, but the English version of a Renaissance Latin crib of the original, thrice removed from the original. And even this ghost of a ghost of a ghost soon fades from the scene, or rather, persists only in echoes of the false name Odysseus gave himself as part of his bloody practical joke on the Cyclops. "*Ou tis*" is that name, No Man, Nobody, an appellation nearly anonymous, and therefore fitting for a poet without a proper persona or voice of his own.

What we hear in *The Cantos* is, finally, Nobody talking in garbled and half-understood tongues about a world in which, culture having become Kulchur, nothing matters. Consequently, despite all the references, literary and historical, the allusions and quotations, the dropped names of the living and the dead, the self-annihilating *Cantos* are about Nothing at all.

Only having realized this will the reader be ready to recognize that the real model for *The Cantos* is not Homer's *Odyssey*, much less Vergil's or Dante's pseudo-Homeric Epics, or even Walt Whitman's *Leaves of Grass*. It is, rather, Flaubert's *Bouvard et Pécuchet*, a thoroughly unreadable work which Pound so extravagantly admired all the same, perhaps because it bears the same parodic relationship to the bourgeois novel as his unfinished, unfinishable poem does to the classic Epic. Flaubert's anti-novel not merely was, but was intended to be, as he warned in announcing it, a book "about nothing." I want to produce, he wrote, "such an impression of lassitude and ennui that as people read the book they will think of its being written by a cretin." Indeed, the same can be said of *The Cantos*, with the substitution perhaps of "madman" for "cretin." Both, at any rate, represent polar, absolute, terminal Parody, parody degree zero, in the sense that no more ultimate parody can be written of either, as I must confess I have tried more than once—producing each time, alas, results less absurd than the original. *Ma questo è divertente.*

Francis Scott Fitzgerald

We have come to consider Scott Fitzgerald one of the major novelists of the early twentieth century, ranking him with Faulkner and Hemingway. Yet of his novels only *The Great Gatsby* is completely successful—coherent in structure and unified in tone, as his others are not. Ironically enough, however, its subject is not success but failure. But this seems only fitting, since despite its posthumous acclaim, its author, like his protagonist, failed both in love and in his quest to be accepted by those lucky enough to have been born rich.

He died, in fact, poor and frantic in Hollywood, the scene of his final failure, leaving behind fragments of *The Last Tycoon*, an unfinishable book about the ambiguity of success. It was his last contribution to the metafiction which he lived rather than wrote, and which has been continued after his death by journalists and gossip-mongerers, as well as young authors who think of themselves as his heirs. Ironically enough, that metafiction is these days more widely known than anything Fitzgerald actually published; and for this he is best remembered and loved. But this would scarcely have surprised him, convinced as he was that in America just as nothing fails like success, nothing succeeds like failure.

Pop Goes the Faulkner:
In Quest of *Sanctuary*

Though I had never stopped reading and rereading Faulkner and attempting to come to terms with his achievement in the privacy of my own head, as the eighties came to a close I realized that I had published almost nothing about any of his books for more than a quarter of a century. During that time, to be sure, my interest had shifted from the art novel to popular fiction, novels which please the many who prefer reading pleasure unmeditated and unexamined, like *Gone with the Wind*, rather than those, like James Joyce's *Ulysses*, which provide opportunities for classroom exegesis and analysis to the few who get their kicks out of such second-hand responses to literature. But I had begun by thinking of Faulkner as a kind of American Joyce; as how could I not in light of the fact that I had been introduced to him by critic-pedagogues who taught me to read *The Sound and the Fury* and *Absalom, Absalom!* as modernist masterpieces, modeled on *Ulysses*.

Disconcertingly, however, as I have since discovered, Faulkner may well have never read *Ulysses* at all; and though certainly he did not read *Gone with the Wind* either (his only recorded comment on it is that no story should take a thousand words to tell) certain Hollywood producers recognized affinities between his work and Margaret Mitchell's. For a while, at any rate, they considered trying to use the nostalgic and sentimental stories about the Old South, eventually gathered together under the title of *The Unvanquished*, as the basis for a film which they hoped would rival, or at least share in the spectacular box-office success of, *Gone with the Wind*. It was a hope for which there seemed some warrant, since most of those short fictions had appeared originally in the *Saturday Evening Post*, most popular of all the family slicks.

To be sure, for this very reason perhaps, Faulkner was never proud of them; or, in any case, he pretended not to be, referring to them in private correspondence as "pulp" and "trash." Clearly he was embarrassed at being able to produce stories which pleased both the editors and readers of a journal in which he appeared side by side with such critically despised panderers to popular taste as Fannie Hurst, Edna Ferber and Octavus Roy Cohen—and was well paid for doing so. It was, indeed, precisely that embarrassment which prompted the infamous and ambiguous introductory note to *Sanctuary* in which he apologized for its weakness, describing it as "cheap because it was deliberately conceived to make money."

Yet all the same, he continued intermittently throughout his career to try to make it commercially—driven not only by economic pressures, as he found it easy to confess, but, as he found it harder to admit, by a desire, a need to communicate with the mass audience he affected to despise. Even less easily was he able to come to terms with the fact that he was good at doing so. Not only could he compete with the pros on the pages of the slicks; he could hold his own with veteran Hollywood hacks in turning out viable film scripts. Of the movies he helped write, *To Have and Have Not* and *The Big Sleep* have achieved the status of minor classics, and other well-crafted but uninspired Class B films like *The Last Slaver* continue to be replayed on cable off prime time.

In any case, both in print and on the screen, Faulkner provided pleasure to a large audience, most of whom would be unwilling to pick up except on assignment, and incapable of understanding, unless guided through them in the classroom, his denser more complex and more critically esteemed fictions, like *The Sound and the Fury* or even *As I Lay Dying*. Finally, as I was moved to observe many years ago, Faulkner managed to please "two audiences, each unaware of the fact, much less the grounds, of the other's appreciation."

The little review essay in which I first made this observation was prompted by the appearance in 1948 of Faulkner's *Collected Stories,* most of which (as well as his extravagantly admired "The Bear") had first been published in popular family magazines. But though I have reprinted that essay twice in the years since, it seems to have made almost no impression on the Faulkner critical establishment; which is, I suppose, why I am moved once more to try to make clear the sense in which Faulkner's "pop" stories (and by the same token, his "pop" novel, *Sanctuary*) represent not works of the left hand, irrelevant or peripheral, but the essence, the very center of his achievement.

In them, certainly, we can find a clue to what is less apparent in his more involuted and pretentious fictions: the fact that Faulkner is more like such nineteenth-century popular entertainers as Dickens and Twain than such alienated authors of our own century as Proust, Mann and Joyce. We must not be misled by Faulkner's own attempts to conceal this by identifying himself with the pioneers of modernism—particularly in the speeches which later in life he gave to academic audiences, from whom earlier on he had fled. In them, drop-out that he was, he assured the Ph.Ds assembled in his honor that he considered Mann and Joyce the greatest authors of the age, and the former in particular the founder of a literary tradition to which he himself belonged. But such remarks seem to me to have been prompted by a kind of second-hand cultural snobbism from which Faulkner never quite recovered, after having picked it up early in life—first from his friend and mentor, Phil Stone, and then from the highbrow bohemian types with whom he associated briefly in New Orleans, Greenwich Village and Paris.

Despite what he said and thought, however, I myself can find no evidence at all of the influence of Mann on Faulkner, and little enough of Joyce—beyond that of his poetry, which was as immune as Faulkner's own to the impact of modernism. To be sure, Faulkner sometimes uses the narrative mode called "stream of consciousness," so spectacularly exploited in *Ulysses;* but by the late twenties such interior monologues had become standard features of even the most provincial fiction. Besides, as I have already noted, Faulkner on at least one occasion asserted that he had never read *Ulysses.* To be sure, he is also on record as having asserted that he lied when he said so; so that it is finally impossible to know (he is a notoriously unreliable source of information about himself) whether or not he was lying about having lied in the first instance.

What we do know for certain is that when toward the very end of his life he accumulated a library for his residence in Charlottesville, Virginia, he included in it none of the master works of high modernism which he had publicly touted, but instead the novels of Cervantes, Hugo, Tolstoy and even Mark Twain's *Tom Sawyer* and *Huckleberry Finn*; though while still in the full throes of his youthful snobbism, he had described Twain as "a hack writer who would not have been considered fourth rate in Europe." But it was, of course, with the complete works of Dickens that he began—as how could he not? It was, after all, from that immensely popular Victorian novelist that his mother had read to him as a boy, and it was from his books too that he had read to his own daughter. *Martin Chuzzlewit,* in particular, seems to have possessed his imagination. Indeed, Sairy Gamp, the obese and drunken midwife, nurse and layer-out-of-the-dead, who steals that novel from its major characters, is re-embodied in Madame Reba, the comic-grotesque brothel keeper, who makes her first appearance in *Sanctuary* and her last in *The Reivers,* two of the most popular—in part for that reason perhaps—of all Faulkner's books.

Yet Faulkner himself nowhere that I know of confesses his indebtedness to Dickens; nor do the major critics of his work acknowledge it. Indeed, in the index to Cleanth Brooks's otherwise exhaustive study of the Yoknapatawpha fictions the name of that earlier novelist does not even appear. Albert Guerard, to be sure, in *The Triumph of the Novel* deals with the affinities between Faulkner and Dickens and Dostoevsky. What interests him, however, is what he takes to be the antimimetic, ludic, nonrepresentational narrative mode of their novels, the sense in which they can be understood to have established an alternative to what F. R. Leavis called "The Great Tradition": a countertradition which climaxes in our own time in the postmodernist fictions of Nabokov, Pynchon, Burgess, Hawkes, Barth and Barthelme. He therefore never pauses to reflect on the fact that both the popular nineteenth-century forerunners of Faulkner, quite unlike their alienated twentieth-century successors, were shamelessly cliché-ridden and unabashedly sentimental; and that it was this, indeed, which kept them unalienated from the mass audience.

But so (despite his ambivalence about making it in the marketplace) is Faulkner. Like Dickens before him—and unlike more recent authors who prefer irony to pathos—the sentimental is for him a prevailing mode. This is conspicuously true of his war stories, whether of World War I or the War between the States, in which the soupiest platitudes of self-sacrifice, blind courage, and honor are unabashedly exploited. But it tends to overwhelm him, too, whenever he deals with wide-eyed small boys, sturdy yeoman farmers and faithful black servants. It manifests itself even in *The Sound and the Fury*, where, despite the nihilism suggested by the Shakespearean quotation evoked in the title ("a tale told by an idiot . . . signifying nothing"), the final word in it is given to the believing Christian—as true blue as she is true black—Dilsey. It is a last minute cop-out reinforced by the phrase devoted to her in the appendix (an instant cliché, if there ever was one), "They endured."

Much admired by the flintiest-hearted elitist critics—afraid perhaps that to denigrate her might seem "racist"—Dilsey seems to me a dismayingly stock character, an Aunt Jemima type, scarcely distinguishable from the Black Mammy in whose arms Scarlett O'Hara seeks refuge at the end of *Gone with the Wind*; or for that matter, from Harriet Beecher Stowe's equally pious and faithful Uncle Tom (the gender difference is irrelevant, since both are essentially sexless). But finally, of course, almost all of Faulkner's females are stereotypes, though few of them are as benign as Dilsey. Besides Black Mammies like her, the only women in Faulkner rendered sympathetically are certain safely postmenopausal white old maids and widows. Fully sexed women are typically regarded with horror; except—in the opinion of many readers, including a few academic "specialists" in Faulkner—Ruby Lamar: that cliché Whore with a Heart of Gold, who seems to me always on the verge of breaking out into a tearful chorus of "He's my May-un." It should be remembered, however, that Horace Benbow, closest thing to a spokesman for the author in *Sanctuary*, finally turns in despair from Ruby, describing her as just another "stupid mammal."

In any case, all the other women in that profoundly misogynist novel, like most of their sisters everywhere in Faulkner's oeuvre, are products of the flipside of Faulkner's sentimental attitude toward their sex: his nauseated rage at them for refusing in "reality" to live up to the idealizing stereotypes of them as inviolate temples, sanctuaries of innocence. As in Dickens, the pejorative antistereotypes cued by that rage in Faulkner become, without ceasing to be stereotypes, caricatures, grotesques, at once horrific and comic. Think of Madame Reba once more—and specifically of the truly Dickensian scene after

Red's funeral, in which he and two other brothel keepers weep for the indignities of their sex—while a young relation of one of them drinks himself silly on the beer he has snitched behind their sobbing backs. It is perhaps because we are asked to laugh at rather than weep over such characters that even those of us totally committed to the aesthetics of modernism continue to find them acceptable. Certainly, ever since Oscar Wilde, the critical establishment has refused to be moved by the plight of such stereotyped monsters of incredible innocence as Little Nell, but has felt no qualms about responding to that of such equally stereotyped monsters of malevolence as Sally Brass and Quilp.

If Faulkner has proved easier for modernists to come to terms with than his Victorian master, this is because though there are in his work Quilps in great plenty (most of them called Snopes) and not a few Sally Brasses, there are no Little Nells. Even little Caddy in *The Sound and the Fury*, whom he once rather disconcertingly described as his "heart's darling," he does not kill off before the fall of puberty as Dickens did Little Nell, but permits her to grow up and lose her mythological innocence; as, indeed, he had foreshadowed from the very start by portraying her in "muddy drawers." In any case, throughout his earliest and best fiction (late in his career he tries, unconvincingly I think, to redeem them) Faulkner vilifies women, drawing on the copious stock of misogynist platitudes current in his time and place.

"No Jiggs and Maggie cliché of popular anti-feminism," I wrote nearly thirty years ago in *Love and Death in the American Novel*, "is too banal for him to use; he reminds us (again and again) that men are helpless in the hands of their mothers, wives and sisters . . . that females do not think but proceed from evidence to conclusions by paths too devious for men to follow . . . that they possess neither morality nor honor . . . that they are capable of betraying without guilt, but also of inexplicable loyalty . . . that they enjoy an occasional beating at the hands of men . . . that they are unforgiving and without charity to members of their own sex." What I did not then add, perhaps because I was not yet ready to confront head-on *Sanctuary*, of which it is the declared theme, is the final item of this pop misogynist credo: "women are completely impervious to evil."

With such views of the second sex, quite obviously the stereotypical Happy Ending of Boy-Gets-Girl, so dear to the hearts of the popular audience, is unavailable to Faulkner. Indeed (as Albert Guerard has so persuasively contended) consummated heterosexual passion is for him a taboo, a forbidden form of love. But in this regard he is scarcely unique among American writers, on all levels from the highest of high novelists to the purveyors of the sleaziest pop, who have managed (as I have been pointing out throughout my critical career) to provide an alternative happily-ever-after, which has pleased many and pleased long: joining together in the wilderness two males, one a white man or boy in flight from the world of white women, the other a nonwhite, red, black or brown, but in any case at home in the wilderness.

Such interethnic male bonding is to be found not only in our classic literature from Cooper to Melville and Twain; but it constitutes the erotic or sentimental center of latterday youth best sellers like *One Flew over the Cuckoo's Nest*. It has become finally a stereotype reimagined over and over in Hollywood movies, like *The Fortune Cookie* or *The Defamed Ones*; and it is a cliché re-embodied on television, especially on the Cop Shows in which a salt-and-pepper pair ride side by side in a squad car or back each other up on the streets, as, for instance, in current favorites like *Spenser for Hire* or *Miami Vice*. Needless to say, it is also to be found in Faulkner's most popular works, including *Intruder in the Dust, The Reivers* and, especially, "The Bear," which has the dubious distinction of being considered by high-tone critics among the best of Faulkner's stories and at the same time having pleased the middle-brow editors and readers of the *Saturday Evening Post*.

Beneath such frozen stereotypes of interethnic male bonding (as Faulkner no doubt intuited) there lies a genuine myth of love, whose archetypal resonance no travesty ever quite destroys. To be sure, its primary appeal is to males; yet females too respond to it, despite its misogynist overtones. After all, though Melville once expressed doubts that any woman could read *Moby Dick* with pleasure, many have—or at least have claimed to; responding positively also to *Huckleberry Finn* and, apparently (some 80 percent of the readers of the journal in which it first appeared were women), "The Bear" as well.

From the very beginnings of our literature, however, writers—principally but not exclusively females addressing a female audience—have exploited another myth of love, as appealing as that of interethnic male bonding to boys and men, or that of Boy-Gets-Girl to readers of both sexes. This is the theme of Brother-Sister incest in all its variations: witting and unwitting, narrowly averted or tragically consummated. Its classic formulation is found, of course, in Edgar Allan Poe's best-loved story, "The Fall of the House of Usher"; but long before Poe it had been exploited over and over in certain best selling women's novels of the late eighteenth and very early nineteenth centuries. Moreover, realizing its appeal, Melville made it the archetypal erotic center of *Pierre*, the only book he deliberately wrote to attract the female audience. It is scarcely surprising then to find it recurring over and over in Faulkner, who instinctively, as it were (it is a talent shared by all truly popular writers), realized how deeply it lay embedded in the collective unconsciousness of America. Not only is it present in *Flags in the Dust, The Sound and the Fury* and, most notoriously, in *Absalom, Absalom!* but it persists even in *Sanctuary*, especially in its first inchoate version, in which Faulkner had not yet disentangled the Popeye-Temple story from the Sartoris saga.

Neither of those two primary erotic myths, however, is to be found in the master works of high modernism, in which they tend to be replaced by the self-serving secondary myth of the *poète maudit*, the unloved alienated artist, alternatively portrayed as symbolically killing his bourgeois father or wandering through the nighttime city in quest of him. Such portraits of the artist as a rejected and disaffected young man are conspicuous by their absence in most of Faulkner's fiction. The closest thing to it, perhaps, is Horace Benbow, who is specifically characterized as an artist in *Flags in the Dust*, but not, interestingly enough, in either version of *Sanctuary*. Quentin Compson, to be sure, seems an artist in embryo in *The Sound and the Fury*, but we know, of course, that he commits suicide while still short of maturity. And though Horace survives into middle age, he disappears from the continuation of his story in *Requiem for a Nun*, being replaced by Gavin Stevens, who typifies the "intellectual" mouthpieces in Faulkner's later novels. Like Horace, he is an overeducated lawyer with a degree from an elite university; but unlike him, he can swap yarns with the old boys on the front porch, sporting a Phi Beta Kappa key which none of them recognizes. He seems to me, finally, to symbolize the nonalienation of the popular artist: functioning not as a distrusted creator of fictions ordinary people cannot understand or as a prophet intruding into the larger community uninvited and unwelcome; but as an amateur detective called upon in moments of disaster and confusion—in short, not merely accepted but *needed*.

It was in large part for this reason that of all pop genres the detective story proved most attractive to Faulkner, who prized it, too, because it preserved the traditional Aristotelian plot structure, which is to say, told a "story" in the old-fashioned sense of the word. But such linear narratives, with a last minute recognition and reveal (the "O. Henry hook" they called it contemptuously) had been disavowed by modernist novelists, who preferred to it the climaxless "epiphany" perfected by James Joyce. Certainly, Faulkner exploited that pop form not only in later works like *Knight's Gambit* and *Intruder in the Dust*, but in *Sanctuary*, his first truly popular book, which outsold everything he had written before it and stayed in print during the long years of critical eclipse when almost everything else he had written had ceased to be available except in libraries. It was *Sanctuary* in any case, which made Faulkner's a familiar name to the general reader, and persuaded Hollywood not just to hire him as a script-writer but to make a film version of the book. That movie, in which he himself had no hand, proved to be very bad indeed, its horrific details euphemized to the point of incoherence, and has deservedly been forgotten; but his versions of the work of others, which its sale helped make possible, were often quite good—best of all (as might well have been expected) his screenplay of Raymond Chandler's detective story, *The Big Sleep*.

It was not, however, only such factors, plus Faulkner's ambivalent yearning to reach the mass audience, which attracted him to that pop genre. Two older writers, whom he admired and emulated, had also tried their hand at it: Dickens, of course, to begin with, and his great-grandfather, as well, with whom he shared a name and sought desperately to identify. The "Old Colonel," it should be remembered, had been not only a heroic warrior, which Faulkner sometimes pretended to be but could not help acknowledging finally was beyond his power; he was also the author of a best-selling novel called *The White Rose of Memphis*, which was a murder mystery, complete with detectives, disguises, false accusations and the final exposure of the guilty; and here his grandson could hope at least to emulate him.

Faulkner, moreover, seems clearly to have been influenced by two of the most popular American detective story writers of the 1920s, S. S. Van Dine and Dashiell Hammett—the former of whom he must have read in hardcovers, while the latter came to him via the pulp magazines which we know he used to read. The evidence is less clear that Faulkner ever bought any of the novels of Van Dine; but it is hard for me to believe he did not; since he had been introduced by Phil Stone to *The Creative Will*, a critical study which Van Dine had published under his true name, Willard Huntington Wright. It must surely have tickled Faulkner to realize that the author, who under that name had written a book attacking all popular art as the refuge of the vulgar and ignorant, under his pseudonym had grown rich and famous by writing mysteries for precisely that despised audience. In those books, moreover, Philo Vance, the amateur sleuth who is their hero, echoes the elitist sentiments of *The Creative Will*, thus compounding the ironies. Finally—in one more turn of the screw—Faulkner seems to have modeled his own favorite sleuth, Gavin Stevens, on Philo Vance, making him, like his prototype, a super-sophisticated, garrulous and grandiloquent amateur given to mouthing highminded platitudes about philosophy, politics, psychology and aesthetics.

In *Sanctuary*, however, Gavin Stevens is absent—except as dimly foreshadowed in the self-pitying, ineffective figure of Horace Benbow, who moves through an underworld milieu of pervasive corruption and violence much like that in which Hammett's pitiless and effective Private Eyes operate successfully. The style of *Sanctuary*, moreover, except when Horace's drunken babbling spills over into its text, consists of short declarative sentences, without subordination, more like those of Hammett than Van Dine, whom, Hammett, in fact, had excoriated in print for his stylistic pretentiousness. The language of *Sanctuary*, too, is more like Hammett's: lean and mean, close to the tight-lipped, hard-boiled speech of the streets. Nor does Faulkner's pop novel resemble Hammett in style and diction alone. Its final ironic plot twist, in which Popeye, who has escaped hanging for murders he has actually committed, is executed for one which he has not, is so closely anticipated in one of Hammett's Continental Cop stories that it is difficult to believe Faulkner had not read and remembered it.

In any case, insofar as *Sanctuary* is a detective story, it is one in the tradition of lowbrow pulp *schlock à la* Hammett, rather than of the kitschy middlebrow slicks so congenial to S. S. Van Dine. Yet Hammett—though he had by that time met Faulkner in Hollywood and they had become mutually destructive drinking buddies—when he finally got around to reading *Sanctuary*, did not esteem it very highly. "Mr. Faulkner," he wrote, "is over-rated by such people as have read him at all. He has a nice taste in the morbid and the gruesome, but doesn't seem to do much with it." Faulkner, on the other hand, has left no recorded response to any of Hammett's fiction, only a strange comment on his character, an incredible valedictory which shocked Lillian Hellman, to whom he observed, "He drank too much."

Nonetheless, even as Hammett and Faulkner expressed such distrust of each other, certain eminent French authors like André Malraux and Albert Camus were touting them both, associating them with each other as presumably neglected American geniuses who had redeemed the *roman policier* by raising that pop genre to the level of Greek tragedy. Yet, as Malraux himself was moved to remark, *Sanctuary* is an odd sort of *roman policier*, being a detective story without a proper detective. Horace Benbow, it is true, equivocally identifies himself as such at one point, when he is asked, "are you a detective?" and answers, "Yes . . . yes. No matter. It doesn't matter." But he is really of course only a small town lawyer, and not a very good one at that, who spends more time worrying about the indignities of being married to a woman married once before and wrestling with his incestuous attraction to his step-daughter and his sister than in solving the case of murder and rape in which he finds himself involved.

His single real feat of detection is discovering that Temple Drake has been present at the scene of the crime and locating her in her whorehouse retreat. But though he seems for a moment to have persuaded her into testifying on behalf of his falsely accused client, Lee Goodwin, she finally clinches the prosecution's case by deliberately lying on the witness stand; thus exculpating Popeye, who is actually guilty, and condemning Lee—not just in the eyes of the jury who sentence him to death, but the larger community who torture and lynch him. To be sure, as we have already noticed, Popeye does not finally escape scot-free either, eventually committing a kind of suicide by refusing to defend himself against charges of having committed another murder of which he is innocent. The reasons for his complicity in his own death, Faulkner never makes clear; but they are (I am convinced) somehow connected to his ambiguous relationship with the woman whose lying testimony has seemed initially to deliver him from hanging. In the end, the only major character in *Sanctuary* who is left not merely undestroyed, but untouched by guilt is that woman herself, Temple Drake, though she is, directly or indirectly, responsible for all the deaths that occur in its pages.

The final effect of *Sanctuary* is, in any event, precisely the opposite of that created by the detective story in its closed middlebrow form, at least as that effect is described by W. H. Auden in his immensely persuasive essay "The Guilty Vicarage." Its resolution, that is to say, does not restore the community in which the crime has occurred to a state of Edenic innocence—by identifying a single source of guilt and thus exculpating all the initially suspected others. Instead, that entire community is revealed as guilty along with the nominal criminal, who is merely a scapegoat ritually punished for its sins; and the question therefore of who is "really" guilty turns out to be irrelevant. But if *Sanctuary* is, in this sense, an antidetective story, so also are most of Hammett's as well as those of his disciples and imitators from Raymond Chandler to Mickey Spillane.

Many critics have, of course, realized the sense in which *Sanctuary* is such a detective, or rather antidetective story, and not a few have recognized as well its indebtedness to the gangster novels and movies, which possessed the imagination of the mass audience in the era of Prohibition, bootlegging and the Valentine's Day Massacre. It is hard, indeed, to miss its affinities to that form; ending as it does with the expected, almost required death of the gangster-in-chief—and evoking along the way most of the stereotypes associated with the genre. Certainly, its criminal characters are stereotyped, from Popeye himself, the gunsel whose phallic power resides only in the killing machine holstered under his arm, to the standard crew of scarcely articulate hard guys who protect him and run his booze—including Red, the handsome stud he engages to pleasure Temple and finally murders. And lurking in the background is the predictable shyster mouthpiece: "the Jew lawyer from Memphis," who apparently orchestrates the final courtroom scene.

Few, however, seem to have realized that *Sanctuary* includes a potpourri of almost *all* the popular genres of the late 1920s. Yet Faulkner himself boasted in his introduction of having put into it everything that "a person in Mississippi would believe to be current trends"—meaning, of course, not what would be considered chic in the realm of high art, but whatever was currently fashionable in the well-paying slicks and the penny-a-word pulps. Notable among these is the tale of "Flaming Youth" or "Our Dancing Daughters," immensely popular in a time when appalled parents stared across a widening generation gap at their jazz-age offspring—liberated by "coeducation," the automobile and the sexual revolution. Certainly Temple Drake, whatever she finally becomes, enters the scene in the guise of a typical longlegged teenaged flapper, as played by Clara Bow or the young Joan Crawford; a co-ed *demi-vierge* in scandalously short skirts, who might well have been drawn by John Held, Jr., the favorite cartoonist of the period. Similarly, Gowan Stevens is a standard college boy type, a callow youth who cannot hold his drinks and learns it the hard way.

The two of them seem, indeed, almost comic characters in quest of an appropriate comic denouement. But this, of course, they do not find; even though, as the book moves toward its close, it becomes more and more humorous. One could, in fact, extract from its otherwise grim pages a collection of "funny stories," which constitute another enduring pop genre. These range from the rather hackneyed, but much admired (*over*admired, I am convinced) "Stupid Rube in the Big City" anecdote, in which a pair of Snopeses take a brother to a hotel, to the Dickensian vignette of the three Mourning Madams and the drunken small boy. My own favorite, however, is the brutally hilarious scene at Red's wake, in which his coffin is upset by his drunken comrades (even as the band plays "Sonny Boy"), and his body is flung to the ground, dislodging the wax plug which had concealed the bullet hole in his forehead. It is a classic example of what we have come only recently to call, though we did not invent it, "black humor": the kind of joke in bad taste which recurs in the last sentences of *Sanctuary*'s penultimate episode, in which Popeye—with the noose already around his neck—says to the sheriff, "Fix my hair, Jack," and the sheriff answers, "Sure . . . I'll fix it for you," springing the trap.

But at this point we are on the borderline between nausea and laughter, which is to say, between humor and horror. And this should remind us that still another pop genre much on Faulkner's mind as he wrote and rewrote *Sanctuary* is the Horror Story as practiced from the time of Poe to that of Lovecraft and Stephen King. "Horrific" is, indeed, the word he customarily used to describe that novel—and horrific it is in good faith. Indeed, there are scarcely any of the stock effects of the horror genre, audio or video, which it lacks: from the tap-tap-tap of a blind man's stick to the rustle of rats in a corncrib, the ominous thud of a muffled gunshot off scene, the crackle of flames from the lynch-mob's bonfire, and the barely audible whisper of blood in Temple's ravaged body. So, too, do the standard grotesques of the Gothic Romance abound: "crips" and "feebs" and freaks, not least of which is Popeye himself—more monster than human, more shadow than substance. "The black man," Temple and Horace call him, aware perhaps that this is a traditional American name for the Devil. And there is, too, of course, the infamous bloody corncob, an icon of unspeakable evil, for which *Sanctuary* is remembered even by those who have never read it; though Faulkner alludes to it only briefly at a point where his horrific tale is nearly told.

But finally—and essentially—the novel which Albert Camus believed to be the greatest of Faulkner's fictions belongs to the most disreputable and unredeemable pop genre of all, being pornography, as the dictionary defines that pejorative term, "a portrayal of erotic behavior designed to cause sexual excitement." Though there are many such portrayals in Faulkner's work of "erotic behavior," including such kinky subvarieties as pedophilia, necrophilia, incest and bestiality, *Sanctuary* was the only one of his books which its intended publisher refused at first to publish, presumably as too "dirty." Yet it is in some ways the softest of soft porn—avoiding not only what were then still considered "dirty" words, but explicit descriptions in any words of the sex act itself. The brutal violation of Temple, for instance, is rendered solely in terms of her fantasies, climaxing in her hallucination of turning into a boy—popping a teeny-tiny penis; though, of course, that male organ is called by none of its grosser street names.

Nonetheless, however soft, *Sanctuary* is sadomasochistic porn in the tradition of the divine Marquis's *Justine* and *Juliette*, ambiguously and disturbingly blurring the distinction between murder and desire, violence and passion, *thanatos* and *eros*. Its central image of love therefore (after all, insofar as he can, Popeye loves Temple, and in her way Temple loves him) is rape. But rape, however abhorrent in fact, is an image of true archetypal resonance, which has provided a mythic erotic center for a large number of works which have pleased many and pleased long. These include not just banned books like de Sade's, but many classics and longtime family favorites ranging from Shakespeare's *Titus Andronicus* and Samuel Richardson's *Clarissa* to *Gone with the Wind*, the Tarzan series (in which everyone she encounters attempts to rape Jane) and those currently popular Women's Romances, whose beautiful protagonists not infrequently end up marrying the balefully attractive males who began by ravishing them.

All such stories represent, in any case, latter-day avatars of the ancient archetype of the *donna fuggita*, the Pursued Woman: a primordial image which, no matter how the actual relations of the sex may change, persists in the deep unconscious of us all. Faulkner, however, ironizes and at the same time heightens the titillation implicit in that archetype by making his rapist impotent, which is to say, not-quite-male, and portraying his intended victim as not-quite-female. Not only do both of Temple Drake's names hint at her androgynous nature, but the sexual role she plays is finally mythically "masculine." Beginning by running always in the wrong direction or not fast enough to foil those who pursue her in lust, then ceasing to run at all—she ends by becoming the sexual aggressor, the pursuer rather than the pursued. So at least she seems, in her last sexual encounter with Red, in which—as Faulkner describes it—"she sprang like a bow, hurling herself upon him, her mouth gaped and ugly like that of a dying fish as she writhed her loins against him"; and we seem to be there watching, at once fascinated and repelled.

"Watching" is the operative word; since *Sanctuary*, like all true pornography, is essentially voyeuristic in its appeal. When reading it, that is to say, we do not typically identify with its erotically active characters, rapist or raped; but with the Peeping Tom author, who compels us to keep our eye glued to the key hole, ashamed but unable to withdraw—as the author himself seems to have been in the first place. Certainly, Faulkner confessed as much in his shamefaced public apology for his novel; suggesting, to me at least, that pornography only really works for us when at some level we feel that the pleasure it provides us with is disreputable; or in any event are uncomfortably aware that others, whom we otherwise respect, consider it so—some indeed wanting to ban or burn it.

But Faulkner made such guilt-ridden voyeurism the subject as well as the mode of apprehending the novel, in which from start to finish someone seems always to be watching someone else watching him or her. Think of Popeye and Benbow staring at each other for two hours across the spring at Frenchman's Bend; or Benbow once more watching in one mirror Little Belle watching him in a reflecting other. The climax of such reflexive voyeurism, however, comes in Faulkner's rendering of the scene in which Popeye slobbers over the bed in which Temple and Red copulate at his command. That scene is represented not directly, but as reported by a black maid who has watched Popeye watching; thus putting us as readers in the position of voyeurs at a fourth remove—watching the author watching her watching them. It is this which makes *Sanctuary* unique: the first (and as far as I know, the only) piece of metapornography for which I have, for reasons I hope I have made clear, long been ashamed to confess my inordinate fondness; and which therefore, I believe, no one who reads it properly can ever be proud of liking.

Looking Back After 50 Years

When *The Grapes of Wrath* was first published on the eve of World War II, it was acclaimed (or at least so it then seemed) by all men of good will. Only pious hypocrites and reactionary yahoos demurred: labeling it "vulgar," "obscene," "false" and "un-American," even as its more extravagant admirers were hailing it as a uniquely American masterpiece, worthy of being ranked with *Moby Dick* and *Leaves of Grass*. Ironically enough, it is this hyperbolic assessment which continues to appear as a jacket blurb on its latest editions. I say ironically because more recently the critical consensus has drastically changed. Indeed, when—after the passage of twenty-five years—Steinbeck was belatedly given the Nobel Prize for Literature, most reputable critics greeted the news with derision and scorn. Typical of the response was that of Arthur Mizener who deplored the granting "of this most distinguished prize to a writer whose real but limited talent is watered down by tenth-rate philosophizing." Moreover, even after another quarter of a century, as distinguished a critic as Harold Bloom agreed, writing that "because he inevitably falls into bathos, lacks invention and is clearly incapable of creating characters with real inwardness," Steinbeck is clearly not one of the "inescapable novelists" of America, like Faulkner and Hemingway, Ralph Ellison and Thomas Pynchon.

But why, I feel impelled to ask, has Steinbeck's reputation thus declined—so swiftly, indeed, that by 1962, as Mizener was able to contend with few to say him nay, "most serious readers" had long since "ceased reading him." Surely this state of affairs cannot be, despite what an ever-diminishing number of hardcore fans—chiefly Californians—argue, because a conspiracy of "Eastern intellectuals" caused *The Grapes of Wrath* to disappear from the required reading lists in the majority of university courses in American literature all up and down our land: lists on which, it is worth noting, other provincial authors, Western, Mid-Western and Southern, continue to appear. To understand the unique reasons for Steinbeck's precipitous decline, we must begin in quite another way, by trying to understand the unique reasons for his initial success.

There now seems little doubt that *The Grapes of Wrath* was originally over-prized because it seemed to embody so perfectly the mood and sensibility, the anti-puritanical morality, the leftist politics—and especially the apocalyptic vision of the thirties. To be sure, that morality, politics and vision were not shared even in that age by most ordinary Americans—certainly not by most blue collar workers or (hard as Steinbeck tries to persuade us of this) the dispossessed sharecroppers of the Dust Bowl. The vision did, however, possess the minds and hearts of some intellectuals and would-be intellectuals in the metropolitan East and Midwest, who controlled the review sections of mass-circulation newspapers and influential magazines. It was they who hailed Steinbeck not just as a consummate artist but one on the "right side"—i.e., one who was a prophet of the coming of socialism.

To make him seem an artist on the level of Melville or Whitman, they had to ignore all in him that was maudlin, sentimental and overblown, which was not easy. But it was even harder to make him seem an unequivocal advocate of a collectivist society as defined by the Communists, fellow-travelers and sympathizers, who at that point claimed to speak for the artists and intellectuals of America. They had to simplify his profoundly ambiguous (not to say hopelessly contradictory) politics; ignoring, for instance, his eccentric biologism, his stubborn individualism, his irrational fear of mechanization, indeed, of modernism and industrialism in general. But especially disconcerting was his essentially reactionary agrarianism—projected in the Joads' dream of living happily ever after in a snug little cottage on their very own little plot of fertile land.

But the more single-minded liberals found it possible to do what they wanted by emphasizing elements in Steinbeck's muddled thought which they found more comfortably orthodox. These elements included the belief that only a violent revolutionary uprising of the exploited classes could deliver America from poverty, injustice and the threat of war; that the mounting wrath of those classes meant that such a revolution was just around the corner; and that, in any case, capitalism was doomed—and with it, the military, the police, organized religion—ultimately, the nuclear family itself. But none of what he and his liberal admirers then foresaw, of course, has come to pass. In the United States, not only has socialism not triumphed, but the very dream of it has died for all but an ever-diminishing minority, chiefly academics with tenure, who write in a jargon comprehensible only to each other. Moreover, not the revolution which Steinbeck prophesied, but World War II, which he nowhere predicts, ended the Great Depression.

Consequently, capitalism has continued to flourish everywhere, not only in America and Western Europe but in rapidly developing countries of the once-underdeveloped Far East; and it begins to make inroads even in the Soviet Union and its satellite states. Nor has organized religion shown any signs of withering away. Rather, for some decades now, we have been witnessing the revival of traditional faiths; and the sects which prosper the best are, alas, the most puritanical, fundamentalist, fanatical and mutually intolerant.

The only social change that Steinbeck foresaw that has actually occurred is the erosion of the nuclear family. Contrary to his expectations, however, it has not expanded into a communal meta-family, a family of all humankind, but has shrunk so rapidly that in my own lifetime I have seen the two-parent family with 1.7 kids replace the multi-generational household swarming with children, grandchildren and at least a grandma in attendance. And that two-parent domicile in turn begins to yield to the single parent family.

Not surprisingly, then, as the hopes and dreams of the 1930s have proved delusive (persisting only in the vestigial nostalgia of unreconstructed "liberals"), the reputations of those books whose popularity depended in large part on embodying the dreams have tended to decline. Not only *The Grapes of Wrath* but also John Dos Passos's *USA* and James T. Farrell's *Studs Lonigan*, novels once also considered masterworks that would live for all time, have not outlived the ideology that informed them. It should not be thought, however, that their recent devaluation is explicable in purely ideological terms. While it is true that many of the latter-day critics (including me) who have devalued those novels are committed to quite different ideologies, this commitment has not prevented us from admiring other writers of the age whose political sympathies were more like theirs than ours. Even as we have sought to exclude Steinbeck, Dos Passos and Farrell from the canon, we have done our best to replace them with writers like Nathanael West and Henry Roth, who, though overlooked or undervalued in their own time, were stauncher supporters of the Communist political line than the former. Unlike Steinbeck et al., however, the latter did not submit to the aesthetic line of the Cultural Commissars in Moscow, who had decreed that realism, "social realism," was the only viable mode for progressive fiction in the twentieth century.

Instead, West and Roth emulated certain earlier *avant-garde*, experimental writers whom those Commissars had condemned as petty-bourgeois decadents. Roth, for instance, made no bones about his indebtedness to James Joyce and T. S. Eliot, and West was clearly influenced by the French Dadaists and Surrealists; both, that is to say, wrote in the tradition that we have come to call "Modernism." Small wonder then that when the American critical establishment, which determines the rank order of our books, came in the first half of the twentieth century to judge these books by Modernist standards, it was Roth and West rather than Steinbeck, Dos Passos and Farrell whom they placed on the top of their lists. Steinbeck seemed to them particularly problematical since, though not a naïf like Farrell, he did not, like the more sophisticated Dos Passos, adopt even superficially the devices of experimental fiction.

Not only did they fault him for being an old-fashioned realist, apparently blissfully unaware of the Joycean "revolution of the word"; they condemned him, too, for his equally obsolescent optimism: his failure to seek, much less attain, the "tragic" view of human existence which they had come to regard as essential to all great art. They found him guilty, moreover, of what seemed to them the four cardinal literary sins: didacticism, sentimentality, stereotyping and melodrama. Rather than remaining remote and invisible behind his text, he consistently (they charged) leans over his readers' shoulders to tell them exactly what he means.

So, too (they further contended), he eschews evasive irony in favor of shameless sentimentality, thereby not only flattening out all nuances and ambiguity but also sacrificing plausibility for the sake of easy pathos. Certainly this sacrifice happens in the infamous schmaltzy scene at the roadside hamburger stand, in which an improbably soft-hearted waitress, counterman and pair of truckers conspire to get into the hands of a couple of Okie kids the candy canes they lust for but which their (poor but honest, of course) parents cannot afford. It all eventuates in a kind of soupy kindness contest, whose winners are indicated when the waitress sighs "reverently" behind their departing backs, "Truck drivers!" It is a sentiment we are expected to share, along with the implicit message that all proles are noble; leaving readers with a more complex view of human nature, rich or poor, more inclined to snigger than sigh.

Such sentimentality depends, indeed, on stock responses to the stock characters who appear everywhere in *The Grapes of Wrath.* Nor is it only supernumerary walk-ons who are clichés out of the common stock of the time. Even the major characters whom he most carefully delineates tend to turn into such stereotypes. The most notorious instance of this is to be found in his set piece in praise of Ma Joad. "Her hazel eyes," Steinbeck writes, pulling out the stops, "seemed to have experienced all possible tragedy and to have surmounted pain and suffering like steps into a high calm and superhuman understanding . . . From her position as a healer, her hands had grown sure and cool and quiet; from her position as an arbiter she had become remote and faultless in judgment as a goddess . . ." Not only does the inflated Mother's Day greeting card rhetoric of this passage have little to do with any actual mothers; it has even less to do with the complex, passionate woman who elsewhere in the text stands off her husband with a jack handle in her fist and murder in her eye. It is as if Steinbeck were somehow compelled to falsify his own vision at its truest as well as life itself.

Such reduction of multi-dimensional characters leads inevitably to simplifying the complex intermingling of good and evil in human affairs to black and white melodrama, in which all the good is portrayed as being on one side, *our* side, all the bad on the other, *their* side. In Steinbeck's case, as is appropriate to the leftist ideology of his time, our side is, of course, that of the expropriated and exploited; while the hated other is identified with the exploiting bourgeoisie: the "shitheels," as the roadside hamburger stand waitress inelegantly calls them, who heartlessly ride by, or over, the starving children of the poor. Such relentless travesty of the rich (only born-again Christians are more brutally caricatured) is especially ironical in the case of an author who was himself the son of a bourgeois family and who was already quite well off when he wrote *The Grapes of Wrath,* which to compound the irony even further, made him as close to filthy rich as any freelance writer can hope to become.

I am not, please understand, putting down Steinbeck's novel on the grounds that it was written in bad faith. Whatever the motives of any author (and they are, in any case, finally inscrutable), a book deserves to be judged on its merits as a work of art. But I do feel obliged to point out that even read with no knowledge of Steinbeck's own class origins or financial status, *The Grapes of Wrath* seems clearly motivated by a kind of guilt-ridden self-hatred, which leads him not merely to vilify his own class but also to ask his readers to condone— even admire—in the underclass, much that we, whatever our class, would otherwise find reprehensible. Examples include not only grossness, blasphemy and a contempt for literacy, but habitual drunkenness, loveless tom-catting, petty thievery and finally mindless violence, from bar-room brawling to wife-beating and murder. Not only are we expected to see the two-time murderer, Tom Joad, as the book's hero, a man more sinned against than sinning; but to sympathize also with his *alter ego*, the infamous Pretty Boy Floyd, for whom Ma apologizes, saying, "He warn't a bad boy. Jus' got drove in a corner."

The only fault of his beloved Okies which Steinbeck does not treat with mingled condescension and envy is their racism, their ingrained prejudice against Blacks and Indians. Disconcertingly—and more than a little implausibly— no Afro-Americans or full-blooded Native Americans actually appear in this account of a pilgrimage which begins on the edge of the Black Belt and passes through the heart of what was once known as the Indian territory, suggesting that the author himself shares to some degree the ethnocentrism of his characters. In any case, he reminds us over and over that they are all 100 percent WASPs, "real Americans" of pure pioneer stock. He refers, however, only in passing—half apologetically, as it were—to the negrophobia for which in the after years the descendants of his Okies have become notorious.

Negroes (invariably called "niggers" in the text) are referred to only twice: first in a passage early in the book in which we are permitted to overhear the song which keeps ringing in Tom Joad's head as he returns home from jail. "And then we spied a nigger with a trigger that was bigger than an elephant's proboscis . . ."; and next in the scraps of conversation at a roadside camp on which we are also allowed to eavesdrop, "a lady back home, won't mention no names, had a nigger kid all of a sudden. Never did hunt out that nigger . . .

couldn't hold her head up no more . . ." It is hard to tell what Steinbeck's own attitude is toward this evocation of his poor whites' sexual jealousy and the unfulfilled threat of lynching in response to black-white miscegenation. But there seems little doubt that he sympathized with the family's view of Indians as the ultimate enemy, since he repeats three times with apparent approval their thumbnail account of their history: "Grandpa killed the Indians, Pa killed snakes for the land. Maybe we can kill banks . . ."

It was finally, however, not on moral grounds, much less political ones (after all, I was still able to admire poets like Pound whom I found even more egregious on both counts), but on aesthetic ones that I originally refused to take Steinbeck seriously. I did not, for instance, discuss him at all in my purportedly all-inclusive study of American fiction, *Love and Death in the American Novel*. In 1960 I judged him and found him wanting (or so at least I persuaded myself) on the basis of the standards for High Art taught to me by the apostles of Modernism. And even now, I still have trouble coming to terms with Steinbeck, despite the fact that I no longer believe in those standards. Indeed, for the past ten or fifteen years, culminating in my latest critical book *What Was Literature?*, I have been doing my best to undermine those standards, arguing that they are no longer viable, if indeed they ever were in a mass society like ours. In the course of doing so, I have felt obliged to redeem the reputation of another thirties book that I once despised, Margaret Mitchell's *Gone with the Wind*, which is, of course, not merely more politically reprehensible than *The Grapes of Wrath* but more flagrantly sentimental, stereotyped, didactic and melodramatic.

Yet *Gone with the Wind* cannot be ignored, I have come to realize, since despite the scorn of elitist critics, it has refused to die, becoming instead the most widely read and best loved of American books world wide; thus passing what Samuel Johnson, himself a super-elitist, declared was the final test of literary greatness. It has pleased many, and pleased long, because (I have slowly learned), though both ethically and aesthetically falling far short of excellence, it possesses in the highest degree archetypical resonance. This quality, however, is overlooked by traditional critics who are aware of the sense in which literature must instruct and delight but blind to the fact that to attain immortality literature must also possess mythopoeic power. It must, that is to say, create characters who—like Mitchell's Scarlett O'Hara and Rhett Butler—live on in the deep imagination of the world, side by side not only with Odysseus and Achilles, Hamlet and Falstaff, but also Tarzan and Sherlock Holmes, Captain Marvel and Superman. That the first four of these characters appear in elegantly crafted and philosophically profound works, while the latter four were created in what initially seemed mere commercial "trash," is finally irrelevant.

What does matter is that all of them have become part of the communal dreams of world culture; that they are, in this sense, true myths, as none of the characters in *The Grapes of Wrath*, alas, are. No one, for instance, in celebration of the fiftieth anniversary of Steinbeck's book, has been moved to peddle ceramic images of Rose of Sharon or of Ma, as such secular icons of Scarlett were offered to all takers in the pages of *TV Guide* when the book in which she appeared reached the same venerable age. Nonetheless, it is true that though no individual character in *The Grapes of Wrath* has achieved mythic status, the lemming-like pilgrimage west of his faceless Okies established itself almost immediately as an archetypal image. But Steinbeck himself helped conceal this fact by insisting (not just in *obiter dicta* but in the book itself) that his ambitions were quite other than those of popular story-tellers with a mythopoeic gift.

Certainly he never spoke of himself as being like Margaret Mitchell or Edgar Rice Burroughs, an amateur wanting only to spin a good yarn that would entertain and make a quick buck. His desire to be taken seriously as an artist is everywhere declared by his attempts at fine writing and, especially, the portentous philosophical and theological reflections, sometimes interpolated in his editorial interchapters, sometimes entrusted—a little improbably—to Jim Casy and Tom Joad. In the latter case, they are rendered in a kind of colloquial baby talk, which not merely simplifies such notions as the Oversoul but also turns them into inadvertent parody. Nonetheless, some critics, chiefly second-rank academics whose "subject" is Steinbeck—have been led to argue quite solemnly about whether the author is finally Christian or anti-Christian and to discuss his debt to Emerson and St. Paul on a lofty level, as no one has ever been tempted to talk about frankly pop books like *Gone with the Wind*.

Finally, therefore, I have decided that despite its continuing popularity in the face of critical disapproval, *The Grapes of Wrath* cannot be properly judged as a pop novel. But neither can it (for reasons which I hope I have made sufficiently clear) be properly judged as art novel. It is finally something a little like but even more different from both: a *tertium quid* which I do not find it easy to define, though for the rest of these remarks I shall try.

Let me take for a starting place a more or less off-hand remark of Edmund Wilson, who once wrote toward the end of a theoretical essay about the nature of art: "You sometimes encounter books that seem to mark precisely the borderlines between what is definitely superior and work that is definitely bad—the novels of John Steinbeck, for instance." I would, however, amend this to read "work that is definitely superior and work that is definitely bad" by Modernist standards of high art or, more simply, between work that is in such terms clearly "highbrow" and that which is unequivocally "lowbrow."

All of Steinbeck's fiction, that is to say, *The Grapes of Wrath* in particular, is "middlebrow" (to use an awkward term which I long ago forswore, but have been able to find nothing to replace) and must therefore be judged by standards different both from those appropriate to highly crafted novels which please the minority audience and from those suitable to indifferently crafted "easy reads," beloved by the majority audience. What makes this judging difficult as well as necessary to do is that middlebrow art aspires to the condition of both. On the one hand, middlebrow writers attempt to persuade the reader of what they often believe themselves: that they are producing high art. While, on the other hand, sometimes quite unconsciously, middlebrow writers provide the satisfaction of the best seller. They want, that is to say, to have their cake and eat it too; and occasionally they manage to do so.

I don't know how I remained unaware of this fact for so long, since the very genre to which *The Grapes of Wrath* belongs has become at this point essentially middlebrow. But it took me a while before I realized that, though it pretends to be a semi-documentary with epic overtones, it is really a pastoral, which the dictionary describes as "A literary work dealing with the life of shepherds or rural life generally . . . typically drawing a conventional contrast between the country and city . . . or court . . . and often using the characters as vehicles for the expression of the author's moral, social or literary views . . ." From the start the pastoral was not written, of course, to be read by the rustics it praised (after all, one of their presumed virtues was their illiteracy) but by aristocrats, whom it amused to pretend that they admired, even envied the rustics. The pastoral remained, therefore, as late as the time of Spenser and Sidney, a courtly or aristocratic genre—the equivalent of what came to be called later "high art."

When, however, it was re-invented in democratic, theoretically classless America as the Western, and when its shepherds were turned into cowboys, its audience became largely middleclass, middlebrow Easterners. Indeed, Owen Wister's *The Virginian*, the first long-lived example of that new genre, was still being urged on me—along with Scott's *Ivanhoe* and Eliot's *Silas Marner*—as a "classic" suitable for one of my age by my sophomore English teacher, who was quite unaware that at that point (I was all of 15) I was already reading James Joyce and Marcel Proust. I was also, however, reading—because no one had urged them on me—the Westerns of schlockmasters like Zane Grey and Louis L'Amour, who at that point had turned the genre into a pop form, which in print and translated to the screen, created—behind the backs of the critics, as it were—one of the most enduring of American myths: the myth of the West.

It is that genre and that myth that Steinbeck, without confessing, or even quite knowing it, attempted to restore to middlebrow respectability in *The Grapes of Wrath*. At any rate, though he may have thought of his ambitious novel as a work of art and "serious" social commentary, the large audience which made it a best seller read it as a middlebrow Western, responding not to its medium or its message but to its re-evocation of the legendary journey toward the setting sun through a dream landscape already familiar from a thousand other books and movies. To be sure, Steinbeck's way west leads not across virgin prairies and perilous trails but down the asphalt of Route 6, which his protagonists travel not on horseback or in covered wagons but in rustling over-loaded cars and trucks. They love their jalopies, however, as dearly as the Lone Ranger loved Silver.

In fact, their affection for their vehicles is the deepest passion portrayed in this anaphrodisiac book, in which, despite frequent scenes of casual sex, there is (as in the classic pulp Western) no real *eros*—except, of course, for the Oedipal bonding of Tom Joad and his mother. But even that loving pair is divorced before the book quite ends, when Tom leaves Ma, like the proper Western loner he has become: the righteous killer with a price on his head, who "lights out for the territory ahead of the rest." He does not, however, leave the scene until the Oedipal syndrome has been completed; which is to say, until the symbol of patriarchal power has been undone, Pa stripped of his authority by his wife and son.

In light of this Oedipal theme, it is fitting that in the novel's final scene the only father figure present is a dying old man, who, in a total reversal of conventional generational roles, we see suckling at Rose of Sharon's breast—impotent as a newborn baby. Her actual child (his father, once more appropriately, not merely absent but disgraced) was—in another ironic reversal, this time of life and death—stillborn. Indeed, at the climactic moment, the child is floating down the river in a box, a shriveled blue mummy of indeterminate sex. That strange conclusion of a revolutionary and intendedly hopeful fable, Steinbeck himself has confessed, forced itself on him unbidden, which is to say, emerged out of his deep unconscious.

Earlier in the novel, there had in fact been two climactic scenes, with which he might have concluded his tale on an upbeat note more appropriate to his avowed politics. The first of these (with which John Ford did in fact end his film version—in homage presumably to F. D. R. and the New Deal) occurs when the Joads discover in the "gov'ment camp," not just food, shelter and flush toilets, but the possibility of controlling their own destinies. And the second comes at the moment when Tom Joad decides to dedicate himself to the religio-revolutionary mission of Jim Casy, who, appropriately enough, considering that he shares the initials of the Christian savior, has already died for the sins of the capitalist world. "Wherever they's a fight," Tom tells his grieving mother as he prepares to disappear, "I'll be there . . . Wherever they's a cop beating' up a guy, I'll be there . . . and when our folks eat the stuff they raise an' live in the houses they build—why, I'll be there . . ."

But Steinbeck apparently could not bring himself to close on such fashionable left-wing soapbox rhetoric. Instead, in the few pages which follow he reinvokes what seems at first an utterly irrelevant image—portrayed over and over in literature and painting since the early Renaissance—of a young girl offering her bare breast to an aged invalid, often her own father. It is an image sometimes pathetic, sometimes quasi-erotic, but never political, and certainly never hopeful. Nonetheless, certain middlebrow critics have tried to persuade us and themselves that in the context of Steinbeck's novel, this bitter parody of the Nativity constitutes a kind of miraculous Happy Ending. "Rose of Sharon," one of them contends, "out of her own need gives life . . . thus removing the curse of sterility from the universe."

It seems to me, however, that the milk of a half-starved Okie girl is not likely to be copious and rich enough to sustain life and that, in any case, the old man she suckles is beyond the point of saving. As far as the cosmic implications of her act are concerned, moreover, the text has already made clear that the downpour which brings so strange a suckling to her withered teat, though the Joads have prayed for it in the drought-ridden wasteland of Oklahoma, creates when it comes in California not fertility but destruction. Certainly, it washes away the futile dikes which they have erected, along with what remains of their scant household goods and their last shelter. And finally it immobilizes their beloved vehicles, making them incapable of further Westering, even if there were a further west. In my opinion, therefore, *The Grapes of Wrath* ends not on the note of pseudo-Emersonian cosmic optimism which it has sustained up to that point but on a note of tragic despair, which, for ideological reasons, Steinbeck had earlier avoided. Yet it is impossible to be absolutely sure who is right in this regard, I or the middlebrow euphemizers, because this time for once Steinbeck does not lean over our shoulders to explain exactly what he means—thus leaving the image with which the book closes to speak for itself, like a myth; which is to say, to remain ambiguous, polysemous, mysterious.

"Mysterious" is, indeed, the final word of the text: a confession on Steinbeck's part, for those able to read it, that he does not understand where his story, here blessedly out of control, has taken him. But it is precisely that perplexity and the ambiguous image it has engendered in this archetypical scene—which I once utterly despised as obvious, tawdry, exploitative—which seem to me now to redeem at the last possible moment the inert stereotypes, the easy pathos, the *ersatz* transcendentalism and the doctrinaire optimism which elsewhere flaw this problematical, middlebrow book.

Robert Penn Warren:
A Final Word

The recent death of Robert Penn Warren has left me feeling glad that I managed to say a final word about his work before all further commentary on him had come to seem depressingly posthumous, memorial. My relationship to what he wrote has always been and remains still a living one. I had, however, published nothing new about him, nor indeed, even spoken about him in public, or for that matter reread anything of his for nearly thirty years, when toward the end of 1987 I was asked to participate in a symposium in his honor at Austin Peay State University. I had, it is true, carefully preserved three little essays which had first appeared in the fifties as reviews of *World Enough and Time, Brother to Dragons* and *Band of Angels,* reprinting them in 1960 in a volume called *No! In Thunder* and then again in 1970 in my *Collected Essays.* It was my way of acknowledging that despite my long silence and the gathering dust on these books in my library, resonating echoes from them (as well as from "The Ballad of Billie Potts" and, especially, *All the King's Men*) have continued to ring in my head, influencing my own subsequent work as a fictionist and poet as well as a critic. Nonetheless, I was inclined at first to refuse the invitation to Austin Peay, in part because I had for so long lost touch with what Warren was doing. But chiefly I hesitated because accepting it, I would have to talk about him in a part of the world in which I am a rank outsider: a stranger in the (to me) strange land in which Warren was so conspicuously at home. To be sure, for many years, he had been an exile in the North; yet he had returned in his imagination—continually, compulsively—to that part of the South where he had been born and grown up. It had, indeed, determined once and for all not just his subject matter and his settings, but the language in which he wrote, the rhythm and diction of his prose and verse. The world, however, which had determined my dreams and the language in which I body them forth was first of all the urban East, then the Midwest, the Rocky Mountain Northwest, even, a little, New England—another America.

When, therefore, I contemplated going to Tennessee, I could not help remembering that in that alien state I had been censored for the only time in my life—my story "Nude Croquet" snatched from the newsstands by irate local citizens. To be sure (as I reminded my listeners when I finally made the trip), I was not entirely without connections in that part of the world, my wife's family having come from Louisville and Mayfield, Kentucky—her great-aunt being, in fact, the author of *Mrs. Wiggs in the Cabbage Patch*. But (as I was also moved to tell them) the one time I dared to confront that family on its own homegrounds, I was made aware that not only was I an eternal outsider in Dixie, but—being a Jew as well as a damn yankee—a comic outsider at that.

All had gone well over the fried chicken, the lima beans swimming in butter and the beaten biscuits; but as the tinkle of the little silver bell signaled it was time to clear the table, my wife's grandmother looked up and smiled not at her but directly at me. "Sally," she said sweetly, apropos of nothing at all, "they're letting Jews into the country club now. *Somebody* has to pay for the new eighteen hole golf course." And suddenly I found myself turning into Woody Allen—knew that I had always been in my relationships with the South just such a clown—especially, when I attempt to deal critically with such laureates of that region as William Faulkner or Eudora Welty or Robert Penn Warren. But, perhaps, I reassured myself, it was precisely my status as a comic outsider that enabled me to perceive certain things about those writers which remained invisible to critics too close to them to attain a proper perspective.

That this is true, at least in the case of Warren, I came to feel, when preparing for my visit to Austin Peay, which despite everything I decided to make, I discovered that more recent commentators on his books continued to refer to observations I had made in my three little pieces: indicating that however unsatisfactory my answers, some of the questions I had raised thirty years before were still of interest to latterday Warren aficionados, including those much more at home in his world than I. From the same sources, moreover, I found that Warren himself had in the intervening decades continued to be haunted by the very works which had seemed to me so tantalizingly suggestive from the start—particularly, of course, *All the King's Men* and *Brother to Dragons*. I felt, therefore, free to concentrate on the poetry and prose which he had written in the fifties in a last attempt to answer satisfactorily (at least to myself) the questions which I had left dangling for three decades.

The first and most important of these is how Warren managed from the very beginning to please two audiences, High and Low, serving, as it were, two masters: the ordinary readers who make best sellers and the literary critics, who determine what is preserved in libraries and assigned in classes in English. Their demands, I believed at that point (influenced in part by the criticism of Warren himself), were utterly incompatible. How, then, could he, I asked myself in bafflement, have been published simultaneously in pretentious literary journals like the *Partisan Review* and the *Kenyon Review,* and in ladies' magazines, such as *Cosmopolitan*? And how, similarly, was it possible for his earlier novels even as they were being solemnly analyzed in academic quarterlies, to be distributed by book clubs pandering to the lowest common denominator of vulgar tastes of *The Literary Guild?*

What most disconcerted me was the fact that *All the King's Men*, which is by critical consensus his most distinguished novel, had been turned (with his consent and approval) into a popular film that won three Oscars, at a moment when such awards were bestowed almost exclusively on crowd-pleasing *schlock*. For such dubious distinctions Warren must have been prepared, since that novel had earlier won the Pulitzer Prize, which then was typically given to fiction meeting the same marketplace criteria. In any case, there is no evidence that any of this disturbed Warren. Nor did the translation of his work from one medium to another seem problematical to him, though it troubled me who still believed at that point that the medium was the message.

After all, *All the King's Men,* which I had first encountered as a novel, had pre-existed (I soon learned) as a play in verse called *Proud Flesh.* And (as I further learned to my further confusion) *Brother to Dragons,* which had made its debut in print as a long quasi-dramatic poem in loose blank verse had originally been conceived as a novel, then re-conceived as a ballad in a pseudo-folk voice. "I once intended to make a ballad of them long ago," the final text confesses in the voice of R. P. W., "but the form/ was not adequate: the facile imitation/ Of a folk simplicity would never serve . . ." The underlying conviction which made such transformations permissible Warren had earlier stated explicitly in some verses included in *Eleven Poems on the Same Theme:* ". . . There is no form to hold/ Reality and its insufferable intransigence."

But this is a heresy; it is not, in light of Modernist literary orthodoxy, which insisted that "a poem should not mean but be"; that it should, indeed, be "like a fruit . . . palpable but mute," "a well-wrought urn," utterly other when it is reshaped, however well or ill. The metaphor "well-wrought urn" is, as a matter of fact, the title of a book by Cleanth Brooks who was also, in collaboration with Warren, the author of the famous/infamous textbook *Understanding Poetry.* That work, indeed, taught several generations of students, including my own, precisely those formalist orthodoxies which Warren's earlier poetry and fiction so insidiously subvert.

To compound the paradox, moreover, *Understanding Poetry* itself became, as no other text book in criticism—certainly no other by a New Critic—ever came near becoming, a best seller. And this seems fair enough, however disconcerting, in light of the fact that Warren's fiction and verse, along with their spinoffs in other media, also achieved marketplace popularity, unlike those of such colleagues and fellow Southern Agrarians as John Crowe Ransom and Allen Tate.

It was not only, to be sure, in his apparent indifference to the medium that Warren undercut Modernist orthodoxy and achieved best-sellerdom. His

novels were based not on the models of High Modernism admired and emulated by his fellow New Critics. Indeed, one looks in vain through the pages
of *All the King's Men* or, for that matter, *World Enough and Time* and *Band of
Angels*, for nuances of sensibility reminiscent of Henry James and Virginia
Woolf, or the fracturing of the narrative line and the eschewal of direct mime-
sis in favor of stream-of-consciousness that characterizes James Joyce's *Ulysses*
and *Finnegans Wake*. No, Warren's books seem more indebted to the example
of the Historical Romance: a disreputable sub-genre still despised by elitist
critics though it is at the present moment—with the possible exception of
SF/Fantasy and Horror—the most widely read of all Pop forms. Warren has,
understandably enough, been uneasy with this fact; in interview after interview, denying that he is an Historical Romancer. But I at least am left feeling
that he protests too much—and after the fact to boot. After all, he did sub-title
World Enough and Time, "A Romantic Novel"; and though he did not do the
same for *Band of Angels,* it cries out for such a generic classification. So, too,
for that matter does the Cass Mastern episode so crucial to *All the King's Men:*
the narrative within a narrative, which Jack Burden must write before he can
come to terms with the past—and, like a true historical romancer, escape "out
of history into history and the awful responsibility of Time."

Moreover, even when Warren departs from the rhetorical strategies
invented by Sir Walter Scott, those to which he turns are the perhaps slightly
more respectable but equally outmoded ones of the realistic or naturalistic
novel as practiced by, say, Emile Zola or Theodore Dreiser. He is, that is to say,
more interested in wrestling with "intransigent reality" and confronting social
issues than in creating elegant structures or finding *le mot juste* or forwarding
the "revolution of the word." Though for a long time Warren seems to have
tried to conceal his somewhat reactionary tastes, perhaps even from himself,
by the late sixties, when Modernism was evolving into what is currently called
"post-Modernism," he had come out of the closet. In one candid interview,
he confessed his distaste for what he dubbed contemptuously "fancy-fancy
artsy-artsy fiction"; then went on to deplore the fact that his brightest and
most "literary" students no longer read, much less loved and imitated such
favorites of his own (writers of "the meat and potatoes school," he dubbed
them) as Maupassant and Dreiser, Balzac and Zola, not even Charles Dickens.
They are all, it is worth noting, nineteenth-century novelists, pre-Moderns.
The only twentieth-century writer Warren mentions favorably is Hemingway,
from whom, he notes, his students have also turned away, perhaps in part
because (as he does *not* note) Hemingway had found his true voice only after
rejecting the temptations of the avant-garde.

There seems no doubt, in any case, that Warren has been profoundly influenced by Hemingway, though his use of the American colloquial seems to

me to owe less to the Old Master himself, than to certain of his Pop disciples, inventors of the hardboiled detective story, like Dashiell Hammett and Raymond Chandler. Certainly, when Jack Burden begins to talk like one of the boys-in-the-back-room, he sounds more like Sam Spade or Philip Marlowe than Nick Adams or Jake Barnes. But, of course, he does not always speak in the voice of a *film noir* Private Eye. Sometimes he philosophizes grandiloquently like the drop-out Ph.D. candidate he is portrayed as being; thus permitting the author, for whom he is clearly a surrogate, to editorialize, leaning over the reader's shoulder as all good Modernists had presumably learned *not* to do. Finally, also in contempt of modernist orthodoxy, Burden is permitted to indulge in a kind of rhetoric, high pitched, shamelessly shrill and insistent, that more closely resembles the style of Willy Stark than that of James or Joyce.

In the verse narrative of *Brother to Dragons,* Warren apparently felt even freer to indulge his taste for a gorgeous, garish, horrific style, long since considered *démodé* by the critical establishment. And why not, after all; since he was attempting to write in an equally outmoded form. Heavily plotted linear narratives in verse had presumably begun to go out of style with the publication of Walt Whitman's *Leaves of Grass* a century before. And certainly no twentieth-century poet admired by the New Critics had made a similar attempt; turning instead to parodic anti-epic forms, patchworks of disjunct lyrics, quotations and allusions, like Crane's *The Bridge,* Pound's *Cantos,* Eliot's *The Waste Land* and W. C. Williams's *Paterson.* Moreover, Warren's subject matter was—unfashionably once more—melodramatic enough to justify almost any excess of language, eventuating in what I was moved to call in my early essay on the poem "bombast." Such a deliberate breaching of restraint and decorum betrays a desire not merely to move the reader, but—in the words of a latterday master of the same rhetorical mode, Stephen King—to "gross them out." Yet, after all, bombast and the genre of Horror literature with which it is typically associated has an ancient and honorable ancestry. It goes, in fact, all the way back to Seneca, then is revived in the plays of his Elizabethan and Jacobean imitators, including Shakespeare's *Titus Andronicus;* and resurfaces in that strange spin-off of the Historical Romance, the Gothic Novel, most egregiously represented by M. B. Lewis's *The Monk.*

As in such earlier works the evocation of the atrocious and the horrific in *Brother to Dragons* verges on the pornographic—meriting, in modern Hollywood terms, an R-rating, if not a downright X. Certainly this is true of the climactic scene of the poem, to which all critics compulsively refer, in which Lilburne Lewis hacks a black boy to pieces on a butcher's block. But so, too, is it of the scene of Lilburne's sexual assault on his wife, which critics typically pass over in embarrassed silence: his forcing her to perform an unspecified—

to her nameless and therefore utterly abominable—act. To compound the horror, moreover, Lilburne asks her, even as he has asked the mutilated black boy, to signify her assent to her violation: to become a collaborator, a willing accomplice.

Even when I still shared the elitist prejudices of modernism, I found these scenes and the extravagant language in which they are rendered not merely moving but somehow finally acceptable; though, I must confess I found some difficulty in coming to terms with them. All the more so do I now, when I no longer consider despicable the popular gothic romances with which they have so much in common, find them and the rhetoric in which they are couched acceptable. Nonetheless, I am still disturbed by Warren's obsessive-compulsive use of the same bombastic language to describe the homeliest and most trivial incidents. When, for instance, he writes of a man taking a piss by the side of the road, ". . . stopping just once to void the bladder/ Under that stunning silence after the tire's song/ The July-fly screamed like a nerve gone wild,/ Screamed like a dentist's drill . . . The sunlight screamed, while the urine spattered the parched soil . . ." it seems to me not merely much too much, but finally ridiculous.

This, however, I have come slowly to realize, is a part of the price Warren has had to pay for the real advantages that accrue to him for having—behind his own back, as it were, as well as that of his colleagues and his more obtuse admirers—chosen to emulate the model of Pop Art in all its vulgarity rather than High Literature in all its discreet elegance. But to say exactly what those advantages are I find it necessary to return in conclusion to Warren's cavalier attitudes to the medium in which he works—examining more closely the strange metamorphoses of *Brother to Dragons* and *All the King's Men.*

Begun (as we have already noticed) as a novel, *All the King's Men* was apparently next sketched out as a play in a loose form intermediate between prose and verse. Only the third time around did it assume its final shape as something neither quite a poetic drama nor a long narrative poem, though, in any case intended to be read rather than watched on the stage. Its stage potential, however, seems from the start to have tantalized not just Warren but others as well. As early as 1955 the BBC broadcast a dramatic reading of it; and some years later it was again telecast in a version in whose writing Warren played no part though he did act in it the role of R. P. W.'s father. Moreover, before the fifties were over he had himself composed a new dramatic version which was staged several times in the following years, altered by its various directors as it toured the country from Seattle to Broadway. By 1974 it had achieved a form which Warren himself considered worth preserving in print, actually revising and polishing it for publication in the *Georgia Review.*

But this was not yet the end. On the basis of what he had learned from actually seeing his multigeneric work performed, he drastically rewrote it in its narrative form as well: loosening its cadences, cutting back its prolixity, sharpening the encounters of its characters. He brought it back a little closer, that is to say, to the "Tale in Verse and Voices" he had originally conceived, to a true closet drama—intended to be played out in the reader's head rather than passively perused.

It is a strange, almost unique development for what seems in other respects a late Modernist poem. Nor does its uniqueness lie only in its generic trans-formations. Even less characteristic is its almost slavish accommodation to audience response and the demands of production—more customary surely in the commercial theatre and Sam Goldwyn's Hollywood than in the world of High Art according to John Crowe Ransom.

But the metamorphoses of *All the King's Men* are still more anomalous. It appeared, for instance, in two different versions as a novel; the English edition dropping (apparently with Warren's consent) the whole Cass Mastern episode, so crucial to Jack Burden's development, and indeed, a thematic center to the book as a whole. But even earlier it had been written as a play in verse and prose, in which Burden, its eventual protagonist, scarcely appears at all. In that form, in fact, it had been staged by Eric Bentley in 1946 at the University of Minnesota, where Warren was then teaching. It would seem, however, that he found that production unsatisfactory. But far from abandoning the dramatic form or what had since become a successful novel, he rewrote the play in prose for a 1949 production. In the next decade, moreover, he kept rewriting it; until in 1960, it seemed to him finished enough to publish between hard covers.

Yet that is by no means the end of the story. Escaping its original author completely, as it were, and entering the public domain, in 1949 *All the King's Men* was turned into an Academy Award–winning movie by Robert Rossen. He, in turn, was so proud of his film script that he published it in 1972, in a volume containing what he thought of as his three best screenplays. But (I thought just recently, watching a rerun on television), how close to trav-esty that movie version becomes: not merely translating from one medium to another, but from one language and one world to another. Rossen, to be sure, tells us that the film was originally shot not from the script he eventually printed (that came later, after the fact) but from the novel itself; meaning that Warren is, in effect, the real *auteur* of the movie.

It turns out, however, that in the course of shooting Rossen managed to de-Southernize completely what had begun as the most Southern of stories: moving the setting of the action to a small town in California, in which all the characters speak a kind of generalized mid-American, bereft of all Southern cadences and idioms. Moreover, Adam Stanton in the screenplay is portrayed (in deference to the director's Hollywood liberalism) as the only character able to see the truth about Willie Stark, rather than—as in the novel—just one more self-destructive blind man in the country of the blind.

Yet watching the movie again after all these years, I could not help feeling that somehow (why else did Warren like it so much or at least bother to say so publicly?) Rossen had not, however he may have simplified, really falsified this immensely ambiguous, truly polysemous and therefore endlessly adaptable fable. He had, instead, revealed the one of its multiple meanings most acceptable to an audience with political prejudices quite different from Warren's. So, too, I suppose (though I have not seen it) did a recent American opera, as well as the various versions for stage, screen and television produced by party-line writers in Communist Eastern Europe. The latter certainly must have made the expected point that all of the United States and in particular the American South is a breeding ground of Fascist violence.

Such presumable ideological "kidnappings" of *All the King's Men* do not, I am suggesting, subvert what we like to think of as the "true meaning" of the work, which is to say, what that work means to us and presumably to Warren himself. Rather, they complement, expand it in ways which are ultimately not merely legitimate but necessary; since all of us anywhere and at any time are prisoners of our own time- and place-bound ideologies. We cannot, therefore, see the total significance of such genuinely meta-ideological fables as Warren's novel. Such myths in fictional form are adapted by their readers or viewers, on a level below that of full consciousness, to suit their psycho-social needs, whatever their conscious allegiances, or, for that matter, their gender, class, generation or level of artistic sophistication.

In this sense, *All the King's Men* is more like *Gone with the Wind* than, say, *Remembrance of Things Past* or *The Magic Mountain*. That is to say, its underlying mythos not merely enters the public domain almost immediately, but seems to have been there even before the work which embodies it appeared. Certainly this is true of the myth of Huey Long which constitutes the subtext of *All the King's Men*. Let me be clear; it is not the actual history of that defunct demagogue's career to which I am referring but a communal dream or nightmare based as much on pre-existing tales and legends as that career itself. Even before Warren's novel appeared, that archetypal story had been turned into published fictions in Adrian Locke Langley's *A Lion in the Streets,* John Dos Passos's *Number One,* and Hamilton Basso's *Sun in Capricorn.* But even earlier it had been created by Huey Long himself and his PR people, then re-created in Sunday Supplements, newsreels and speeches in Congress or on street corners. I cannot help recalling that I myself made my debut as a public speaker in the mid-thirties with a vitriolic attack on Long as the Fascist bugaboo-in-chief of the time.

His rise and fall had, in short, become a part of the folk mythology to which Warren turned over and over throughout his writing life, from "The Ballad of Billie Potts" and *Brother to Dragons* through *World Enough and Time* and *Band of Angels* to *Chief Joseph of the Nez-Perce*. Warren's most authentic and moving works, that is to say, do not, like such modernist masterpieces as *Ulysses* and *The Waste Land* allegorize, euphemize and ultimately parody stories which had long been a part of standard mythology. Instead, they re-create archetypal stories which none of us yet realizes will achieve full mythic status, though reading them we feel that they are not being told for the first time nor ever will be for the last.

It is, at any rate, for their ability to evoke primary myths, their innate mythopoeic power, I am convinced, that the fiction and poetry of Warren on which I have been meditating will be remembered and loved. Nor will those who prize them be confined to academics and elite critics who think that literature is "words on the page." They will include also ordinary readers who instinctively know that not the medium but the myth is the message. As a matter of fact, I firmly believe that the only books destined to please many and please long are those which possess such archetypal resonance. Some of them, to be sure, are distrusted and despised by the critics, despite or rather perhaps because of their popular success, yet they stubbornly stay in print—like the novels of Harriet Beecher Stowe and Bram Stoker, Edgar Rice Burroughs, Margaret Mitchell and Stephen King. Others, however, often for reasons hard to understand, are not merely praised by the critic-pedagogues but become required reading in classes in English—like the works of Sophocles and Shakespeare, Dickens and Mark Twain, William Faulkner and, of course, Robert Penn Warren, who like those others will survive even this final indignity.

Capote's Tale

This collection contains one extraordinarily good story plus three or four others less good but still memorable that should help redeem Truman Capote, the writer, from that other Capote, the creature of the advertising department and the photographer. Risen from the couch that adorned the jacket of his last year's novel, he leans for this volume, epicene among lush blossoms—very tender, very young. The boy author has been a standard feature of our literature ever since the beginnings of romanticism, and I suppose our generation is entitled to one of its own, but surely Capote deserves better than being fixed in that stereotype.

True, his work shows the occasional over-writing, the twilit Gothic subject matter and the masochistic uses of horror traditional in the fiction of the boy author ever since the eighteen-year-old Lewis wrote his *Monk* 150 years ago. But Capote has, in addition, the ability to control tone, an honest tenderness toward those of his characters he can understand (children and psychotics) and a splendid sense of humor—seldom remarked upon. In the best of his stories, "Children on Their Birthdays," he grasps a situation at once ridiculous and terrible, creating out of the absurdities of love and death among children a rich tension lacking in his other stories, even such successful performances as "The Tree of Night" and "Miriam." On the whole, the level of achievement of these shorter pieces of fiction seems to me a good deal higher than that of Capote's novel, *Other Voices, Other Rooms*, where occasional triumphs of style or characterization are undercut by poor structure and a general air of padding and pastiche.

Mr. Capote is not yet ready to sustain a novel, but as a teller of tales he has a genuine and peculiar talent. He has, however, certain disturbing faults even in the shorter forms, most notably an inability *to hear* and reproduce common speech; so that when he tries occasionally to tell a whole story through the mouth of a simple or vulgar character ("My Side of the Matter"), he fails dismally. But in his hands the fairy tale and ghost story manage to assimilate the attitudes of twentieth-century psychology without losing integrity by demanding to be accepted as mere fantasy, or explained as mere symbol.

The bogeyman, though he fades sometimes into the delusion of the paranoiac, remains a *real* bogeyman still. He is indeed scarcely ever absent from these stories, reappearing in various guises, as a constant antagonist: the buyer of dreams who is also Master Misery in the story of that name, the old man in "Miriam," Mr. Destronelli in "The Headless Hawk," Lazarus the Man, Who Is Buried Alive in "A Tree of Night," a voice on the telephone in "Shut a Final Door." These are not symbolic representations of evil but genuine spooks: what the child, having learned in the whispered tale, finally believes in, but what the adult absurdly denies and is destroyed by.

> I call him Master Misery on account of that's who he is, Master Misery. Only maybe you call him something else: anyway he is the same fellow, and you must've known him. All mothers tell their kids about him: he lives in the hollows of trees, he comes down chimneys late at night, he lurks in graveyards, and you can hear his step in the attic. The sonofabitch . . .

In Capote's stories the fairy world, more serious than business or love, is forever closing in upon the skeptical secure world of grown-ups. But his children—and the natural allies of children, clown or lunatic—are competent to deal with the underground universe of the incredible. Consequently they are Capote's most credible characters; especially the *Wunderkind*, the precocious child, sometimes flesh and blood, real if not quite canny, like Appleseed or Miss Bobbit, sometimes fading into a haunt like the title character in "Miriam."

Mr. Capote writes not merely of children but from their side; his stories are the kids' imagined revenge upon maturity. Adults find neither mercy nor tenderness in these tales; for to have denied childhood or to have lost faith in its terrors—by simply growing up—is such a loss and denial, that, except for the mad, it invites the nemesis which Capote's children, as the bearers of this mystery, never have to endure.

Only in "Children on Their Birthdays," the most complex and satisfying of these tales, is there an ironical reverse, when the astonishing Miss Bobbit, the little girl who has shocked, cowed and bullied a whole town of grown-ups, is killed, at the point of leaving for Hollywood (the child's paradise), by the six o'clock bus, blind on its adult business. This story alone is enough to make the volume worth reading, but there are rewards too in the other pieces, and it is a pity that fewer people will read it than have read *Other Voices, Other Rooms*, since it represents Mr. Capote's essential achievement so far.

The City and the Writer

This is, to begin with, an extraordinarily handsome book. The jacket, the Stieglitz photograph which serves as a frontispiece, the drawings by Marvin Bileck and the typography all conspire to give the volume an aspect of the physically prepossessing, an initial air of conviction. There is a certain irony in all this elegance as a décor for recollections that proceed from Brownsville; but there is justice, too; for Kazin has succeeded in imposing a beauty of honesty and coherence on the seediness and squalor of the world where he began. And the make-up of the book is at once a tribute to that beauty and an attempt to render it in other terms.

Though the work refuses to become a "novel," its honesty is not the brute honesty of fact, but the *arranged* honesty of a reminiscent fiction whose motive is love. Hence it continually risks, and, I am pleased to say, continually escapes, the falsification of the sentimental. It rejects the double technique we are used to thinking of as the sole guarantee of authenticity in such recollections; eschewing the passionate documentation and the immediate cold representation that mark works stemming from a pure spasm of revulsion (one thinks, for instance, of Farrell's South Side of Chicago). Kazin begins on a second convolution, on the pulse of nostalgia: compulsively re-seeking the scenes he had fled in quest of the freedom, the breaking-out that was at one stage the whole of his life, in search of a limiting pastness, a breaking back in, needed now to complete the definition of his existence. There is no question of surrendering what one has gained, merely of looking back from it, rather than forward to it. Indeed, after a certain point, when one is incredibly living in what has always been a desperately pointed-toward "future"—the only way to preserve the pure wonder of that "future" is to redeem the past. Such a redemption means, of course, mythicizing a little what one has lived through. We are surely all sufficiently aware by now that memory is no transparent medium, but rather a cagy and poetic ally, remaking what was merely given into the needed.

Such a redemption Kazin has attempted for his own years among the working-class Jews of Brownsville, when the whole world "outside," even the city of New York just across the river, seemed incredibly remote, an untouchable though visible utopia. For him freedom was the City, and the City was America, toward which his parents had sailed in the steerage of the Stieglitz photograph, but on the verge of which they had somehow disastrously beached without love or God. From the despair and insecurity (mitigated by the warmth of family life and the color of the streets) of Brownsville, Kazin had to complete the journey into the mythic America that no ship could attain. And especially in the schools, those outposts of the Real America, he felt himself continually tested under the gentile stare of his teachers, to see whether indeed he were worthy of Success—an alternative name for what his parents meant by America. I have never come across anywhere else so apt a description of the Kafkaesque relationship between the Jewish schoolchild and his alien Guardians.

It is one of the (dearly bought) splendors of Jewish existence in America that it provides such apt and unforced metaphors for outsideness and quiet terror. And it provides, too, as Kazin realizes (though this is considered in some quarters more politic and "liberal" to deny), the clue to an understanding of radical politics in this country. Even among the first-generation immigrants (one is tempted to say "among the parents," because they had consented to become almost exclusively that) the image of Socialism had been set up beside that of Success-America, as the first easy vision of stepping from shipboard to belongingness had failed; without hypocrisy, the two visions managed to exist side by side: the dream of "the children" becoming rich and respectable, along with the vote for Debs and the discussions in the Workman's Circle. And as the children grew into a post-Bolshevik world, the parents' dream of worldly success was driven more and more underground (who dared confess it in the pit of the Depression!), and the Soviet Union more and more replaced America as the image of freedom. There began a looking back eastward over one's shoulder for the vision that had once glimmered on the western horizon; and it was no accident that some of Kazin's friends sailed back over the tracks of their parents to die in the Spanish Civil War. There has always been in American Communism, so much the product of the children of East European Jewish immigrants, this exasperation at the mirage of hope appearing in precisely the place one has just left, and consequently the general air of one running frantically from line to line before a post-office window, as the line one is *not* in seems always to move faster toward its goal.

But the young "Bolsheviks" of the second generation (Kazin himself remained a "Socialist," though one attracted toward the pole of the Soviet Union) entertained a contradiction as deep and unperceived as that of their parents: a loyalty to the unorganized fraternity of the "isolated" artists of all times and places and beliefs: Whitman, Eliot, Beethoven or Emily Dickinson, along with an allegiance to the working class and its Party to which loneliness was the unforgivable sin. When that odd and untenable amalgam fell apart for Kazin, it was toward the "isolates" that he turned in his typical development;

but not before some of his friends had sailed off in search of barricades with the *The Waste Land* in their pockets.

The key image of Kazin's book is walking, alone or with a girl, but chiefly alone: the erratic, desperate exploration of his world by a young man, moving beneath walls he cannot believe will ever open to him, but moving at least to his own internal music (the music, one recalls, to which *Ulysses* also unfolds, a characteristic modern music). Here is no marcher in a parade, no comrade lost among the millions in the "march of history," but the unredeemably lonely walker in the City. The City, with its parody of sociability, its interposition of a false fate of *things* between man and his destiny, is the proper end of the pilgrimage to America. No modern mythology is possible that is not an urban mythology, from the image of the Artist as Stephen Dedalus to the avatar of the Hero as Captain Marvel; and it is finally just that the individual finding his own and our America should have come the long way from Walden Pond to Brownsville.

It is because the young Jew as writer and thinker is the very symbol of our urbanization (as also our ambivalent relationship to Europe, the atomization of our culture and our joyful desperation) that *A Walker in the City* takes on an additional weight, seems central to our plight. It is his sure sense of this *central-ness* of his experience which saves Kazin from the temptation to cheap exoticism inherent in his material. It would have been only too easy to have submitted to the familiar I-remember-momma-over-the-lox-and-bagels routine, and to have become the Molly Goldberg of the anti-television set; in the world of enlightenment and good will, everyone is eager to chortle warmly over the difference of the immigrant Jew, when it is precisely his sameness that matters. Yet Kazin does not deny himself completely the warmth inherent in his material; avoiding the more obvious uses of irony, he dares risk exploiting the "soft" sensibility which this century has taught us to regard as inherently false.

It is the *seriousness*, the religious tone (if one can use the adjective without implying mawkish piety) of the book which overcomes its various temptations: sentimentality, local color and finally the impulse to become just another "first novel," the pseudo-fictional confession which is a bore before it is told. We have here, to be sure, another portrait of the artist as a young man, and one, indeed, which is constantly reminding us of the Joycean prototype. But Kazin has not, in the typical loss of nerve, retreated back to older fictional forms from Joyce's almost total demolition of all that makes the conventional novel. He has rather pushed on into a kind of non-novel, whose possibilities Joyce made apparent in his *Portrait*, but from which he himself turned at the very last minute when Stephen's ultimate vision showed him only a way back into art. Kazin's book, being a religious one, becomes in a way a reversal of the

Joycean procedure (I do not mean, of course, to overshadow him by evoking the great ghost, but the comparison demands to be made); Joyce is attempting all the time to show that so-called moments of mystical insight are, when they are genuine, "aesthetic," while Kazin seems to me to be attempting to redeem the Joycean "epiphany" from literature to something more like the traditional meaning of religion.

A Walker in the City is, in the end, the account of a series of illuminations, strung on a strand of reminiscence; the evocation of deep intuitive experiences of unity with the otherness of nature and man and God, which does not deny but in an unforeseen way fulfills loneliness. And this also is an America, discovered, as it were, inadvertently by a boy from Brownsville in search of a much simpler belongingness.

Style and Anti-Style
in the Short Story

Surely there has never been so favorable a moment for the short story! In the past few months, the publishers have given us a more imposing list of short fiction than we have ever seen in a comparable period; after years of assuring us and themselves that the publication of such books is the surest way to bankruptcy, they have set to printing them with so infectious an air of abandon and self-congratulation that one finds oneself grinning triumphantly at the mere *fact* of the volumes before him. Here are book-length monuments to a lifetime of work in the field (Conrad Aiken, Faulkner and W. C. Williams), and early collections for which the younger writer has undergone the initiation of a first novel (Mary McCarthy, Paul Bowles); and here are the familiar O. Henry and Martha Foley anthologies, which we have come to greet with the sort of genial grumbling due dull but faithful friends. There is even in the air a sense of all this virtuous publishing activity having been rewarded more spectacularly than anyone could possibly have foreseen. Has not the Faulkner collection already been chosen by one of the largest book clubs!

True enough, there is no note of elation in the prefaces to the anthologies; and one remembers despite oneself the diminishing number of stories appearing in the literary magazines, the paucity of new writers and their quick turning away to the novel under pressure from agents and publishers, the progressively slower production of the established fictionists (Katherine Anne Porter) or their loosening down into a more and more meaningless flurry of productivity (Kay Boyle). And yet it seems churlish at the very moment that so fat a goose is set down before us to play Scrooge to the publishers' tiny Tim, by insisting on the hopeless confusion of standards and the over-all poverty of performance in the actual short story.

Surely, it is disconcerting to find in the two collections of the year's "best" work in the field only one story in common; even allowing for the tendency nowadays to choose sides on all questions of evaluation on the threadbare basis of the "open" versus the "hermetic," the split is disturbing, and disturbingly uncommented on. No one seems to me sufficiently exercised by the well-known fact, only underlined by the present divergence, that we have no common agreement about what the short story is.* And yet this places upon the writer the unnecessary burden of defining his genre at the same moment he is seeking to establish his particular use of it. On the one hand, this gives to certain short stories (the work of W. C. Williams is a case in point, and among stuff not represented here, the essay-tales of Isaac Rosenfeld) too much the air of critical manifestos doubling as fictions; and on the other hand, it leads to the establishment of certain chummy little groups trying to live up to the canons of a particular kind of story as if it were "the short story." It is this sort of confusion that helps give to the *New Yorker* or the "Kafka" story that air of smug parochialism so annoying to the outsider, so invisible to the insider. There are some especially unfortunate examples of the former kind (not all from the magazine which gives them a convenient name, of course) in the O. Henry collection—pieces by Cheever, Newhouse, Parsons, etc.

The lack of a definition of the form has left the way open for publishers to name certain pieces and collections of pieces in accordance with a non-aesthetic hierarchy of their own. Since a novel sells better *per se* than a collection of short stories, groups of short fictions, lacking all novelistic line or coherence, like Mary McCarthy's *The Company She Keeps* or Faulkner's *Knight's Gambit*, are called "novels." From the other side, in a day when the term "familiar essay" evokes only images of aging English Professors, anglophile and of attenuated sexuality, standard familiar essays like Mary McCarthy's "The Friend of the Family," W. C. Williams's "The Colored Girls of Passenack" or Aiken's "Gehenna," are jumbled together with fragmentary memoirs and lyric poems in prose, as well as more strictly specified prose "imitations." It is not a question of demanding an impossible purity of genres, but of resenting the judging by unwary critics of quite different intentions by a single body of standards.

Certainly the first step toward clarity is the frank recognition that the short story has fallen heir to various alien obligations since its institution. On one side, it has had thrust upon it certain functions of the lyric poem, most importantly the symbolic realization of an immediate emotional response, and on the other hand, it has had to come to terms with various obligations of the essay, learning to take in its stride discursive and witty commentary. The essay has other avatars, book reviews or letters to the editor, but for most of us the short story is all the poetry we now have. From the beginning, certain writers like Poe were able to achieve in the short story effects that eluded them in their verse. It is fitting, therefore, that Faulkner, the best writer of the group before

*During the past two or three years a body of short-story texts have been appearing, anthologies intended for college classes, but edited by critics and writers, Tate, Scherr, Heilman, etc. These seem to me to be attempting to establish a canon based primarily on the practice of Joyce and Chekhov, but they are mainly pedagogical in intent.

us, be a *poète manqué*; and that Conrad Aiken attain in a few of his stories ("Silent Snow, Secret Snow," for instance) an economy and precision of lyric form that ordinarily is fumbled in his verse. Williams provides another sort of case. One of the functions of his prose is apparently to provide a touchstone beside which his poetry will seem unequivocally verse. Poetizing as he does on the last possible margin of prose, he is driven to postulate an absurdly prosaic prose, which attains, when it does not fall into dry fragments, an incredible austerity. But generally speaking, it is precisely the Romantic traditions of High Rhetoric, the stance of self-conscious virtuosity, so contemned in contemporary poetry, which succeeds in the current short story, whether openly as in Aiken and Faulkner, or somewhat abashedly (with a resultant added tension) in Hemingway and his followers—represented here only in the other *lumpen* efforts of Raymond Chandler and the writers of Science Fiction.

The strain inherited from the essay has not countered but rather strengthened the impulse toward a high artificial diction, whether the result be the DeQuincyish elaboration of an Aiken, or an Oscar Wildish play of ornamental wit as in Mary McCarthy.

Certainly, the two influences have joined to undermine the prestige of "plot" in the short story, crushing it between the upper and nether millstones of theme and symbol. Even in the detective story, where the fable with its archaic reversal and recognition seems essential, writers like Chandler (claiming a direct laying on of hand from Dashiell Hammett) have been hacking away at the importance of the puzzle-solution structure, the last stand of the rational plot in Christendom, deliberately losing the dénouement in a sloppy unraveling covered by a heavy baroque style. In recent issues of the *New York Times* book review supplement, Chandler and John Dickson Carr have been fighting out, for the last time, one hopes, the importance of "plot." One remembers Marx's quip about history repeating itself on the level of comedy.

The amazing downfall of plot is made evident I think by the irony, increased from year to year, of calling a respectable collection of short stories by the name of O. Henry. Despite an annual pious reference by the editor of the collection to the "patron saint" of the form, I suppose it is embarrassingly clear to everyone that O. Henry, who could only plot in the ultimate mechanical sense, never wrote a short story at all.

We find now such talents as Miss McCarthy's and Mr. Williams's, lacking completely any "invention," turning without qualms to the short story. "Invention" has, as a matter of fact, become in many quarters as suspect as draughtmanship in painting; it seems beside the point. Of course, the ability to contrive fables is honored still in the slick magazines, where it is so cynically pledged to the embellishment of formulae, that complete dishonor may seem preferable. In more serious magazines, "invention" is permitted to function only under the aegis of Kafka, that is in devising ingenious literal levels for allegories of the unconscious; but in such areas where a dénouement is irrelevant, and a story is ideally left unfinished, invention is turned from the making of "plots," whose mounting tensions and resolutions imply rationality, to embodying apprehension of an unresolvable irrationality.

It is presumably because the general essay is without status that such discursive minds as Mary McCarthy's turn to the short story. Certainly, the pleasures provided by her intended fictions seldom seem different from those afforded by what she used to call drama reviews in the *Partisan Review.* Occasionally, when life has been kind enough to provide a fabulous frame for her self-laceration and wit ("The Cicerone" is the most nearly successful effort in the present collection, though it does not nearly reach the baleful fascination of "The Man in the Brooks Brothers Shirt"), she gives us the proper formal pleasures of fiction, in addition to that rare sense she can provide of shameful enjoyment, so that participating in her writing becomes the equivalent of retailing an especially vicious bit of gossip, or peering, in abysmal shame and fascination, through a keyhole. It is, I suppose, because she is so utterly at the mercy of experience for fictional occasions that her present collection is eked out with essays and memoirs.

In the place of invention, the writer of short stories has become, above all, an exponent of "focus"—and one has the sense of much performance in this field as the lucky or carefully plotted "shot," and of the writer as the candid camera man, hanging by his feet from the window sill, or crawling on his belly in the midst of life's traffic, in pursuit of the "angle" that alone gives meaning to the event thrust up by the aimless shuffle of circumstances. William Sansom's "My Little Robins," the first story of his collection of "aspects and images," gives us a piece which is at once a description of such a method and its result—but in his work the pure "shot"-effect is marred by an intrusive style, which hints continually that the meaning of the event may have been as much in the writer's sensibility as in the painfully achieved "angle." W. C. Williams provides us with the most unmitigated instances of the technique, his "epiphanies" (the term is from Joyce, of course, to which Williams is often compared, though *The Dubliners*, with its highly patterned rhythms and rich, almost *fin de siècle* romantic metaphor, is quite another matter) given through an almost transparent medium. In "Make Light of It," the focus is all; the artist has reproduced, but ostensibly has not retouched, a given middle, only adding to it by the simple process of "cutting" a significant beginning and end. Williams's stories do not, of course, always proceed by the mere cold process of excision to which he pretends; their intent is marred occasionally by a warm, often embarrassing sentimentality, a veneration of the Passenack Polack as noble savage, sometimes rationalized as "communism"; but on the whole, he is reasonably faithful to his method.

The general inadequacy of the actual short story is the failure of style, and that in turn depends both on our inability to achieve a critical justification of style, and on a more deeply underlying inability to make enough of essential contemporary experience amenable to the control of language. And yet, logically, it is style which should be doing the work of faith in rational form rested upon a loss of faith in the rationality of common or shared experience of this world; but in its place, we have come to entertain a deep belief in the organizing power of individual feeling, the coherence of sensibility. But style, that is to say, diction, metaphor and rhythm, does for sensibility what action once did for the reason. No writer realized this more clearly, and acted more successfully on his realization, than Henry James.

It is no surprise, therefore, to find him much honored by contemporary writers; but it is discouraging to find him emulated only on the most superficial level in the contemporary short story. I actually find his influence working, not merely bowed to, in the only one story before me, my own "Fear of Innocence," and there I may be influenced by the knowledge of my intentions. Certainly *The Injustice Collectors* of Louis Auchincloss, which evoked James in a blurb, and displays on the jacket the external signs of the world in which he moved, provides only a blasphemous parody of the master, bringing to a kind of sub-life in the midst of the Jamesian décor a series of poorly imagined, feebly managed O. Henry contrivances.

In Aiken and Faulkner one finds the sort of strategic hesitancy, the palpable brooding on point of view, the willingness to commit a more than reasonable burden to language, that reminds one strongly of James—but in these older writers his typical exaggerations and excesses have been made very much their own, regionalized to Aiken's post-Freudian Boston, and Faulkner's "South," so indistinguishable from our own inner darkness. The lesson they have learned essentially is that blessed lesson of *excess*. Without *hubris* the short story is no damned good, and certainly the most interesting writers in my lot (whether finally good or bad, the only ones with a chance to be good in a way that will concern and move me) are the excessive ones: Aiken, Faulkner, Miss McCarthy, Sansom, who is not as good here as when performing inside the Kafkaesque world of "fireman Flower," Raymond Chandler and Paul Bowles. These share at least the quality of the outrageous which separates them from the glutinous gray mass of the two collections, Shaw, Sykes, etc. One is tempted to apply to the latter dull throng the Dantean advice on the spiritual mugwumps: *Non ragioniam di loro, ma guarda e passa;* but Heaven is not my immediate goal, and I must pause to discuss their plight.

The impression one gains from the anthologies in particular is that most current writers are so busy knocking wood and staying out of the rain that they cannot write a sentence capable of compelling a reader past the first paragraph. It is not merely, I think, a matter of too many disparate writers torn from their familiar surroundings and compelled to huddle together, without benefit of Thurber cartoons or holes in the magazine covers; it is their likeness that their new contiguity reveals, their carefulness, their anti-style.

Such a story as the Stegner prize piece in the O. Henry ("The Blue Winged Teal"), or practically any of the stories of Irwin Shaw, are so well-behaved, from their pat, unshifty symbols, carefully indicated in the title, to their carefully muted endings, that they are *really* (I mean unless one is a subscriber to the *New Yorker* or *Harper's* and has painfully learned to read them) unreadable. It is hard to realize at first that the carefully unrhythmical sentences, the rejection of metaphor and rhetoric, is a deliberately espoused and practiced technique. Writers who will allow themselves the disorganized opening of Stegner's story, or the shameless and unconvincing letter-device that makes Shaw's well-known "Act of Faith" go, would be ashamed to yield themselves up to the gayety or terror of language. There is nothing more offensive than offhand amateur psychoanalysis, but one can hardly doubt that the fear of language masks an essential fear of experience. The child's world is the world into which such writers plunge by preference—a manageable world toward which they can condescend a little with the gentlest of sentimentalities.

Christopher Sykes, who comes to us inexplicably touted by Evelyn Waugh, appears to be a British version of the anti-stylist at home. He seems always on the verge of implying some larger ethical framework against which his offhand stories would take on a further range of meaning, but he is so intent on reassuring us that he is really a good fellow after all, who gets the point and likes his bit of fun, that he never breaks through the polite chatter of his style. The resolvedly old-fashioned structuring of his stories ("Saint George" is a sufficiently dismal example) helps not at all.

When writers like Mr. Sykes on his side or Mr. Shaw on his are tempted to deal with such matters as the War, they reduce its terror to occasions for the sort of laughter or tears which barely rises above the level of boredom. And I suppose, after all, that one of the functions of the anti-style is precisely this: to give us a false sense of power over our environment, much as the set happy ending does, by bringing it down to the level of our easy contempt or acceptance, as the case may be. These writers are the Fannie Hursts of our period, and there will be just the same astonishment twenty years from now when we discover them inside the covers of our "best" collections, as there is now at finding Fanny in the earlier lists. (It would be ungrateful not to name the few writers in the collections who escape completely the sort of enmity to language I have been describing: Paul Bowles, Saul Bellow, George P. Elliot.)

Irwin Shaw deserves special comment, perhaps, for he has fallen only gradually into the production of the highly finished, eminently salable, but still somehow respectable article—the sort of cake that one eats and has. I remember feeling how aptly his *The Young Lions* was used in the recent movie *Sunset Boulevard* as the off-time "serious" reading of a young hack writer and gigolo. His work is precisely what the weary, liberal writer of bad movie scripts dreams he might turn out if he were only "free"—the sort of work in which social awareness and fundamental decency are entrusted with the work proper to the imagination. I have a great deal of respect for Shaw as a "case"; when I was in college, his play *Bury the Dead* found the precise clichés to express the political opinions of the leftish young, and I have sympathized with his more recent desire to withdraw it in light of what we have learned on either side of the last war. In a story called "Main Currents of American Thought," he has drawn a picture of the hack who attempts to keep alive his self-respect by buying Parrington's *Main Currents* . . . But it is precisely at this point of aspiration that his irony lapses into sentimentality, and he makes of the whole world of terror, bounded by memories of Clifford Odets and the time when every young writer was a Commie, something unrecognizably bereft of terror and ambiguity. He is the slickster *par excellence* of that good liberal mind which has lost touch with imagination and rhetoric and serious wit, and is defenseless against patness and self-pity.

Faulkner, windbag and Dixiecrat (at moments disconcertingly the Senator Claghorn of literature), and Miss McCarthy, the sort of spiritual Trotskyite that any right-minded liberal instinctively hates, are able more easily to honor the imagination—as well as that failure of love and triumph of terror, so essential to our world, but so unseizable by any journalistic or political substitute for the imagination. It is in the free activity of metaphor that the true stylist most spectacularly reveals himself; he has an almost anarchist attitude toward the autonomy of figurative detail within his fiction, whereas the anti-stylist is an aesthetic totalitarian whatever tickets he votes. The outrageous writer gives to the Devil of the irrational his due, and as always more than his due, in his handling of the trope.

Miss McCarthy's metaphors are the wittiest—at first glance, the most nearly autonomous of our lot; they not only compel from us a little shudder of recognition, but they betray us momentarily out of her given fictive world. But in the end they cohere into an organized system, a double series, perpetually suggesting the two other worlds that frame and define the intellectual society to which the action of the series is confined. One level of similitude threatens to reduce the world with which she deals to the realm that defines it from below, the world of things, especially machines or machine-made products: "he looked like an English cigarette," his eyes were "like strange green headlights on an old fashioned car"; Europeans become "fortune-telling machines." At the same time, another level of similitude is insisting on comparisons with an upper world of spirit, in terms of a religion in which none of her protagonists confess they believe. A woman mutters, "*Ite, missa est*," as the black market transaction is completed; through the polite gestures of the cicerone one senses "the swing of the censer" and "the swish of the altar-boy's skirts"; the self-deceit of an unsympathetic husband is a "cardinal article of faith," and his closed view of his relationship with his wife is "his authorized version." It is this larger, half-ironic acceptance of a triple world, material, human, spiritual, preserved at the metaphoric level where the limitations of conscious allegiance are forever defeated, that opens Miss McCarthy's stories out beyond her declared intent.

The metaphorical world of Mr. Aiken is less intellectualized, its irony more latent. His is the conventional world of Romantic tropes, what makes against his post-Freudian understanding of symbol a strange tension, not unlike that in Dylan Thomas's poems. When his 1920-ish Freudianism is bluntly stated, Mr. Aiken is likely to appear hopelessly old-fashioned, but against the even more old-fashioned counterpoint of "hawk-bright and frost-blue," against the inevitable comparison of swiftness to swallows and arrows (but we know all about swallows and arrows!) the effect is redeemed to freshness. The very title of one of his better stories, "A Pair of Vikings," is such an accepted soft image—but within its Romantic insights, Mr. Aiken is able to achieve a fine and rewarding irony.

In Faulkner, imagery is used obsessively; his images are in the first instance fully, almost "Homerically" developed, and they are repeated over and over at points of pressure strategically chosen, like the recurring end-words of a *sestina*, to give the effect of an attempted flight brought up again and again on the same snag of feeling and terror. Two of the best stories in the current collection, "Barn Burning" and "Death-Drag," provide striking instances of his skill with metaphor. The images of the "depthless man" in the former, the man without a shadow, the stamped-out man of tin in the iron coat, cluster about a boy's reluctant recognition of the evil of his barn-burning father; they are images that exist by their own right inside of this single piece, but that gain in force and texture when one knows them in Faulkner's other work, as applied to Popeye or the later Snopeses. In "Death-Drag" it is the double image of the man who is a shark in the plane that is a ghost which helps specify an obsessive vision of the defiance of terror become itself a more ultimate terror. In Faulkner the larger story symbol controls the minor tropes, but he never, like the anti-stylists, confines all his figurative impulses to one neat central symbol; his objective equivalents of horror remain always stubbornly frayed around the edges, give a final feeling of controlling rather than being controlled. Faulkner is different from the more resolutely "high-brow" writers like Miss McCarthy or even Aiken in devotion to plot—reinforced by a lifetime of writing and re-writing his pieces for the slick magazines that demand the apparatus of action. Indeed, it is often the function of his language, musical and figurative, to defend him from the consequences of that devotion, countering the impulse to make of the story a machine by leaning too heavily on stock surprise or suspense (as in "A Courtship") or by depending on the gimmicky double plot twist that almost ruins "A Rose for Emily" in the last sentence.

Raymond Chandler is, in the field of metaphor, the poor man's Mary McCarthy. It is hard to get past his own motions of what he is doing, especially since he has published in four separate places an essay called "The Simple Art of Murder," in which he claims to have rescued the detective story from commercialism and the "flippers of the trained seals of the critical fraternity"— for "Realism" as defined by Hemingway and Hammett. Taken on his own terms, Mr. Chandler is a little ridiculous in that sentimental, back-room vein that has come to be called "hard-boiled"; but understood as a popular pastoral poet, the creator of a world of the incredibly drunk and lush, and the untiringly nymphomaniac babe, through which the wise-cracking Swain as Private Eye walks to the inevitable beating he so richly deserves, Chandler has contrived the most successfully atrocious prose style since Lyly's Euphues, but one which, we should realize, does for the reader to whom literature comes flanked by ads, for sure cures for piles and correspondence courses in becoming a detective, the work of poetry. "He looked about as inconspicuous as a tarantula on a slice of angel-food cake."

Despite the best efforts of Chandler, however, the detective story seems to have failed for its public, as much contemporary writing is failing for other more "serious" publics, in domesticating terror, at a moment when, from within and without, horror is threatening to engulf us. Politics have failed to stem the tide; the only hope is the imagination. I suppose that the mass reader feels with the most cliquish of us, that no "naturalistic" literary genre which fails to pay sufficient respect to magic and myth can survive among us; so that, just as we turn from Hemingway to Kafka, or from Horney to Wilhelm Reich, the pulp-reader turns from the detective story to Science Fiction, or STF as its devotees prefer to call it.

Surely there has never existed in America such a "movement" in the full European sense of the word, right down on the most popular level. STF satisfies a fundamental hunger for the *merveilleux* starved for a long time. Commercial interests have taken advantage of the fervor, and middle-brow muddlers have moved in with various inappropriate vocabularies, but one senses beneath it all the only lively spontaneous manifestation in the contemporary short story. The actual level of writing remains still quite low, often not much above the primitive effort not to use the same word too frequently in the same sentence, despite the almost frenetic critical fervor of readers, who fill page after page with letters of sub-aesthetic comment, and despite the flood of genuine little magazines in the field, called "fanzines," apparently completely unsubsidized, and sporting such titles as *Amoeba, Eusifano* and *Spacewarp.* The advantage of the popular genre lies in the opportunity it provides for the writer and reader to remain unaware of what is really at stake in the developing form. It remains to be seen whether STF will be able to stand up under the strain of slumming expeditions from the high-brow world, or the efforts of founders of Dianetics and advocates of non-Aristotelian semantics to "raise its level." At the present moment, much irrelevant chatter is going on, directed at separating out the truly "prophetic" STF piece from the story of gadgetary interest, and the Bug-eyed Monster thriller. Meanwhile the writers, a rather gloomy bunch, must attempt as best they can to fit their neo-Orwellian, anti-Utopian apprehensions into a formula which demands a reasonably happy ending. What counts, of course, is not what is demanded of them, but what they can get away with—and what they are getting away with is the exploitation of pure terror and the revival of magic, all under the honorific rubric of "science." They are redeeming science for the imagination by mythicizing it, and immunizing the spirit against the indignities of the concentration camp and atomic mutilation by popularizing horror in its most up-to-date avatars.

It is the business of more serious writers, I feel, to be moving into this field in an attempt to redeem neo-Gothic horror for the total, subtle mind, as Poe redeemed it from the early German exponents of *schrecklichkeit.* I do not think the way is to allegorize it blatantly as C. S. Lewis has done in his popularizing novels; Charles Williams has come close to a legitimate metaphysical use of the new terror and magic, but his work was confined to the novel and he has left us no exemplars in the short story. "The Portable Phonograph," of Walter Van Tilburg Clark, represents an essay in the right direction, with its STF theme of the cave-huddling remnants of humanity, just after the final war, defending the remnants of culture with a lead pipe. Clark, however, has only a dim sense of magic, preferring to move downward from the human toward the brute animal experience, and his special talent lies in the *tour de force* of articulating the inarticulate aspiration of the bestial, the hunger of the hawk.

It is Paul Bowles who does for the intellectuals what STF has done for the pulp-reader, compels from us the shocked, protesting acceptance of terror as an irreducible element of being. The whole impact of his work is the insistence on the horrible, and his stories seem only literary by accident, despite their having appeared in very little magazines, and despite the astonishing ease and rhythmical beauty of the style. Like the tales of the science-fictionist, his work denies the world of our everyday living for landscapes more easily allegorized for his purposes; his mythic North Africa and Latin America has its reality in the nightmare, like the trans-galactic worlds of space fiction. He suffers from two basic faults, however, which keep him from achieving the effect upon us he seems always on the verge of attaining. The first arises out of his speaking to intellectuals; driven to deal with ideas, he soon reveals his total inability to make intellectual notions as real as feelings, to specify men thinking as convincingly as he can specify men undergoing castration. The second is a fault endemic to this whole new enterprise; like Chandler and the writers of STF, with their endlessly sapped heroes and their victims stripped of all skin and screaming forever in a saline solution, he is a pornographer of terror, a secret lover of the horror he evokes. It seems to me that he suffers in this latter respect because of the breakdown of a tradition.

Historically there have been only two subjects for the short story proper and one of them is terror (the other is isolation)—but the recent collapse of our long-honored Western attitudes toward force and suffering in the face of concentration camps, compulsory confessions and mass bombing, have left us in a situation much like that in which we found ourselves not long since in regard to sex. We are waiting, I suppose, for a Lawrence of the world of horror. Our more venerable models seem absurdly inadequate. One gets the notion from the Gothic Novel that the Monk Lewises could not really believe in pure terror, but only *wanted* to; and Poe with his heavy costuming and pseudo-antique décor seems to have suffered from the remarkable delusion that horror had to be protected against the encroachments of a world of progress and machinery. Our own need is to make the clean, oiled machine a terror in a tale like the witch or the Inquisitor.

But we cannot seem to strike the right note. We vacillate between censorship and pornography. Here on the desk before me lies an ad for *The Happy Mother Goose*, an expurgated collection in which the famous three mice are not blind but kind, and the Farmer's wife cuts off not their tails but a slice of cheese to feed them; it is all meant, of course, to assure our young that there is no brutality or unkindness in all the world. Beside the new Mother Goose lies a copy of Bowles's *Delicate Prey*, open to the dedication: "for my mother, who first read me the stories of Poe." Having already been twice through the title story in which a young Arab has his sliced-off sex thrust into an incision in his belly, I can only see the tender childhood the dedication evokes in terms of a Charles Addams cartoon—the happy vampire and son at home over the "Cask of Amontillado."

We must, somewhere between the limits of squeamishness and abandon, learn to come to terms with horror; one way is, perhaps, to move again toward a belief in mystery and magic, to a mythic apprehension of reality, to the realization that, in a quite real sense we have not appreciated for a long time, the old gods of darkness are not dead. But to *play* at such a belief, while forgivable enough in cozier Victorian times, when one had to try to shudder, is for us unpardonable. To write the "ghost story," evoking with coy ambiguity antique versions of what haunts us, Wandering Jew or magician or sea nymph (as in Conrad Aiken or Faulkner's "Doctor Martino"—or even Mr. Sansom's almost successful "Poseidon's Daughter"), is to be insufferably beside the point. Nor will it do to evoke the terror of war or politics or personal relationships in the muted style based on the assumption that sociology or psychology or even common sense could explain it *all*. It is not true that with a (revised) Marx and Freud under one arm, one can easily hold the burden of mystery in his free hand.

I suspect that for terror to be truly redeemed, humanized for use in moving and substantial human fictions, it must be understood as *real evil*; without such a belief, the evoked evil one will remain our good old unconscious in a child's false-face. Miss McCarthy comes close to this sort of metaphysics (which entails the denial of the well-behaved style), but she refuses to make the next step that would bring her insights to their final point. She will not recognize the world of innocence, and she is left with the snob's religion: a devil and no god. William Faulkner, in great, clumsy exasperation, makes the final leap—or rather, one regrets to say, *made* it once, for his latest trivial sentimental stories indicate that he has lost the terrible full vision of his greatest work. It is easy enough to ask from the comfort of the reviewing stand for so terrible and committed an awareness, but it is not easy to live by it full time, much less to make of it beautiful fictions.

It is Faulkner's own region that he has so redeemed, the region of us all in so far as it represents that nightmare encounter of black and white from which we all strive to awake, but other areas remain to be redeemed for myth and style and understood terror. The whole of the last war evades us still; we have not yet chewed through the clichés of expectation with which we protected ourselves against its fact; and we have scarcely begun to approach in terms of its inner terror the experience of a whole generation in the Communist Party (Shaw in various places and John Cheever, in a story called "Vega," touch this area with aggravating superficiality—and Williams feints at it several times). If only a talent might arise capable of dealing with these polar experiences with all the cold, precise control of horror that a Bowles squanders on symbols of irrelevant sadism in an exotic landscape; and if only that talent could find a metaphysics and a style able to seize our own parochial terrors in all their rich local involvement with ideas and baffled innocence and stuttering love, the short story might truly flourish among us. Surely it is permitted to believe that the form will rise to its terrible obligation as the unforeseen poetry of our perhaps ultimate hour.

The Higher Unfairness

I am sure that a good deal of the pleasure I find in reading Mary McCarthy arises out of my sense of how offensive she is (and cannot help being) to a certain kind of reader whom it is important that somebody offend. There is a particular kind of "right-thinking" mind that is reduced to a frantic rage not only by what she says, but by her tone, her metaphorical habits, the very shape of her sentences. I should say that it is impossible to have voted for Henry Wallace in 1948 and to admire the cold, underground wit of Mary McCarthy—the wit from which she seems recently to be unhappily relaxing; but which made her drama reviews in *Partisan Review* and her earlier stories so painfully attractive, and which flickers fitfully in *The Groves of Academe.*

Her original gift seems compounded not only of the traditional detached virulence of the satirist (with its roots in self-hatred, and its hostility to pride), but also of the special bitterness of the rebel, grown hard and cagey in his fight against a society which he cannot even persuade to listen to his declaration of war. If in the past Miss McCarthy has often turned her cold eye on the individuals and types on her own side of the (theoretical) barricades, it has not mattered finally; since she has flayed and pilloried them from a point of view impossible for the "soft" liberal or literate philistine to share, even for the sake of rejoicing in the discomfiture of a despised category of intellectuals. Mary McCarthy's appeal has been a snob appeal of a particularly fortunate sort, since the group for whom she has written, far from considering themselves a "happy few," have prided themselves on being a very miserable minority indeed—and she has represented with rare agility and grace the ability of that group at once to despise themselves and the society from which they have withdrawn.

The proper milieu for such a mind was provided by the avant-garde magazines and their readers; and it seems to me that both Miss McCarthy and that milieu have suffered since their separation from each other. As a kind of Apostle to the Gentiles, mingling unnoticed among the contributors to *The New Yorker*, and expounding to its readers (not a few of whom have, of course, always found *Partisan Review,* for example, "negative and Trotskyite") the vagaries of "one side of contemporary American intellectual life," Miss McCarthy has tended to lose precisely those troublesome spiritual qualities, once her greatest asset.

I think it becomes (alas!) more and more possible to read her with the sense that *someone else* is always being satirized, and without the acute and embarrassing awareness of the indignity of being human which she once so masterfully controlled. There are basically two kinds of satire, I suppose: the kind that attacks eccentricity with the comfortable feeling that the writer belongs to the group which embodies a true center and norm (this is preeminently represented among us by *The New Yorker*); and the kind that finds the human condition essentially ridiculous. The first kind is often rooted in a smug, conservative sort of optimism (confusingly known in our world as "liberalism"), while the other kind usually tends toward a religious point of view (often concealed in our world under the rubric of "radicalism"). There had always seemed to me the possibility that Miss McCarthy's wit might flower into such a Christian-Swiftian sort of satire, when its bitterness had recognized itself as a sign of humility; but I do not find such a flowering in her most recent work.

The Groves of Academe has found a subject which seems especially apt as a vehicle for Miss McCarthy's insights and hostilities, dealing as it does with the confrontation of the Liberal and the Underground Man (just such a confrontation as Mary McCarthy's own work provides a certain kind of reader). The scene is the campus of a small "advanced" college; the antagonists Mulcahy, a seedy Machiavellian and self-despiser, obviously "chosen" by his immense unattractiveness to be the Victim of a hundred minor persecutions, and Maynard Hoar, a handsome, loved, earnest and empty Liberal with no sense of how complicated it is to be human. These two have come to seem by now almost archetypal figures, confronting each other over and over again in Congressional committee rooms and before the bench, in the tragi-comedy of revelations about Communism that have filled the columns of our daily newspapers for the last several years.

But Miss McCarthy with a rare comic twist (it is the first successful gimmick she has ever come on, having no essential talent for the machinery of fiction) has made Mulcahy *falsely* accuse himself of having been a Communist, in an involved strategy to hold on to his job as professor of literature in the school of which Hoar, a pledged friend of freedom, is president. The book does not quite live up to the promise of its device, though there are, indeed, many delightful and telling passages—in particular, the description of a poetry conference, that typical cultural event of our time, heretofore not memorialized in fiction. In a sentence here and there, a turn of phrase, an unexpected metaphor, there is a touch of the old wit, but what is lacking in the style is the *excess* that once characterized Miss McCarthy's work, the overloading of each sentence, the lovely vicious gags thrown away out of the sheer fertility of her malice and invention.

Besides, though the book asserts a claim to being a novel, it contains none of the rich novelistic texture of interwoven relationships, none of the large rhythms of change which mark a true novel. Miss McCarthy's talent lies in the framing of sentences, and in the art of composing what used to be called "characters"—set pieces of static description in epigrammatic phrases, the *fixing* of individuals and types in a way essentially hostile to the dynamics of fiction. It is a shame that the older genre has disappeared; or that Miss McCarthy cannot, at least, continue to practice it under the guise of writing drama reviews—for as a novelist she cannot move, in any of the senses of the word.

I do not mean to say that Mulcahy is not magnificently realized, or that certain aspects of student life (though there are no real students in the book) and academic procedure are not neatly caught, or rather, caught out—but nothing happens, it is all *presented*. The secondary plot of the book, a fable of initiation into the dark tangle of human motives, involves a most improbable ingénue, called Domna Rejnev, who convinces us neither that she is Russian (though she talks about Tolstoi and insists on importing tins of *borscht* into the groves of academe), nor, indeed, that she is a real person.

As a matter of fact, none of Miss McCarthy's "control" characters—those normal types against whom the eccentricity of the eccentrics is defined—are at all convincing. The juvenile, an over-solemn neo-orthodox Protestant, the vestigial Proletarian Poet (an egregious example of the sort of pastoral glorification of simple types into which Miss McCarthy occasionally falls), the incredibly principled Alma neither amuse us nor impose their reality upon us. It is only in contriving "humors" and caricatures that Miss McCarthy is at home.

She is even less adequate in stating abstractly the center of values from which the eccentric deviates than she is in creating the innocents who embody those values. Explicit "ideas" are even less her forte than ingénues; and when she is *telling* us why progressive schools are false utopias, why it is wrong to teach students to be "critics rather than readers," or why certain kinds of modern poets are despicable, she falls into a smugness and flatness that betray the wit and unmercifulness of her simple seeing. When she descends, for instance, to a quip about the poet who cannot find time enough to attend all the poetry conferences eager to hear his remarks on the Neglect of Poetry, she is engaging in the satire of condescension rather than that of implication. It is the *other* who is seen as absurd, with a merely vulgar kind of unfairness, quite different from that Higher Unfairness, that unwillingness to pander to any aspect of our own or her self-esteem, which once marked Miss McCarthy's work, and to which I hope she will return.

Encounter with Death

A Death in the Family is not a completed novel, but a collection of brilliant narrative and lyric fragments given *editorially* the semblance of a novel. In its present state (fixed by the premature death of the author), it hesitates between two ambitions, one of which would have made it a tight, highly unified novella, covering only some three or four days; the other of which would have expanded it in the direction of thick, family saga, spanning in its main action five to ten years—and including by indirect reference many more. Only the novella-germ seems to have been worked out in anything like final form; while the saga survives as a handful of trial studies, not integrated into the main fiction by the author but somewhat arbitrarily placed in the present book by the editors.

The single unifying factor of the novella and saga—aside from their common raw material of family history—is the mind of a small boy, the death of whose father and the coming to moral maturity of whose mother are the center of the three-day narrative. Yet here, too, there is confusion; for Agee had apparently not yet solved the problem of point of view; and the book, as it has been patched together, shifts disconcertingly from a post of observation just behind the head of the small boy to one which moves nervously. The incomplete work hovers between the subjective and objective, between the lyrical and the novelistic.

The book turns, it seems to me, about four major themes: the threat and temptations of drunkenness, the clash of utterly different families joined in a marriage resented by both, the terrible illumination implicit in the face of death, the conflict of Protestantism and Catholicism. The last two are sufficiently rendered, in a discreet and subtle poetry, within the limits of the novella. The first two are only suggested in the fragments of the saga which survive. The family of the dead husband, for instance, comes to life briefly in the opening, is further illuminated by a visit to his great-grandmother in the deep country (the opposition between the families involves that between urban and rural, instinctive and intellectual), but is lost at the book's close—where that family simply drops out of sight in a lapse unforgivable in a finished work.

In a strange way, the basic limitations of the book (insofar as they can be divined in its present form) are indistinguishable from its basic virtues. It is not sufficient to say merely, as I have said so far, that the book suffers from a conflict between Agee's essentially lyric gifts and the novelistic obligations he accepts. John Peale Bishop and Robert Penn Warren, for instance (writers he is most like in background and thematic concerns as well as technique), solve similar problems with some success, finding, each in his own way, fictional strategies not incompatible with their poetic ambitions. The point is, I think, that Agee's talent is peculiarly *visual*, that the world comes to him in sharp, fragmented sights—all detailed foreground. He paints his scenes sometimes like a miniaturist, and this hovering, scrupulous attention to detail obscures both the kind of infinitely receding background and the sense of forward motion necessary to the novel.

Yet it would be ungrateful and unforgivable not to say what *pleasure* there is in his visual revelations. The sights (and though primarily these, beyond them, the smells, tastes, textures, sounds) of Knoxville, Tennessee, some forty years ago, are rendered with an astonishing tact and precision, with a kind of freshness that belongs, for most of us, only to the memories of childhood. It is in the lyrical, free, sensual evocation of a boy's world as seen for the first time, the world of experience upon which our others depend and from which they hopelessly decline that Agee excels.

The tone of the book (at its novella-heart) is nostalgic: a longing to recapture the seen-for-the-first-time, to relive the child's sense of warm, safe involvement in love, to believe again that such security is immune from death and change, to be what we were before we felt the need to identify ourselves. Yet the nostalgia is seldom sentimental; for it is essentially religious. It does not, that is to say, deny the reality of death or pain or suffering, the necessity of the fall from the child's peace or the exclusion from the child's Great Good Place; it only affirms that that peace and that place are real, too; and somehow they survive the disappearance of the people and the houses, the sights and sounds which sustained them. To attempt to translate the book's meaning out of its expression is to realize that, whatever its failure to achieve novel form, it is, in the full sense, poetry: an unanalyzable fusion of theme and image, significance and language. It is the language of the book, at once luminescent and discreet, the language of Agee, *Agee*, that remains in the mind in this time of meager, undistinguished prose, the prose of authors pledged to pretend they are not really there.

A Homosexual Dilemma

For what seems a long time but surely can be no more than a few years, I have been watching James Baldwin's work—not merely reading it, but watching it, warily, hopefully—a little incredulously. I have had the sense that here for once was a young Negro writer, capable of outgrowing at the same moment both qualifications and becoming simply a writer. *Giovanni's Room*, whatever its limitations, is a step in this direction—that is to say, a step beyond the Negro writer's usual obsession with his situation as a Negro in a white culture, an obsession which keeps him forever writing a first book.

I do not mean to imply that the writer who is also a Negro can afford to ignore the deepest passions and conditions of his growing up, and Baldwin has, indeed, treated those passions and conditions in his earlier novel, *Go Tell It on the Mountain*. But he must, I am convinced, *break through*, find ways of registering his identity and outsidedness through other symbols than the accidental, autobiographical one of skin color. Our very concern with Negro-white relations has tended to make a cliché of every aspect of them, and the writer who accepts them as *the* subject lays up for himself a life of exasperation and frustration. It is not easy to make poetry of sociological banalities, especially if one approaches them already committed to righteousness and self-pity.

There is not only no Negro problem in Baldwin's new book: there are not even any Negroes—and this, I must confess, makes me a little uneasy. His protagonist, David, is a shade *too* pale-face, almost ladies-magazine-Saxon, gleaming blond and "rather like an arrow": but this is not what troubles me finally. It is rather the fact that he encounters no black faces in his movements through Paris and in the south of France, that not even the supernumeraries are colored; so that one begins to suspect at last that there must *really* be Negroes present, censored, camouflaged or encoded. It is a little like the feeling of Trilling's *Middle of the Journey,* in which no Jew is permitted to enter a world of intellectual Communists and fellow-travelers. In the mature novel toward which Baldwin is progressing, surely Negro characters will be present, at the periphery or in the center, as the exigencies and probabilities of the story demand—a full world fully rendered.

Giovanni's Room does not create such a full world in any sense. It is a tightly focused book, a novella rather than a novel—dense at its best moments, thin at its worst, but always spare. There are only three characters who count: David himself, the American girl Hella, and the Italian homosexual Giovanni. David, who has never faced up to anything in himself, is driven to make a choice between marriage to Hella and a life with Giovanni in the miserable room on the outskirts of Paris that serves as a symbol of the shoddiness, the isolation, the appallingly naked intimacy of such an affair. Not even choosing in full awareness, but drifting and fleeing, he abandons Giovanni, who in his desolation and poverty is led to commit a murder and is finally guillotined. But David cannot in the end marry Hella at all, her very touch having become repulsive to him; and he is left to a life of degradation and self-reproach, punctuated by furtive affairs with sailors.

It is all very moral and melodramatic, almost a little morality play in modern dress, in which the characters tend to become allegorical and life is portrayed as exacting consequences more bloody and final than its usual fumblings attain. There is something quite old-fashioned about the basic fable: indeed, David's despair after his unalterable rejection of Giovanni recalls phrases from books long confined to the ten-cent tables of second-hand bookstores. "All my vivid realization of how utterly base I myself had been, and of your unspeakable agony, caused by me, your despair, your humiliation, all my remorse . . . my sense of what I had wantonly flung away, and lost beyond all recovery . . . in a word, all my love—love that had lain as I supposed dead, now suddenly had come to, never to let me rest any more . . ." The feeling is the feeling of Baldwin's book, but the words are those of a character in a novel published in 1887 and called *The Yoke of the Thorah*.

Indeed, there is a clue here. The earlier protagonist, a Jew, has reached his final pitch of despair by refusing to marry the Gentile girl with whom he was truly in love, by failing to cast off the "yoke of the Torah." But he might well have been (and *was* in the novel of a few decades later) a white boy giving up his Negro mistress, a social climber rejecting the poor (and pregnant) girl for an heiress: it is a basic American plot—a staple of popular fiction wherever it dares approach the problematical. But it is the gimmick of Baldwin's book to have made the poor but worthy girl a poor but worthy fairy, and thus to have dissolved the sentimental assurance of the older versions into a quite contemporary ambiguity. A writer need be only a little enlightened to recommend (heartily or tearfully) breaking through economic or religious or social conventions to marry the girl one loves. But what if the girl is a *boy*? The moral concern remains, but where is the assured moral answer?

"You are the one who keeps talking about *what* I want," Giovanni insists at one point to David. "But I have only been talking about *who* I want." In terms of Baldwin's novel, this conflict between the "what" and "who" approach to love comes to stand for a deep conflict of the American and European conscience.

It is David, the American, who feels driven to ask not "Can I love Giovanni?" but "Can I love a *man?*", just as his ancestors, of whom, despite his expatriation, he is so proud ("My ancestors conquered a continent, pushing across death-laden plains . . .") might have asked: Can I love a Jew, a Negro, a dissolute woman, one older than myself? We are back now to *The Ambassadors*, to Henry James and the clash between the recent American notion that experience is itself a good and love the great experience, and the more ancient American conviction that there are clean and unclean loves and that only what is clean is good.

It is the most amusing of Baldwin's wry ironics to portray the last stand of Puritanism as a defense of heterosexuality. But if David is our latest Last Puritan, he is by that very token the most uncertain of them all. He knows he cannot endure the stench of Giovanni's room, of Europe; but no more can he return to the well-washed Hella, to a clean America. And what of Hella, what of women in a world where men are as lost as David? "David," she cries, "please, let me be a woman . . . It's *all* I want . . ." But what *he* wants he does not know, and it requires his confidence in his own maleness to define her. "But if women are supposed to be led by men and there aren't any men to lead them, what happens then?"

I do not finally believe in Baldwin's sense of "the lack of sexual authority" in our world; but I believe he believes in it and feels the consequences of such a belief as he renders them in this book. Beneath the melodramatic statement, he is attempting a tragic theme: the loss of the last American innocence, the last of moral certainty—that the mirror does not lie, that little boys are boys, little girls girls. Once more, Hella is his mouthpiece: "Americans should never come to Europe . . . It means they never can be happy again. What's the good of an American who isn't happy? Happiness was all we had." But Hella sees only partway; if beyond happiness there is despair, beyond morality bewilderment, past despair and bewilderment there is God. Baldwin is finally a religious writer, though his religion is desperate and tentative in the expected modern manner. The last word, after all, is with David, who has betrayed everything, in his appeal to the "heavy grace of God," and in his cry to his deepest self, "I must believe. I must believe . . ."

The Noble Savages
of Skid Row

Not all writers are lucky enough to get their first novels written first. Some write them all their lives; some never make it at all. Nelson Algren has finally got to his—six books deep in his career and at just the point where his reputation begins to jell, when everyone has the feeling he has always been there.

In *A Walk on the Wild Side*, he touches directly the critical moment of his life, the juncture at which he took on his pose, his stance, the platitudes and the sentimentality that have informed his work ever since. The place was New Orleans (more precisely, Storyville); the time, 1931; the mood, that half-paralyzed depression-bred self-pity which it was once possible to think of as revolutionary fervor. In that place, at that time, out of that mood, Algren re-created himself from a journalism-school student on the make to the bard of the stumble-bum.

That there is more than a little fraud involved in his pose can't, I think, be held against him. For the American writer, the one thing impossible is to speak in his own voice; such obvious honesty never seems to him honest *enough*. If Algren seems heading from the start toward the annoying jacket portrait showing him ankle-deep in back-alley garbage, so was Hemingway always aiming at the candid shot of "Papa" coming out of the African bush, or Faulkner at the post on the porch behind the colonial pillars. Most American novelists share with farmers and shopkeepers the notion that a writer is less *real* than a junkie, a planter, a big-game hunter or a pug. If Algren's stance apologizes for his art and betrays his lack of faith in his very function, he is in good company; if he had more talent it would not really matter.

ADVENTURE IN NOSTALGIA

Certain talents he does have: the natural novelist's uncanny gift of recall—so that every barroom conversation, every grifter's confidence lives on indefinitely in his mind. His books are always little encyclopedias of offbeat information, unprinted articles from a scandalous *National Geographic*. In the present book we can learn the names and habits of railroad cops over a score of states, the self-imposed "legal codes" of men in jail, the color of jeans worn at a certain time in a certain small town in Texas.

And then Algren can be really funny. In this novel, a rocking chair, a red-and-green coffeepot, a shameless and greedy Negro girl and a mosquito are worked into a scene of howling farce. When Algren grows serious, however, he is embarrassing. It is not merely a matter of his impossibly arty prose, his truncated sentences which, aiming at effect, end in incoherence, his inability to pass by an assonance or a jazzy rhythm; in any style, he is able to tell the truth only about *facts*. His people are not rendered as seen, but recast by sentimentality and the desire to make a soapbox point.

In a strange way, Algren, for all his desire to come to terms with an impossibly "real" life, is isolated from the life of his time. He was made, unfortunately, once and for all in the early 1930s, in the literary cult of "experience" of those times. He has not thought a new thought or felt a new feeling since. He has merely recapitulated and stood still, more and more lonely, as our literature has moved on and left him almost a museum piece—the Last of the Proletarian Writers. Naturally, the technical conservatism of his writing and his old-fashioned "new" ideas have not impeded his popularity; the reader knows in advance what he is up against, and the reading of one of his books is an adventure in nostalgia. That is why it seems quite proper for him to come home at last in his latest novel, to put back into the context that bred them the poor platitudes by which he has lived ever since: "'Nobody goes hungry' said Little Round Hoover, wiping chicken gravy off his little round chin. A man with the right stuff in him didn't need government help to find work. That would make him lazy . . . Self-reliance for the penniless and government help to the rich, the Old Guard was in again." It is as if the *Anvil* had never died, the *New Masses* never shrunk. If only it were all so simple, and we all so young again!

Algren is finally a political writer and a moralist, though his politics is largely sentiment and his morality pure corn. Behind his present account of New Orleans pimps and whores there is a point, a gin-soaked pill of bitter wisdom. Indeed, the narrative of *A Walk on the Wild Side* is slight and perfunctory; a major portion of the book is local color and almost all the rest editorial. The climax of the novel is a little sermon in pseudo-popular prose that surely must represent Algren's own point of view, since it is completely improbable in the mind of the character who presumably thinks it: "All I found was two kinds of people. Them that would rather live on the loser's side of the street with the other losers than to win off by theirselves; and them who want to be one of the winners even though the only way left for them to win was over them who have already been whipped."

Just to be sure we've got it, Algren buttonholes us once more on the jacket, his own exegete: "The book asks why lost people sometimes develop into greater human beings than those who have never been lost in their whole lives."

Ultima Skid Row

These are not, of course, ideas but sentimental indulgences—a refusal to see the very characters the author imagines or remembers except through a haze of forgiving tears. Why the small-time con man or pander seems to Algren nobler than the "Do-Right Daddy," the successful banker, say, whose methods the cheap operator is emulating as best he can, is never made clear to the mind, however compellingly put to the feelings. Rich and poor, all men are liars to themselves, all lost.

Surely, mere material failure is no distinction in the tragic world where all fail. But Algren's world is not tragic; it is melodramatic, the arena for his strange version of the Class Struggle between bum and banker, freak and real-estate owner. There is no room in this expurgated universe for workers or teachers or clerks, no room for anything that does not qualify for a place in an edifying nightmare. Algren's is a world of exotics—the last jungle, inhabited by the last of the Noble Savages, the final goal of literary tourism.

It is, then, as an exotic, a romantic purveyor of escape literature, that Algren must be read—this apparent "realist" whose fictional world is at the ultimate remove from any reality his readers know. Beyond Tahiti and Samoa, there exists the last unexplored island: Ultima Skid Row, on which nothing is merely dull, grimy and without savor, but all grotesque and titillating in the lurid light of Algren's "poetic" prose. It is to the last Romantic America that he takes us, to the last dream turned nightmare, this strange cicerone. What final pleasure we find in his novels we find, alas, as *voyeurs*.

Up from Adolescence

I am not sure why I have liked so much less, this time through, a story which moved me so deeply when I first read it in *The New Yorker* four or five years ago. I mean, of course, "Zooey," to which "Franny" is finally an appendage, like the long explanatory footnote on pages 52 and 53, the author's apologetic statement on the jacket, the pretentiously modest dedication: all the gimmicks, in short, which conceal neither from him nor from us the fact that he has not yet made of essentially novelistic material the novel it wants to become.

It was, I guess, the novel which "Zooey," along with a handful of earlier stories, seemed to promise to which I responded with initial enthusiasm: the fat chronicle of the Glass family which might have caught once and for all the pathos and silliness of middle-class, middle-brow intellectual aspiration— the sad and foolish dream that certain families, largely Jewish, dreamed for their children listening to the Quiz Kids perform on the radio two long decades ago. For the sake of that novel, Salinger seemed at the point of making a new start, of breaking through certain bad habits picked up along the way from *Good Housekeeping* to *The New Yorker*. Certainly in "Zooey" Salinger had begun untypically to specify the times and circumstances of his characters; to furnish patiently the rooms through which they moved; to eschew slickness and sentimentality and easy jokes in favor of a style almost inept enough to guarantee honesty; to venture beyond an evocation of adolescent self-pity and adolescent concern with sex titillating chiefly to adolescents themselves.

But there is, as yet, no novel—only "Zooey," well-leaded and in hard covers, flanked by apologies and new promises, but still unfulfilled: and it is this, I suppose, which has left me baffled and a little disappointed. In a magazine, Salinger's documentation seemed not quite so irrelevant, his furnishings not quite so disproportionate to the events they frame, the awkwardness of his writing not quite so much a tic of embarrassment or a posture of false modesty.

"Franny" itself, which I had not read before, seems to me an eminently satisfactory piece of reportage, turned in as evidence (at the demonstration trial of the generations, in which it is not clear who is the plaintiff, who the defendant) by a middle-aged eavesdropper on station platforms and at restaurants where the Ivy League young ritually prepare for watching games and getting laid. It is, at least, scarcely ever cute, like much of "Zooey" and all of the mere apparatus with which it ekes out a book; and it ends ambiguously before its author, whose resolutions are often disasters, can manage to be either sentimental or sage. In "Franny" for once Salinger demonstrates that he can write of adolescence without disappearing into it; but "Franny," alas, is completed by "Zooey," which itself completes nothing.

We have been, I begin slowly to understand, living through a revolution in taste, a radical transformation of the widest American literary audience from one in which women predominate to one in which adolescents make up the majority. Controlling the market (it is, for instance, largely to reach them that the more expensive paperbacks were invented and marketed in new ways by new generations of editors scarcely older than themselves), they control also the mode. And the mode demands, in lieu of the teenage novelists who somehow refuse to appear, Teenage Impersonators, among whom one might list, say, Norman Mailer, Jack Kerouac, even William Burroughs—certainly the Salinger who wrote *Catcher in the Rye* and invented Holden Caulfield, a figure emulated by the young themselves, though not by all the young.

Each of the Impersonators I have mentioned speaks only for a portion of our youth: hip or beat or square, straight or queer or undecided. No one writes for all, but inevitably takes his stand: with those who "turn on" or those who do not, with those who write papers on Kierkegaard and Flaubert or those who scrawl on the walls of saloons "Ez for Pres." Salinger, of course, speaks for the cleanest, politest, best-dressed, best-fed and best-read among the disaffected (and who is not disaffected?) young; not junkies or faggots, not even upper-Bohemians, his protagonists travel a road bounded on one end by school and on the other by home. They have families and teachers rather than lovers or friends; and their crises are likely to be defined in terms of whether or not to go back for the second semester to Vassar or Princeton, to Dana Hall or St. Mark's. Their *Angst* is improbably cued by such questions as: "Does my date for the Harvard weekend *really* understand what poetry is?" or "Is it possible that my English instructor hates literature after all?"

I do not mean by reduction to mock the concerns of Salinger's characters; they cannot, in any case, be reduced, and I should mock myself making fun of them. For better or for worse, a significant number of sensitive young Americans live in a world in which the classroom and the football game provide customary arenas for anguish and joy, love and death; and to that world, Salinger has been more faithful than it perhaps deserves. Which is why in the end he is a comic novelist or nothing. If the Temple Drake of Faulkner's *Sanctuary* stands as the classic portrait of a coed in the twenties, the Franny of Salinger's Glass stories bids to become her equivalent for the fifties, and the decline in terror and intensity from one to the other, the descent toward middle-brow bathos is the fault not of Salinger but of the times. Temple's revolt was against vestigial Puritanism and obsolescent chivalry and her weapons were booze and sex; Franny's is against literature and the New Criticism and her weapon is the "Jesus Prayer."

Certainly, this is fair enough; for, in the thirty years that separate the two refugees from college, the Culture Religion of Western Europe has replaced Christianity as the orthodox faith for middle-class urban Americans; and the pastors to whom our hungry sheep look up in vain are Ph.Ds in Literature and the "section men" who are their acolytes. In a society presided over by this new clergy, to play with Vedanta or Buddhism or even Catholicism, except as these are represented in certain recent poetic texts, *i.e.*, to seek a salvation beyond the reach of art, is considered heresy or madness or some blasphemous compound of both. Franny, at any rate, who will not write the proper papers or go out for the next college play, seems, not only to her elders and her peers, but to herself as well, a heretic guilty as charged and therefore self-condemned to what her world calls a "nervous breakdown."

I am less sure this time though than I was the first that Salinger really understands just how splendid and horrifying a joke this all is, but begin to suspect that he has only stumbled on the comic possibilities of his subject in pursuit of a more pathetic theme which has obsessed him ever since the writing of his poplar little tearjerker, "For Esmé—with Love and Squalor." It is this theme which lies at the center of *Catcher in the Rye* and which becomes the main interest if not of "Franny," certainly of the much longer "Zooey." I am referring, of course, to Salinger's presentation of madness as the chief temptation of modern life, especially for the intelligent young; and his conviction that, consequently, the chief heroism possible to us now is the rejection of madness, the decision to be sane. What suicide was for the young Werther or running away from home for Huck Finn, the "nervous breakdown," Salinger urges us to believe, is for the sensitive adolescent of our time. Having been taught, chiefly by the psychoanalysts (who haunt Salinger's books, ambiguous and omnipresent almost as his teachers), that insanity itself lies within the scope of choice, we have been able to make of it a theme for debate, our own to-be-or-not-to-be.

Before the present volume, Salinger had always presented madness as a special temptation of males; perhaps because, in the myth he was elaborating, it is a female image of innocence that, at the last moment, lures his almost-lost protagonists back from the brink of insanity: a little girl typically, prepubescent and therefore immune to the world's evil, which, in his work, fully nubile women tend to embody. The series which begins with "Esmé" goes on through "A Perfect Day for Bananafish," where the girl-savior appears too late to save Seymour, oldest of the Glass family; and reaches an appropriate climax in *Catcher in the Rye*, where the savior is the little sister and the myth achieves its final form. It is the Orestes-Iphigenia story, we see there, that Salinger all along had been trying to rewrite, the account of a Fury-haunted brother redeemed by his priestess-sister; though Salinger demotes that sister in age, thus downgrading the tone of the legend from tragic to merely pathetic.

In "Zooey," where the brother saves, the sister is redeemed and neither is a child, the myth struggles back toward the tragic dimension; and it is for this, too, perhaps that I responded so strongly at first to the story, to its implicit declaration of Salinger's resolve to escape what had become for him a trap. Yet though the girl-savior does not operate in "Zooey" to produce the pat Happy Ending of *Catcher in the Rye*, she floats disconcertingly in and out of its action, a not-quite-irrelevant ghost. It is, for instance, the chance meeting with a four-year-old girl at the meat counter of a supermarket that prompts the long letter from his oldest surviving brother, Buddy, which Zooey is reading as his story opens; and in that letter, we are permitted to see at last the haiku found in Seymour's hotel room after his suicide: "The little girl on the plane/ Who turned her doll's head around/ To look at me."

Buddy, however, released from long silence by his little girl and the memory of Seymour's, has tried to save Zooey, through the mails, by advising him to "act" (Buddy is a teacher of writing, Zooey a TV star); and Zooey, trying in turn to save Franny, can only repeat in Buddy's voice and over Seymour's still-listed telephone the same advice. Behind it all, at any rate, is the inevitable little girl, her message echoed and re-echoed through the linked ventriloquist's dummies of the three brothers, who seem sometimes only three versions of the single author, listening faithfully to Esmé down the years.

But "Zooey" is, at last, a fable of reconciliation as well as of salvation; for the saved Franny, we are left to believe, will return perhaps to school, certainly to "acting," as her brothers recommend, not so much for her own sake as for the sake of what Seymour had been accustomed to call, in their Quiz Kid days, the Fat Lady, *i.e.*, the audience out front. But the Fat Lady, Zooey announces as his story ends, is Christ; the mass audience is Christ. It is an appropriate enough theophany for a popular entertainer, for Salinger as well as Zooey, and the cue for a truce with all the world, with bad teachers, mad television producers, bad psychoanalysts, bad everyone.

Finally, like his characters, Salinger is reconciled with everything but sex. The single voice in his novella which advocates marriage is the voice of Bessie Glass, a stage-Irish comic mother married to an off-stage comic Jew; but she raises it in vain in a fictional world where apparently only women marry and where certainly no father appears on the scene. It is to Zooey she speaks, the one son of hers not already killed by marriage like Seymour, or safe in monastic retirement, secular like Buddy's or ecclesiastical like his Jesuit brother Waker's. Zooey, who fears his own body and his mother's touch on it, turns her aside with a quip; though he might well have repeated what he had cried earlier in deep contempt, "That's just sex talking, buddy . . . I know that voice." These words, too, he had addressed to her; since for him men and women alike are "buddy," as if unlike the actual Buddy, he needed no little girl to remind him of what Seymour had once tried to teach them all: that "all legitimate religious study *must* lead to unlearning . . . the illusory differences between boys and girls . . ."

To unlearn the illusory differences: this is what for Salinger it means *to be as a child*. And the Glasses, we remember, are in this sense children, holy innocents still at twenty or thirty or forty, Quiz Kids who never made the mistake of growing up, and whose most glorious hours were spent before the microphones on a nation-wide radio program called "It's a Wise Child." The notion of the Quiz Kids, with their forced precocity, their meaningless answers to pointless questions faked by station employees, as heroes, sages, secret saints of our time is palpably absurd. But Salinger himself ironically qualifies what he seems naïvely to offer by the unfinished quotation he uses to give his only half-mythical program its name. It is with his collaboration, we remind ourselves, that we are able to say of his hidden saints, when they become insufferably cute or clever or smug, "The little bastards!" Surely, this is Salinger's joke, not just one on him and on his world.

The Divine Stupidity
of Kurt Vonnegut:
Portrait of the Novelist
as Bridge over Troubled Water

I first read Kurt Vonnegut, Jr., as I now know was proper, in paper, and at the urging of a fourteen-year-old son. He came to me, that is to say, not off the shelves of a library, but from the same world of disreputable entertainment to which comic books and beloved bad movies belong: the world of the pleasure rather than the reality principle, the world of the young rather than the old.

I grew up, for better or worse, in a generation and a class for which literature seemed more a duty than self-indulgence. And I was a father before I was prepared to admit that books, even the very best of them, can, maybe should, be used to subvert the world of duty and work and success. I don't mean that I did not in fact make such uses of some of them when I was myself still a son and an adolescent, merely that I insisted they be kosher, which is to say, checked out as classics and/or avant-garde masterpieces by accepted critics.

At any rate, I began, at the behest of my son, with Vonnegut's *Player Piano* (then called, as I remember, *Utopia 14*), which moved me oddly, though I still managed to avoid having to come to terms with it by tucking it away in the category of "Science Fiction." And I continued to read his books as science fiction whenever they came to hand on supermarket bookstalls. I am, like everyone else I know, an inveterate impulse buyer and commodity consumer.

Then, just three or four years ago, I was reminded that for some almost as young at this moment as my son was when he first introduced me to Vonnegut, his books seemed more scriptures than commodities. I had been asked for the first time to a university not under the auspices of the English department, but on the invitation of the students themselves; and at the end of my three-week stay was given two books which, to my hosts, represented the kind of writing that compelled their deepest assent: Claude Lévi-Strauss's *La Pensée Sauvage* and Vonnegut's *The Sirens of Titan*. It was still the point before student aspiration had been fully politicized; and I suspect that now such secret scriptures are more likely to be Maoist or Trotskyist than structuralist and fantastic. Still, in this area one nail does not necessarily drive out another; and only last year a group of English students (who would supply me, before the official release date, with lyrics of new Bob Dylan songs) were asking that two books be added to a reading list of post–World War II novels: Ken Kesey's *One Flew over the Cuckoo's Nest* and Kurt Vonnegut's *Cat's Cradle*.

But Vonnegut seems an odd choice really, being not only immune to Left politics, but neither a pothead like Allen Ginsberg, nor an acidhead like, say, Ken Kesey—or even a reformed heroin addict, like William Burroughs. He is—or so he claims in autobiographical asides—only an old-fashioned juice-head, a moderate boozer, now a couple of years past forty-five; and given— when liquored up—to remembering *his* war, which is to say, World War II, rather than World War III which didn't happen, or those smaller ones which did, in Korea or Vietnam. But it is those other wars which possess the imaginations of the young, especially the last, which may, indeed, be the first ever fought by Americans on marijuana rather than whiskey. What, then, has made Kurt Vonnegut an underground favorite of the young?

It is partly, I suppose, the fact that structurally, archetypally speaking, the space-odyssey is the same thing as the "trip"; and that having chosen the mode of Science Fiction, Vonnegut has subscribed to a mythology otherwise sustained by smoking grass or dropping LSD, or, for that matter, simply sitting half-stunned before the late, late show on TV. In a certain sense, it can be said that the taking of drugs is a technological substitute for a special kind of literature, for fantasy—an attempt to substitute chemistry for words; and it can thus be understood as a kind of midterm between science fiction and actual manned flights into outer space, those trips to the moon or Mars, which can be read as the final expression of technology imitating art. And, of course, becoming art once more as television records them.

Not Proust-Mann-and-Joyce, those "thick" books dense with realistic detail, symbol and psychological analysis, but the Western, Science Fiction and Porn, "thin" books all fantasy and plot and characters in two dimensions, possess our imaginations now; or at least so certain writers whom young readers prefer have come recently to believe. Novelists nurtured on the tradition of High Art and avant-garde, and therefore initially committed to a dream of surviving on library shelves and in classroom analyses, learn now that only the ephemeral lives the real life of literature these days, in living hearts and heads; and they begin, therefore, to emulate the Pop forms, which means begin to aspire to making it in paperback.

The long-predicted death of the Novel turns out to be the death of the Art Novel, the "poetic" novel read by an elite audience to whom high literature represents chiefly the opportunity of verifying their own special status in a world of slobs committed to the consumption of "mass culture." Quite "serious" writers, writers who kid neither themselves nor their readers, register their awareness of this in ways many of their most ardent readers seem not yet quite to understand. But only in this context is it possible to see clearly what John Barth was up to either in *The Sot-Weed Factor*, where in re-creating Pocahontas he created the Dirty Western, or in *Giles Goat-Boy*, where he married Rabelais to Science Fiction. So, too, the more recent work of William Burroughs, *The Ticket That Exploded*, for instance, only makes real sense to one who realizes how much in it comes from releasing the standard images of run-of-the-mill science fiction in a haze of junk. And he, too, begins now to move toward the classical form of the Western, first and most authentic variety of American Pop—that tale of the male companions, red and white, in flight from women and in quest of the absolute wilderness, which has recently been reborn in books as various as Ken Kesey's *One Flew over the Cuckoo's Nest*, Truman Capote's *In Cold Blood* and Norman Mailer's *Why Are We in Vietnam?* It was all there in James Fenimore Cooper to begin with, has remained there in the Pop underground ever since, and rises to the surface whenever an American writer wants to indulge not his own exclusive fantasies of alienation and chosenness, but the dreams he shares with everyone else.

Some American writers, John Updike, for instance, and Philip Roth, have been too inhibited by their own parochial commitments to the provinces of High Art as defined by *The New Yorker* or *Partisan Review* to make it back into the world of the Western or up and out into the world of Science Fiction. They, too, have felt the pressure to move toward the world of Pop and have responded by creating—in *Couples* and *Portnoy's Complaint*—fantasies of sex rather than of the Virgin Forest or Outer Space, turning to what Alberto Moravia once described as the last place where urban men (and who more urban than Roth, more suburban than Updike) live in nature. "I am not a Jewish sage," Roth has said recently, talking of his newest book, "I am a Jew Freak like Tiny Tim!" It is his instinct for survival which is speaking; and how splendidly he has survived the death of the Jewish Art Novel the record of sales for *Portnoy's Complaint* sufficiently indicates. But woe to writers, Jew and Gentile alike, who do not respond as he does, since the Novel must cease taking itself seriously or perish.

Vonnegut has had what we now realize to be an advantage in this regard, since he began as a Pop writer, the author of "slick" fiction, written to earn money, which is to say, to fit formulas which are often genuine myths, frozen and waiting to be released. Fortunately, though he has sometimes written to suit the tastes of middle-aged ladies who constitute the readership of the *Ladies' Home Journal*, he has tended more to exploit the mythology of the future. But he has, in any case—as writers of, rather than *about*, mythology must—written books that are thin and wide, rather than deep and narrow, books which open out into fantasy and magic by means of linear narration rather than deep analysis; and so happen on wisdom, fall into it through grace, rather than pursue it doggedly or seek to earn it by hard work. Moreover, like all literature which tries to close the gap between the elite and the popular audiences rather than to confirm it, Vonnegut's books tend to temper irony with sentimentality and to dissolve both in wonder.

Inevitably, however, critical approval has overtaken him; and he appears now elegantly produced between boards—misrepresented, as it were. And who could wish it otherwise, for criticism's sake at least, since he is a test case for the critics. When I was young, literary critics thought they knew for sure that it was their function to educate taste: to rescue a mass audience, largely middle-aged, from an addiction to outworn sentimentality and escapism, to prepare them to read what was newest and most difficult. Suddenly, however, it is the mass audience which leads the critics, educating them, for now it is the critics who are middle-aged, the big audience that is young; rescuing them from an addiction to outworn irony, and teaching them to read for the sake of a joy deeper than that of mere culture-climbing. Understandably enough, many survivors of the old critical regime find it difficult to persuade themselves that if, recently, they have come to esteem Vonnegut, it is not because they have been converted to the side of Pop, but because—though they did not at first realize it—he has all along belonged to the other side of High Art.

Confusion in this regard extends even to Vonnegut's publishers, or at least to the writers of his jacket copy, who assure us that "Once mistakenly typed as a science-fiction writer, he is now recognized as a mainstream storyteller." But all is presumably set straight; for we are also informed he has taught at the University of Iowa Writers Workshop. It is true, of course—however belatedly the universities and copy writers have come to acknowledge it—that Vonnegut *does* belong to what we know again to be the mainstream of fiction; it is not the mainstream of High Art, however, but of myth and entertainment; a stream which was forced to flow underground over the past several decades but has now surfaced once more.

To be, for a while, thus invisible is, in any case, not necessarily bad; art renews itself precisely in the dialectical process of disappearing, reappearing, disappearing. And just as the invisibility of the avant-garde, its unavailability to contemporary criticism at the beginning of the twentieth century, was a source of health and strength for an elitist, neoclassic tradition; so the invisibility of Pop, its immunity to fashionable judgment, seems in mid-twentieth century to have been a source of health and strength to what we now recognize as the New Romanticism: an art which prefers sentimentality to irony, passion to reason, vulgarity to subtlety. But sentimentality and passion and vulgarity had long been consigned to the outer darkness by such reigning critics as T. S. Eliot and Cleanth Brooks. And, as always when seeking renewal, art had to descend into that darkness which exists on the blind side of the critics' heads.

Moreover, for young readers the invisibility of Pop in general, Science Fiction in particular, has seemed a warrant of its relevance, a sign that by virtue of being unavailable to their elders, it belonged especially to them, to *their* "underground." And yet they could not forebear bringing the buried treasure they had discovered to the surface, bugging their presumed betters, urging their parents and teachers to share the pleasures of Pop—in Vonnegut, or, for that matter, Andy Warhol and Roy Lichtenstein, or vintage comic books or movies starring John Wayne. To do so, however, is to make the invisible visible, the hidden manifest, to translate certain artists from the paperback shelves or pornographic bookstores to the classroom and the required reading list, which creates confusion for all concerned.

And yet finally who can regret the whole ironic process; since to writers like Vonnegut, on the border between New Pop and Old High Art, their initial invisibility is a torment which leaves scars, if not disabling traumas. To check through the *Book Review Index*, for instance, and discover that from 1952 to 1963 no book of Vonnegut's is recorded as having appeared or been reviewed is to understand the persistent defensiveness which underlies his playful-bitter references to his status as "a writer of science fiction." Even in his latest collection of short stories and articles, which appeared in 1968 under the title of *Welcome to the Monkey House*, he is still fighting it out, saying ironically, "Here one finds the fruits of Free Enterprise"; then going on to explain, "I used to be a public-relations man for General Electric, and then I became a free-lance writer of so-called slick fiction . . . Whether I improved myself morally by making the change I am not prepared to say. That is one of the questions I mean to ask God on Judgment Day . . . I have already put the question to a college professor who . . . assured me that public-relations men and slick writers were equally vile, in that they both buggered truth for money." The self-doubt in this latest comment is undercut by the irony. But Vonnegut was not always even this secure about what he was doing; since a writer, however much a pro, lives only days by what his stories earn him, must get through his nights on remembering what the critics say.

Perhaps Vonnegut's initial difficulty on this score, which turns out to be a final advantage, is that he is a transitional figure in a time of transition, a period in which we are rapidly leaving behind the values of Modernism: the notion propagated by such Modernist high priests as T. S. Eliot that "Culture" belongs to an elite, a tiny remnant saved by being able to appreciate an abstruse, hermetic, highly allusive and symbolic form of art. To the Modernist,

Pop is a vice of the weak-minded majority, or alternatively, a sop thrown to the exploited by the Madison Avenue lackeys of their exploiters; to the Post-Modernist it is the storehouse of fantasy in which the present Future we now live was prefigured, the twenty-first century pre-invented.

Vonnegut is of two minds on the subject, alternatively, simultaneously. On the one hand, he has lived from the beginning by appealing to the great Pop audience on its own grounds, and yet something in him has always yearned to be a "serious writer," to win the respect of those professors whom he affects to despise, but whose colleague he has recently become all the same. And that something is betrayed in his habit—untypical in Pop fiction—of putting writers and artists at the center of his books. But this habit belongs essentially to the kind of Modernist book whose subject is art, whose hero the artist; and whose classic instance is Joyce's *Portrait of the Artist as a Young Man*.

Vonnegut has never, consequently, seemed to the first generation of hard-core science fiction fans a major figure in the genre, even Kingsley Amis in *New Maps of Hell*, the one broadly inclusive survey of the genre, dismissing him with a single friendly sentence. The older aficionados—weary scientists and hardworking technicians, for instance, to whom Science Fiction seemed a device for escaping rather than expanding their own sense of reality—have always preferred figures like Robert Heinlein, in whose earlier books the familiar conventions of the thriller and the detective story were transferred without fundamental change to interplanetary regions. But Heinlein ever since *Stranger in a Strange Land* has been remaking his own work on the model of Vonnegut's—using images of pursuit and discovery in Outer Space to indicate the possibilities of creating in Inner Space new values, a new language, in short, just such a New World as the New Romantics dream.

Meanwhile, Vonnegut himself, however, has been moving uneasily away from his Science-Fiction beginnings; in books like *God Bless You, Mr. Rosewater* and *Slaughterhouse-Five*, ironically playing with the form he once quite simply practiced. But disengaging from science fiction, Vonnegut seems on the point of disengaging entirely from words, and perhaps it is a weariness with the craft of fiction itself, with, at any rate, telling stories, i.e., making plots or myths, that impels him; as if he suspects the Pop Novel may be as dead as the Art Novel. More and more, he is impelled toward abstraction, the making of constellations or patterns, which may explain his recent statement that "I would enjoy becoming a painter for a while."

To understand how Vonnegut has moved, however, it is necessary to look more closely at his work to date, in particular at the six novels he has written since 1952. His short stories, collected in two volumes, *Canary in a Cat House* (1961) and *Welcome to the Monkey House* (1968), I shall refer to only in passing, since they seem to have been written with his left hand (he himself described them as "samples of work I sold in order to finance the writing of the novels"), and he has no special talent for short fiction in any case.

Vonnegut's first novel, *Player Piano,* appeared in 1952, when he had just turned thirty, and was widely (if not always favorably) reviewed as a "serious" book; since, despite its projection into the future and its Science-Fiction gimmicks, it represented quite obviously the kind of earnest social criticism which suggests comparisons with quite respectable writers like Aldous Huxley and George Orwell. In its earlier pages especially, it seems now, in fact, *too* bent on suggesting such comparisons, more committed to morality than play, more concerned with editorial than invention; grimly intent on proving (once more!) that machines deball and dehumanize men—and that the huge corporation, called the Ilium Works but evidently modeled on the General Electric plant in Schenectady, for which Vonnegut once did PR, corrupts those it nominates as an elite even as it strips of all dignity those it finds unworthy to program its computers. But before *Player Piano* is through, Vonnegut's sense of humor has mitigated his indignation, and he is pursuing (quite like those younger contemporaries, Jules Feiffer or Joseph Heller, for instance) any possibility of a joke, no matter how poor or in the midst of no matter what horror: anticipating, in fact, the mode later called, ineptly enough, "Black Humor."

What *Player Piano* conspicuously lacks, however, is a writer-spokesman at the center. Its point-of-view protagonist is a skeptical technocrat, an engineer who has lost faith in a world fashioned exclusively by those who share his skills; and among his enemies are included the kind of Pop writers who, in a world controlled by machines, provide ready-made dreams of man in a state of nature, whether bare-chested bargemen on the Erie Canal or Tarzan swinging homeward toward Jane in the treetops. Yet Vonnegut is at his best in the book when he himself indulges in Pop fantasy—anticipating what he can do best, as he invents the Ghost Shirt Society: that association of rebels against the white man's technology, who assume the bulletproof magic garb of those desperate Indians who fought vainly to stem the tide of European immigration in the late nineteenth century, and who, like their Indian counterparts, go down to defeat, destroyed by the technology of men too stupid to know the truth of magic.

Yet he seems not to have known how to deal with what he had begun to guess; for *Player Piano* is followed by seven years of silence—seven years in which he published no novels at all, only stories for the slicks. But he emerges from that silence with a pair of books which between them constitute his main achievement: *The Sirens of Titan,* which appeared in 1959, and *Cat's Cradle,* which was published in 1963. In these two fictions, at any rate, he seems at ease—in a way he was not earlier and would not be later—with Science Fiction; finding in its conventions not a kind of restriction, but a way of releasing his own sentimental-ironic view of a meaningless universe redeemed by love; his own unrecognized need to write a New Gospel or at least to rewrite the Old; his distrusted longing to indulge his fantasy without providing the unimaginative one more occasion for idle masturbation; his unconfessed desire to escape both the stifling inwardness of the traditional Art Novel and the empty virtuosity of avant-garde experiment.

The Sirens of Titan appeared as a paperback original, perhaps because hard-cover publishers would have nothing to do with him. And yet, in a sense they did not intend, the publishers are right; what he begins in *The Sirens of Titan*, confirms in *Cat's Cradle*, does not belong in hard-covers at all—being admirably suited to the not-quite-book snatched on the run in airports or picked up to allay boredom in bus terminals. Acquiring them so we are not tempted to hoard them, but to lose them as good things should cheerfully be lost (sitting down to write this article, I discovered that *all* of my Vonnegut books had been mislaid or borrowed and not returned); and reading them, we are not tempted to believe ourselves set apart by the rareness of our pleasure or the subtlety of our understanding. Like all Pop Art, they confirm our solidarity with everyone who can read at all, or merely dream over pages devoted to evoking the mystery of space and time, or to prophesying the end of man.

Mother Night, however, which appeared two years after *Sirens*, in 1961, temporarily interrupts Vonnegut's continuing exploration of the potentialities of Science Fiction—representing perhaps a desire to be more immediately topical, more directly political, more "serious" in short. It is not unsuccessful in its own terms, but finally irrelevant to Vonnegut's special vocation, though deeply concerned with Germany and World War II, which is Vonnegut's other obsessive subject matter: the past he remembers, rather than the future he extrapolates or invents. *Mother Night* does not quite manage to deal with the American bombing of Dresden, through which Vonnegut actually lived as a prisoner of war—but it flirts with it throughout. This past year, he has come closer in *Slaughterhouse-Five;* but even that novel is less about Dresden than about Vonnegut's failure to come to terms with it—one of those beautifully frustrating works about their own impossibility, like Fellini's *Eight and a Half.* And it is inevitable, perhaps, that Howard W. Campbell, Jr., the protagonist of *Mother Night*, appears in the later book as well, quoted one more (final?) time in the tale Vonnegut could not make him tell first time around.

Eschewing Science Fiction in *Mother Night*, however, Vonnegut turns to another, more established Pop form, the spy novel. It is, in fact, dedicated to Mata Hari, the evocation of whose name introduces a disturbing note of irony; since she has become not merely a byword, but a comic one. The story itself is, however, serious enough: the tale of a double agent, unable to prove for a long time that he was really in the pay of the US Government and unwilling, finally, to save himself from hanging when that proof is unexpectedly offered. Self-condemned and self-executed, Howard W. Campbell leaves behind a book intended to testify that one is always—hopelessly, irrecoverably—what he pretends to be, pretends to himself he is *only* pretending to be.

Campbell is, in fact, the first major author-protagonist in Vonnegut; and, like his own author, a Pop artist before history makes him an autobiographer. He has become for the large German public a successful playwright; and for the smaller public of two, constituted by himself and his wife, a private por-nographer. Once the war is over, however, and he has fled back to his native America, his works fall into the hands of a Soviet writer who achieves a second round of best-sellerdom, claiming the translated versions as his own. And why not, since such fables are anonymous, international—pass not only from hand to hand, but from country to country as well. This Campbell does not really understand—but it does not deeply trouble him. What really does is the fact that his Russian counterpart has published (with illustrations) a large edition of his own private porn—titillating the great public with what was intended for the tiniest of elites.

And if Campbell responds so extravagantly to having become, inadver-tently, a pornographer, this is surely because his author is especially hung up on the subject of porn, the sole Pop form which, in fact, evades him—despite a theoretical dedication to freeing men to lead full sexual lives. Vonnegut can-not ever quite manage to talk dirty enough to be explicit about sex; though (because?) he is haunted throughout his work by a vision of his own books ending up in the display windows of pornographic bookshops, confused by owners and customers alike with hard-core pornography. He is aware really that the confusion is, on the deepest level, somehow valid; that the best of Science Fiction has in common with the shabbiest sort of erotica, not sex but "fantasies of an impossibly hospitable world."

But he is not really at ease with the fact; and throughout his work, espe-cially as it grows more and more unguardedly confessional, there appears over and over the image of that first of all pornographic photos, in which a girl is vainly trying to screw a Shetland pony: produced, he tells us, by the favorite student of Daguerre, and therefore an apt symbol of revolutionary art becoming (quickly, quickly) a Pop commodity, to be peddled to the unwary on street corners. Yet what bugs Vonnegut even more is the awareness that in his own time pornography is practiced, and accepted, as revolutionary Art itself, a special way of telling the truth about the society we live in; and he parodies mercilessly, in *God Bless You, Mr. Rosewater,* a novelist presumably dedicated to absolute candor who ends up writing: "I twisted her arm until she opened her legs, and she gave a little scream, half joy, half pain (how do you figure a woman?) as I rammed the old avenger home"—which one suspects is intended as a put-down of Norman Mailer.

In the end, however, the spy novel proved for Vonnegut almost as unsympathetic as pornography itself—more unsympathetic, in fact, since the story of espionage posits a world of total alienation rather than one of impossible hospitality. He could not find room in it, moreover, for magic and wonder, the religious dimension so necessary to his view of man. Campbell is a writer, a popular artist, but he is not a guru, and Vonnegut could scarcely imagine him writing a new bible. What religious leaders appear in *Mother Night* are presented as comic nuts gathered together in a tiny American neo-Nazi Party: a defrocked priest and a dentist-minister, convinced that a man's teeth are the key to his character, and founder of the Western Hemisphere University of the Bible, by which, it turns out later, the witch doctor in *Cat's Cradle* has been ordained.

That shadowy figure of Dr. Vox Humana represents, in fact, the sole link between *Mother Night* and the book which follows it, in which Vonnegut returns again to the kind of Science Fiction he had already so successfully exploited in *The Sirens of Titan*, his best book, I think—most totally achieved, most nearly dreamed rather than contrived. In it, he evokes all the themes, along with their sustaining images, for which we remember him with special affection and amusement: the unreality of time and the consequent possibility of traveling therein; the illusory nature of free will and the consequent possibility of heroism and sacrifice; the impossibility of really choosing one's mate and the consequent necessity to love whomever, whatever happens to come to hand. It is, moreover, his most *chutzpahdik*, his most outrageously and attractively arrogant book; for in it he dares not only to ask the ultimate question about the meaning of human life, but to *answer* it.

But what sets *The Sirens of Titan* apart is that, inventing it, Vonnegut has escaped from the limitations of an imagination narrower and more provincial than it is ever possible quite to remember. Despite his dedication to a form predicated on space-travel, Vonnegut is oddly earthbound, American-bound really; there are, in fact, only three localities in which his invention is at home: Ilium, New York, the country around Indianapolis, and Cape Cod—not, one notices uneasily, any of those mythological metropolises so congenial to the minds of most writers of Science Fiction. In *The Sirens of Titan*, however, he imagined for the first time Tralfamadore, the transgalactic world he is to evoke again and again, but to which none of his space-travelers ever actually go; until, perhaps, the Billy Pilgrim of his last book [*Slaughterhouse-Five*], and which we are free, therefore, to understand for the absolute Elsewhere, more easily reached by art of madness than by mere technology. And he has also described in its pages Mars and a Moon of Saturn called Titan, to and from which his protagonist, Malachi Constant, shuttles, returning at last to Indianapolis, where he dies waiting for a bus.

More central, though, to Vonnegut's own development is the antagonist, who is whirled at the book's close quite out of our solar system and our ken; that Winston Niles Rumfoord, who is both author and guru, as articulate and omnipotent as Prospero on his Island, and who seemingly wants to rule the world but turns out only to have longed to create a religion. He manages in fact to launch from Mars a doomed expedition of brainwashed mercenaries, whose intended defeat causes all men on Earth to recoil from conflict and self-delusion, and to live together in peace, worshiping according to the tenets of the Church of God the Utterly Indifferent, whose messiah-scapegoat is Malachi Constant himself. But in the end Rumfoord proves as little in charge of his own destiny as Constant; since not only his two books, but all of his complex maneuvering of men—and, indeed, the whole course of human history which made his actions possible—are revealed as having been plotted, by almost immortal Tralfamadorians, intent only on getting a spare part to one of their messengers, stranded on Titan with a trivial communication to another planet far across the universe. This is not, however, the work's final word, Vonnegut's final position; for that very messenger, it turns out, through an intricate machine, has learned somehow to love in the aeons he has spent as a castaway; and he provides—like a kindly Pop artist—a vision of Paradise to sustain Malachi's dying moments; a false vision sustained by posthypnotic suggestion, but sufficient to make dying more palatable than living. It is as much of a Happy Ending as Kurt Vonnegut could imagine at this point in his career, as much of a Happy Ending—he tries to persuade us—as we need or can use.

But in *Cat's Cradle*, his next work of Science Fiction, he does not even offer us this token Happy Ending, for that book begins and ends with a vision of the total destruction of mankind, to which only an eternal gesture of contempt is an adequate response. It is a book which has nothing to do with Heaven except insofar as it is not there ("No cat! No cradle!"), though it takes place largely on an island paradise in the Caribbean, which stirs in us once more memories of that Master of Illusion, Prospero. This time, however, the Prospero who regulates the actions of everyone else is dead before the fiction begins; a certain Dr. Felix Hoenikker, referred to throughout as "the father of the Atomic Bomb." He is a more equivocal figure even than Rumfoord, the hero-villain of *The Sirens of Titan*.

The name Rumfoord appears over and over in Vonnegut's stories and novels, always signifying the kind of Groton-Harvard-educated WASP, before whom—as a Midwestern German American—he feels that fascinated repulsion all of us Americans experience confronted by some absolute alien who happens to have got here before us. The Hoenikkers, father and children, like Vonnegut bear a name which memorializes their connection with a European people who made soap of dead Jews and were themselves roasted, boiled, turned to tinder by bombs from American planes. And before those Germans he feels the fascinated repulsion all of us Americans experience confronting the particular people abroad from whose midst our ancestors fled, but who persist still in our flesh, our dreams; and with whom therefore we die a little, when we come to bomb them.

Cat's Cradle is presented as if told by an almost anonymous narrator (we learn his first name John-Jonah, are left to guess his last—Vonnegut, perhaps?), who begins by trying to write the history of total destruction (called in his case, *The Day the World Ended*), with which Vonnegut himself was still wrestling in vain. For John-Jonah, however, it was to be a book about Hiroshima rather than Dresden, and in the end he does not even manage that—his imagination (and Vonnegut's) pre-empted not by the Atomic Bomb, which did not quite end the world, but by Hoenikker's next, posthumous invention, which did: not by the final fire, but the final ice—a kind of super-ice, called *Ice-Nine*, which melts at 114 degrees Fahrenheit, and with which Hoenikker was playing like a child at the moment of his death.

John-Jonah moves among the heirs who share the invention—old Hoenikker's children, along with their lovers and friends—learning slowly, painfully how to become yet one more Vonnegut sacrificial victim: the patsy and reluctant messiah of yet one more true, i.e., false, religion. At the book's close, he lies frozen for all eternity, his thumb to his nose and a history of the world clasped to his side. He has learned this sacred gesture of contempt for the God or not-God behind the universe from Bokonon, a Black Prophet who is Vonnegut's most impressive rebel-guru; and who, just before his own suicide, composed the final sentence of his Scriptures, as if for John-Jonah's special benefit: "If I were a younger man, I would write a history of human stupidity; and I would climb to the top of Mount McCabe . . . and I would make a statue of myself, lying on my back, and thumbing my nose at You Know Who."

Indeed, the not-quite nihilism of the book's close is a product of the tension between the religion of Bokononism, which advocates formulating and believing sacred lies, and the vision granted to the dwarfed son of the Father of the Bomb of the emptiness behind all lies, however sacred. The voices of the White Dwarf and the Black Prophet are both Vonnegut's, and they answer each other inconclusively throughout; creating an ambiguity quite like that produced by the opposite claims of High Art (the Dwarf, an avant-garde painter, renders his view in monochrome abstraction) and Pop Art (Bokonon, an entertainer, sings his creed in calypso form).

But, as ever in Vonnegut, something more is presented than the unresolvable conflict of mutually exclusive theories; namely, the possibility of actual joy. John, at any rate, is revealed as having experienced two great joys before his tale is told: one slow and long-continued, as he learns who are the other members of his *karass*, the handful of others in the world with whom, willynilly, he must work out the pattern of his destiny: one intense and momentary, as he plays footsie with the blond Negress, Mona, whom he, and everyone else, loves: their naked soles touching in the ecstatic union called by Bokononists *"Boko-maru." Cat's Cradle* is then a book about loving; but it is even more, as my own language has been teaching me, the words that suggest themselves to me as I describe it, a book about learning, which means, inevitably about learning a new language. It is Vonnegut's great good fortune to know this, and to be able to invent such new languages: to create terms like *karass* and *Boko-maru*, which seem to survive, in the heads of his readers, his plots and even his jokes.

Since *Cat's Cradle,* Vonnegut has written a pair of books, *God Bless You, Mr. Rosewater* (1965) and *Slaughterhouse-Five* (1969), which constitute, in fact, a single work, with common characters, common themes, common obsessions and a common whimsy—and which together rifle his earlier books for other characters, themes, obsessions and whimsical asides; as if he is being driven to make his total work seem in retrospect a latter-day Human Comedy or Yoknapatawpha series. But the last novels are quite different in their tone and effect, being essentially autobiographical rather than mythic: quasi-novels really, in which the author returns to his early material reflectively rather than obsessively—and so ends writing *about* it, rather than simply writing it; and thus falls, for better or worse, quite out of the world of Pop art. It is, perhaps, because of this fall that Vonnegut has become more available to established literary critics; or maybe his acceptance is only the inevitable triumph of time. Any writer who has lived so long (and he *has*) tends to seem at least respectable, even admirable—particularly if he is the sort of writer on whose behalf children tirelessly propagandize their parents.

Yet it is wrong finally to learn to love the late Vonnegut first, and to come to his earlier books backwards through the ones which followed. Ideally, a reader should learn his territory as he revealed it: be introduced to Ilium, New York, in *Player Piano;* to Indianapolis and Cape Cod and Tralfamadore in *The Sirens of Titan.* Vonnegut has, to be sure, returned in his last two novels to his three favorite American provinces and the single transgalactic dream world in which he feels at home; but those worlds are oddly transmogrified. Tralfamadore, especially, has been distanced and ironized into the place "where the flying saucers come from," and serves no longer to release Vonnegut into the world of Science Fiction, but only as an occasion to make rueful jokes about it.

God Bless You, Mr. Rosewater is not Science Fiction at all—not even like *Mother Night* a spy story—but a work of "mainstream literature," in which Vonnegut has transposed from the Future and Elsewhere to the Present and Right Here the themes which he once mythologized in popular, fantastic modes: the compelling need to love the unlovable, whose ranks industrialization has disconcertingly swelled; the magical power of money and the holy folly of renouncing it; the uses and abuses of fantasy itself. But the profoundest and most central concern of *God Bless You, Mr. Rosewater* is new for Vonnegut; seems in fact more closely related to Norman O. Brown or Michel Foucault or R. D. Laing than what he himself had dealt with earlier. We remember the novel chiefly as a book about madness, or more particularly, as one about the relationship between madness and holiness; since Eliot Rosewater—a millionaire who becomes a Volunteer Fireman and one-man Counseling Service—is the first of Vonnegut's gurus who lives *in* madness rather than *by* lies. He does not, that is to say, choose deliberately to deceive for the sake of the salvation of mankind, but is hopelessly self-deceived; insane enough to accept as truth what Rumfoord was forced to justify as useful fictions, or Bokonon to preach as *foma,* "harmless untruths."

But if *God Bless You, Mr. Rosewater* is not Science Fiction, it is compulsively *about* science fiction; and this time the writer nearest to its center (Eliot Rosewater himself has only the unfinished scraps of a fantasy novel in his desk) is Kilgore Trout, the author of scores of neglected and despised Science Fiction novels. As the name itself betrays, however (it contains precisely the same number of letters as "Kurt Vonnegut," and, indeed, the four letters of "Kurt" insist on detaching themselves from the rest), Trout is a comic, self-deprecatory portrait of his author—or rather of what his author might have been, in some sense *was,* up to the moment he wrote the book in which Trout appears. As inappropriate to one on the verge of ambiguous success, Vonnegut portrays his alter ego as an absurd failure, driven to earn his living by supervising paper boys or redeeming Green Stamps, and obsessed by the fact that his books are only available in shops that peddle porn.

Yet it is given to Trout to play an equivocal St. Paul to Eliot Rosewater's absurd Christ: to rationalize Eliot's madness in terms acceptable even to his tycoon father; and yet to prepare Eliot himself for lapsing back into insanity, alcoholism and obesity, after he has been cured of all three by a regime of tennis and tranquilizers in a madhouse. And in *Slaughterhouse-Five,* Trout returns to play a similar role for a similar sub-messiah, this time an optometrist called Billy Pilgrim, who had, as a matter of fact, been introduced to the work of Trout by Eliot himself in the psycho-ward of a military hospital during World War II.

But Billy, unlike Eliot, travels in space and time, actually reaching Tralfamadore itself (invented first by Vonnegut in *The Sirens of Titan*, then reinvented by Trout in *God Bless You, Mr. Rosewater*), where he is displayed naked in a zoo, at work, at play, on the john and in the arms of Montana Wildhack, a Hollywood starlet imported for mating purposes. Oddly enough, however—as Vonnegut pointedly informs us—Trout had already imagined the zoo episode in fiction, and Billy had read it before living it, or dreaming it, or falling through time and space into it. Vonnegut will not, to be sure, let us side with the cynics and realists who would, by psychiatric means, cure Billy of his belief that he has been and is forever on Tralfamadore, but he leaves suspended, not quite asked, much less answered, the question of whether he travels there through Outer Space or Inner, via madness or flying saucer—or merely by means of Pop fiction, in which each of these is revealed as the metaphor of the other.

Perhaps Vonnegut does not know at all what he is really doing in his last book *Slaughterhouse-Five*. Perhaps he even believes what he so stoutly maintains in those sections of it which are more reminiscence and editorial than invention and fantasy; believes that he is at last writing the book he ascribed to John-Jonah in *Cat's Cradle*: the book which he precisely cannot, should not write, which is called archetypally *The Day the World Ended*, and which comes to him not out of his writer's imagination, but out of the duty he feels imposed on him by the fact that he himself lived through the fire-bombing of Dresden.

But though, like his author, Billy Pilgrim lives through that event—and returns to it eternally in contempt of time—he, like his author once more, can only return to it the way of Tralfamadore, which is to say, a world more comic and terrible and real than that of apocalyptic history. And if at last Vonnegut does not understand, all the better for him and for us. What he does not understand is precisely what saves him for readers like me who are disconcerted and dismayed as he grows more and more conscious of more and more in himself, turns more and more from fantasy to analysis.

Perhaps the process has begun to reverse itself, however, in *Slaughterhouse-Five*, or at least in those pages of it in which Billy takes his author back with him into the world of Science Fiction. I at least find occasion for hope in such passages, as I do in some remarks Vonnegut has included in a recent statement about his future plans and prospects. "I expect," he writes, "to become more and more stupid as time goes by." God bless him.

Notes on Philip José Farmer

Philip José Farmer seems now to have reached the point of public recognition, and I for one am feeling a little dismayed. I don't suppose that publication in *Esquire* alone is enough to make an unfashionable writer a *chic* one, but it is a real, perhaps irrevocable, step in that direction. I liked it much better when a taste for Farmer's fiction could still seem a private, slightly shameful pleasure, or a perverse affectation on the part of a scholar, an eccentric vice. In those days, he belonged chiefly to readers who did not even suspect that the novel is dead—to an audience which took him off the racks in drugstores or supermarkets or airports to allay boredom—and with no sense certainly that they were approaching "literature." Beyond them, there were, of course, a few others, some themselves more highly touted writers of Science Fiction, who knew that he was something very special; but they wanted to keep it a secret.

To be sure, Farmer had won a Hugo Award or two, one for his earliest work and another a decade and a half later. And a third, in 1972, for the novel *To Your Scattered Bodies Go.* But he was never the object of cult adoration, like Robert Heinlein, for instance, after the appearance of *Stranger in a Strange Land*; nor was he regarded, like Kurt Vonnegut, by *his* group of the faithful, as a hidden "great writer." To tell the truth, Farmer does not behave much like an aspirant to "mainstream" greatness. With all the modesty of a hack, he inclines to throw even his best conceptions away—writing hastily, sometimes downright sloppily; so that we are likely to be left with the disconcerting sense that his work, especially when it aspires to novel length, runs out rather than properly finishes. ("To preserve the Freudian tone of this article, I would have said 'peters out.'")

Nonetheless, he has an imagination capable of being kindled by the irredeemable mystery of the universe and the soul, and in turn able to kindle the imagination of others—readers who for a couple of generations have been turning to Science Fiction to keep wonder and ecstasy alive in times apparently uncongenial to those deep psychic experiences. That wonder and ecstasy, wherever it is found in Science Fiction, is ultimately rooted in our sexuality; and the best writers of the genre, during its period of flowering after World War II, appear to have realized instinctively that to succeed in their enterprise they had somehow to eroticize machines, gadgets and the scientific enterprise itself—or at least to exploit the preexistent erotic implications of the paraphernalia of a technological age.

Philip Farmer was, however, during the fifties, the only major writer of Science Fiction to deal _explicitly_ with sex. He constituted, therefore, a singular exception, an eccentric case—in a genre whose leading authors created protagonists themselves apparently desexed, though they and their adventures implicitly symbolized or projected sexuality; since they constitute, as it were, the communal dreams of a technological, urban civilization. And that civilization knows in its sleep what it denies waking, that at this point, it must eroticize the Industrial Revolution or perish, just as it thinks it knows waking, what it denies in its sleep, that sex must be re-imagined as machine technology or rejected out of hand. The latter is the task of modern pornography, even as the former is that of Science Fiction.

It was inevitable, therefore, from the start that Farmer would, at the climax of his career, produce two works at once fantasy and bald, explicit pornography— "hardcore pornography," as the cant phrase has it: _The Image of the Beast_ and _A Feast Unknown_. Both books were published by the same subrespectable firm and distributed through channels ordinarily unsympathetic to any work not aimed exclusively and directly at simple-minded titillation, "jerk-off literature," in short. Never mind that _A Feast Unknown_ begins with a quotation from May Swenson's poetry and ends with an apologetic Afterword by Theodore Sturgeon, in which he insists that this piece of sado-masochistic porn, whose hero can only have an orgasm over the bleeding body of his victims, represents somehow "the very core of the healthy truth expressed in the slogan, 'Make love, not war.'"

A Feast Unknown is a hilarious parody of the pop literature of super-heroic adventure; but its essential characteristic is a shamelessness beyond all possible apology. To speak of the imagination which informs it and its predecessor (in whose key scene an extraterrestrial girl with sharp iron dentures goes down on an unwary cop) as "healthy" is an inadvertent error or a deliberate lie. They are about as healthy as the works of the "divine" Marquis de Sade himself; which is to say, they may function therapeutically, but only by releasing in us, or exploding out of us, fantasies in themselves sick. And they have, in fact, helped pave the way for a new brand of Science Fiction, which deals frankly with human passion, "sick" and "healthy"; providing us with real phalluses and wombs, against which we can measure their symbolic projections in spaceships and underground cities on unknown planets. The paperback periodical, _Quark_, for instance, in which Farmer himself has been published, has also printed the work of younger writers, his debtors and descendants—in the form of candidly-worked-out genital fantasies, often by recently liberated women, eager to excel him in the candor of their language and the brutality of their images. But Farmer was there first.

I remember reading many years ago my first Farmer story, which was called "Mother," and being astonished and gratified (a little condescendingly, perhaps) to discover certain Freudian insights into the nature of family relationships, ingeniously worked out and made flesh, as it were, in the world of intergalactic travel and an endlessly receding future. My surprise and delight were not only cued by the prejudice which then possessed me utterly—my conviction that pop fiction was necessarily immune to the insights of depth psychology; but arose also because the mythology of Freud was based on the belief that the neuroses were rooted in the past, and that, therefore, the revelation of sexual secrets depended on retrospection. It needed a writer like Farmer, committed to the anticipation of the future, to turn psychoanalysis in the direction of prophecy. The concerns first explored in "Mother" and the other tales later collected in a volume called *Strange Relations* have continued to obsess him, reaching their culmination in his Hugo Award winning story, "Riders of the Purple Wage." In that tale—whose title puns on Zane Grey, of course (as he is always punning on names out of earlier literature, popular or elitist), and whose not-so-secret motto is "the family that blows is the family that grows"—he has taken advantage of the greater linguistic freedom of the past decade. And he has thus been able to render even more explicitly the vision of a cloying and destructive relationship between Mothers and Sons, with which he began nearly twenty years ago.

One of Farmer's major obsessive themes, as a matter of fact, is precisely the theme of Mother as a threat to freedom, a temptation to regression, a womb turned prison. And closely connected to it is the second of his major themes, the discovery of new religions in a new world; for those religions always turn out to be matriarchal and are presented as an overwhelming challenge to the patriarchal faith of Christianity. Yet, it is a Roman Catholic padre, more son than father though he is called Father John Carmody, who in various short stories and the extraordinary novel, *Night of Light*, somehow comes to terms with those alien mythologies and rituals; or even manages to defend them and his own *machismo* simultaneously with gun and fist.

In any case, the Cults of the Great Goddess have always obsessed Farmer; and, indeed, there seems something deep within him that yearns for a time, real or imagined, in which the male was not a Hero but a Servant of that great principle of fertility, as in the bawdiest of his subpornographic novels, *Flesh*. Yet Farmer's third obsessive theme comes into direct (and perhaps irreconcilable) conflict with this fearful nostalgia for the matriarchal security each of us has known in infancy. And this is the myth of The Hero with a Thousand

Faces, the lonely, phallic *übermensch* triumphing by his ability not to create but to kill. Farmer's favorite name for the extravagantly male super-hero is "Tarzan"; a killer presumably suckled by a she-ape rather than a mere female woman; but really created out of his own head by a god or devil called Edgar Rice Burroughs, and endlessly re-created by a subsidiary deity or demon called Philip José Farmer.

In five major books at least, he has returned to that key figure—who also flickers in and out of his other fictions sometimes quite irrelevantly: in *Lord Tyger, A Feast Unknown, Lord of the Trees, The Mad Goblin* and most recently in *Tarzan Alive*. The first of these deals with a boy brought up in the jungle by a mad scientist (a caricature of Farmer himself?) eager to save Burroughs's honor by proving that a Savage Noble can indeed survive under the conditions described by Tarzan's original biographer. The second is a sado-pornographic account of a struggle to the death between "Lord Grandrith" (the *true* Tarzan) and "Doc Caliban" (the *true* Doc Savage): a struggle which reaches an initial climax when the two super-heroes duel with erect phalluses on a knife-edge of stone bridging a chasm, and ends with both of them deballed. The third and fourth, issued as a double paperback—this time without the warning, "ADULTS ONLY"—represent, in Farmer's own words, "something unique . . . the only spinoff of 'clean books' from a 'dirty' book."

In all of them, however, "clean" or "dirty," Farmer insists not only on Tarzan's virtual immortality, but—even more strongly—on his extraordinary sexual endowment: his superiority in this respect to his primate pals and his Black neighbors (though he argues heatedly that Tarzan is no "racist")—as well as, one presumes, to his author and his readers. The same themes obsess him still in the fifth, to be published soon—but already excerpted in *Esquire*. It is in all respects the culmination of the others: a delightfully monomaniac attempt to "'prove' through the use of quasi-scholarly tools . . ." that Tarzan is (a) "a close relative of such modern heroes as Professor Challenger, Holmes and Wolfe, Lord John Roxton, Denis Nayland Smith, Bulldog Drummond, Lord Peter Wimsey, Raffles, Leopold Bloom, and Richard Wentworth (who is not only the Spider but was once G-8 and is at the same time the Shadow) . . ." and (b) "that Tarzan is the last of the Heroes of the Golden Age, Nature's final expression . . ."

But Tarzan, for all his encyclopedic comprehensiveness, represents only a small part of Farmer's larger attempt (at once absurd and beautiful, fore-doomed to failure but, once conceived, already a success) to subsume in his own works *all* of the books in the world that have touched or moved him. For him, the traditions of Science Fiction provide a warrant for constructing Universes of his own: worlds whose place names turn out inevitably to demand as many footnotes as T. S. Eliot's *The Waste Land*—Dante's Joy, Baudelaire,

Ozagen (Oz again!); and which are inhabited not only by new species but old friends, fictional or real—Hiawatha, Alice in Wonderland, Sir Richard Burton, Ishmael (Melville's) and Herman Goering.

Particularly in his "pocket universes" series and in his more recent River-world Books, *To Your Scattered Bodies Go* and *The Fabulous Riverboat*, all that seemed to have died here on Earth (everywhere at least except in the head of one voracious reader) is resurrected—or at least reconstructed in quasi-immortal form by omniscient computers in Worlds Out There. Obviously, it is the deepest level of childhood response which Farmer has reached in this pair of novels, in the first of which Sir Richard Burton pursues amorously Lewis Carroll's chastely loved Alice Liddell; while in the second, Mark Twain searches with equal passion for his lost wife, Livy, and for iron ore deposits rich enough to make possible the building of a paddlewheel steamer. The primary images seem erotic, even genital; but in the Riverworld there turns out to be more detailed description of eating than of sex. And, indeed, the most important gadget in its extraterrestrial technology is the "Grail," a kind of portable short-order kitchen provided by the invisible masters of a warmed-over universe.

But this is fair enough; since throughout Farmer's work he demonstrates himself to be the most oral of men—his heroes being more typically blown than laid; his image of ultimate horror a bitten-off penis; and his vision of utopian bliss a kind of not-quite-kiss, in which the partners (functionally neither totally male nor female) move their lips ecstatically around a pale snakelike organ which wriggles out of the mouth of one into that of the other. In this light, it seems appropriate to describe Farmer's cultural imperialism as a gargantuan lust to *swallow* the whole cosmos, past, present and to come, and to spew it out again.

Farmer wants even to eat and regurgitate himself; the industrious hack who writes his books, plus that hack's fantasies of what he secretly is or might be. And in the end, he does manage to mingle almost unnoticed among super-heroes and mutants and monsters, as if the character Philip José Farmer were as real as any fiction: the writer without real fans, who, for twenty-five [*five* is correct] years, tried to make it in Southern California, baffled by apartment house living among Jewish neighbors, improbably married the whole time to the same wife—and fleeing at last back to Peoria, Illinois, where he was born [correct place of birth: North Terre Haute, Indiana]. Usually his self-portraits are betrayed by the initials, P. J. F., as he himself points out: "Kickaha (Paul Janus Finnegan) is me as I would like to be. Peter Jairus Frigate (*To Your Scattered Bodies Go*) is me as I (more or less) really am."

Finally, I suppose, Farmer must dream of swallowing down his readers, too, or at least of "taking them in," as the telltale phrase has it, with jokes and hoaxes and "scholarly" proofs. And there is something satisfactory, after all, about imagining ourselves, complete with wives, kids and worldly possessions, disappearing into an utterly fictional world along with Alice and Tarzan and Kilgore Trout, the Scarlet Pimpernel and Jack the Ripper and Samuel Clemens. But not before we have managed to say, as I am trying to say here: *Thanks for the feast.*

The Return of
James Branch Cabell;
Or, the Cream of the
Cream of the Jest

I first read James Branch Cabell's *Jurgen* in 1932 or 1933 as a gesture of contempt (I was then fifteen or sixteen years old) to the world of my elders: a way of asserting my independence of the taboos imposed on me in particular—and more generally on all writers and readers of the time—by what I had already learned from H. L. Mencken to call the " booboisie," and what Cabell himself taught me, long before I discovered Matthew Arnold, to refer to as "Philistia." *Jurgen*, I knew before I picked it up, had been not so many years earlier a banned or almost banned book. And I thought of it, therefore, in the context of other once-forbidden novels like Dreiser's *Sister Carrie*, Lawrence's *Lady Chatterley's Lover* and James Joyce's *Ulysses;* so that flaunting it in the face of parents and teachers seemed to me quite as revolutionary an act as publicly reading Marx's *Das Kapital* or joining the Young Communist League—which I also did at the same moment, with a similar sense of daring, and none at all of the contradictions involved.

That Cabell despised Joyce and Lawrence, the whole adventure of modernism with which I had misguidedly identified him, I was as blissfully unaware as I was that, quite unlike those avowed enemies of convention and organized religion, he quite dutifully attended church, appeared in formal dress at cotillions and refrained from typing on Sundays lest he offend his stuffier neighbors. Nor did I suspect that his politics were as far to the right as mine then were to the left, though it was already on record that he wished Hindenburg had triumphed in World War I and Stonewall Jackson had carried the day in the Civil War. In any case, I still believed the main point was to *épater la bourgeoisie* from either flank; and that a chief weapon in that fundamental conflict between an enlightened Us and a benighted Them was the production of what They considered pornography. I was dimly conscious, though it scarcely seemed to matter, that what Cabell wrote was a special *kind* of pornography—soft, genteel, perhaps a little pretentious; which is to say, pornography euphemized and camouflaged with recondite literary allusions, learned mythological references and quotations from acknowledged "great books," preferably in Greek and Latin, or at the very least, French.

I would, moreover, have denied vehemently that the pleasure I found in reading *Jurgen* (culture-climbing adolescent that I was, for all my radical jargon) had anything in common with the titillation derived from the same book by those "chorus girls" who Heywood Broun had reported thumbed through its pages, ignoring everything but certain "phallic" passages of which they had heard on the subcultural grapevine. And certainly I, a boy from the streets of Newark, New Jersey, felt nothing in common with those other young ladies in suburban or semirural finishing schools whose continued sniggering interest in his book prompted fan letters which enraged Cabell. Nor did my appreciation of his erotic masterpiece, I assured myself, resemble even the somewhat more sophisticated response of Zelda Fitzgerald, who, pleading that she could not find a copy in her local bookstore, wrote to ask Cabell to send her one; backing up her plea (she knew a nympholept when she encountered one) with a particularly fetching photograph of her very young and quite beautiful self.

Yet, now I realize, whatever my aesthetic or political rationalizations, I must have turned with relief (and the kind of thrill appropriate to my age) from the dutiful perusal of grim texts like Friedrich Engels's *Anti-Dühring* or Lenin's *What Is to Be Done?* not just to *Jurgen*, but to such other purportedly antibourgeois soft porn as James Huneker's *Painted Veils*, Anatole France's *Penguin Island* and Pierre Louÿs' *Aphrodite*. Such books were available in those days in garishly illustrated cheap reprints, along with erotic "classics" like Flaubert's *Salammbô* and Boccaccio's *Decameron*, as well as more blatant examples of up-to-date mytho-pornography like Viereck and Elridge's *My First Two Thousand Years*. And they were typically stacked up on bargain tables in chain drugstores and cut-rate *schlock* emporia, which peddled them side by side with exploding cigars and cutesy genre pictures of sleeping nude boys whose peckers were being nibbled at by geese.

I first read *Jurgen*, that is to say, in the context of a kind of exploitative popular culture against which I thought I had been immunized by long exposure to "high art," particularly in its avant-garde manifestations. Was I not, at the very moment, for instance, following breathlessly in succeeding issues of the *transition* sections from the book which eventually became *Finnegans Wake*, but was then known by the few who were aware of it at all as *Work in Progress?* And had I not long since graduated from taking seriously the kind of *fin de siècle* pop novel which Cabell had begun by imitating, Anthony Hope's *Prisoner of Zenda*, for example, and Henry Harland's *The Cardinal Snuffbox?* Even the romances of Booth Tarkington, about which Cabell remained

ambivalent to the end of his career, the unspeakable *Seventeen* and the insufferable *Monsieur Beaucaire*, I had left behind in junior high school. Nor had
I ever really developed a taste for the kind of middle American, middle-class,
pseudorealistic best sellers by Harold Bell Wright and Gene Stratton Porter,
which Cabell felt obliged to vilify long after they had lost their mass audience.
It was as if he never outgrew the need to prove (to himself, to certain forgotten newspaper reviewers, like Burton Rascoe, to readers like me) that he was
something altogether different: neglected, perhaps, by most Americans, but
for his virtues rather than his faults.

What was Cabell to do, however, when he came—thanks not only to professional enemies of Philistia like me, plus finishing-school students and chorus
girls, who were at least young, but to the very middle-aged Philistines who
read Wright and Porter—a best seller? This was, indeed, the cream of the jest
(but on *whom?*): a jest belatedly compounded by the fact that even now, if any
of his books is remembered at all, it is likely to be that anomalous marketplace
success, *Jurgen*. Long before his death in 1958, Cabell had recorded, not once
but many times, his dismay over the fact that this single book had overshad-
owed all the rest—most movingly perhaps in a much rewritten novel, entitled
appropriately enough, *The Cream of the Jest*.

In it, an author called Felix Kennaston (one of Cabell's many thinly disguised fictional surrogates) is described as having produced after some distinguished failures a best seller, *Men Who Loved Alison*—"one of those many
books which have profited very dubiously indeed, by having obtained, in one
way or another, the repute of being indecent." Such books, which Cabell-
Kennaston tells us include "the sloppy and soporific catalogues of Rabelais . . .
and the unendurably dull botcheries of Boccaccio," are read, he goes on to
explain, by an audience consisting of "immature persons who are content to
put up with the diction and stylistic devices for the sake of the atoning talk
of unnatural amours, which, however sparsely . . . adorns and opens the pornoscopic reader's laborious way." Despite the multiple ironies, Cabell's point
is clear. There are two types of best sellers: those read by a mass audience
responding to the trash they really are; and those (usually erotic or suspected
of being erotic) responded to for what they are *not* by the kind of reader who
finds their essential best a distraction and a bore. But it is to the latter category
that Cabell, despite everything, believed *Jurgen* to belong.

To have confessed otherwise, even to himself, would have undercut not
only his aesthetic faith in himself as essentially different from the darlings of
the literary marketplace but also his political belief that the majority of Americans (perhaps the majority of mankind) is always wrong in its choices in the
bookstore as well as the polling place. Had he not declared as early as 1919 in
Jurgen itself that "The religion of Hell is patriotism, and the government is an

enlightened democracy"? And was he still not insisting, looking at the best seller lists of 1945 and finding them as disheartening as those of his youth, that "a nation which upon three separate occasions and running re-elected Franklin Roosevelt has abandoned all claims to intelligence"? Like most Americans by the end of World War II, I found such unreconstructed anti–New Dealism absurd, and the antidemocratic bias it betrayed reprehensible; yet even at that point I was no more able than Cabell to grant that in the literary arena as well as the political, popular judgment might sometimes be superior to that of a self-appointed aristocracy of taste.

But in the case of Cabell's *Jurgen* at least, time has proved the mass audience right. *Jurgen* (contrary to what Cabell himself thought) *is* the best of his novels—not despite its pornographic passages and because of its "fine writing," but despite that "fine writing" and because of its appeal to prurience. Had Cabell or any of the critics who first touted him understood so much, they would have been able to surmise what they did not in fact foresee: that his work was ironically destined to survive not as "high literature," belles lettres, "serious art"—but as a kind of "pop" appealing primarily to adolescents of all ages. Indeed, in this sense, his fate resembles that of Edgar Allan Poe, another native of Richmond, Virginia, and the only nineteenth-century American author he could bring himself to praise without qualification; though Poe, who like Cabell considered himself a "dandy" in the realm of art, has ended as the favorite reading matter of high school students and the source of plots for the kind of Class B movies they prefer.

Certainly, I myself did not realize this essential truth about Cabell even after my first enthusiasm for him wore out. At that point, I not merely stopped reading him, I stopped thinking about him at all. If I recalled occasionally my former affection for *Jurgen,* it was as a juvenile lapse of taste, indulged in shamefully after I was old enough to know better; a yielding not only to what Cabell would have called my "pornoscopic" impulses but also to a taste for overwriting and ingroup allusiveness—obvious appeals to reigning fashion and the snobbism of the culturally insecure, to which I had believed myself immune. Even my change of heart, however, turned out to be in tune with the changing times; for as the depression grew deeper, it no longer seemed possible to praise his effete efforts as H. L. Mencken and Burton Rascoe, for instance, once had. Besides, I asked myself, who the hell were *they* anyhow, those newspaper hacks without real standards or any deep theoretical understanding of what literature was? Almost imperceptibly, I and my contemporaries had begun to think of our times not as a postwar but as a prewar era; which is to say, memories of Wilson's ill-fated War to End All War, which so obsessed Cabell, faded, and intimations of FDR's war-to-come began to haunt our troubled sleep.

It was "realism," in any case, which carried the day in the thirties, whose preferred novelists were Dos Passos and Farrell and Steinbeck: that very "realism" against which Cabell had vainly protested all his life long; though he had exempted from his censure such twenties forerunners of that movement as Sinclair Lewis and Theodore Dreiser—largely because they were his friends and had publicly touted his work. Other twenties writers whom he admired and praised, however, like Joseph Hergesheimer, came to be considered in the gray days of the depression too effete, elegant, involuted, affected and "decadent" to be endured. Nor were their reputations redeemed in the post–World War II reaction against the ideological excesses of the thirties. Though by the time the fifties arrived, critical consensus had begun to turn against not just Farrell and Dos Passos and Steinbeck but Lewis and Dreiser as well, this did not mean the rediscovery of Hergesheimer and Cabell. Rather like their realist contemporaries and successors, such dandies of the twenties were measured by post–World War II critics against two somewhat younger contemporaries, Faulkner and Hemingway, who came—however slowly and with whatever ups and downs—to represent the major achievement in fiction of the post–World War I sensibility.

But Cabell refused, with what seems at this remove a touchingly transparent defensiveness, to measure himself against them. Urged by literary correspondents to read them and register an opinion, he responded, "I cannot protest that Hemingway is quite my favorite author," and "as goes Faulkner, I have to date [he is writing in 1953] read none of his books, I confess blushingly. They did not attract me somehow and besides that I felt duty bound to dispose of *Gone with the Wind* [first]." The last sentence is intended, of course, as the ultimate put-down, since he had already declared of Margaret Mitchell's super–best seller in 1936, "I did not find *Gone with the Wind* to be even readable, far less a masterpiece."

The conjunction of the two authors and their simultaneous dismissal, though natural enough, inevitable, perhaps, is also symptomatic and revealing. After all, Faulkner is far and away the chief contender for the title of greatest southern novelist of the twentieth century, to which Cabell had clearly aspired; and Margaret Mitchell (also a Southerner, committed to imprinting on the popular imagination that region's myth of the Civil War and Reconstruction) had written the most successful best seller of the century, as Cabell seemed for a little while to fear (but, one cannot help suspecting, also to hope) he might have done. Such a rejection of the two chief fictional spokesmen for the American South seems consistent, at first glance, with his interior expatriation: his attempt to write from his retreat in Richmond if not quite as if from outside the South, at least from outside the South as part of America—from outside of America.

He sets the action of his most characteristic books in an imaginary king-dom whose boundaries may be vague, but whose climate is Mediterranean and whose language is French, or rather, I suppose, Provençal; and he attaches himself to a literary tradition rooted in late medieval France and Restoration England. No wonder then that he was contemptuous of what he called the "spiritual descendants of Walt Whitman," especially Waldo Frank, whom he parodically portrays as calling out, "Come, let's be sturdy and fearless pioneers, and grow real hair on our chests, and develop our splendid innate qualities without truckling to tradition and effete foreigners." The moment at which Cabell was travestying the cultural rediscovery of America was, however, precisely the moment at which not just for younger native writers but for the whole world, the literature produced in the United States in the middle of the nineteenth century was becoming an inspiration and model. "Classic American Literature," D. H. Lawrence called that flowering of prose and verse which for him climaxed in *Leaves of Grass*; and the American critic F. O. Mat-thiessen labeled it even more honorifically "The American Renaissance." But Cabell is apparently as immune to the appeal of the fiction of that period as he is to its poetry. Of the author of *Moby Dick*, for instance, he remarks coolly that "When it comes to Melville, I feel I lack appreciation." And this is com-prehensible enough after all; since as Cabell himself never managed to say, but must somehow have intuited, the erotic myths of chivalry and gallantry, dominei and the service of women which inform his fiction have little in com-mon with the peculiarly American myth of interethnic male-bonding which moved novelists otherwise as different from each other as Cooper, Melville, Mark Twain and Faulkner.

There is oddly enough one American book which appeared at that magical point in the mid-nineteenth century about which Cabell has a good word to say; though it is one ignored by both Lawrence and Matthiessen, and dis-trusted by almost all elitist critics—precisely because, perhaps, it has been a favorite of the popular audience everywhere in the world except the American South. I am referring, of course, to Harriet Beecher Stowe's *Uncle Tom's Cabin*, of which Cabell was driven to write, despite his abhorrence for Mrs. Stowe's abolitionism, her shameless sentimentality and her unflattering portrayal of the region he loved, "It is badly written, and has nothing to do with any South which ever existed, but its power is undeniable." What moved him to such a declaration was not simple perversity, as I was at first tempted to believe, but that deep yearning for the "romantic" rather than the "realistic" which joined him to the most frivolous readers of best sellers and separated him from the "serious" critics of his time. "I grieve to report," he said by way of explanation, "that as a romance the book is excellent."

His instinctive and unquenchable love for the romance, moreover, not only

separated Cabell from the neo-Whitmanians, populists, nativists and realists, who flourished largely in the Northeast of the United States, and whose
politics were more often than not left of center. It drove a wedge also between
him and that rival school, the self-styled New Poets and New Critics, many of
whom (from John Crowe Ransom to Allen Tate) were not merely Southerners
like him, but shared both his rightist politics and his distrust of the author of
Leaves of Grass. Though like Cabell, they, too, turned to Europe as a source of
inspiration, their models were the *symbolistes,* the founding fathers of modernism, which Cabell despised. Not only did he eschew *vers libre* in favor of
conventional stanzaic form, refusing either to "break the iamb" or abandon
the clichés of traditional poetic diction; he disavowed as well their favorite
European novelist, James Joyce. T. S. Eliot, on whose taste the southern Agrarians based their own, had given *Ulysses* his blessing; but Cabell contemptuously associated its prose style with the empty rhetoric of American politics.
Looking back on certain popular books he had loved in his earliest youth,
for instance, he observes that he now finds them "to be as sad twaddle as a
Congressional Record or the effusions of the late Gertrude Stein and James
Joyce."

Once more, his judgment is consistent with his practice, since the definition of the modern novel, the art novel, implicit in *Ulysses* challenges the basic
assumptions about the nature of prose fiction which underlie the mannered
prose, the whimsical structure, the romantic tone of the legend of Manuel
and his descendants. Indeed, so long as the critical establishment continues
to share Joyce's assumptions rather than his, Cabell stands little chance of
being considered ever again (the words are V. L. Parrington's and were written at the peak of his fame) "the supreme comic spirit thus far granted us."
Despite the heroic efforts of Edmund Wilson to refurbish his fading reputation in the years immediately before his death and the continuing adulation
of a shrinking circle of parochial admirers, Cabell has in fact disappeared
almost completely from the consciousness of practicing writers and literary
pundits. Not only has it become impossible to think of him any longer as a
"great writer," but even as a minor one of real interest; so that Frederick Hoff-
man in a comprehensive book on literature of the 1920s published in 1955 did
not even list him in an extensive bibliography, much less discuss any of his
novels at length.

Yet in 1980, at least seven of his books, all from the Poictesme cycle, were
once more in print as paperbacks, and were displayed side by side with current
best sellers in the bookstalls of airports and supermarkets. But this time
around they are presented under the aegis of "fantasy and science fiction," in
a series which also includes reprints of L. Frank Baum's Oz books and is clearly

aimed at the audience which has turned the *Rings* trilogy of J. R. R. Tolkien, Frank Herbert's *Dune* and Robert Heinlein's *Stranger in a Strange Land* into pop classics. Cabell, that is to say, at the very moment of his exclusion (permanent and irreversible, I fear) from the ranks of "high literature" threatens to return as a "youth best seller," sharing the fate of certain of his nineteenth-century predecessors like Bram Stoker and H. Rider Haggard, who were remanded to the outer darkness by the critical establishment, but—in part for that very reason—prized by a student underground. And this seems scarcely surprising in the light of the facts which I have been reminding you, particularly the early popularity of *Jurgen*.

This time, however, Cabell appeals to a new generation of what he considered the mindless young (the grandchildren of his original audience) not as a pornographer or an old-fashioned spinner of romantic yarns, but as a writer of up-to-date fantasy. Cabell is "probably the only American fantasy writer of genius," Lin Carter writes of him, apparently forgetting that other Richmond author, Edgar Allan Poe. But we are dealing with "hype" rather than criticism: an introduction to a series of Cabell reprints which Ballantine Books obviously hoped would reach in the late seventies the ready-made audience for what Edmund Wilson was already describing in 1956 as "juvenile trash," meaning specifically *The Lord of the Rings*. At that point, Wilson still thought it possible to distinguish between the fairy tales of Tolkien, which he was proud to despise, and the fantasy of Cabell, which he was not ashamed to admire. The former, he believed, demanded of adult readers, eager to share the enthusiasms of the young, the abrogation of all "standards," ethical as well as aesthetic, normally associated with maturity and sophistication.

It seems to me, however, that though there is a real difference between the two, it is one of degree rather than kind, Cabell substituting for the naïveté of extended childhood the callowness of prolonged adolescence. The pleasure, therefore, which despite myself I continue to find in his fiction, seems to me an understandable but rather ignoble response to what are essentially the wet dreams of an eternal fraternity boy, wish-fulfillment fantasies set in a realm between dawn and sunrise, in which time is unreal and crime without consequence. In this crepuscular Neverland, all males are incredibly urbane and phallic, all women fair and delightfully stupid up to the point of marriage. After that dread event, the former becomes genitally inadequate, and the latter shrewish and nagging, though dedicated, for reasons never made quite clear, to nurturing and protecting their doddering mates so that they can produce romances celebrating not those wives, of course, but certain phantom girls whom they have not married and who consequently remain forever desirable and eighteen.

How is it possible today to respond without guilt to Cabell's travesties of male/female relations, when women everywhere around us are protesting such stereotypes of them and us? Indeed, they had already begun to do so at the moment Cabell was publishing his first books; nor was he unaware either of that protest or the leveling politics which underlay it; the inevitable extension, it seemed to him, of egalitarianism from class to gender. Nonetheless, though he observed in 1935—with typical snide irony—that "the lady is climbing down to full equality with the butler and the congressman," he refused to give ground; declaring that as a "Romanticist" and a member of what he liked to call "the gentry," he could never agree to "regard women as human beings." Yet guilty or not, we who do regard our sisters as human, read him still in large part, I suspect, not in spite of his "sexism" but because of it; since in the unreconstructed dark underside of our minds the notion of the eternally unattainable lady which we do not dare confess in full daylight continues to lead a crepuscular life.

Indeed, it would seem as if popular "fantasy" exists precisely in order to indulge "immortal longings" in us which our conscious pities and allegiances have taught us to continue. Cabell, to be sure, had completely different notions about the function of nonmimetic art. To him the enemy was "realism," which he identified not just with the bourgeois world of compromise and accommodation, but with the best sellers that celebrated its values. His elite "romances" he thought of as subverting and transcending that world in the imagination, thus preparing a chosen few for achieving in fact an evolutionary leap to a new level of humanity. But the survival of his books as merely another kind of best seller (preferred above all others at the moment by the youth audience) suggests that their function may all along have been "regressive" rather than "progressive," though therapeutically so—encouraging, as the psychiatrists would put it, "regression in service of the ego."

They afford us, that is to say, ways of expressing, harmlessly, symbolically, certain juvenile wishes and primordial fears that we have learned to be ashamed of but from which we can never quite deliver ourselves: ways—to use a metaphor which might well have appealed to Cabell, but somehow did not—of "giving the Devil his due." Though a working title of the novel eventually called *Jurgen* was "Go to the Devil," and Cabell actually described in it a Black Ritual invented by that infamous Satanist and sexologist, Aleister Crowley, he was deeply embarrassed when a grateful Crowley hailed him as "a world genius of commanding stature." He refused in fact ever to answer his insistent letters, dismissing him as one of the nameless "hordes of idiots and prurient fools . . . of dabblers in black magic" from whom in genteel dismay he sought to dissociate himself. Yet it is surely dishonorable motives rather like Crowley's which have made it possible for me to return to Cabell; ten of whose novels I read with unseemly relish before I could manage to stop, preferring this time around *The High Place*, a work really wicked, rather than, like *Jurgen*, merely naughty. And surely I could not have done so, if I had not realized that I was dealing not with "high art" but with "juvenile trash," which like all trash—indeed, like all books which "please many and please long"—was of the Devil's party without knowing it.

Who Really Died in Vietnam?
The Cost in Human Lives

It is often said that the war in Vietnam has divided our society, pitting generation against generation and class against class; like much that is "often said" about public issues, this is true—but not deeply revealing. It is more revealing, I think, to say that the war in Vietnam has mercilessly brought to light a profound division in our society by demonstrating that the actual fighting of war has become more and more exclusively an occupation of the exploited and dispossessed, while protest against war has been more and more preempted by the privileged and economically secure. As any newspaper reader with a feeling for statistics must have noticed, since about 1962 it has been by and large the obligation of the children of the poor to die in a war they do not understand, while the sons and daughters of the rich are demonstrating at home against that same conflict, which they have come to understand too well to endure.

The place in which the children of the rich have come to their understanding, and then mounted demonstrations, is the university, where their status as students has exempted them from combat. It has been, in fact, the prestige of higher education that has converted universal selective service from a democratic to a discriminatory institution, thus turning the Vietnam War into the first war of which it can be said unequivocally that it is being fought for us by our servants. Yet the university system in the United States is the least elitist of any in the world. Some 25 percent of our young people between eighteen and twenty-four attend college, and we are presumably on the way to fulfilling the goal of universal higher education implicit in the constitutions of the Land-Grant colleges, which pledge that their doors will remain open to all and that "the tuition shall be forever free."

How did such anomalous inequities arise from the conjunction of two democratic dreams: the dream of sixteen years of schooling for all who desire it and the utopian vision of a citizens' army? From the first there were attempts to subvert the dreams by buying military substitutes, for instance, but not until Vietnam was the privileged evasion of service sanctioned by law. Of course, the exemption of college students would not have made so flagrant a difference had not the population of the universities already been so out of line with the ethnic and class balances of the larger community. Certain groups, such as the Jews, enroll more than 70 percent of their children in universities, while the blacks have reached only half of the national average and the Indians half that of the blacks.

The reasons for such imbalance are complex, but the facts are simple and clear. In our armed forces, drawn from the less favored segments of the community, barely 5 percent of all enlisted men have made it through college—which is to say that those most likely to die in Vietnam are Americans who were first of all educationally deprived. It would surely be worse, as Sen. Edward Kennedy has argued on the floor of the Senate, if we were to substitute a volunteer army for our present mixture of conscripts and volunteers. But matters are bad enough as they stand—too bad, in fact, either to ignore or to seem to justify by a comparison with what would be even more monstrously unjust.

It was not the statistics, however, that first led me to reflect on the paradoxical relationship between participation and protest in the Vietnam War. Rather, it was the slow-dawning realization that I had never known a single family that had lost a son in Vietnam, or, indeed, one with a son wounded, missing in action or held prisoner of war. And this despite the fact that American casualties in Vietnam are already almost equal to those of World War I. Nor am I alone in my strange plight; in talking to friends about a subject they seem eager *not* to discuss, I discover they can, they must, all say the same. As far as the university community in which I live and work is concerned, the war in Vietnam happens—on the level where blood is shed and lives are lost— primarily to others, though of course, in social, moral and psychological terms, we are all touched, suffering along with other indignities the final one of being physically immune.

At this moment some Vietnam veterans are coming to the campuses, but I have still to meet one on my home grounds at the university in Buffalo. And I learn, consulting the statistics once more, that, though nearly half of those already released from service have taken advantage of their educational GI rights, more than half of that group have chosen vocational over university training.

No, the single person I have known well who went as a soldier to Vietnam (and returned) was black to begin with and had never been to college at all. On the other hand, I have been more or less familiar with hundreds, perhaps thousands, of young men—white and educated to the BA or beyond—who have protested the war they never saw. I do not mean to impugn the courage or sincerity of any of them, though they have ranged from conscientious objectors to back-row stowaways, from draft-card burners to connivers who have baffled their Selective Service boards by zonking themselves out on speed or reciting semifictional tales of their homosexuality, drug addiction and psychosis. My own contemporaries present a mixed bag as well: organizers of teach-ins and raiders of draft boards, passers of petitions and visitors to the war zone who have gathered evidence of defoliation, terror bombings and the burning of children. Nor have they all escaped unscathed, since even among the combatants in this less spectacular war against the war there have been casualties, too: busted heads, broken limbs, disrupted lives, expulsions, arrests, vindictive sentences, even some deaths.

No one has died on my own campus, to be sure, as at Kent State. But for a little while we, too, were occupied territory: 400 police marching smartly between the library and the parking lot, smacking their puttees with their night sticks—more, I would suppose, to reassure themselves than to terrify us. It was they who were on enemy ground, bugged by phone calls from their angry wives wanting to know when the hell they would stop playing soldier and come home. Before it was all over, there had been four nights of battle, tear gas against hurled rocks and Coke bottles, even a couple of students peppered with buckshot.

It was a battle between the students and their parents, really; between the elders who loved, if not the war in Vietnam, at least the society that supported it, and the youths who hated both that war and that society—and most of all, perhaps, those members of the society they knew best. Of course, the parents were not there when the firing began, having called the cops in to do their dirty work; which is to say, having mustered a squad of uniformed men quite like, in class origin and degree of education, the forces in Vietnam. It was a second war being fought for them by their servants; but, since the enemy this time was their own children, it turned out to be a class war as well, with college kids confronting those who had not made it onto the campus until trouble began. On the campuses, however, those servants did better than in the rice paddies of Vietnam, for the victories of the students were small and transitory, consisting only of the political eclipse of Lyndon Johnson; a few antiwar bills introduced and defeated in Congress; the emergence of new strategies for losing a presidential election; and especially the momentary elation of the demonstrations, the mass ecstasy subsiding into frustration and baffled rage as the first war, the big war, the war elsewhere, continued.

If the students achieved relatively little, the risks they ran were relatively light. For in the cold war between the bourgeois generations there was less direct confrontation and less retrospective vindictiveness, as judges with LLDs mitigated what cops with high school diplomas had done earlier, dismissing cases, suspending sentences, in effect, abrogating martial law. This détente give us the chance, perhaps, to see the struggle in a larger context, to understand that the students' war, quite like the colonial war against which it is directed, is part of a greater whole: in this case the total war against affluence and the university, waged as much on account of as in spite of the fact that together these enemies made possible that other war.

Having realized so much, we can begin to count all the casualties incurred in the war at home: not just those caught in the line of fire, but those who died of drug overdoses and in crumpled Volkswagens; those who were the victims of homemade bombs, whether their inept makers or some late-working researcher, as innocent (or guilty) as his assassins; those killed by Charles Manson and his girls, along with the less ideological patsies of big dope deals gone wrong. These are the "combat deaths," and there are the "wounded" as well: those stricken by hepatitis from improperly sterilized needles or by VD, which has grown virulent again among those at odds with uptight hygiene and AMA professionalism. And finally there are the mad—a new category on official casualty lists, but surely not unknown in earlier wars. Now I recall that I have, after all, known one casualty in Vietnam: a "hippie" merchant seaman, carrying combat supplies into the war theater and dope out of it, who came unstuck in the middle of the Indian Ocean and sent me a telegram reading: "I am the Messiah. My father is dying."

But the greater number of casualties have occurred in Vietnam, of course, where not only God (whom we have listed as dead for a century or two anyhow) but many men continue to die, though fewer and fewer of them have been Americans in recent years. "Vietnamization" has mean that our Oriental servants are doing more and more of the dying for us. From the start, however, this has been a conflict in which nonwhites have died at a disproportionate rate, and not merely because it happens to have occurred in a country inhabited by nonwhites. By the middle of October the total number of American dead was 56,164, whereas the "enemy" dead came to 900,909, and the South Vietnamese had lost 181,906 combat troops. If one adjusts these figures by subtracting the nearly 6,000 black dead from the U.S. total and adding them to the nonwhite total, the final result is approximately: US, 50,000; Them, 1,000,000 . . . When the nearly 425,000 South Vietnamese civilians are taken into account, the disproportion becomes even more staggering.

Although perhaps not that surprising. The war in Vietnam seems about to turn into one in which no whites at all die. And yet it remains very much *our* war, the war we have dreamed ever since the first European set foot on American soil only to find the land he lusted for inhabited by a nonwhite people—in short, the undeclared, three-hundred-year-long war against the Indian, in the course of which we whites first became "Americans."

Into the image of our first alien enemy we have assimilated all the other nonwhites encountered in our imperialist adventures ever since: the long series of swarthy Others whose homelands we were sure destiny intended to be our own and whom we therefore battled, as the Marine Corps hymn puts it, "From the halls of Montezuma to the shores of Tripoli . . ." Fixed in a hundred thousand works of art and sub-art, the image persists. "Remember the Alamo!" the embattled politician cries, or "Remember Custer's last stand," an apologetic journalist writes of this very war, and the proper responses arise. We are at home, back in the familiar nightmare once more.

But this time around we do not quite dare to say aloud, "The only good Injun is a dead Injun," for racism is no longer fashionable (at least among the polite), not dead, to be sure, but driven underground, into the undermind. And so we endure the pangs of a society that has outlived a value system whose mythological foundation remains firm. It has been a long time since we permitted ourselves officially to declare our hatred and fear of "gooks" and "wogs," which we still confess in our private abusive names for the Others. No official voice, for instance, cried "Yellow Peril" to justify the Second World War, which Vietnam in some sense continued, but private voices in the heat of combat cried worse. This deep-seated hatred for nonwhites may finally have been the reason why we were able to drop the atomic bomb on the Japanese though not on the Germans, on nonwhites but not whites, on Them but not Us. Certainly, the shameful war in Vietnam seems to confirm the suspicion that a lust for genocide rather than mere strategy cued the double bombing of Japan. For how can we read, without the aid of such mythology, the strange conflict in Southeast Asia that rejected even the traditional name of war while providing us with daily "body counts"? How unendurable they finally became, those totals reckoned in each morning's newspaper: for every enemy soldier killed, we soon learned, a three-day pass, quite like the seventeenth-century bounty of five pounds for every Indian scalp. It was as if we were moving grimly to the point where, checking the last figures, we would discover we had them all, *all!*

But even though the dream of total destruction is thus inadvertently confessed in the press, we have denied ourselves the instrument of total destruction this time around: no Big Bomb (though certain reactionary voices continued to call for it), only hand-to-hand combat, sniper answering sniper, the helicopters swooping low on missions of rescue and supply. To be sure, there are "little" bombs in great plenty, but somehow these do not register in our mythological imaginations, only in theirs. For us the prevailing image of the war is one of infiltration: the sneak attack from their side; from ours the war against the very trees, the burning out by jellied fire of the forest that conceals and the guerrillas that it conceals. And always no atomic bomb! It is not just a last delicate scruple of hypocrisy, the resolve to destroy utterly without quite seeming to do so—for what is the difference between a single payload of atomic magnitude and thousands of smaller raids adding up to the same total?

It is also a deliberate decision—not less deliberate for being secret even from ourselves—to reinvent and reenact Indian warfare, in what must surely prove the last episode of our long combat with the nonwhite world.

Maybe, if we had been able to say aloud, "The only good Injun is a dead Injun," this war would have been over long ago and the next would have begun. But in the face of fact and probability we talked instead of national interest and containment and the threat of Communism (which somehow no hawk has ever been able to persuade us to fight in Europe, only in Asia). When will we realize that, in the bad dream our longest-lived myth has become, those "Reds" we fight turn out to be not Communists but *Peaux-Rouges*—Apaches, Mohicans and Custer-killing Sioux?

James Fenimore Cooper: The Problem of the Bad Good Writer

We are gathered here to honor an American writer—the first American writer, we sometimes boast, to have achieved world-wide literary eminence in his own time and to have maintained it undiminished into ours. Yet we are all uncomfortably aware, as Cooper himself had become aware before his death, that it is only five of his books (one tenth of his literary production) which anybody but the most fanatic scholar-specialists can persuade himself are worth celebrating. Moreover, these five Leatherstocking Tales, though they stay in print and are read still by a substantial though diminishing audience, chiefly juvenile, are quite unlike what we ordinarily think of as Classics or "Great Books." They are, in fact, on most counts—on all counts, if judged by rigorous critical standards—bad books: ineptly structured, shamelessly periphrastic, euphemistic and verbose; at last, unforgivably boring, particularly in their ponderous introductions and the all-too-frequent *obiter dicta* of their garrulous anti-hero.

Even when they are intermittently interesting, they interest us not for their technical virtuosity or executive skill, much less for their wisdom, morality or insight into the labyrinth of the human heart. No, they interest us—once the editorializing has ceased and the woodland pursuits and evasions begun; once tomahawks flash through the darkling air and rifles are discharged out of the shadowed underbrush, while canoes glide stealthily across lakes impossibly virgin and more beautiful than any nature has made—as much we call "escapist trash" interests us. Like all such trash, they are, not accidentally but essentially, violent, melodramatic, sentimental and, above all, trite, reassuringly platitudinous, familiar before the fact; so that they can move us to shudders and tears, yet leave us feeling not shaken but reassured.

Re-reading, for instance, just the other day that scene in *The Last of the Mohicans* in which Uncas is recognized by Tamenund and the doom of his race prophesied, I found myself weeping; as I have always wept since I first encountered it at the age of twelve, yet satisfied, gratified now as I was then. It is not merely that I have come to expect that scene after many re-readings, would feel cheated if it were not there, but that somehow I had expected it from the first; as if the very shape, the nature, the genre of the novel had promised such archetypal satisfactions. It is, indeed, this keeping of implicit promises which makes all popular genres finally reassuring, no matter how many calamities befall their characters along the way. Knowing, for instance, that *The Last of the Mohicans* is an historical Romance, as classically formulated and launched into eternal best-sellerdom by Sir Walter Scott, we know also that in the end some almost faceless boy will get some almost anonymous girl (no matter what loneliness awaits Natty Bumppo), and that some satisfactorily egregious villain will go down to bloody defeat (no matter how many foredoomed sub-heroes he takes with him).

Yet precisely this formulaic quality, the predictability of its ritual conclusion is one of the reasons why in our time—when Henry James and Flaubert have taught us that in "serious" literature the anti-cliché must prevail: the boy lose the girl, the girl the boy, or even worse that they get each other and live to regret it—the historical Romance has been consigned to the realm of paraliterature, popular culture. That once honorable genre belongs now to the marketplace rather than the library and the English lit classroom, as the veriest tyro, the Freshman dreaming of becoming a literature major, is likely to know. And if he does not, he can learn it reading the head notes to almost any standard collection of American poetry and prose. The relevant passage, for instance, in an anthology for class use compiled by Cleanth Brooks, Robert Penn Warren and R. W. B. Lewis, informs us that "Cooper's defects as a writer are indeed real and great, and his worth is of an order peculiarly vulnerable to the change of taste following the work of Flaubert, Henry James and James Joyce."

Brooks is, of course, one of the earliest American spokesmen for what came to be known as the New Criticism, an academicized and peculiarly genteel version of Modernism as adapted to WASP culture by T. S. Eliot. Relentlessly formalist on the level of aesthetics, anti-bourgeois and anti-populist (often, indeed, fascist) on the level of politics, such New Critics were by definition hostile to whatever pleased the many by touching depths of the psyche where form and execution, along with medium itself, became irrelevant. To them, literature is the medium: words on the page, a shapely text, a well-wrought urn, which, in the poetic tag that became for them a rallying cry, "does not mean but be." Never really at home in the realm of prose (even narrative poetry of any length baffled them, since they had no real understanding of "story"), they preferred novels with the dense texture of poetry: complicated, hermetic works available only to patient analysis, like the late novels of Henry James; though in a pinch, they would admit into their canon such "loose and baggy monsters" as *Moby Dick*, provided they were mystifying enough to allow for endless exegesis.

The New Critics—whose views Warren and Lewis, as well as Brooks, still avow, though they have been replaced for most of us since the end of World War II by neo-neo-Formalism, French-style, and neo-Romanticism, American-style—were from the start sworn enemies of Romanticism in any form, especially in popular literature. The insidious temptations of sentimentality and the cliché they feared as their Puritan ancestors had feared the wiles of the Devil—avoiding the first with defensive irony, and the second by a relentless pursuit of the New. They have tended, therefore, to scorn, or at best condescend to writers (invariably sentimental and cliché-ridden) beloved by the untutored mass audience; especially those who, like Fenimore Cooper, deliberately wooed that audience—refusing to take themselves seriously as "artists," but preferring to regard themselves as amateur entertainers or commercial entrepreneurs.

How then did Cooper make it at all (as he in fact did, despite their apologies) into the pages of Brooks, Warren and Lewis? Can it have been their paradoxical desire to produce a best-selling classroom anthology celebrating a contempt for everything that makes a best seller? Or was it merely that vestigial chauvinism present in even the most anti-democratic of us: an unwillingness to cast out utterly the single early nineteenth-century American novelist with even the shadow of a claim to being a "good writer."

If, however, Cooper is in any sense "good"—valuable, memorable, moving, capable of outliving his own time—it is because, contrary to the teachings of the New Criticism, literature is not, finally, its medium; not words at all, but something beyond, behind, before, above or below words. Whatever the quality, the gift which has insured Cooper's survival, it is one which associates him not with Flaubert and James and Joyce, not even with Hawthorne and Melville; but with Harriet Beecher Stowe, Margaret Mitchell and Taylor Caldwell, Edgar Rice Burroughs, Conan Doyle, H. Rider Haggard and L. Frank Baum. Only Mark Twain is comparable among American novelists regarded by an overwhelming critical consensus as of first rank; since Harriet Beecher Stowe is as problematical for critics as Cooper himself. Yet, paradoxically enough, Twain launched a devastating attack not just on the Leatherstocking Tales, but on the Professors, the critical establishment of his time, who—dishonestly, incomprehensibly, it seemed to Twain, as it still seems to me—touted Cooper's pop romances as "Great Literature."

In a hilarious and disrespectful little essay called "Fenimore Cooper's Literary Offenses," which, fittingly enough, has become the best-known piece of pop criticism in the world, Twain directed his venom chiefly against a certain "Prof. Lounsbury" of Columbia and "Prof. Brander Matthews" of Yale; signing himself, to make even clearer his hostility to universities in general and the Ivy League in particular, "Mark Twain M.A., Professor of Belles Lettres in the Veterinary College of Arizona." That Prof. Lounsbury found *The Pathfinder* and *The Deerslayer* "pure works of art," and Prof. Brander Matthews thought Natty Bumppo "one of the very greatest characters in fiction" Twain purported to find explicable only on the grounds that they had never read Cooper at all. And in a sense, which I hope I will be able to clarify before I am through, they had not read him—not certainly as they read Spenser or Milton or Keats. Indeed, they could not, any more than we can, read him that way; but they did not realize this, enchanted, as it were, by a magic imperceptible to conventional literary analysis.

Though Twain's irreverent essay has been often reprinted, becoming in the years since 1895 a kind of anthologist's chestnut, it has never, I am convinced, been taken seriously enough. But this is, of course (as is appropriate for a response of one popular writer to another), because it is written in a style available to both their readerships rather than to the academic critics it attacks. A series of outrageous jokes, it lacks the low seriousness, pedantry and grim rigor which we have come (alas!) to associate with proper literary criticism. We find it as easy, therefore, to laugh away Twain's exaggerated calumny of Cooper's style as we do to laugh away his hyperbolic diatribe against the German language. The writer has been as little affected by his scorn as the language, we assure ourselves. To what else, indeed, does this occasion testify?

Yet we laugh with Twain rather than at him because his humor (involving always, as Freud convincingly argued, a "release of the repressed") serves to release both our otherwise unconfessed resentment of the longeurs and ineptitudes of the Leatherstocking Tales, and the shame we feel at responding so positively and passionately to what we know is schlock. But we do not easily acknowledge this, trying instead to explain Twain's case away, as if he were the problem rather than Cooper and our uneasy relationship to him. After all, we tell ourselves, Twain was a self-educated, provincial author of best sellers who longed to be accepted as a cultural equal by the Boston Brahmins; and was therefore desperate to prove that one could be simultaneously the darling of the popular audience and a skilled craftsman. Besides, as he never admits in this essay but betrays elsewhere in his work, there stands between him and the Leatherstocking Tales, in which a key role is played by almost intolerably noble Redmen, a Westerner's pathological hatred of Indians, acquired when he was a tenderfoot in the mining camps: a conviction that the only good Indian is a dead Indian.

Most damagingly of all, Twain seems to have confused the conventions of mimetic and fantastic art; demanding of self-declared Romances (projections of nightmare and dream) a kind of verisimilitude, a faithfulness to fact and probability only appropriate to the Novel proper (renditions of waking life). Yet Twain, after all, is the author of that prototypical American fiction, *Huckleberry Finn*, from which, as Hemingway asserted, all our subsequent novels have descended; and his objections to a series of books for which a similar claim has been made must be taken very seriously indeed. Besides, a great deal of his most damaging negative criticism is irrefutable.

If there are really "rules" (as Twain argues) "governing literary art," then surely they include: "using the right word, not its second cousin; eschewing surplusage; not omitting necessary details; avoiding slovenliness of form; employing a simple and straight forward style." And Cooper, as Twain demonstrates in considerable detail, fails on all these counts, so that it is hard to dissent from his summary indictment of *The Deerslayer*:

> A work of art? It has no invention . . . no order, system, sequence, or result . . . no lifelikeness . . . no seeming of reality . . . its characters are confusedly drawn . . . its humor is pathetic; its pathos is funny; its conversations are—oh! indescribable; its love-scenes odious; its English a crime against the language.

But the decision has gone against Twain in the twentieth century, even among modernist novelists and critics, to whom the Victorian taste of Professors Lounsbury and Matthews seems an ultimate abomination in all other respects. D. H. Lawrence, for instance, in his *Studies in Classic American Literature*, calls *The Deerslayer* "one of the most beautiful and perfect books in the world: flawless as a jewel and of gemlike concentration." To be sure, Lawrence is more interested in the mystic import of Cooper's novel than in its form. But T. S. Eliot, that self-styled "Classicist," to whom structural and linguistic excellence is all-important, concurs (as he does with no other opinion of Lawrence, on sex, politics, art or the destiny of the human race); calling the essay from which this quotation comes "probably [Eliot always hedges his bets a little] the most brilliant of critical essays on Cooper . . ." Even Marius Bewley, official spokesman on American literature, for the school of F. R. Leavis, admits Cooper into a "Great Tradition" of the novel, so narrowly defined that it excludes not only Scott, Cooper's avowed model, but Smollett and Sterne and (until Leavis's deathbed repentance) all the most characteristic fiction of Charles Dickens. Why then has modernist criticism, which has almost totally revised the Victorian canon of American literature, preserved Fenimore Cooper from the fate, say, of Stevenson and Scott? On aesthetic grounds, he is indefensible; and the majority of such critics are on record as refusing to defend any writing on "extrinsic" moral grounds. It is, in any case, hard to argue either that Cooper's formal ineptness is made up for by the nobility of his vision of life, or that it is redeemed by his insight into the American destiny. To understand—as the historian or the enlightened statesman strives to understand—that conflict of alien cultures in the New World with which our nation began, Cooper is of no value whatsoever. But to understand the mythological grid through which the original European conquerors and settlers perceived that conflict, and through which, willy-nilly, we all still perceive both it and any further imperialist ventures (the recent war in Vietnam, for instance) which can be assimilated to it in our deep imaginations, he is very valuable indeed.

Yet that mythological grid, brought to the level of full consciousness, tells us things about his undermind and our own of which it is not easy to be proud; revealing to us not what we consciously believe or would like to believe are our values and motives, but what really continues to move us below the level of daylight awareness: the dark side of our ambivalence to the nonwhite alien others with whom we continue to live in America. The attitudes and assumptions embodied in the Leatherstocking Tales—judging not by what is asserted in editorial asides, but suggested in encrypted form through plot and character— are regressive, reactionary, downright wicked in terms of the enlightened moral consensus of the late twentieth century. They are, that is to say, racist, sexist and anti-democratic; based on an ethnocentric, culturally imperialist and hierarchal view of society which serves to perpetuate, indeed celebrates the subservience of Red and Black men to white ones, of females to males, and of the uncultivated poor to the lettered rich. Cooper believes that such a rank order of races, sexes and classes is not only actual but desirable. To upset it, he tells us through his mouthpiece, Natty, would be as unnatural as snowfall in summer; and even in Heaven it will persist unchanged.

Most of Cooper's ardent admirers have been the literate sons of fathers who, if not successful, have been at least white and, preferably, Anglo-Saxon: a race, according to Cooper, just a little whiter than any other. Not all of them by any means have confessed even to themselves that they shared the doctrine implicit in his fiction: that Western Culture, i.e., White European Christian Civilization, was destined to conquer not only dark-skinned America, but all the non-White World; and that those born to other cultures have the choice of accommodating to it, or disavowing it, to die in a genocidal war which they have no chance of winning. In their secret hearts, however, such readers respond to that message; thrilling to a vision of the vanishing dark Other embodied in the image of the noble Mohicans, whose ultimate nobility is proved by a willingness to immolate themselves, like Chingachgook, in order to make way for the higher civilization which the Christian God, in his inscrutable wisdom, has destined to replace theirs. It did not bother Cooper that his God operated through the agency of dedicated, chivalric (and, of course, white) warriors, who made the New World safe for the Christian virtues of charity and forgiveness, not by practicing them—but by shooting straighter, fighting harder, killing more efficiently than their pagan enemies.

In real history, the inter-ethnic war of extinction which Cooper dreams did not prevent certain White men from taking to themselves Indian brides, or, less frequently, perhaps, certain White women from settling happily into the wigwams of Indian braves. But in Cooper, the miscegenation taboo is seldom challenged, and never with impunity. In his novels, it is absolutely forbidden to mingle white and non-white in lust or holy matrimony, thus creating a race neither white nor Red. Even the best of Good Indians for him is not quite good enough to mate with a white maiden. Whatever the Indians themselves may believe is their unredeemed folly. If not downright satanic like Magua, that ultimate rapist and phallic killer, they are, like Uncas, disturbingly Dionysiac— passional, sexual, bloody and cruel.

The only love capable of mitigating, for a little while, the essential hostility of Red man and White is inter-ethnic male bonding in the forest, a union achievable only outside the settlements, where pearl-pale virgins, devout wives and austerely virtuous mothers rule. Fruitless, blossomless, temporary and evanescent as a dream, this union never, of course, confesses in action its sublimated homosexuality, stopping short of the carnal. But it less successfully conceals its essential misogyny, its condescension to and veiled contempt for the women who accept a passive, passionless role and its fear of the sexually experienced, threatening hussies who reject it.

If Cooper had expressed such ideas openly, many of his more liberal secret sharers would, in our time certainly, feel compelled to condemn him. In his five dream books, however, what is most at odds with our conscious pieties is encrypted in a form which passes easily as "mere entertainment" or "a good old-fashioned yarn." Cooper is not, I think, deliberately devious; he simply, as Twain charged, did not know what he was doing. And this turns out to be more blessing than curse, enabling him to release in his meta-verbal texts primordial images, prelinguistic archetypes whose political implications lie buried too deep for rational analysis. The question of belief or non-belief is not posed at this mythic level, so that we can respond sympathetically to Cooper's obsessive images, even when they imply values and social attitudes utterly different from our own.

The ability to evoke such images and to impose them on others depends on a certain mythopoeic power: a mysterious "gift" which has nothing to do with intellectual endowment, moral insight, purity of the heart or even verbal skills beyond the most elementary. The "goodness" of the kind of popular writer who is "good" only or chiefly in this sense can therefore co-exist with aesthetic "badness," and even ethical "wickedness." Such literature is not Art, not Belles

Lettres, much less secular wisdom, but a sort of disreputable Secret Scriptures accepted on faith—and if need be, in the teeth of authority. And as such, the good-bad Leatherstocking Tales represent our homegrown, wicked-holy Old Testament, from which all other mythic novels in our Classic tradition (dominated by WASP male fantasy) derive. Notable among these is, of course, *Huckleberry Finn*, in which, despite Twain's theoretical contempt for Cooper, Huck and Jim on the raft re-enact the archetypal comradeship of Natty and Chingachgook. Similarly, in Moby Dick, Melville re-dreamed that relationship in the salvational love of Ishmael and Queequeg; the Noble Indian becoming a brown-skinned Polynesian, once we had penetrated the South Pacific, as easily as he had turned Black after our rape of Africa.

Wherever we Americans have confronted cultures alien to our Christian Humanist version of "civilization," the good dream of inter-ethnic male-bonding—inextricably tangled with the nightmare of racism and misogyny—has been reborn. And in the age of the imminent conquest of space, we have invented in anticipation, as it were, an analogous bonding with extra-extra-terrestrials: Captain Kirk (in the TV series and the film now breaking attendance records in all the theaters of America) joined in "a love which passeth the love of men for women" with the green Vulcan, Mr. Spock. In short, then, if in one sense (the formal, verbal) all American fiction comes out of *Huckleberry Finn* in another (the archetypal, mythical), it derives from the Leatherstocking Tales, or more precisely, perhaps, *The Deerslayer*. In this, the last of the series, Cooper, nearly twenty years after he had, almost inadvertently, stumbled on his proper subject, dared finally to write a true anti-Historical Romance disguised as another example of the genre it subverted. Here finally, I am suggesting, he permitted the archetype of White/Red male bonding (which came to him from God knows where: out of trappers' autobiographies, tales of Indian captivity, the American ambiance itself—certainly not anything thought of, then or now, as "literature" worth emulating) to triumph over the monochrome boy-gets-girl stereotype of the Historical Romance. And here, therefore, there occurs for the first time in a full-length American novel (it had been anticipated only in Washington Irving's short story, "Rip Van Winkle") the truly American anti–Happy Ending, anti-marital, anti-domestic, anti-female.

The Deerslayer is, to be sure, as most critics have observed, an initiation story in which the protagonist becomes a man not by being inducted into sex, European-style, but into murder, American-style. More than this, however, it is a book in which scarcely any boy gets a girl or vice versa, though desire—vain and foolish where not tainted and vile—moves almost all of the characters. Hurry Harry does not get Judith, nor does Hetty get Harry, nor the Indian Widow of Natty's first Indian victim Natty. No one gets Natty, not even

Judith, who though white is fallen, soiled and, therefore, ends in the arms of a corrupt officer, a professional seducer who offers her not Christian marriage but a life of comfortable degradation. In this bleakest (though somehow also most lovely) of Cooper's forest romances, only the Indians Chingachgook and Hist achieve a real marriage; but they sustain it just long enough for her to bear the mythological Last of the Mohicans. Then she duly dies, summarily executed by an author eager to prepare the one truly idyllic union he can imagine: the anti-marriage in which Natty and Chingachgook, forsaking all others, cleave unto each other, to have and to hold till death do them part . . . This is the Paradise Regained of our mythic tradition—an anti-Eden from which Eve has been banished so that the new American Adam can live in peace with the Big Serpent (which is, in fact, what the Indian word "Chingachgook" means). To be worthy of his woodland mate, however, Natty must first lose his innocence—not erotically, since he is by definition forever virgin, unfathered and unfathering, without mother or wife—but thanatically. What phallic power is in him resides not in his genitals but in his rifle. A product of high technology, magically named like an amulet or a sword, it nonetheless remains a toy, even as he remains a boy, until it is used to kill another man rather than a deer or other lesser beast. To become an American, the male offspring of a nameless, forgotten European father must learn to kill rather than beget, as well as to remain forever true to his male comrades while rejecting all women. Yet he must also serve, with humility and chivalric deference, both those women, or at least the ladies among them, and the Christian culture they represent; firing at the snap of a twig with uncanny precision until no skulking savage is left to threaten their honor or their lives.

But the genocidal anti–Happy Ending has proved as delusory as the marital Happy Ending it sought to replace. The Vanishing American refuses to vanish. The dark-skinned savage shot down in daylight, hopefully once and for all, rises again to ravage and pillage, not only in the guilt-ridden fantasies of the night, but also in the nightmare which is history, the nightmare from which we strive vainly to awake. In America itself, Native Americans occupy Alcatraz and resume hostilities at Wounded Knee; while their mythological equivalents rise up against us wherever our missionary zeal, our commercial greed or our Cooperian lust to spread our brand of civilization takes us. In Japan, the Philippines, Korea, Cuba, Nicaragua, Vietnam, the West Bank of the Jordan and Iran, it turns out—no matter how hard we pretend that among the swarthy enemy there still are, there must be dark-skinned comrades as true to us, despite their alien skin color, as Chingachgook himself—that they are all Bad Indians. There is not a Vanishing Noble Mohican in the lot: only endlessly reduplicated Maguas, treacherous, given to torture; pledged to unremitting revenge against all of our color for the wrongs we cannot deny we have done them—but which we vainly hoped they would understand were regrettable incidents along the path to their redemption.

And in the course of the brutal battles they have ensued: the endless war fought, typically, in a wilderness territory, where they are at home and we are not, we have been forced to fight as they have always admitted fighting (and we pretend we do not); shrinking from no atrocity, however vile; sparing, in their style, neither women nor children. And in the course of such warfare, which we begin now to suspect we can never win, we have become Bad Indians ourselves: shameless defilers of the dead, takers of scalps, bounty hunters, ever less and less like Natty, more and more like Old Hutter and Hurry Harry. Only the dream of redemptive male-bonding has survived, plus a desperate faith in the ideal of manliness bred by such comradeship and the skills appropriate to it: the ability to take down with a single shot to the heart first the elusive deer, then the mortal enemy, grown so shadowy in the thickening woods that we can scarcely tell him from our own "shadows cast upon the trees."

A decade or so ago, I predicted (in a talk on the changing mythology of American Wars, delivered to a group of political scientists) that when a myth was made of the war then still happening in Vietnam, it would represent one more, perhaps final, recension of the myth first formulated in the Leather-stocking Tales. And this has proved to be true; though this time the archetypal story has not been retold in print, a bound book destined for required reading in the classroom; but a popular film seen and loved by millions of ordinary Americans, even while it was being condemned by self-righteous intellectuals as a distortion of history (which it is), an arrantly racist slander of the Vietnamese people (which it both is and is not) and a glorification of murder and mayhem (which it is not).

Called in open acknowledgement of its debt to Cooper *The Deer Hunter*, it is a film—according to its director, Michael Cimino—not primarily about war, much less the War of the moment, but about "male-bonding." To be sure, a good deal of its action occurs in a mythologized Vietnam, but quite as much is set in a steel town in Pennsylvania and in the wooded hills beyond it, where we see the newest avatar of Natty Bumppo instructing his presumed successor in the art of killing beautifully, bringing down a deer with a single shot. That Natty has been reborn—for the last time, it becomes clearer and clearer as the movie progresses—as a second-generation Russian-American factory worker seems apt enough; since in the dying twentieth century the only unashamed Americans are such unreconstructed proletarian ethnics. But the forest in which the New Natty has learned to bring down in love and reverence the totem animal of his prototype is protected parkland, an artificial preserve; and the wilderness in which he first learns to turn his skill against a human is a Southeast Asian jungle, in whose clearings not wigwams rise but cities long since corrupted by civilizations more decadent than our own. Neither at home nor abroad, in any case, does he find Noble Savages with skins darker than his to whom he can bond himself in *macho* love.

It is only with some white comrade in arms, younger, more frightened, less skilled in the wilderness arts than he that he can join to create an anti-family: sole bastion in a world without women, against the faceless savages, who, acting by a code he cannot ever understand, perpetrate what seem to him barbarous atrocities. But the bastion does not hold; that love cannot prevail—not even when the latest Natty Bumppo, driven to a candor none of the early avatars ever attained, confesses to his friend the love hitherto without a name. "I love you," he says, reaching out in vain to stay the hand of his doomed beloved, who has been saving his last best bullet for what both of them know now is the true enemy, the real Bad Indian, i.e., himself: the White American gone mad in a war against darkness and savagery, which we can no longer believe is somewhere Out There. After such knowledge, what is left for the survivor except to put down forever his deer-rifle, and join with the other survivors (or are they ghosts?) in singing "God Bless America." And for me leaving the theater in tears, what remains to do except remember James Fenimore Cooper, our worst, best, wickedest and truest laureate.

Mythicizing the Unspeakable

In Memory of Enrique Garcia Diez

The response to the late, ill-fated war in Vietnam in recent American films and fiction is in almost all cases mediated through earlier films and fiction, which had created a grid of perception that determined in advance how the war would be perceived by participants and nonparticipants alike. If, therefore, we would properly understand, say, *The Deer Hunter* or *Apocalypse Now*, we must come to terms first with earlier fiction. I am not thinking of the works to which those movies directly (and somewhat confusingly) allude, Cooper's *The Deerslayer* and Conrad's *Heart of Darkness*, but of the three novels by major authors responding directly to World War I, in which a peculiar American antiwar myth was first established. In John Dos Passos's *Three Soldiers*, E. E. Cummings's *The Enormous Room* and especially, perhaps, Ernest Hemingway's *A Farewell to Arms*, the message is that it is not sweet and fitting to die for the fatherland; and the true enemy of all men of goodwill is not the ostensible foe but armed conflict itself, no matter in what cause it is ostensibly fought. It follows, therefore, that the truest heroism is to be found in the anti-hero, who makes what Hemingway calls "a separate peace" by fleeing from battle, deserting his own side.

To be sure, World War I, in which these three authors were engaged, was in fact a struggle between competing imperialist powers, none of whose hands were clean and among whom it was consequently difficult to choose. But even when in World War II, the enemies of the United States and its allies were Fascist Italy, Nazi Germany and Feudal Japan, brutal and reactionary states despised by all men of goodwill, the metapolitical myth of "a separate peace" persisted still. To be sure, most American artists and intellectuals supported that War; yet the fictions about it which we most highly prize, like Norman Mailer's *The Naked and the Dead*, Joseph Heller's *Catch-22* and Kurt Vonnegut's *Slaughterhouse-Five*, follow the model of *A Farewell to Arms*, deliberately subverting values of patriotism and combat heroism.

In Mailer's book, the nominal Japanese enemy is almost invisible, and the real war is revealed as the class war between officers and men; while Heller's satirical dark comedy portrays the self-defeating absurdity not just of the military bureaucracy but of war itself. Finally in Vonnegut's best-selling novel (a favorite of younger readers ever since the dissenting sixties) the central image of evil is not the concentration camps of Hitler and the destruction of the Jews, but the bombing by Americans of the open city of Dresden: suggesting that our own side (whichever it may be) is always and inevitably the real Enemy. Similarly, cinematic box-office successes like *Dr. Strangelove* recall not the Japanese sneak attack on Pearl Harbor but our dropping of the Atom Bomb on Hiroshima and Nagasaki, evoking in the audience not satisfaction in justified vengeance but lingering doubt and guilt. In any case, such antiwar sentiments, with the underlying conviction that no national cause is worth dying or killing for, had come to possess the deep imaginations of most American writers and intellectuals, academics and university students, as well as certain pretentious journalists and TV commentators, even before John F. Kennedy had begun that tentative involvement in Vietnam which was destined to become a fatal engagement.

It must be understood, however, that despite the marketplace success of some of the works which sustained it, the myth of a separate peace was never shared by the majority of Americans, including the less sophisticated members of the middle class and petty bourgeoisie, farmers, workers, the underclasses. Their countermyth was sustained by pop movies and television shows, pulp magazines and comic books, in which the value of fighting for God and Country is not questioned and combat heroism is glorified. In such works the American Hero is portrayed as the lonely individual confronting the forces of evil without support from a cowed or corrupt or impotent community; adapted, that is to say, to the archetypal image embodied in Tarzan of the Apes, Superman and Batman, as well as the cowboy protagonists of movies like *High Noon* and such incorruptible Private Eyes as Sam Spade and Philip Marlowe. Indeed, the heroes of popular prowar films were often played by the same actors as had appeared in these other genres: Gary Cooper, for instance, playing Sergeant York and John Wayne storming the beaches of Iwo Jima.

For a little while, it seemed as if—on the very eve of our final commitment in Vietnam—the two audiences might be joined together for once. After all, the Special Forces, who represented a first step in that direction, had been sent there by John F. Kennedy, with whom many antiwar intellectuals managed to identify, despite the fact that he seems to have thought of himself as a Cold War hero in the best Superman tradition. But that improbable alliance began to fall apart with the fiasco of the Bay of Pigs; and the old division returned stronger than ever after Kennedy's assassination left the waging of the undeclared war in Southeast Asia in the hands of Lyndon B. Johnson, a crude peasant whom upper-middle-class intellectuals found it as easy to hate as they had to love his Harvard-educated predecessor.

From that point on, the mass support of the war came chiefly from the undereducated lower classes, who were, of course, actually fighting it—dying in places of which they had never heard; or returning, physically or psychologically crippled, to the jeers or silent contempt of the children of more favored classes, who (thanks to the vagaries of the draft laws) were able to demonstrate against the war safely at home. It is not, I am suggesting, the mere fact of the opposition to the War in Vietnam which makes it uniquely difficult to mythicize, but the class nature of that opposition. There had been antiwar riots during the Civil War (in one of which—in New York City—scores, perhaps hundreds of protestors had been killed by the troops which put it down), and this, too, had pitted class against class. In that earlier case, however, the protestors were working men, chiefly recent Irish immigrants, facing a draft from which the sons of the privileged WASP upper classes could buy themselves out. Moreover, many of the most visible and audible demonstrators against the war in Vietnam, unlike the considerably smaller numbers who had refused to serve in World Wars I and II, were not hardline pacifists on religious or political grounds, but only, as it were, Cold Warriors on the other side. Rather than taking a stand against violence in whatever cause and condemning combat heroism under whatever flag, they were apologists for violence and terrorism as long as it was directed against the armed forces of the United States in Vietnam, and actual practitioners of it against cops on their own grounds.

After all, they, too, had grown up reading the Superhero comic books and were not immune to the heroic myth they embodied; though, unlike their redneck and blue-collar fellow citizens, they imagined the justified killers of their juvenile fantasies re-embodied not in the Green Berets but in Vietcong guerrillas. To do so, however, they had to euphemize the atrocities of the North Vietnamese, denying that they killed women and children in South Vietnam and brutally tortured American prisoners of war. Or, forced to admit the truth of such charges, they argued that such terror was justified, since it was practiced by dedicated socialists who sought thus to hasten the emergence in their invaded homeland of a Utopia in which exploitation, oppression and warfare itself would forever cease.

But, as it turned out, before any of the truly mythic works dealing with Vietnam had appeared—certainly long before the three films that I propose to analyze had been released—it became harder and harder for the "Doves," who sought thus to mythicize the Vietcong as archetypal heroes, to explain why a victorious Utopian socialist state has ever since broken the peace by launching a series of imperialist forays against its neighbors, including that other presumable socialist Utopia, Kampuchea. Nor was it easy to explain why a constant stream of refugees, largely ethnic Chinese, sought to flee (to capitalist America, of all places) from a society where theoretically ethnic and class oppression had disappeared. Especially embarrassing, however, because it had been for so long so vehemently denied was the overwhelming verification of the fact (finally admitted, however reluctantly, by Jane Fonda herself) that helpless, disarmed American POWs had been inhumanely abused by their captors.

Nonetheless, the "Hawks," who had mythicized the Green Berets as the Good Guys battling the Powers of Darkness, found small satisfaction in the discomfiture of their former adversaries, because subsequent events undercut their mythic scenario even more damagingly. That is to say, those whom they still had desperately to believe were the Good Guys had not only committed atrocities of their own, but, even more disconcertingly, despite their presumed superior virtue and combat skills, they had *lost!* And Americans are not accustomed to thinking of themselves as losers but as winners; though, to be sure, as anyone familiar with our popular literature is well aware, there is at least one notable exception to this. The South was, of course, defeated on the battlefield in the War between the States, but it has triumphed ever since in print and on the screen. I am thinking particularly of Margaret Mitchell's *Gone with the Wind,* whose apology for the Klan and glorification of the Confederacy has been applauded by audiences for more than half a century, and not just in America alone. Interestingly enough, the film version of her novel was the first movie asked for by the North Vietnamese, when cultural relations were restored between their country and ours at the end of hostilities: testimony, surely, to the fact that like all truly mythic literature, *Gone with the Wind* binds together at a level below full consciousness those divided on the level of conscious belief and allegiance.

As this century draws to a close, no novel or film I know of has similarly mythicized for all audiences, popular and elite, Hawk and Dove, victor and vanquished, the defeat in Vietnam of not just our forces but our illusions. The three movies to which I alluded earlier have, however, come close to performing that formidable task; in part because they are all three of them sufficiently ambiguous to reflect the doubts which these days undercut the one-time certainties of the most hawkish and dovish. It is, indeed, this quality that has led some critics to speak of them as ideologically muddled, politically confused, when they are in fact, like all truly mythic texts, meta-ideological, metapolitical; and, by the same token—despite certain gestures at realism—contemptuous of what historians, journalists, and social scientists consider "facts."

Especially misleading in this regard is Michael Cimino's *The Deer Hunter,* which begins with a slow, patient documentation of the ordinary life of working people: second-generation East European ethnics, which is to say, exactly the kind of naïve 100 percent Americans who not merely fought the war in

Southeast Asia, but deeply believed in it. Their ghettoized society is one which no upper-class student protestors ever entered, and where, indeed, not even a distant echo of their antiwar, antipatriotic slogans was ever heard. Yet what we are watching, as the film's title has made clear, is not a slice of proletarian life but the re-enactment of a fable, a legend as old as America itself: a post-Vietnam version of the myth classically formulated in James Fenimore Cooper's *The Deerslayer* and *The Last of the Mohicans*. It had, however, been invented even earlier in certain self-styled wilderness chronicles intended to justify the three-hundred-year-long bloody conflict with the Indians: the dark-skinned aborigines with whom pale-faced European immigrants contended for the virgin land—finally winning, though only after they had learned to fight Indian style. It is the dream of winning a similar guerrilla war fought in another wilderness against other alien nonwhite forces that possesses the undermind of the blue-collar white warriors of *The Deer Hunter*, who have sharpened their hunting skills in the virgin hills surrounding their small town. For them, that is to say, the jungles of Vietnam were already translated before they had ever entered them into the mythological woods of *The Last of the Mohicans;* and the "Reds" against whom they fought into Redskins: hostile Savages reborn in a living dream turned, alas, nightmare—since this time the encounter is destined to end in defeat rather than victory for the white invaders.

None of this is transmitted (in this most cinematic of films) through dialogue, much less editorial voice-over—or even in narrative. It is instead entrusted to the images: beginning with the shot of the squalid industrial town in the midst of the pristine beauty of the hills reflected in the eye of a half-drunken hunter, a refugee from church and the family, intent on bringing a 12-point buck down with a single shot. Some literal-minded critics have argued that no such magnificently antlered beast could possibly have been present in that place at that time of year. But this is, of course, utterly beside the point; since that impossible animal is the iconic embodiment of a deep wish, like the images which possess our dreams.

And so also are the repeated images of Russian roulette that come to dominate the later part of the film. To them the critics have raised similar objections: calling them improbable, implausible, absurd—not really because they fail to recognize their symbolic significance but because they do. They realize, that is to say, that the "game" of Russian roulette represents in oneiric form quite real atrocities committed by the North Vietnamese against captured South Vietnamese and Americans. Moreover (as the movie re-creates another archetypal American story beloved by Cooper, that of Indian Captivity and Escape), the weapon loaded for Russian roulette is turned against the would-be torturers—becoming an instrument of deliverance rather than destruction. Nor is this the final metamorphosis of a polyvalent symbol for all in war that is random, irrational, gratuitously brutal and hopelessly out of control.

In its final recurrence, Russian roulette has been turned into a kind of blood-sport: a parody, played out for fun and profit, of the conflict which is stuttering to a close around it. At that point, a symbolic last American in Vietnam—the ultimate victim of his and our dream, for whom there is no other way out—manages to take control of his destiny: *willing* the suicidal shot that releases both him and his friend, still futilely dreaming of other, more benign methods of escape. "One shot," the suicide says, echoing the cry of that friend, who was the hunter on the hill with which it all began; thus making clear what the idyllic dream of Fenimore Cooper has been all the time meaning, revealing that we ourselves have been from the very start the Beast in View. But though this is the final appearance of the gun with a single bullet in its chambers, it is not yet the end of the story. For antiwar and antiviolence as it finally is (the hunter on the hill is last shown *not* shooting the deer in his sights), *The Deer Hunter* is not anti-American—or even anti–American Dream.

In the concluding scene of the movie, the survivors of Vietnam, side by side with their womenfolk and their buddies who stayed home, are singing together "God Bless America"—not, it is worth noting, the official national anthem, but a pop patriotic hymn by a tinpan alley songwriter, also an immigrant from Eastern Europe, though this time a Jew. Nor is this a sentimental cop-out, as some have charged, much less a piece of covert irony, as others embarrassed by such charges have argued. Singing it, the aging survivors pledge allegiance to the traditional values to which their parents had earlier painfully learned to assimilate: the values of a middle-aged middle America, symbolized not just by the flag they bless, but the church, home, marriage and the family to which they have returned. What defeat in the war has delivered them from is the illusions by which adolescents think they can live forever, a false Utopia of irresponsibility, male bonding, booze, casual sex and justified murder.

Apocalypse Now, unlike *The Deer Hunter*, is talky and didactic—forever telling the viewer what it means in dialogue and editorial voice-over. It is, moreover, not the product of a single voice, like Michael Cimino's film, a single mind in touch with the collective unconscious of the mass audience. It represents rather the joint effort of an oddly assorted team of super-self-conscious would-be intellectuals, moved not just by conflicting ideologies but quite different myths of war. The author of the script from which Coppola's film was eventually made was John Milius, a right-winger, whose earlier screenplays include *Red Dawn* and *Conan the Barbarian*. The first of these makes clear that he is an unreconstructed Cold War apologist; and the second reveals that he is a true believer in the comic book cult of the Savage as a kind of primitive

Superhero, immune to all civilized notions of Good and Evil. Even in his original script, however, Milius had apparently already begun to fuse the figure of the amoral Barbarian with that of Kurtz, the European gone native, who in Joseph Conrad's *Heart of Darkness* learns that such a Savage lurks deep in the heart of even the most civilized among us—and that this is the ultimate horror.

To confound confusion even further, Milius had drawn heavily on a journalistic chronicle of what had "really" happened in Vietnam, written by Michael Herr. Herr, moreover, was finally drafted to do the film's running voice-over narrative. In it, Conrad's rather baroque English is translated into tough-guy American street speech, reminiscent of Dashiell Hammett or Raymond Chandler; thus suggesting that what happened in Vietnam is less a historical event than a crime, and that any true account of it, therefore, must be in some sense a whodunit. In any case, Herr was, is—despite some ambivalence—basically a Dove, antiwar and *pro*-Vietcong. But so, too, is Coppola and, for that matter, Marlon Brando; who not merely inadvertently parodied every scene in which he appeared (a *fat* Kurtz is already a parody), but quite consciously helped determine the final form and ideological slant of the film. As a result, *Apocalypse Now* is politically confused, ideologically conflicted; which explains in part why its director is driven to try to say in unequivocal words what remains hopelessly ambiguous in the movie images.

Some of those images are—despite their ambiguity—quite striking. Indeed, especially in the first half of the film there are some that linger in the mind long after its "message" is forgotten. Most notable among them, perhaps, is the scene of the hard-ass American officer manically surfing under enemy fire, and that of the Playboy Bunnies being snatched by helicopter from the threat not of enemy violence but of the lust they have aroused in our own watching troops. There is, however, no central image of archetypal resonance comparable to the scenes of Russian roulette in *The Deer Hunter*. One which might well have performed that function is the scene of the Vietcong cutting off the arms of their children after they have been inoculated by American doctors: a fitting symbol of that heroic savagery beyond morality which Kurtz yearns to emulate and, to some degree, does. But it is kept off camera, reported only in words. Similarly, we are—in the final version of the movie—not permitted to see the ultimate holocaust, the *Götterdämmerung* promised by the title. Finally, therefore, though Coppola's Kurtz, like Conrad's before him, cries out "The horror! The horror!", it is hard to feel much less to say exactly what this means.

Part of the problem, surely, is that Conrad's essentially racist myth of the civilized white European confronting dark-skinned hostiles, which Coppola deliberately sought to adapt, is undercut by a quite contradictory American myth, from which neither he nor his collaborators can free themselves. Conrad clearly believes that though the white imperialist Hero may temporarily triumph in the alien dark world by adopting its bloody rituals and ruthless amorality, he thereby loses his soul to the heart of darkness. But the corresponding myth as formulated by Fenimore Cooper suggests that by thus accommodating to wilderness ways in a world he hopes ultimately to make his own, the paleface ex-European is able to defeat his dusky enemies at their own game and on their own home grounds. In the course of doing so, moreover, he becomes a *tertium quid,* neither civilized nor savage, neither white nor non-white, as these terms have been traditionally defined—but something new under the sun, which is to say, an American.

In any case, by thus "going native," Coppola's Kurtz temporarily prevails in the wilderness world of Vietnam: making himself King and God of the Montagnards with acts of brutality that shock even the callous American military. But we are left uncertain as to whether he is more admirable or despicable, ultimately saved or lost. In the end, Coppola cops out, quite like Willard, his eye and spokesman on the film, who finally rejects the destiny that might have redeemed him, and retrospectively, Kurtz. Instead, that is to say, of becoming Kurtz's successor, a reincarnation of Divine Leader as the ritual slaughter at the film's center seems to promise, Willard simply turns tail and goes home; reassuring himself that by doing so he has, like a good soldier, both fulfilled his assignment and disassociated himself from the evil military bureaucracy which made it. In any case, Coppola fails to create a new heroic myth capable of assuaging the psychic wounds of Vietnam, contenting himself with interpreting an old one—in the tradition of High Modernist literature, as the rather pretentious references to T. S. Eliot and Frazer's *Golden Bough* remind us. Though it comes closer, Cimino's reimagining of Fenimore Cooper fails in this regard, too; as also do those innumerable "War is Hell" films like, say, *Platoon,* which rehash but cannot quite revive for a society traumatized by Vietnam the pattern of World War I antiwar flicks derived from Hemingway's *A Farewell to Arms.*

Improbably enough, that formidable task was accomplished by Sylvester Stallone: a shameless purveyor of schlock, with no artistic pretensions, whom hightone critics therefore condemned sight unseen even before his first Vietnam movie had appeared. Yet he had already created in Rocky a kind of pre-portrait of the post-Vietnam hero in the guise of an Italo-American, lumpen-proletarian pug, able to whip to a pulp uppity niggers and ruthless Russian strongmen. Even as Rocky, that archetypal figure had already entered the public domain of mass consciousness—his very name becoming, as it were, a common noun in the languages of the entire world. How much more this is true of Rambo, in whom Rocky is reborn as a psychopathic survivor of the war in Vietnam; and who therefore satisfies even more urgent psychosocial needs not just of Americans, though of Americans first of all.

Despite all this, however, the critical establishment has continued to greet the Rambo series with unmitigated scorn. And why should they not; since what seems for them to matter is the undeniable fact that the Rambo films are incredibly ill constructed and poorly acted, as well as melodramatic, sentimental, gratuitously violent—and, of course, politically reactionary. Nor are they troubled by the fact that the same charges could be leveled at other masterpieces of American Pop like *Tarzan of the Apes* and *Gone with the Wind,* which have entered the hearts and deep underminds of moviegoers everywhere. So, too, *Rambo* is doing at the present moment, his name as familiar as those not just of Tarzan and Scarlett but of Don Quixote and Huck Finn to a majority audience who could not identify a single character out of *The Deer Hunter* or *Apocalypse Now* or *Good Morning, Vietnam.*

It is for this reason that the makers of a TV futurist fantasy set in Los Angeles of the twenty-first century, called *Alien Nation,* feel free to show in its introductory shots a movie marquee reading "*Rambo VI.*" There is nothing surprising about this; but I was, I must confess, a little astonished to learn that during the recent revolution there, a reporter had found a band of Maoist guerrillas in the Philippines watching *Rambo* on their Betamax. But why not, after all, since those same guerrillas were, he also tells us, wearing Mickey Mouse T-shirts and eating Dunkin' Donuts. In short, though we may have lost militarily in Southeast Asia, our popular culture has triumphed everywhere; whatever their overt politics, on a deeper level even Communists these days share the values that culture embodies—as we were made aware when the masses of East Germany surged through the fallen Berlin Wall into the Supermarkets of the West.

It is, however, a defeat rather than a victory of the West to which the myth of Rambo responds. But to understand the sense in which this is true, we must remind ourselves that Stallone's series was made not while the war was still going on in Vietnam but after its disastrous end. They are, that is to say, postwar, postdefeat films. Even in the very first of the series there are no actual scenes from the war itself, except for a couple of brief flashbacks, and even these are not of combat but of the imprisonment and torture of Americans by North Vietnamese. It is their plight which stirs in the protagonist a rage that he vents not on his alien enemies but on his fellow citizens, who fear and despise him when he returns home, and on the cops and courts, who harass and jail him as a vagrant, a disturber of the peace. They are Americans one and all to whom his presumably 100 percent American heroism has come to seem in retrospect an embarrassment and source of guilt.

Even in *Rambo II*, his righteous wrath is directed at an American enemy. This time, however, it is the bureaucrats, military and civilian, who, though they have been pressured by public opinion into sending him on a single-handed mission into Vietnam to rescue Americans reported as still being held there, make his task as difficult as possible. What they desperately need to believe is that there are no remaining POWs; that it is all over. They are, therefore, embarrassed by the continuing existence of him and his kind, at home as well as abroad; and would be pleased if his mission ended in his death. But, as it turns out, such prisoners do exist; and he does not die, though he is left to combat the Vietnamese jailers and their massively armed Russian allies with only the weapons he can carry, chiefly a knife and a bow and arrow. Thus accoutred and stripped to the buff, he turns before our very eyes into the mythic figure of the white man gone native, like Natty Bumppo and Tarzan: thus enabling Stallone to imagine a version of the War in Vietnam in which the grunts rather than the gooks play the role of the Noble Savage. Moreover, Rambo is not, we learn as the plot unfolds, the European ethnic prole we have taken him for at first, but a breed, half-Indian and half-German. And it is to the Native American of his heritage he reverts, as in the wilderness he brings down helicopters and stops the tanks of his enemies with a single shot of his bow, frustrating advanced technology with primitive woodcraft.

This is, however, not the only myth out of Cooper embodied in the Rambo series. Indeed what we remember longer and what touches American viewers even more deeply (responding as it does to the psychic wound inflicted by our ignominious defeat) is the story of Indian Captivity and deliverance, updated into a fantasy of rescuing the American POWs presumably still being held and tortured in the jungles from which our forces have long since withdrawn. There is, of course, no proof that such prisoners really exist; indeed, there is every reason to believe that they do not. But large numbers of ordinary citizens continue to believe that they do; not just politicians in quest of a cause, but the parents, mates and children of soldiers still listed as missing in action. It is they who write letters to the papers, sign petitions and demonstrate before the White House.

What is involved is not an error of judgment but an act of faith; like the equally widespread and passionately held belief (despite the lack of confirmatory evidence) in Flying Saucers, Big Foot, the Abominable Snowman and the Loch Ness Monster. All of which, I suppose, is just another way of saying that the myth of the still-unrescued POWs is a genuine myth, that is, a lie which tells the truth. And the truth which it tells is that a piece of the essential identity not just of every combat veteran, but of all the rest of us—whether we cheered them on toward destruction or jeered at them for being fools and child-murderers when they returned—remains still captive in Vietnam, left behind in our precipitate retreat. Indeed, the three films I have discussed, along with a score of others, plus countless books, articles and TV shows, represent a symbolic effort to bring back home again what we hope can be recuperated in imagination if not in fact: a not ignoble part of us all squandered in an ignoble war.

The Legend

For more than a century now the image of Buffalo Bill has captured the deep imagination of Americans. Most of us still see in our mind's eye that erect figure astride a white horse, ten-gallon hat in hand or pushed back just a little to reveal the ruddy complexion, the startlingly brown eyes, the silky mustache and goatee—becoming, like his almost shoulder-length hair, whiter and whiter with the passage of the years. "Buffalo Bill," we say to ourselves, and the magical name evokes the legend that, though it may these days trouble rather than inspire us, refuses to die. Not only has it outlasted the Old West that was its setting, the Indian wars that were its immediate occasion and even William F. Cody, the actual man whose not very extraordinary life it transformed into a unique American dream; it has survived as well the vogue of the illustrated pulp fiction and the popular drama in which it was first embodied.

The Western frontier was already closing by the 1880s, and the last large-scale slaughter of Indian "hostiles" by white troops began with the shooting of Sitting Bull in 1890 and culminated two weeks later with the massacre at Wounded Knee. Cody himself was not present at either event, the first of which he had in fact futilely attempted to prevent—thus losing his chance of dying in an Indian ambush or shootout, as the myth that he had lived seemed for a while to demand. To be sure, there was a war in progress in 1917 when he finally died, and America was becoming involved with it; but it was a European conflict removed from his myths of westward expansion and heroism in the "Great Desert" of the Plains. In any case, Cody had by then become embroiled in the anti-mythic world of business and domesticity, fighting his last battle not at Ypres or Verdun but in a Wyoming courtroom, where he sued for divorce his embittered wife, convinced she was trying to poison him. It was she who emerged the victor, however—or at least had the last laugh—since the divorce was not granted, and she was therefore able, despite Cody's expressed wish, to have him buried far from the Wyoming city that bears his name but does not even now possess his remains.

His spirit, however, lived on after his death for nearly two decades in the Wild West, the open-air historical pageant and equestrian display that he had first mounted in 1883, and in which he starred until 1916, when he could no longer sit in a saddle but entered the arena holding the reins of a horse-drawn carriage—a tremulous old man, bewigged and grease-painted into an unconvincing simulacrum of his former self. None of this mattered, however, any more than it mattered that the ownership of his show had long since passed into the hands of Pawnee Bill—who combined it with his own "Far East"—and the Sells-Floto Circus, which combined the remnants of Buffalo Bill's original cast of Indians, cowboys, trick riders and sharpshooters with freaks, sword-swallowers and tattooed ladies. All that those last audiences required was Buffalo Bill's physical presence, his hand lifted in a valedictory gesture that countless repetitions did not stale, turning it rather into a ritual reassurance that a vanishing America and the breed of American who made it had not *quite* vanished from the earth. Not yet.

Even his actual demise seems to have made little difference in this respect; for though it moved old rivals to posthumous judgments (Pawnee Bill observing, "He was just an irresponsible boy") and new poets to elegiac verses (E. E. Cummings writing, "Buffalo Bill's/ defunct . . . Jesus/ he was a handsome man . . ."), the Wild West continued on, as if he had never died at all. Symptomatically, however, the last two such shows, both of which closed in 1938, were produced by a pair of film cowboys, Tim Holt and Tom Mix, whose quite different icons and myths the oldsters among us remember as projected in the darkened theater rather than acted on a dusty field under the open sky.

But almost no one living any longer recalls the illustrated dime novels or the stage melodramas in which the image and legend of Buffalo Bill were first created. In fact, well before 1938—when the Great Depression was about to end and World War II about to begin—Ned Buntline, who wrote the first of those novels and the second of those plays, was nearly forgotten; and Prentiss Ingraham, who produced more Buffalo Bill fiction than any other author, was fast fading into oblivion. Even novels signed if not actually authored by Cody himself were already gathering dust in attics and on the shelves of children's libraries, along with the various versions of his *Autobiography* and his sister's account of his life—once sold on street corners for a dollar (a ticket of admission thrown in free) by the advance men for his show. As they died from memory, so too did the black-and-white steel engravings, "The First Scalp for Custer," "Bloody Work of the Squaws," "A Hurricane of Buffalos," with which they were adorned, as well as the full-color reproductions of the same motifs on the hundred-sheet billboard posters, and the autographed photos of Cody and his fellow performers. The pictures had gone into oblivion along with the words.

Or if not quite into oblivion, into the hands of PR men eager to attract tourists to one or another of the competing Buffalo Bill Centers in Colorado and Wyoming, or scholars dedicated to discovering the "historical truth" behind the icons and myths. To be sure, Cody had always claimed that it was just such "truth" ("Everything genuine!") that was enacted in his Wild West, which he would therefore never allow anyone to call a "show." Yet from childhood on, the evidence seems to indicate, he had longed to become a showman, telling his sisters in intervals between "playing Indians" (he, the sole surviving male member of his family, was always the scalper—they invariably the scalped) that "I believe I'll run a show when I get to be a man." And when they objected that this ill befitted one destined—as a fortune teller had revealed to their mother—to be President of the United States, he answered, "I do not propose to be President, but I do mean to have a show."

He ended, moreover, as he had begun, playing "Cowboys and Indians"—at first, just behind the elusive frontier at North Platte, Nebraska, where in 1882 he celebrated the Fourth of July with "Old Glory Blowout," then in the parks and fair-grounds of urban centers like Chicago, Boston and New York, Paris, London and Rome. But for ten years before he had impersonated in the independent theaters of countless cities and towns a mythological hero called by his name, who night after night killed Indians and delivered female captives from a fate worse than death. It was a plot first naturalized for America by James Fenimore Cooper, then readapted to the prairie West by Ned Buntline, Prentiss Ingraham and other best-selling novelists in quest of a new theme. But on the stage, they discovered, such stories had an added appeal when enacted by frontiersmen and scouts, like Cody himself or Texas Jack Omohundro and Wild Bill Hickok, who joined him in some of his first dramatic ventures.

It scarcely mattered if these men forgot their lines or broke character, since the audiences came in large part to see them not *in* but *through* the parts they played, returning, once the season was over, to their part-time roles as real killers of beasts and men. Buffalo Bill, in particular, as all readers of newspapers and magazines were kept aware, had never abandoned the wilderness life that had first made him famous. When the theaters closed for the summer or 1872, for instance, he went back to his old haunts as guide to a buffalo-hunting party that included the Grand Duke Alexis of Russia. And four years later, between theatrical seasons, he rejoined the 5th Cavalry, just in time to avenge Custer by scalping an Indian called Yellow Hand. That redoubtable deed he apparently performed dressed in a particularly splendid costume he had first worn on the stage, and in the presence of an audience of newspapermen. Furthermore, no sooner had he gotten back to "civilization," than he appeared in a new play called *The Red Right Hand; or Buffalo Bill's First Scalp for Custer*—as if fact and fiction were not merely continuous but indistinguishable.

The confusion between reality and illusion, history and myth was even further confounded by the fact that with the opening of the Wild West show, no one wrote a fictional script; and the reenactments of fact directed by Buffalo

Bill himself employed not professional actors but real cowboys, real Indians, real cattle and horses and mules and bison. Consequently, when Custer's Last Stand was reenacted in the arena, half of the cast—all Indians, of course—had participated in the original battle.

Finally, even the most infamous "hostile" of all, Sitting Bull, joined the show for one season, and when he left, he took with him two presents from Buffalo Bill: a size eight white Stetson and a dancing horse he particularly admired. Indeed, even as he was gunned down in a tragicomedy of errors by a fellow tribesman who was trying to prevent his arrest, that horse, taking the shot for his customary cue, went into his customary dance. And who was to say that he was wrong, that what happened was not, in some sense, a part of Buffalo Bill's ongoing mythological show.

Fair enough, then, that when in the troubled 1960s the history of the American West was being rewritten, Buffalo Bill, flanked by Sitting Bull, reappeared in the theater not as "The Last of the Great Scouts," but as a showman playing a part. In Arthur Kopit's *Indians*, a play produced in New York in 1969, Cody enters bowing to an unseen audience from the back of a palpably fake white stallion. He is a ghost called back not to the real world but to an equally ghostly stage—or rather a spectral "Wild West," which, like him, cannot quite die. It is metatheater with which we are confronted, theater about theater; though the play within a play, once so vast it could scarcely be contained in acres of open fields, can now be enclosed by a proscenium arch. Buffalo Bill has likewise been reduced in scale, along with Wild Bill Hickok and Ned Buntline, and indeed everyone involved—except for the Indians, who are larger than life, larger than death, and for whom the play is therefore named.

Nor is this inappropriate to a time when revisionist anthropologists were glorifying the Indian way of life and revisionist historians recasting them as the "good guys" rather than the "bad" in the struggle for the Western Plains. There were also revisionist novels and films, which—in response to growing feelings of white guilt and self-hatred *vis à vis* the native people of America— travestied and traduced all myths justifying Westward expansion. Sentimentalization of the "Noble Savage" had had a place in our literature from the start, but it had typically been balanced by vilification of his "innate barbarism." In the late '60s, however, the latter was neutralized and the former reinforced by the mounting protest, occasioned by our involvement in Vietnam, against not merely all war and racism, but against the very concepts of patriotism and combat heroism—except as practiced by warriors of another color.

The favorite reading matter of the period, especially among the young, included Claude Lévi-Strauss's *La Pensée Sauvage,* John G. Neihardt's *Black Elk Speaks,* Theodora Kroeber's *Ishi in the Two Worlds,* Dee Brown's *Bury My Heart at Wounded Knee,* Vine Deloria, Jr.'s *Custer Died for Your Sins,* Ken Kesey's *One Flew over the Cuckoo's Nest* and Thomas Berger's *Little Big Man*—all of them defenses of Indian culture and attacks on the whites who sought to destroy it, some directed specifically at George Armstrong Custer. Once Custer had been thus "debunked," however, Buffalo Bill's legend was doomed, since he was in some sense the General's *alter ego.* The Plains Indians called both by the same name, Pahaska, or Longhair, and in fact they bore an uncanny resemblance to one another—which Cody seems deliberately to have exploited, modeling his persona on that of the professional soldier who had gone down to defeat before the Wild West show began. So faithful was his impersonation that seeing him in the arena years later, an old black maid of the Custers was stunned to discover in him the express image of her former master. But he had the right, Cody would have protested, since he had not only served under Custer but had "avenged" him with the scalping of Yellow Hand.

Moreover, not just their icons but their myths were the same, the archetypal meanings of the Wild West and the Battle of the Little Big Horn being finally one. We are used, however, to looking for myth in story; and at first glance, Cody's "exhibitions" seem to have had no more narrative line than a three-ring circus. Yet once we have understood that the sharpshooting, the rodeo events and the general highjinks are secondary—a concession to the audience demand for entertainment and vicarious tourism—we can locate in the Wild West, if not a continuous story, at least a mythic center, represented by such standard features as the attacks on the Deadwood stagecoach, the immigrant train or the settler's cabin; the duels with Tall Bull or Yellow Hand; and Custer's Last Stand itself.

Reflecting on these, it becomes clear that the theme of Buffalo Bill's Wild West was more specifically guerrilla warfare, in which individual combat skills still counted—as they had not in the Civil War, whose outcome was decided by technology rather than personal heroism. By the time Cody's theatrical career began, the dreadnought and the machine gun had already been invented, and before his last appearance in the arena, the armored car, the tank, the zeppelin and the combat plane were already in action. Nonetheless, the forces of good in the Wild West continued right to the end to fight on horseback and with Colts and Winchesters against a similarly mounted and armed enemy, who possessed such weapons and mounts in the first place because they had been given or sold them by the whites.

What motivated them to do so is hard to say—blind greed, perhaps, or even some dim sense of fair play, or even an unconscious desire to make possible the last war white America could unequivocally win, and the reassuring mythic drama into which Buffalo Bill converted it. In any event, it is almost impossible to tell where the real Wild West ends and the Wild West show begins, since they have the same cast: Indians and cowboys, horses and soldiers. Of these, it is the Indians and horses whose names we remember (Long Bull and Sitting Bull, Brigham, Powderface and Charlie), while their white opponents fade to an anonymous blur—except, of course, for Buffalo Bill himself. Cody's Indians, moreover, moved, like him and his horses, back and forth between history and show biz, which is to say, warring and playing at war. Indeed, one of the strangest aspects of the spectacle he created was in the defeat of the "Redskin hostiles" as acted out by the defeated themselves—repeating endlessly, as if in a recurrent nightmare, the events that had turned them from fighters against the white man's culture to actors in a white man's show.

Most of the Indians were, it is true, wards of the government; many actual Prisoners of War, like the survivors of the Ghost Dance, nineteen of whom were released in Cody's custody for one of his grand European tours. But why they consented to re-enact their humiliation before an audience of their conquerors I find puzzling, though—even more oddly—earlier commentators on the Wild West seem not at all troubled by so unprecedented an event. To be sure, conditions were bad back on the reservation, and the Indians were paid well by Cody, fed well, provided with cigarettes and transported to foreign lands where they were paid a great deal of attention and admired. The world of illusion, moreover, was one in which they felt at home. Indeed, one recent anthropologist has called the whole culture of the Plains Indians "as make-believe as the set of a Western movie." Even in war, they seemed motivated more by a desire to win the applause of their peers than to destroy their enemies; so that ritually touching the body of a foe in combat was deemed as authentic a "*coup*" as stabbing him in the heart. But in this case, it was on their living bodies that *coups* were counted over and over, and to endure this, they must in some sense have subscribed to the myth as well as to the fact of their defeat.

Indeed, it is reported that Short Bull, one of the organizers of the Ghost Dance (that last piece of "make believe" in which the Sioux came to believe they would be delivered from the white man), said of Cody, "He killed us because we were bad and because we fought against what he knew was best for us . . ." But what "he knew was best" was, of course, that "the inferior must give way to the superior civilization . . . Their doom is sealed . . . The total extinction of the race is only a question of time." These words were written by Cody's sister, who framed them with a reference to Cooper's *The Last of the Mohicans*—in which the Myth of the Vanishing American was first formulated—and a quotation from Kipling's "The White Man's Burden." Elsewhere, moreover, Cody himself further specifies what his sister means by "white," insisting that the

West can only be redeemed from "Savagery" by "the march of the Anglo-Saxon race," at whose head his more ardent fans liked to imagine him, a White Knight on a White Horse.

If the chivalric metaphor out of Sir Walter Scott reminds us uncomfortably of the sheeted riders of the Ku Klux Klan, it is fair enough, since Ned Buntline, who first launched Cody's legend, was also a leader of the American Protestant Association, that other, earlier sodality dedicated to preserving the purity of White Protestant America. And there seems to me little doubt that to many in his audience Bill Cody represented the savior of the WASPs (the line of descent from him to John Wayne is unbroken) who, even as they were exterminating the dusky enemy in the West, were being threatened from the opposite direction by immigrant hordes out of Eastern and Southern Europe, almost equally dusky and dangerous.

Different as he was from such new Americans, however, the mythic Buffalo Bill, self-made, self-educated and of humble origins, was equally unlike certain rich and privileged older Americans, who though kin to him ethnically, had grown fat and flabby in the effete East. To them he seemed a kind of Noble Savage, a White Indian, doomed like the Red Ones to "vanish" before the advance of the civilization for which he had cleared the way, but in which he could not survive. This, at any rate, is the way in which he and his cohorts were perceived by such representatives of that world as Frederic Remington, an aging athlete from Yale, full of self-hatred and ambivalent love for the "human brutes" of the West, to which he returned again and again as a tourist and illustrator. "As a picture, perfect; as a reality, horrible," Remington wrote—and it is difficult to tell whether he is talking about cowboys or Indians—yet he was a faithful fan of the Wild West.

When the legend of Buffalo Bill passed into the hands of the descendants of East European immigrants, however—new Americans mythologically not quite "white" and politically rather to the Left—they found him not "poetical and harmless" (as Remington had also said of the show) but racist and reactionary. They were, therefore, not inclined to mourn, even condescendingly, the passing of his kind—aware that, in fact, his heirs still survived as unreconstructed "rednecks," ready to resist with force the renewal of Indian nationalism at Alcatraz or Wounded Knee.

There is a kind of vestigial, qualified sympathy for Cody in Kopit's *Indians,* a sense that to be trapped as he was in an outlived myth, even of his own making, was at least pitiful, if not downright tragic. However, in the film "suggested" by that play but drastically rewritten by Robert Altman and Allan Rudolph, Buffalo Bill fares much worse, which is particularly ironic in light of the fact that his icon and myth had until then proved unamenable to screen treatment. In Altman's film, *Buffalo Bill and the Indians, or Sitting Bull's History*

Lesson, Cody is portrayed as a bluster and bluff, a hopeless drunk, an aging swinger on the verge of impotence—and especially as an exploiter of Indians whom he neither loves nor understands.

It is Altman's Sitting Bull, magician and prophet, who understands everything, and chiefly that Buffalo Bill is the enemy and his myth of the West, a "lie." But among the whites no one heeds his "lesson" except for Annie Oakley, who is portrayed sympathetically—in accord with the liberal clichés of the time (it was 1976 before the film appeared), which demanded that women like Indians be shown as wiser than white males. Between them, in any case, they baffle, defeat and finally abandon not just Cody but his myth.

The anti-myth that Altman and Rudolph seek to substitute for Cody's proves also to be a "lie," though one more responsive to the psycho-social needs of the time. What documents survive indicate that Sitting Bull and Annie Oakley really loved and trusted Buffalo Bill to the end of their lives, the former saying to a relative who dared lay hands on his white Stetson, "My friend Longhair gave me this hat. I value it very highly for the hand that placed it on my head had friendly feeling for me," while the latter wrote of Cody, "I travelled with him for seventeen years ... And the whole time we were one great family loyal to a man ... His words were more than most contracts ..."

But such discrepancies are finally irrelevant, since no age can tell—or, indeed, know—the "truth" about its past, but can only replace old myths with new ones, for a little while believing them to be "facts." So with the myth of the Winning of the West and the subjugation of the Plains Indians. Yet no matter how much that myth has changed in response to our changing attitudes over the past century or more, the icon of "The Last of the Great Scouts" has remained unchanging at its center: an aging horseman charging toward us as if forever in a cloud of dust, his hat in one hand, the reins in the other, long white hair streaming out behind him. And who can doubt that as long as America lasts and memory endures, somewhere at the heart of the next myth we take for truth will be the dream figure of Buffalo Bill. "Jesus/ he was a handsome man ..."

Getting It Right:
The Flag Raisings
at Iwo Jima

For nearly eighty years I have—as a student and teacher—dutifully gone to school. Only once in 1942, overwhelmed by a desire to be where history is made not taught, I played hookey. Though I had a wife, a child nearly two and another on the way—as well as a full-time teaching job—one day I slammed my office door behind me and did the closest thing I could to "going to sea." I enlisted in a navy program that sent me back to another college town even farther from the nearest ocean. There I spent fourteen of the most tedious months of my life learning Japanese, after which I was certified as an interpreter and sent to Pearl Harbor.

"Pearl Harbor," I thought, "the real thing." The name alone evoked images of golden beaches and swaying palms under a hailstorm of bombs. By the time I arrived, however, Honolulu had become a seedy and crowded way station to more distant sites of combat. Moreover, I was greeted not by hula girls bearing leis, but by a gaggle of surly dock workers shouting, "You'll be so-o-o-ry!" And sorry I was because my assigned duties kept me deskbound every day from three to eleven, translating documents that seemed of little interest to me or anyone else.

For a while I managed to allay my ennui by spending some of my earlier free hours soaking and blistering on the beach of Waikiki and many of the later ones getting drunk in downtown Honolulu. But this soon wore out, so in desperation I began to apply for a transfer to any place where I would be closer to the action.

I got no response to any of my applications, however, because—I eventually realized—my commanding officer was intercepting them. And when I complained, he waved me back to my desk and said, "Go shit up a rope." He must have finally relented because when I was on the verge of, as they say on the Islands, "going pineapple," I was assigned as an interrogator to the command ship of an attack force headed for the Island-fortress of Iwo Jima. I was thrilled, of course, at the prospect of an end to boredom, then a little terrified that I would not live long enough to enjoy it, since I had no notion of how to behave under fire, never having had any combat training. When I asked my commanding officer what I could do about it, he answered, "Just watch what the guy in front of you is doing, and whatever it is, you do it too."

As it turned out I need not have worried, since I did my interrogation of prisoners not in the muck and confusion of a battlefield but instead quizzed them safely tucked away in a trim and tidy ship, whose uptight captain required us to wear ties at dinner.

Once for a couple of hours on D-day plus two I traveled the fifteen hundred yards that separated me from the shore. No prisoners had been sent out to us during those first two days. I surmised this was because the few Japanese who let themselves be captured were killed by their captors, whose basic training had conditioned them to kill first and think later.

But since they had also been conditioned to obey any command from an officer, I felt that if they were not just urged but *ordered* to spare the life of a prisoner they would do so. It was in quest of someone willing to issue such an order that I had come ashore, where finding a couple of marine officers willing to listen, I made my plea. I did not cite the Geneva Conventions or the biblical passage about "doing unto others." Instead I reminded them that a dead POW was of no use to anyone, but a living one might provide information that would save American lives. When I had finished, the officers nodded as if in assent but said not a word, just turned about abruptly and left.

After they had departed I still had some time left before my transportation back to the ship was due so I jumped into the ocean for a quick swim. Swimming is for me a mode of meditation, and in a hundred bays and inlets, streams and ponds, I have found momentary peace. But off Iwo Jima even the illusion of peace proved impossible. I could not take two successive strokes without crashing into a splintered spar, a spent shell, a twisted hunk of plastic or metal—even something that looked enough like a severed human arm that I did not examine it too closely. Moreover, I could not block out the thump, crackle and whine of guns and bombs coming from a battle going on just over a ridge a thousand yards from where I struggled in the surf.

As I retreated toward the shore, I could see a very large marine was crawling over the ridge on his belly, holding out an object I could not identify. As he came nearer, I could make out that he was yelling, "What would you give for a *real* Jap helmet—a real souvenir?" Thrusting it in my face, he turned it over so I could see it was indeed a *real* helmet, holding half a Japanese skull in a puddle of *real* blood.

"Get the hell out of here, or I'll . . . I'll . . ." I yelled back; but before I could say what I would do, he was pleading, "What do you think it's worth? Make me an offer." But seeing he would get no offer, he shrugged, started to climb back to where he had come from, muttering something that sounded like "Stingy old Jew." At the crest of the ridge, noticing my stripes for the first time perhaps, he grinned and more loudly and clearly added, "Sir . . . have a good day, Sir."

Somehow this started me laughing, and I laughed all the way back to the ship. No sooner had I hit the sack, however, than I blacked out and slept until the morning wake-up call, when I discovered that a small boat had pulled alongside of us, and in it a tiny Japanese prisoner squatted as an oversize marine stood over him, a baseball bat in hand. With it he was swatting the prisoner, first on one side of the head, then on the other—not hard enough to knock him out, but hard enough to really hurt.

Though conscious and able to talk, the first of my prisoners was so weak from the battering plus a half-dozen minor wounds that the ship's doctor insisted we lay him out in sick bay, where Doc could tend his injuries while I questioned him, as I questioned almost all my other prisoners, feeling a little smug at the thought that I and the doctor sought to keep alive the enemies whom everyone else on our side was trying to kill. But I felt guilty too, since in addition to not killing those others I had made it most unlikely their killing me. Indeed, when the fighting was over it turned out that not a single navy interpreter was included in the list of the dead or mortally wounded, though half the American forces involved and 90 percent of the Japanese had been killed. Small wonder then that when I got back home, I was plagued by nightmares in which some of the POWs I had questioned and who had died either on Iwo Jima or after they had returned home would reappear. Two especially came whenever sleep would not.

The presence of the first was signaled by the sound of squishy flesh on hard steel—appropriately enough since though both his legs had been blown off just above the knee, he had insisted on climbing up the ship's ladder on his bloody stumps rather than allowing himself to be hoisted aboard. He never spoke a word, unlike the second prisoner who kept screaming in a childish treble the words he first screamed in sick bay when, prepping him, Doc started shaving off his pubic hair. Apparently believing he was about to be castrated, he pissed all over himself, me and the doctor. Then realizing that he had disgraced himself, he cried out, "*Hazukashii, shoben demas.*" "Shame, shame, my piss is trickling out." Sometimes on waking, I would think it was I, not he, who had cried out those words; and in fact in that very sick bay where he had disgraced himself I had come very close to doing the same.

I was always a claustrophobe, and one of my fears when I enlisted was that I would be assigned to a submarine. Though I never was, I might as well have been, since our sick bay, with its low overhead, absence of portholes and single escape hatch, was much like a compartment in an undersea vessel. The ventilator in the walls circulated not real air but a stale residue of air heavy with the odors of sweat and excrement, disinfectant and blood. The first time

I breathed in this noxious combination, I came close to puking my guts out or shitting in my breeches.

But by swallowing my own bile and breathing through my mouth I managed not to do so until Doc had tied off his last stitches. Then I sprang like a sprinter out of his blocks and ran full speed up ladders and through hatches to an open-air upper deck where I could breathe without threat of nausea. Early on, I noticed that looking over the rail from that lofty perch, I could see what was happening at that moment on shore, framed like a television picture. Thus witnessed, everything seemed somehow both more and less real and no matter how horrible, more tolerable.

Therefore when I had grown used to sick-bay routine, I would often retreat to that deck to watch whatever was "showing." No matter what it was, however, the burial of a hundred marines in a bulldozed grave or a single Japanese burned to ashes by a flame thrower, I would grow so relaxed that sometimes I actually dozed off.

I must have been in that state on D-day plus four when I was jerked awake by a realization that what I was only half watching was the ceremonial raising of an American flag much like one I had seen earlier. But who had tried, I asked myself—indeed, why had anyone tried—to duplicate an event that by definition could happen only once?

In quest of answers I questioned anyone who would listen to me, even a particularly boring reporter whom I usually avoided. Though he followed the official navy line, insisting that there had been only one flag raising, he was able to give me new information about the cameraman who had photographed it: an "old buddy" of his called Joe Rosenthal, whom he described as "a Michelangelo with a lens," and whose picture was indeed "a shoo-in for a Pulitzer Prize."

His prediction of course turned out to be true. Rosenthal won not just that one, but many prizes. It was, moreover, reproduced in media ranging from comic strips and comic books to postage stamps and coins, ceramic statuettes and finally the impressive monument that remains to this day a chief attraction for tourists to Washington, D.C.

Worshippers before such icons have not apparently been disturbed by the fact that finally so many skeptics charged that Rosenthal's photograph has been in some sense a fraud that the navy itself has felt obliged to admit and try to explain away that before it was taken another picture was made of an earlier flag raising on the same spot. The navy has recently revealed that that picture still exists, along with a list of the names of the marines who appear in it. Those names, however, have been kept a secret more closely guarded than that of the atom bomb, and those to whom they belong have never in any way been honored for having first occupied the dominating height of Mt. Suribachi.

There has, I suppose, always been some fraud involved in religious relics and icons, from the "True Cross" to "Veronica's Veil," and there is in addition something especially appropriate about an American icon, since the country of its origin is the same country that produced P. T. Barnum.

But the flag raisings on Mt. Suribachi are something new under the sun, being, it seems to me, the first instance of dealing with war in the same way in which the masters of popular culture have long taught us to deal with what is real in current events and various forms of entertainment. Rosenthal, that is to say, deserves credit for realizing that the popular audience could be persuaded to accept his reality, the same kind of counterfeit they had long accepted in quiz shows, wrestling matches and self-styled documentaries. It seems to me only proper that the pioneer in combining show biz and combat should have been a man who, as his name indicates, was Jewish, as were most of those who had earlier persuaded the mass audience for movies, TV and sports events that reality is something that is made rather than what merely happens to be. It was some such thought that persuaded me when I imagined what Rosenthal must have been saying when he drafted his amateur actors for a second shot: "Just one more take, *boychiks,* and it's a wrap. But this time let's try to make it *real!*" which sounds a bit like Samuel Goldwyn.

At this point I began to understand that a meditation on this strange merger could and probably should be made a key part of my book about Iwo Jima. In it, however, I would have to deal not just with aesthetics, ethics and politics, but also with technology, since not until the invention of still photographs, movies and television would battles begin to be lost and won on film as well as in the field. Consequently, since Iwo Jima our most recent wars have seemed to be more and more "acted," "performed" or "played," thanks ultimately to Rosenthal.

Since he had in common with me not just the fact that he was Jewish, but that in the midst of armed forces he carried no gun, only a camera, I longed to meet with him and for a while tried. But I finally realized that he would have been unable to tell me anything I still wanted to know about those who had made the decision about what to include and what to exclude, what to tell the truth about and what to lie about as to what happened on Mt. Suribachi. After all, to have made the radical changes in publicity and the disposition of forces necessary for what actually followed needed someone with high rank and strong authority, like, it finally occurred to me, a Marine Corps general or a navy admiral, who were quartered close to me on our ship.

Though I saw them almost every day, however, I and others of my low rank, from the black seaman who swept our cabins and made our beds to junior officers, were invisible to senior officers. I had once, to be sure, been noticed by the Marine Corps general when we had literally bumped into each other in one of the narrow corridors of the ship. "And who the hell are you, anyhow?" was what he growled before shoving me aside; six more words than the admiral on whose staff I was officially listed ever managed to say, until that day when I heard over the ship's intercom an anonymous voice urging Lt. j.g. Fiedler to lay up to the admiral's quarters. I was sure that what prompted this must have been his decision to reprimand me for some failure in my work. But when I finally passed through the door of his cabin, he was sitting relaxed and congenial behind a table on which was displayed an oversize, lavishly illustrated book entitled *Maryland's Colonial Charm as Seen Through Her Silver*. "I hear," he said, "that you are a writer. Well, as you see, I am one, too. Let's have a drink and really *talk* to each other." He passed across the table a glass of sherry and raising his said, "Cheers." Looking at me instead of just through me, he waited for me to respond with something writerly, I suppose; but the only thing that came to my lips was the Yiddish toast, *"L'chaim."*

As incomprehensible to him as his flagrantly goyish behavior had been to me, this convinced him that he would never hear from me the latest gossip out of Harlem or Greenwich Village, or the Left Bank, so he decided to try another tack. "Don't be shy, son," he said, "in my quarters you can say what you wouldn't dare to any place else, repeat the worst things the enemy says about our side. Atrocities, for instance . . ." He filled both our glasses and continued, "You know, we commit them too. All the stuff you've heard about what we were supposed to have done to the Japs on Guadalcanal is true. You know, even the . . ." he stuttered to a full stop, as if the rumors about our troops cutting off the petite penises of the enemy and stuffing them into their mouths were too truly atrocious to put into words. But he should have known of course that this was a horror story that every side in every war has told about the other side, which no doubt has sometimes even been practiced by both. Most often, however, cruelties practiced in the midst of combat tended to be more banal than monstrous, more comic than melodramatic like those I had witnessed myself, whose proper voice-over was not *Danse macabre* but "Take Me out to the Ball Game."

"Only that is atrocious," I said, "which we feel obliged to lie about, as we lie about the raising of the flag on Suribachi, the second raising." He reacted to this not with surprise or indignation as I had foolishly, boyishly expected, but with the boredom with which full adults react to what is shockingly new to the young but routine to them. If he had ever really known about those flag raisings, I decided it was just a matter of housekeeping to him, something to be attended to and then forgotten. In any case, he said nothing, only began to look at his watch as if he had just remembered that the time was up that he had budgeted for discussions like this, and a moment later I found myself out on the deck looking back at his closed door. I felt no anger at him, only at myself for not having realized that to him and perhaps everyone else but me the subject of the flag raisings seemed as inconsequential and irrelevant as *Maryland's Colonial Charm* seemed to me.

I knew, then, that I might someday actually write something about Suribachi. All the same, it could never be a central theme for my book. Certainly it no longer seemed as intriguing a subject as the experience of living my own death, which I had after my failed meeting with my fellow author, when a single Japanese plane managed to slip through our defenses and was not spotted until directly overhead. Eventually it went down in flames, but not until it dropped a pair of bombs, one of them terrifyingly close to where I had been stationed, for once in full combat gear, and where for the only time I felt under fire, that I thought I had died.

I had in fact come closer to really dying on a couple of other occasions. The first was when Doc and I were opening the last folds of a filthy blanket in which a comatose POW had been wrapped and discovered the notice reading: DANGER! GAS GANGRENE! HANDLE WITH CARE! "Too late," Doc muttered, "too fucking late," which it almost was, since for the next week or two I believed he was about to die and I would follow fast. Ironically, however, the only actual death was that of the Japanese POW, for whose life we had inadvertently risked our own.

My second close encounter with death came from what is called "friendly fire," when our own shipmates, celebrating the end of the war in Europe, were using for fireworks loaded handguns. Too drunk to fire safely into the air, they lay down a deadly waist-high barrage into which I—not quite sober myself—stumbled; I might have ingloriously died, had not one of the revelers shoved me out of the way just in time. On neither of these occasions did I have the hallucination of living my own death, which is bred by the combination of combat exhilaration and combat fear. But when the second bomb dropped there was a sudden enhancement of my hearing that enabled me to hear every word screamed by our lookout, which until then had been blocked out by sirens, whistles, gunshots and screams. "The sneaky little Nip is right over us," that lookout was shouting; "the slanty-eyed bastard is gonna . . ." Then my acute hearing was gone as quickly as it had come, followed by the fading out of all the other senses and eventually consciousness itself.

After a while the only thing I knew was that I could not smell, taste, hear or see; then I no longer knew that, and finally I did not even know that I did not know. *"This is the vanishing point,"* I thought. *"I must be dead."* Yet I was somehow aware that if I could think anything, I must still be alive, which, in fact, I was.

The shadow of death never fell on me again because even when a general alarm was sounded and all hands ordered to battle stations, I was waved back to sick bay to deal with the next batch of POWs who, never having been informed of their right to reveal nothing but their name, rank and serial number, blurted out everything they knew so abjectly and obsequiously that our sessions seemed disturbingly like the inquisitions of the powerless by the empowered, which I had always found distasteful enough when empowered neighborhood cops interrogated disempowered, unemployed black adolescents. I found it even more disturbing, however, when the inquisitors were colleagues of my own and those being interrogated were captive enemies. I was aware, of course, that some of my colleagues sometimes played the role of Bad Cop in their interrogations but I myself from the very beginning chose to play the Good Cop, though those same colleagues argued that to do so served only to delay our victory in the war against racist tyrants.

At first I dismissed this argument as not even worth taking the time to answer, but when the war did in fact seem as if it would drag on forever, I began to fear that playing the Good Cop, though quite different in its results, was no better. Treating the POWs who fell into my hands sympathetically and respecting their humanity seemed to many of them, I began to realize, just another trick of the evil round eyes, a total fraud. The more gung-ho of my colleagues, however, who found it quite real were equally disturbed by it, because it seemed to them that not merely was it delaying our eventual victory but that thus coddling the enemy turned those who coddled them into a kind of double agent.

It seemed to me finally then that I and perhaps all interpreters were caught in a trap. If we played Bad Cop, we turned into the sadistic psychopaths we pretended to be; and if we played Good Cop, we ended up in some sense and to some degree as moles or traitors. Though this dismayed me, it also seemed to me to provide a subject which could become a valuable new center for my book. To do it justice, however, I would have to explore more deeply the relationship between the questioner and the questioned; and my last best chance for doing so came when I was ordered to oversee the transfer of the POWs we still held to other ships for eventual transfer to the large holding center in Honolulu.

The few brief trips needed to do this have blended in retrospect into a single scene that begins with the crew of the vessel we were about to board crowding against the rail brandishing knives and yelling obscenities at our POWs. To those more fortunate American sailors, the unfortunate humans we were transferring to their ship were just anonymous incarnations of the alien Other. To me, however, they were separate and distinct individuals whom I had known in a relationship as intimate as that of lovers or siblings. Consequently, as each of them disappeared from me forever I would think not there goes one more Jap, but there goes the old man with whom I once sat looking at pictures of his grandchildren, both of us in tears; or, there goes that high school teacher of French with whom I swapped quotations from Mallarmé and Baudelaire; or, there goes the sneaky little sergeant who stole from the other prisoners whatever they had not carefully guarded.

What they all thought of me at the time of parting I never really knew because almost none of them said anything at that point, except for the one whom I knew least well. At the very last moment he who had played dumb through most of our time together turned and screamed, "I love you . . . I love you . . . take me home with you." And for daring to speak, the officer of the day hurried him on his way with a quick hard shove on the back. It was that same dapper young officer to whom somewhat earlier I had recited the Geneva Conventions on the rights of prisoners of war. He clearly had not listened to a word I said, however, but kept looking back and forth between the gleaming side arm he wore on his hip and the empty place on my own where I should have been wearing one but was not. His contempt for a fellow officer presumably in charge of prisoners of war who did not carry a weapon but worried about whether those prisoners got their proper ration of cigarettes was obvious. I could see clearly on his lips the question that he did not ask, "Which side are you on anyhow?" to which I would have answered like a true double agent, "Neither," or maybe, "Both."

Obviously, the war was over for me, and I was more than ready to go home, so I was delighted when we were finally told that there were no more prisoners left to transfer, feeling that was a sign that the battle of Iwo Jima would be ending quite soon; but not so soon that I would not be able to finish the book, which I now saw should be primarily about the interrogator as a double agent and which I felt should be finished before my running away from home had also ended.

Though the combat on Iwo Jima came to an end quite soon thereafter, my returning home was delayed. It turned out that none of us would be released until the next big battle had been fought and won, with the invasion of the main islands of Japan. My new orders read that my job would be to rescue any surviving Kamikaze pilots. Surviving that operation would indeed be difficult, and it seemed to me that I would not make it through. Therefore, during the couple of weeks we waited on Guam for the final assault on Japan, I invested all my energy in getting and staying too drunk to remember I knew what lay just ahead. One night, however, when I was actually monitoring the broadcast of Radio Tokyo, I learned that atomic bombs, whose very existence had been kept a secret from me, had just been dropped, first on Hiroshima and then on Nagasaki. I felt as if I had been reprieved at the last moment from a death sentence; but once more I was shipped off in the wrong direction, not east back to America but west on to China, where I spent the next three months in

Tentsin helping to repatriate Japanese civilians. I might well be there yet had not the Chinese themselves, who first greeted us as liberators from Japanese oppression, decided that we were no better and began to shout, "Yankee go home"—and someone in Washington listened.

But when I finally did get back to a wife I no longer really knew and two kids I had never gotten to know in the first place, I was so sick of war and the talk of war that I couldn't even tell anybody I knew what happened to me, much less write about it for total strangers to read. The only thing I could think of to do with the past four years of my life was to forget them, along with everything associated with them, including the language I worked so hard to learn. Despite this willed amnesia, I was not totally silent. In fact, once I had hunkered down behind my familiar old desk, words and phrases began to flow freely again. They were, however, not about my recent warring past but about the remoter peaceful times before the first mass technological war, as reimagined by Mark Twain in *Huckleberry Finn,* which I was then reading to my sons. Thanks to him I was able only a short time after my discharge from the navy to write "Come Back to the Raft Ag'in, Huck Honey," the infamous little essay about the unique American myth of interethnic male bonding.

I was unable to do anything, however, with what happened to me on Iwo Jima for more than half a century. Yet as early as the mid-fifties I had begun to try, aware that the battle I had witnessed had become a real myth; which is to say, that like only a very few others, Waterloo, for instance, and Gettysburg, its memory was preserved not only on the pages of history but in the dreams of ordinary Americans. I could not, however, properly begin until 1984 when I discovered a packet of letters written to my wife from Iwo Jima that I had thought lost forever. I remembered them as containing only shipboard gossip and declarations of love but discovered they also included a detailed daily log of my experiences, constituting in fact a first draft of the book I was still trying to write; so that using them as a pony, I could easily and quickly finish the book I had so many times begun. In a burst of euphoria, therefore, I fired off a letter to the editor of my last book, telling her that I would have shortly a new one whose contents I listed (interestingly enough, they did not include the raisings of the flag) along with a request for a contract and an advance on royalties.

No check arrived by return mail, however—only, after considerable delay, a politely unenthusiastic response. By the time I received it, moreover, rereading my letters from Iwo Jima I realized that their accounts of my past were radically different from what I thought I remembered. Most disconcertingly, events I had once considered of great importance were scarcely mentioned, most notably the duplicate raisings of the Stars and Stripes. In the end, what I learned was what I should have known to begin with, that like all history, autobiographies are really fictions. This insight seemed to me to suggest a new way to begin, but my attempts to do so produced only fragments, and finally I came to a complete standstill.

Therefore, when three or four years later the letters, which had been lost, then found, were again lost, reduced to a sodden, almost illegible heap of papers by a catastrophic house fire, I felt this was an omen, a sign that what I was trying to do was undoable, and so I again abandoned my projected book about Iwo Jima, this time, I thought, forever.

That "forever" lasted only as long as the millennium into which I had been born; for as it and I both drew to a close I was asked by a local newspaper to do a piece on the decade of the past century I found most fascinating, but "in no more than 1,200 words—please." I answered that for many years I had been trying unsuccessfully to write a book-length study of the 1940s and the battle at its center and that although it seemed to me impossible to say what I had to say in fewer words, I tried once more. When I did I was surprised that I could deal adequately with most of what had seemed worth preserving in a longer book.

This included not just much of my theorizing but also anecdotal material like my temporarily abandoned account of the second flag raising. This was, I suppose, predictable enough, since as the debate over the authenticity of Rosenthal's photograph reached its peak, the navy finally admitted that what it portrayed was only a revised version of an earlier one; but in its changes not intended to fool anyone but merely to replace a flag almost invisible to many still fighting on lower ground with one more visible to all. Many skeptics, however, continued to contend that it had been a shameless hoax, a plausible lie from the very start. Others felt that whatever its beginnings it had finally become a genuine myth, which is to say, though still a lie, the kind of lie that tells a truth that cannot be told otherwise. More recently, they argue, it has become a stereotype or cliché that is also an icon, a form of myth visible and therefore available to everyone.

Though in my little newspaper piece I made only a brief reference to the problem of the raisings of the flags, the responses to it were almost entirely concerned with that question. The two negative ones that actually were printed in the letters to the editor column of our local paper consisted mainly of abusive name calling, which indeed I expected. But the single positive one that was sent to me at home surprised me since it was not just a sympathetic and intelligent response to what I had really said, but contained information that, if true, would change radically what everyone, including me, had earlier believed about the flag raisings. Its truth seemed to me guaranteed by the fact that the writer, who signed himself Calvin Scott, was the last living member of the group that had built the set for Rosenthal's picture: the seventh hitherto unknown and invisible buddy of the six, whose faces and names have been made recognizable by Rosenthal's picture and its many reproductions—so at least Scott claimed in an interview he gave on the fiftieth anniversary of the battle of Iwo Jima, when he himself was approaching seventy and spending his last years making stained glass in the small town where he had been born.

From that interview, a copy of which he sent me, I learned that on February 23, 1945, when he had turned just eighteen, Scott had found himself near the top of Mt. Suribachi. He was not a fighting marine, but an unarmed stretcher bearer—having got rid of the weapon he had been issued to make room for something more useful to him as a tender of the wounded. Though he thought of that as his primary function, he was ready to collaborate in any other kind of action he was called on to perform. It happened that at that very moment there was just such a call: a broadcast request for help in replacing the tattered little flag raised by those who had originally driven the Japanese from the heights, yet had not hung high enough to be seen by and boost the morale of everyone concerned. A larger, more photogenic flag had already been obtained, but what was still needed was an appropriate standard from which to hang it.

It was Scott, apparently, who found the piece of pipe long enough to do the job; and it was he, too, who tied on the new flag and began the process of planting it on the crest of the hill. Since he must have then been in the forefront of the group Rosenthal was proposing to photograph a little later, it is hard to understand why his face did not appear side by side with those of the six others, which have become as familiar as pictures in the family photograph album and whose names have become household words.

It was because, Scott explained in his interview, before that picture was taken "some guy bumped me off the knoll." Tumbling backwards, he continued, he found himself blocking out the rest of the group that Rosenthal was about to capture on film and crouched down low so that the picture could be shot over his head. Though he apparently realized that he had thus collaborated in his own disappearance from history, there is no trace of regret in his account, nor any suggestion of resentment. It apparently never even occurred to him that one of those who stayed in the picture might well have been the guy who, to make sure he himself got in, "bumped him out of the picture." In any event, Scott clearly does not intend to distract from the fame and glory of the other six. To be sure, honesty compelled him to make clear that the second flag raising was not a military but a cosmetic operation, carried out not under fire but on a spot that only a few hours before had been cleared of any Japanese military presence. Scott also reminds us that before the fighting on Iwo Jima was completely ended all of the original flag raisers who remained were wounded, three of them mortally, and those who survived did not live very long. In fact, when Scott fifty years later was writing his reminiscences, none of them was left alive. They had, however, become immortalized in a way in which Scott never was. If he continues to haunt anyone in the world after he himself has reached the end of his life, it will be as a kind of anonymous filmy specter. How different has been and presumably will be the fate of some of the other flag raisers, especially Jack Bradley, whose name was being prominently displayed in newspapers and magazines at the very moment I was writing this, since his heroism was being celebrated in a book written by his son James, called appropriately enough, *Flags of Our Fathers.*

From the very start, Bradley was the figure in Rosenthal's photograph featured above all the rest. Certainly, of the whole crew he is the first one to have been officially celebrated as a war hero. Moreover, he became sooner and more securely than any of the others a show business and media celebrity and, finally, a myth. This happened not simply because he outlived all the others, but because physically as well as spiritually he seemed an embodiment of the symbolic role in which Rosenthal had sought to cast everyone in his picture: the sturdily handsome Anglo-Saxon defender of our flag against the lesser breeds of the world. It was for this reason, too, that Bradley all his life long was bombarded by fan mail, though he apparently never answered any of the letters; and for the same reason, too, he was advertised as chief attraction at war-time fund raisers, one of which, thanks to him, set an all-time record for money raised. So too, Hollywood cast him to play himself in a movie called *The Sands of Iwo Jima,* in which he is portrayed fighting side by side with John Wayne, another macho, one-hundred-percent American type, whose audience seemed to have forgotten the fact that he had never fought in any war anywhere in the world.

Bradley's appeal to the mass audience is understandable enough, but that this most visible of all the flag raisers was found equally appealing by the least visible one of all is not. In the interview of Scott, the name most often mentioned is Bradley's, whom at one point Scott refers to as "a good friend of mine." He then goes on to tell us that it was Bradley he asked to hold the pole he had found while he tied on the flag.

Disconcertingly though, Scott calls his "good friend" only "John," though by everyone else he is called nothing but "Jack" or "Doc." In his own account Bradley, even more disconcertingly, claims that he had been given the pole not by Scott but by a marine called Mike Strank. Finally, Scott seems to have been as absent from Bradley's memory as he was from Rosenthal's picture. Bradley, however, seems to have had a gift for not seeing what was right in front of him, including Rosenthal as well as Scott. This is so, at least according to his son who asserts flatly, "My father did not know the picture was taken. He wasn't looking at the camera. None of the guys knew their picture was being taken."

But of course James felt obliged to deny everything that seemed to indicate that the picture that had brought such glory and honor to his father had been in any way staged.

He could not, though, deny that his father had willingly appeared in other restagings like, for instance, the John Wayne movie. But finally, what makes it impossible to take seriously James's assertion that Rosenthal's famous picture is the one and only representation of the battle of Iwo Jima is the fact that it was not the last any more than it had been the first picture of the flag raising on Iwo Jima. Somehow dissatisfied with it, Rosenthal tried one more time to get it right. What Rosenthal said this time to the twenty-five or thirty amateur actors whom he drafted for this third and presumably better photograph, Scott reported in his reminiscences: "Rosenthal told us to throw our rifles in the air or wave our helmets and yell to beat hell." The picture that resulted, alas, seems to me a total failure, trite, unconvincing and looking more like a schoolboy's celebration of victory in a football game than a solemn ceremony appropriate to the successful climax of a major battle. But Rosenthal apparently liked it more than the one almost everyone else prefers, and he seems even to have believed for a while that it was for this photograph he was extravagantly praised during the weeks that followed.

But though that third version was reproduced once in a popular magazine on the tenth anniversary of the flag raising, and again in a sidebar to a newspaper account of Scott's interview, it was only known to a few people, most of whom seemed to have soon forgotten it. This is truly regrettable, since only in it does an image of Scott actually appear. Though it is unsatisfactory in many ways, since he is barely visible, a shadowy, almost unidentifiable figure lost in a cloud of dust at the far edge of a crowd, it is the only evidence that there was actually a Calvin Scott and that he had been present for the flag raising on Iwo Jima.

Consequently, the fact that this third version has disappeared along with Scott into the gap in the history and legend of Iwo Jima created when the existence of the real raisings of the flag were declared officially nonexistent has persuaded me to make my own third attempt at telling this often mistold tale and finally getting it right.

Mythicizing the City

For millennia now mankind has been moving inexorably into cities—streaming from forest clearings and lonely farms, hillside hamlets and island villages to found Athens and Rome, Cairo and Jerusalem, Kiev and Odessa, Shanghai and Tokyo, São Paulo and Mexico City, San Francisco and New York—until the whole world promises or threatens (it can be, has been, felt either way) to turn into the City, Metropolis, Megalopolis. But, alas, though we have desired this, we have forgotten why. Once, once we knew, and the memory is preserved in the frozen etymology of certain words: "civilization" (the creation of human culture by clustering together in the *civis*, which is to say, the city); and "politics" (the science of living together in large numbers, of creating communities bigger than the family or the tribe in the polis, once more the city). "Outside the polis," Aristotle taught, "no one is truly human, but either a god or a beast." And for a long time we believed him, or at least acted as if we did.

Moreover, looking around now in what will always be for me the city *par excellence,* in Newark where I was born and my father before me, I can see still the institutions which this city, like all cities, created, institutions for which the city was a necessary pre-condition: the Library, the Museum, the University. Though I did not go to college in Newark, I was—as I have written before—educated in this library, this museum; but also I learned what museums, libraries and schools cannot teach in Military Park. There in my lunch breaks at the tedious job I started at age thirteen or fourteen, I listened to the political speakers and evangelists on soap boxes, the drifters and hobos who sat beside me on the benches, and the wino who read aloud from Jack London's *The Iron Heel.* But this, too, is what cities alone make possible: the confluence of many people, preaching and remembering, lying and telling the truth, asking and answering—until not just dialogue happens, but the dialectic is invented. Nor is it invented once and for all in, say, the Agora of ancient Athens, but over and over, wherever the traffic of buying and selling turns mysteriously into the traffic of ideas. And what I had begun to learn passively and in silence, I finished learning by talking to crowds gathered on urban street corners, where—long before I had stood behind a desk in the classroom—I first tried to teach over the catcalls of hecklers. "Patiently to explain," Lenin called that art, which he also described as "the first duty of the revolutionary." But patience is a virtue we all acquire in cities, a necessity for urban survival.

Yet somehow we grow impatient with cities themselves, that growing majority of us who continue to crowd into them, or who, like me, return to them after a temporary flight to the boondocks. Nor is that impatience, that dis-ease the product of a belated discovery (not in my own case surely, since I have always known it) that the city creates along with the Agora, the Library, the Museum and the University unprecedented human indignities. Squalor and poverty have always been part of human existence, but never somehow so visibly. And though violence and terror are also a part of recorded history from the very beginning, organized crime is something new under the sun; as is organized repressive force, the sanctioned counter-terror of the uniformed police.

But the dis-ease, the impatience of which I speak, existed in the literature bred by our deepest nightmares long before the Industrial Revolution had radically transformed the more humane *polis* into an impersonal hub of communications, a center for mass production, marshalling yards, slaughterhouses and assembly plants. At first, indeed, that transformation seemed a blessing rather than a curse for the city poor, since it created more work, more goods and eventually lifted more men and women above the subsistence level. But simultaneously it raised expectations even higher, making those still excluded and deprived ever more aware of their suffering, while rich and poor alike became conscious of the price paid: the growing alienation of all humankind from the natural world in which we first become human, and which in turn we have humanized by making it a part of our essential mythology, the perceptual grid through which we see and understand our identity and destiny.

But though our poets and storytellers have striven valiantly to mythicize the city, too; to make it a fact of the imagination as well as of geography, demography and sociology—like the Sun, the Moon, the Desert, the Ocean, the Forest, even the King's Palace and the Peasant's Hut—it has proved oddly resistant to any mythic images except for certain negative, dark, infernal ones, which reinforce rather than neutralize our sense of alienation. Very early on, to be sure, the notion of a city, one's own city (Babylon, let's say, or Rome or Jerusalem or Byzantium) as the center of the world, the navel of the Universe, was part of the official legends of certain imperial powers. And some of these parochial myths continue to influence our political behavior to this very day. Think, for instance, of how the mythological competition of Jews, Christians, and Muslims over the "Holy City" of Jerusalem helps to determine, even in the face of rational self-interest, war and peace in the Middle East.

But the attempt of Christianity to adapt that myth to its own universalist theology, by making it the model or prototype of the "Heavenly City," has somehow failed to fire the imagination even of its own communicants. The single Christian poem which continues to shape our deep fantasies, whether we are believers or not, follows the opposite strategy, using the City as the model or prototype of Hell: a symbol of absolute alienation rather than total fulfillment, of shared misery rather than communal bliss. In Dante's *Divine Comedy,* Heaven is compared to the boundless ocean and at its heart to a great white rose, while Purgatory is portrayed as a lofty mountain on a lonely island—all three images derived from the world of pre-urban, if not pre-human, nature. But Hell is figured forth as a walled city, much like the poet's own Florence, which had exiled him forever but continued to obsess him to the end of his days. *"Per me si va nella città dolente"* reads the inscription upon its gates. "Through me one goes into the mournful city."

And when some 600 years after the writing of the *Divine Comedy,* T. S. Eliot is evoking, in the major urban poem of the post–World War I era, his—and our—real, unreal city ("Falling towers/ Jerusalem Athens Alexandria/ Vienna London/ Unreal"), it is other lines from Dante's *Inferno* which come inevitably to his mind. "A crowd flowed over London Bridge, so many/ I had not thought death had undone so many . . ." It is, however, not only this reactionary American expatriate, appalled by the Russian Revolution and trembling on the edge of madness ("I think we are in rats' alley/ Where the dead men lost their bones") for whom the Dantesque metaphor of Hell as the City becomes the modern metaphor of the City as Hell.

Among Eliot's contemporaries as well as his immediate predecessors and successors that mythological equation is echoed and re-echoed: in Baudelaire and Ezra Pound, Stephen Crane and Hart Crane and William Faulkner, Dostoevski and Zola and Samuel Beckett. Politics makes no difference, nor does sex. Leftists as well as rightists are possessed by the image—women (think of the infernal city of *Waiting for Mr. Goodbar* and of Joan Didion's Los Angeles) as well as men. Nor is it confined to Europeans and Americans of European descent. For Afro-Americans like Richard Wright and James Baldwin and Ralph Ellison the streets of the City are the byways of Hell; and Amiri Baraka confesses his debt to Dante openly, calling his most ambitious effort in prose (whose setting is, of course, Newark) *The System of Dante's Hell.*

The instances I have cited all belong to the nineteenth and twentieth centuries; but the Dantesque metaphor did not slumber through the long centuries between the late Middle Ages and the modern world. It appears sporadically throughout the Renaissance; most notably, perhaps, in Shakespeare, whose urban plays—*Coriolanus, Timon of Athens, Measure for Measure, Troilus and Cressida*—tend to be his most horrendous. It scarcely matters whether they are nominally set in Rome or Athens, Vienna or Troy (one suspects he is always thinking of London); he portrays the urban milieu as a culture in which disloyalty and disease thrive, a place where love is sold for gold, and syphilis eats away the human body, once thought to have been created in the image of God. Similarly, in our own mid-nineteenth-century Renaissance, the infernal myth of the City reappears in full force, especially in the fiction of Herman Melville.

Remembering *Moby Dick,* we tend to think of that tormented novelist as exclusively a laureate of the sea; but in *Redburn* and "Bartleby the Scrivener," and especially in *Pierre,* he returns to the land, evoking visions of London, Liverpool and New York as terrifying as anything in Dante or Shakespeare. The eponymous hero of *Pierre* has, as a matter of fact, been reading both of those authors even before he leaves the idyllic countryside for New York. And when he enters Manhattan after nightfall, the inscription on the Gates of Inferno is still ringing in his head, so that it seems inevitable for him to describe the city jail where his nightmare journey ends in Dantesque language: "The thieves' quarters, and all the brothels, Lock and Sin hospitals for the incurables, and infirmaries and infernoes of hell seemed to have . . . poured out upon earth through the vile vomitory of some unmentionable cellar."

But Melville has also been reading certain Utopian socialist novelists of the earlier nineteenth century, authors of best sellers like Eugene Sue's *Mysteries of Paris,* George Reynolds's *Mysteries of London* and the American George Lippard's *The Monks of Monks Hall,* in which he lubriciously describes the rape and seduction of working-class girls by rich Philadelphia voluptuaries, while preaching that "Literature merely considered as an ART is a despicable thing . . . A literature which does not work practically, for the advancement of social reform . . . is just good for nothing at all."

If critics have failed to notice the influence on Melville of the urban "Mysteries," which won a large audience of newly literate working-class readers, largely male, by combining revolutionary doctrine, soft porn and Gothic horror in a city setting, it is because these books have long since lost their mass appeal without ever having won the approval of the critical establishment. But they seemed once to represent a breakthrough in fiction of real political importance (Karl Marx devoted a large part of his first book, *The Holy Family,* to an attack on Eugene Sue) as well as aesthetic interest. And this seems fair enough in light of the fact that they represent the first fully self-conscious attempt to create a new Myth of the City as an arena for class warfare rather than a symbol of infernal horror.

But unfortunately, Sue used as his model James Fenimore Cooper; convinced, perhaps, that even as "the American Sir Walter Scott" had achieved popularity by mythicizing the virgin Forest of the New World and its "savage" inhabitants, he could succeed with the mass audience by mythicizing the "wilderness" of the Old World cities and their "savage" inhabitants, "the barbarians in our very midst"; which is to say, the lumpen poor and the "criminal classes," whom he describes as gathering to plot murder and mayhem in a "mysterious language full of dark images and disgusting metaphors."

The fascination with crime, however, takes Sue and his followers away from the factories and workshops and the daytime streets where workers demonstrated for their rights into the nighttime, nightmare region typically called by one of the traditional names of Hades, "the underworld"; which is to say, the secular Hell which underlies the Earthly Paradise, into which Utopian dreamers (some of them the very authors of these books) dreamed the cities of the world could be transformed with the coming of socialism. At the very moment, however, that Eugene Sue was writing about the old, corrupt, fascinating, shadowy Paris, it was being changed in ways he had not foreseen; the Baron Hausmann supervising operations which would break through the old tortuous byways and alleys that had become the refuge of outlaws and revolutionaries, in order to open great boulevards, down which the rich could ride in splendor and the police charge without obstruction to maintain Law and Order.

But even where socialism has triumphed, the more the city has changed, the more it has remained the same; since essentially, not accidentally, "it contradicts nature . . . denies all nature . . . [the words are Oswald Spengler's, who for once speaks the truth] the gigantic megalopolis, the city-as-world . . . suffers nothing beside itself." And it is a sense of the contradiction implicit in this insight between what our conscious needs demand, i.e., civilization, the city-as-world, and what our instinctive, impulsive undermind yearns for, i.e., nature, the persistence of the pre-human, a world we never made, which nurtures our underground resentment of the City and our image of it as a Hell to which we are self-condemned.

There seems (at least as far as the evidence of literature can be trusted) no way out of this trap. Just as the genre of the "Mysteries," invented at the same moment and out of the same impulse as "The Communist Manifesto," submitted finally to the infernal myth, so too its successor, modern science fiction, which is born with the "New City" and constitutes the storehouse of both its mythology and that of the technology which begot it. For a while in its beginnings, some of its founders, themselves often Utopian or "scientific" socialists, did their best to imagine the future in terms of a benign super-city (*Looking Backward* is the earliest example which comes to mind); and occasionally such attempts are made even now. By and large, however, science fiction, on either side of the ideological split which presumably divides our world (it is a genre most of whose truly successful practitioners come either from the Anglo-American world or the immediate orbit of the Soviet Union), when it imagines an urban future, imagines it in grimly, bitterly, blatantly dystopian terms. Indeed, the pattern was set very early with *The Time Machine* of H. G. Wells, the first novelist to leave behind a body of work universally admired and recognized as unequivocal science fiction. In later life, Wells tended to discount his first romance as the product of youthful pessimism; but he was already at the point when he wrote it a self-declared socialist. It seems therefore significant that the new genre (as if it had a mythic essence, if not a will of its own) imposed on him a vision of the remote future not as a classless society but one even more split along class lines than his own. Moreover, what looks to the Time Traveller at first glance like an Earthly Paradise, in which mankind lives at peace with nature, turns out to be merely a kind of super-garden suburb presided over by effete and sterile consumers, the Eloi. Beneath the sunlit world which they inhabit, lies a hidden industrial city of perpetual darkness, inhabited by bestial workers, the Morlocks—who emerge out of their living hell from time to time under cover of night, and, in the guise of slavering demons, quite literally consume the consumers.

Once invented, this notion of locating the working-class ghetto on which the prosperity of the industrial city depends underground, which is to say, in the very place in which the cosmology of the pre-Death-of-God imagination located Hell, proved very attractive. It appears, for instance, in E. M. Forster's much-anthologized tale of the future, "The Machine Stops," and in the first real science fiction film, Fritz Lang's *Metropolis*. But above ground or below, the city of science fiction remains infernal in key works of science fiction in all media, from dystopian classics like Aldous Huxley's *Brave New World* and George Orwell's *1984* to more recent favorites like Anthony Burgess's *Clockwork Orange* and Samuel Delany's *Falling Towers,* whose title is intended to remind us of Eliot's *The Waste Land* and behind that of Dante's *Inferno,* where it all started.

Nor are such extrapolative works confined to the capitalist world, where urban alienation has presumably been exacerbated by shameless profit-seeking and the exploitation of labor. At least equal in horror are visions of the urban future dreamed in the cities of "socialist" eastern Europe. Beginning with Zamyatin's *We,* which appeared in Moscow not long after the Bolshevik Revolution of 1917, such books reach a grim climax in *The Futurological Congress* (1971), of Stanislaw Lem, a Polish writer who was born in Łwow, and has lived since the annexation of his part of Poland by Russia, in Cracow. In the opinion of many (including me), he is the greatest living writer of science fiction; and though his Marxist philosophy is orthodox enough to insure him publication in the Soviet orbit, he seems unable to imagine a post-industrial urban future in which, no matter who owns the basic means of production, humankind will flourish. In *The Futurological Congress,* for instance, he projects the society of 2089, the world as dying city, the city as dying world, in which sixty-nine billion legally registered inhabitants—plus another twenty-six billion in hiding—struggle to survive, though the annual average temperature has dropped four degrees and the return of the glaciers lies only fifteen or twenty years ahead.

The actual inferno these men of the future inhabit is made bearable only by the final invention of the advanced technology which has produced it, i.e., psycho-chemicals, secretly introduced into the water supply, which create shared euphoric hallucinations that everyone takes for the "reality" of their lives. Everyone that is, except for Lem's hero, Ion Tichy, who by dosing himself with an antidote to the hallucinogens is able to see the hideous truth behind the glorious illusion: a world of wrecked machines, rusted robots, collapsed buildings and monstrous mutant humans who tread a perilous way through frozen accumulations of rubbish, until stumbling over obstacles they never see, they themselves freeze to death—not even knowing it until the last spark of altered consciousness flickers out. But Tichy, who has read his Dante, is scarcely surprised, observing only, "I thought there would be ice in hell."

Yet though the very pit of Dante's Hell is ice, into which Satan himself is frozen forever, the walls of his City of Dis are lit by eternal flames; and, indeed, in the popular imagination of the Christian West, it is fire which represents the ultimate torment of the damned. So, too, many writers of modern science fiction and urban fantasy imagine the end of Megalopolis in terms of fire rather than ice. Think, for instance, of fire-bombed Dresden in Kurt Vonnegut's *Slaughterhouse-Five,* a book banned in the pious provinces of America for denying the existence of God, which nonetheless ends in a Dantesque apocalyptic vision; or the fantasy of "The Burning of Los Angeles" which possesses Tod Hackett at the conclusion of Nathanael West's *The Day of the Locust.* Guilt and terror are the feelings evoked by Vonnegut, by West, who, like his artist-protagonist, imagines Hollywood in flames with something more like relish than fear or foreboding.

And reflecting on this, I am led to the final question evoked by this meditation. Do those who imagine the end of the City, whether in fire or ice, wish it or dread it—or, like me, dread they wish it, wish they dreaded it? Certainly, I at least, who have fled the city and returned in fact, but flee it still in my troubled sleep, am caught in an unresolvable ambivalence. And I suspect that those others, too, endure fantasies bred by their love/hate for the City the world threatens/promises to become. I have been forced to confront this doubleness in myself, since the last story I have written but not yet published, a kind of dream-fugue entitled "What Used to Be Called Dead," which started out to be a fairy tale set in a magical wood, insisted on turning into science fiction; taking me back at the moment of transition to where I found myself in an underground cavern (womb or tomb, place of refuge or simply Hell once more) under the statue of the Wars of America in Military Park. Above me, the city burned in a fire from which I an old man grown young again—with a handful of long-dead shoe salesmen beside whom I worked nearly fifty years ago—had somehow managed to escape:

> No matter. The old man was not there, but lay in the bosom of his boyhood, grounded in a dark concrete chamber far underground. And before he quite knew it, he was remembering why. The city had burned for two days and three nights. But what had started the fire no one could guess. The Blacks, perhaps, eager to destroy the rat-infested ghettos in which they lived. Or the Whites no longer able to abide the reproach of their misery. Or others, neither Black nor White and more like trees than men, whom no one had ever seen in daylight, though both Black and White dreamed them nightly. Or perhaps it had only been the long hot summer that had dried everything up: sidewalks and plateglass show windows, wood and stucco and brick and the streetside maples in their jackets of wire mesh, cats in back alleys and dogs breathless beside stone lions on the stone stoops—parching everything to a dryness that could grow no longer, only burn under the unremitting assault of the sun.

But notice, please, as I had not noticed until I re-read my little parable for the purposes of this essay, that my city burns not in a future close or remote, but has burned in an irrecoverable past, before my character's, *my* fifteenth birthday; which means I have never left Newark, but have always been there, been *here:* in a womb, a tomb, a place or refuge or a chamber of Hell, far beneath the threatening flames, the city streets and the monument to our futile wars.

Whatever Happened
to Jerry Lewis?
That's Amore . . .

I was no more than five or six and not yet able to read when my mother, because a baby-sitter failed to show up, felt obliged to take me with her to a showing of *The White Sister* (1923), starring Lillian Gish. This premature venture into the world of adult magic made me an addict of moving pictures. Indeed, in the years since, I have seen more movies than I have read books, though it is for doing the latter that I have come to be paid. From the start, however, I wanted not to be just a passive watcher of films but to participate in making them. This seemed possible since, as was true of many Jewish American families, members of my own had played a part in the production of Hollywood's ready-made dreams. A cousin of mine was a property man; his two sisters worked in casting; and his daughter, whose first visitors after she was born were Charlie Chaplin and Theda Bara, had led the MGM lion onto the set for the first time. All these relatives, however, had not created films but had only done the small chores that made it easier for the directors, script-writers, choreographers, musicians and actors to create them. Although some of these jobs required skills I did not have, there were two I felt at least qualified to try. Some of the stories I had published had been optioned, and for two of them screenplays had actually been written. But neither *The Second Stone* nor *Nude Croquet* had made it to the screen.

For a while it seemed as if I might have more luck as an actor, since my performances in several amateur productions and a semi-pro off-Broadway one had been favorably received. But none of my stage appearances was filmed until, in the late 1950s, I began to be invited to participate in talk shows, in which I appeared so often (and was paid scale) that I had to join AFTRA (the American Federation of Television and Radio Artists). On these shows, however, I played only the same role I lived offstage, that of an anti-academic academic and a part-time social critic—called by the producers of such programs a "nut," as were Allen Ginsberg and Norman Mailer, who were their first choices. But finally these shows gave me a chance to diversify my act. One night when I confessed before the cameras that I desperately longed to play any other part, someone apparently had listened. As I opened the door to my home in Buffalo, the phone was ringing; and when I picked it up I heard a strange voice asking if I could come to Hollywood for six or eight weeks to play the part of a gypsy caravan driver in a full-length film. I said immediately, "Yes, yes, yes," and before I knew it I was in California wearing tights and a plumed hat and rehearsing my lines in what turned out to be a movie called *When I Am King* (1981). It was so badly written, directed and edited that though it had in the cast competent veteran actors like Aldo Ray and Stuart Whitman, it never made its way into any theater, and its producers eventually disappeared without a trace.

Nevertheless, thinking back I find that time to have been one of the most satisfactory in all my life—mostly because it was so unreal. I was put up in a room in the venerable Roosevelt Hotel, looking down from whose windows I could see the tourists gathering before the even more venerable Grauman's Chinese Theater. From there I was picked up every morning and driven to a location familiar to me from a thousand sleazy Westerns, in one thousand and one of which John Wayne had starred. My driver was a fellow actor, a dwarf and former circus clown who arrived each day already drunk and got even drunker from the beers he gulped as we sped down the freeway. From the start I had the sense of being in not a real Hollywood but a mythic one that existed only on the pages of Nathanael West's *The Day of the Locust*. It was as if the Screen Actor's Guild contract I had been given was a passport into that magic space behind the movie screen that I had longed to penetrate.

That visit to Neverland, however, turned out to be my last as well as my first. A couple of years later my name appeared in the credits of a much better film called *Exposed* (1983), starring Rudolf Nureyev and Nastassja Kinski, but I never appeared in the flesh. What the camera did close in on, in an opening scene, were some lines from my *Love and Death in the American Novel* being written on a chalkboard by a professor played by the director of the movie. In a later scene the book itself was shown pressed to the breasts of his students, including Nastassja.

Yet, though I never participated in the making of any other movie, I did continue to watch them and even, reluctantly, to write about a few of them, such as *Beyond the Valley of the Dolls* (1970), *The Immoral Mr. Teas* (1959) and *The Birth of a Nation* (1915); all of them works that annoyed someone or other enough to be condemned, picketed or banned. I did not, however, deal with any of the films of Jerry Lewis until I was asked to contribute to this collection and realized that he, who was once a super–best seller, had become virtually taboo because he had treated the crippled and handicapped as ridiculous rather than pitiful.

His defense by European snobs who typically like only what Americans despise proved to be a kiss of death. Moreover, his American detractors were not convinced by the French defenders, who defended him on aesthetic grounds rather than on the ethical ones of which he was condemned in his own country. They seem not to have been aware of what I would have pointed out: that the portrayal of cripples as laughable is one of the three main ways in which writers have traditionally treated such unfortunates. Homer, for instance, portrays all malformed characters as appropriate targets for ridicule, whether they are mortal monsters such as Thersites or immortal ones such as Hephaestus. Nor is such portrayal of the disabled as comic absent from the culture of our own country. In fact, the minstrel show, a form of popular theater unique to America, began with "Daddy" Rice "Jumping Jim Crow," which is to say, doing a wild dance that he claimed was based on that performed by an old black slave so crippled by rheumatism it was both wonderful and funny that he could dance at all.

The second traditional way of portraying the handicapped is as monsters, ugly in their souls as well as in their bodies. Best known of these is Shakespeare's *Richard III,* to whom he gave a hunchback he never really had but who turned out to be not just hated and feared but loved and admired by actors and audiences. So, too, in the later nineteenth century, malicious amputees such as Long John Silver and Captain Hook fascinated as well as terrified small boys and their fathers. But in Victorian England and America there was a sentimental backlash against the negative portrayal of the disabled as vicious and ridiculous. This created a vacuum that was filled to overflowing by a third way of presenting the handicapped, as beautiful souls trapped in unbeautiful bodies. The best remembered of these saintly cripples is Charles Dickens's Tiny Tim. It was largely because of him that *A Christmas Carol* became a best seller and has remained one right down to the present. By the end of the century in which it first appeared, however, more sophisticated readers began to feel, and were candid enough to confess, that all of Dickens's cripples moved them not to weep but to laugh. Given the choice, they found he was truer to himself when he portrayed the handicapped as comic or grotesque than as pathetic, as in the case of Quilp, the character who he once said was the closest thing to a self-portrait he had ever created.

Jerry Lewis, by contrast, never forgot his primary obligations as a comedian: to keep the audience laughing all through his movies and to leave them feeling happy. Since the kind of comedy he wrote was slapstick farce, in which violence is present everywhere, this was not easy to do. Yet he somehow always managed to make the poke in the eye, the slap on the face, the kick in the ass, the hit on the head and the pratfall, which was his trademark, seem not to matter. In any case, he presented them so that the audience did not respond with gasps of horror but continued to giggle and chortle, as also did the other characters on the stage. Only the protagonist never laughed but responded with a wordless cry of anguish, at which the laughter of everyone else was doubled.

To some of his critics it seemed that he did this by exploiting the shameless tendency of us all to be more delighted than dismayed by the calamities that befall others. It seems to me, however, that what we really laughed at in Jerry's films was not the otherness of the suffering but the sameness to our own. We are all cripples, he seemed to be saying, both those we call handicapped and we whom they call TABS, meaning "temporarily able-bodied."

The same message is contained in the riddle the Sphinx poses to Oedipus in Sophocles' tragedy, when she asks, "Who walks on four legs in the morning, two legs in the afternoon, and three legs in the evening?" Oedipus correctly answers, "Man"—which is to say, all humans, who begin crawling abjectly on all fours in our infancy, then stride proudly on two legs in our prime and, when we are old, hobble unsteadily with the aid of a third leg, a crutch or a cane. To be sure, this melancholy thought is more compatible with tragedy, whose final words of wisdom are "Let no man consider himself happy until he is dead," than with comedy, which concludes with "happily ever after."

Jerry's typical endings, however, though they are not tragic or even melodramatic, are not what most people call happy either. It is hard to find any proper name for his endings, since they do not end with a victory for the protagonist; and what victory would be possible for the nerds who are the anti-heroes in the stories Jerry tells? Defined from the very beginning as losers, they cannot kill a dragon, find the Holy Grail and become saints or kings; nor can they be convincingly portrayed as overthrowing a tyrant and freeing his oppressed people—or even getting rich and being elected Lord Mayor of London. The world in which Jerry's protagonists find themselves is one in which politics and religion play no important role. State houses and churches seem to be permanently closed, and the only well-lit places are the classrooms, gymnasiums, laboratories and auditoriums of seedy second-rate colleges flanked by sleazy nightclubs, bars and soda parlors to which the students flee when school is out.

The potholed streets over which these protagonists move from place to place seem much to me like those of Newark, New Jersey, a city that began to die before it began to live. It was there I once worked in a shoe store side by side with a crew of losers, one of whom was Danny Levitch, Jerry's father. Although he boasted constantly about his rosy prospects in the theater, he always seemed to end up working as an extra salesman. His father's habitual failure must have haunted Jerry and fueled in him a relentless desire to succeed, but that desire is not shared by the comic creeps who survive in his films. None of them seems to be dreaming of success or, indeed, any other fully adult goal. Instead they yearn for what is called, in the jargon of the young, "popularity," hoping to be accepted, applauded and loved not for what others believe and they fear they really are—namely, wimps—but as sleek and loveable hunks, which they hope they can become or at least seem to become by finding the right style of dress or shade of lipstick or way of dancing. The reward for thus renewing themselves is perhaps the oldest of all happy endings: "getting the girl." Sometimes they modernize this dream of their fathers and grandfathers by making it "getting the girls." The shift from singular to plural, however, makes no real difference, since whether they strive to have and to hold just one woman until death do them part or to bed down many, their beloved turns out to be the same bubble-headed blonde shiksa, whom his protagonists think they desire but whom Jerry himself probably could not have stood for a single minute.

There is a slight note of irony in all his portrayals of such females, as he did not realize fully, until Dean Martin had become his inseparable stagemate, that he really thought of those women as rivals for his true love, who was not a woman at all but a glib, sexy, self-confident male much like Martin. The series of movies in which Jerry explored in depth his ill-fated relationship with Dean and Dean's rejection of him—from *My Friend Irma* (1949) to *Hollywood or Bust* (1956)—are not only the saddest and funniest he ever made but absolutely unique.

To be sure, the concept of male couples joined by a sublimated passion "which passeth the love of a woman" yet is "indifferent to men and their erections" is central to many American works, from the minstrel show to such classics as *The Last of the Mohicans, Moby Dick* and *Huckleberry Finn,* about which I have written at length. But the love that joins Jerry and Dean is in many ways different from that which joins the paleface audience to the black actors in the minstrel shows and Huck Finn to Jim, Ishmael to Queequeg, Natty Bumppo to Chingachgook. These all have a racist, political dimension, since in all of them a white and a nonwhite male, though their people back at home are fighting each other, discover it is possible in the wilderness or at sea to find temporary peace and love in a relationship physical but not fully sexual. But Jerry and Dean both would have been more likely to be considered black than white by the WASPs who wrote those books, since one was a Jew and the other Italian, and both therefore too swarthy to be placed on that high rung of the evolutionary ladder WASPs occupied. Of course, the first generation of Italians and Jews were deeply suspicious of each other because of their different religions and cultures, but their children born in America began by playing together on the streets of their neighboring ghettos and, in their quest for upward social mobility, ended up with similar careers as gangsters, boxers or actors. It was in the theater that Dean and Jerry entered into their bond, which, like many such theatrical unions, they announced to the world by fusing both their names into one, calling themselves Martin and Lewis. But unlike Abbott and Costello, Laurel and Hardy, Burns and Allen, they were as drastically different from each other as the stereotypes of their races: the kike Jerry Lewis (née Joseph Levitch) sober, modest, hardworking but afflicted by self-doubt, chiefly sexual; the wop Dean Martin (née Dino Crocetti) charming, articulate and talented but with an unfortunate propensity for getting drunk. One thinks of him primarily, however, as he apparently thought of himself: as one of the mythological Italo-American lounge lizards like Rudolph Valentino and Frank Sinatra.

There were no such mythic erotic role models for Jerry, yet it was he who truly loved, rather than Dean, who would only let himself be loved. And it was Dean who ended the marriage, of which Dean never seems to have been fully aware. So, too, he was not aware of how traumatic was their final separation, which sent Jerry back to his legally married wife and family. But even there Jerry could never forget the cruel words Dean had spoken to him at the moment of what Jerry felt as a divorce: "You can talk about love all you want. To me, you're nothing but a dollar sign," Dean said and then continued his career as leading man and singer of schmaltzy Neapolitan love songs without interruption.

Jerry, however, made fewer and fewer movies, filling his growing hours of idleness with busy work as national chairman for the Muscular Dystrophy Association, whose activities on behalf of victims of such neural disorders climaxed in a Labor Day telethon that since the 1960s has collected millions of dollars. But life has not otherwise been kind to Jerry. As he has grown older he has suffered other disasters, including prostate cancer, a heart attack and a general failure of his body—which he felt for many years was invulnerable. Especially his buttocks and lower back, on which he had fallen hundreds of times, were wracked by pain so bitter that he turned to Percodan for relief. Instead of giving him a surcease of pain for which he hoped, that drug left him only with an addiction that lasted for fifteen years. Nevertheless, I do not like to think that Jerry ever regretted the tortures to which he submitted his flesh for so long, since they had given real pleasure to so many. Among these I count myself, to whom his routines seemed so attractive that I learned how to do some of those falls myself to entertain friends and break up dull parties.

Despite his multiple afflictions, Jerry kept trying to compose a movie with a happier ending than the one that seemed to lie ahead of him in real life. To do this, he was aware he would have to exorcise the ghost of Dean Martin, which continued to haunt him, by rewriting the story of their love. Ultimately, he did so. As late as 1982, Jerry agreed to appear in Martin Scorsese's *The King of Comedy* (1983), which contains an account of his relationship with Dean

Martin, with their roles reversed: that is, Scorsese cast as the unattractive loser, hitherto portrayed by Jerry himself, Robert De Niro, who is of the same ethnic origin as Scorsese and Dean Martin. He then used Jerry to play the part of the successful "king" of showbiz, who rejects De Niro/Jerry.

But Jerry years earlier had made, in *The Nutty Professor* (1963), a more radical revision of their relationship in which only one member is real. The Jerry-like protagonist is called Professor Julius Kelp, while the Deanlike character, called Buddy Love, is not the real antagonist he seems, only an imaginary alter ego. When the film starts, however, nobody seems to know this, not even the professor himself, who feels that to win the heart and hand of the woman he thinks he loves he must turn himself into that younger, more attractive male. The woman is also convinced that it is the nonexistent Dean-figure she really loves. In the end, however, she discovers that she wants and needs someone much more like the unbeautiful professor, and it is that professor she is about to marry when the movie ends.

This seemed to me such a totally satisfactory ending to the story that I could not imagine why anyone would or could add anything to it. I was therefore astonished and a little dismayed when, as we entered the third millennium, I saw a notice in the *TV Guide* that another movie called *The Nutty Professor* (1996) was playing on cable. When I actually saw it, I discovered it was indeed a continuation of Jerry's original film, though his name was not listed as one of the writers or actors but only as one of its executive producers.

It had, moreover, a new ending in which the professor turns out to be a double winner, getting both "the girl" and "the girls." He can do this because, in the new version, he is a kind of Dr. Jekyll, able to turn himself into Hyde with the chemical compound he has invented. This makes it possible for him to be shown, as the action draws to a close, asleep in a bed where he has earlier made love to three lusty bimbos and then, on waking, dressing himself in the proper garb for a marriage to the blonde young starlet he was always convinced he desired. She, however, has changed too, being now no longer a bubble-head but a serious graduate student and also, despite her yellow hair, black. So are most of the other major characters, including the professor, who is played by Eddie Murphy, an African American actor much admired by young people both white and black and whose name alone seemed to guarantee a large audience for the film. This time, moreover, the professor comes onscreen looking not like a medical textbook figure or a terminal victim of muscular dystrophy but instead a grossly fat, aging man destined apparently to get even fatter—a disability at which it is possible to laugh without stirring up the strong negative reactions prompted by Jerry's earlier mocking of the maimed.

These multiple changes make clear what Murphy realized was always true, though less evident earlier: that the major theme of this movie was not disability or interethnic male bonding or even race but reality and illusion. This play on what is and what merely seems Murphy made even more complex by announcing to the audience in publicity releases that he himself was a kind of shape-shifter who would be playing not only the professor but some six or seven other characters. He does indeed play them in full sight in the most hilarious scene of the film, which takes place at a family dinner for the professor: Murphy is made up as the professor, sitting in the midst of three generations of his family, clearly also played by him. This involves, of course, Murphy appearing simultaneously as male and female, old and young.

This kind of age- and gender-bending, as well as the trifling with illusion, seems more characteristic of high art than of pop. Certainly, it is to be found in the Mannerist literature and painting of the fifteenth century and also in the avant-garde schools of art of the twentieth century, such as Surrealism, Dada, Futurism and Postmodernism. But it is also to be found in the popular minstrel show, in which nothing is as it seems and the audience knows it. Those who pretend to be black turn out to be white, and those who come on in the garb of women turn out to be men, and that which seems a typical Southern plantation is revealed finally as a stage of the theater actually located in Buffalo or Boston or New York City. To be sure, so that the movie audience does not miss this affinity, Murphy in the key dinner-table scene makes his characters speak, move, and relate to one another and to the audience in ways much like those characteristic of a style first used by blackface minstrels and later transmitted to the purely white audience of vaudeville, musical comedies, and "talking movies" by an older generation of Jewish American actors such as Al Jolson, Eddie Cantor and, to be sure, Jerry Lewis. It is Al Jolson whom we best remember, but Murphy reminds us that Jerry actually made a best-selling record of the minstrel-show tune "Rock-a-Bye Your Baby with a Dixie Melody" some thirty years after Jolson had made it a hit.

But thirty more years after that release, Jerry seemed about to disappear not just from the stage and screen but from the memory of the audience; or worse yet, it seemed as if he might end up being remembered only as the celebrity announcer who every Labor Day presides over the Muscular Dystrophy Telethon and whose picture is displayed, between those genteel money-raising orgies, on posters everywhere in this country.

On those posters, he who was once accused of slandering the disabled is portrayed as their smug and kindly benefactor. Lest anyone miss the point, he is shown hugging a photogenic child purported to be a victim of muscular dystrophy. Typically these victims are girls, usually white, and always scrupulously clean and with the fixed smiles of professional models. Though they have come to be officially known as "Jerry's Kids," I think of them as "this year's Tiny Tim," and of the portly, solid citizen who beams down on them as this year's Scrooge: not the earlier Scrooge who is almost indistinguishable from a "stingy old Jew" but Scrooge after his conversion into the professional founder of the feast for all the deserving poor.

Thanks to Eddie Murphy, however, Jerry has been delivered from this ignominious fate, his older, truer self having been resurrected, as it were, and displayed once more on screens, actually being watched by a new audience that includes the young as well as the old and the black as well as the white. It seems, in fact, that Jerry will not die again for a long time, since the box-office success of the first blackface version of *The Nutty Professor* was so notable that it has been followed by another, *The Nutty Professor II: The Klumps* (2000). This seems to me to be the single-handed accomplishment of Murphy, who was cool enough to appear before the cameras pretending to be a white man pretending to be black—or rather, perhaps, pretending to be a Jew pretending to be a white man pretending to be black. We therefore owe him thanks for having restored to us in a strange new form the original Jerry Lewis, one of the makers of that mulatto culture that is America's gift to itself and the rest of the world.

SAMUELE F. S. PARDINI (1969–), a native of Tuscany, holds a Laurea Degree in Letters and Philosophy from the University of Pisa and an M.A. and a Ph.D. in Comparative Literature from SUNY Buffalo. His work on Italian Studies, American Studies, Literary Criticism and Popular Culture has appeared in *Acoma*, *ArtVoice*, *BuffaloReport*, *Interdisciplinary Humanities*, *Modern Fiction Studies*, *The Cambridge Dictionary of Christianity*, and *The Bruce Springsteen Reader*. He has edited and translated into Italian two collections of Leslie Fiedler's essays, *Vacanze Romane* (2004) and *Arrivederci alle Armi* (2005). He has taught at SUNY Buffalo, UCLA and Vanderbilt University. Currently, he is a Visiting Assistant Professor of Italian and Interdisciplinary Studies in the Department of Foreign Languages at Elon University.

Printed in the United States
by Baker & Taylor Publisher Services